To Papa
From Irene & Jim
Christmas '95

PORTRAIT OF A REVOLUTIONARY

Portrait of a Revolutionary

GENERAL RICHARD MULCAHY

AND THE

FOUNDING OF THE IRISH FREE STATE

Maryann Gialanella Valiulis

IRISH ACADEMIC PRESS

This book was typeset by
Seton Music Graphics, Bantry,
for Irish Academic Press Ltd,
Kill Lane, Blackrock, Co. Dublin.

First edition, June 1992
Reprinted July 1992

ISBN 0-7165-2494-5

This edition is not for sale in North America, the Philippines and Japan,
where the book is published by the
University Press of Kentucky.

Printed and bound in Ireland by Colour Books Ltd, Dublin

IN MEMORIAM
MY MOTHER
MARY DELLA FERA GIALANELLA

Contents

List of Illustrations

Credits: ills 4 and 5, courtesy of the National Library of Ireland; ills 13–15, courtesy of the Military Archives, Dublin; all other illustrations are courtesy of the Mulcahy family.

Preface

This book grew out of my interest in General Richard Mulcahy and his role in the army mutiny of 1924. Through the years I have been working on this project, I never ceased to find Mulcahy an engaging historical figure whose career spanned a fascinating period in Irish history. Although I originally planned to write a full-scale biography of Mulcahy, I chose instead to concentrate on what I perceived to be the most important segment of his life. I hope the reader, however, will be able to draw an accurate picture of the man, Richard Mulcahy, as well as one of the general. Parts of the last two chapters of this book are drawn from my previous work on the mutiny.

I would like to thank the staff at the National Library of Ireland and the State Paper Office for their help in researching this book. Commandant Peter Young of the Military Archives was most helpful in making records available and in explaining aspects of military life not readily apparent to a non-military person. I am deeply grateful to Ms Kerry Holland and Mr Seamus Helferty and the staff of the University College, Dublin, Archives for their kindness and patience in helping me navigate my way through their rich collections.

I am indebted to my colleagues in Irish history in both Ireland and the United States for sharing their insights and knowledge with me. I am also very grateful for the help and hospitality which the Mulcahy family accorded me over the years. In particular, I am most appreciative of all the assistance which Dr Risteárd Mulcahy gave me. His graciousness and kindness were unfailing.

On a personal level, I would like to thank my colleagues at the Newcomb College Center for Research on Women for their tolerance and support; my research assistants Catherine Buckman, Randall Collins and Kathleen Fitzgerald for their help in preparing the final draft of this manuscript; my friend Joelle Grospelier for listening patiently to my seemingly endless ramblings about land-mines, executions and the like; my aunts, Ellen Della Fera and Phyllis Marchesani, for helping me find the time to write; my daughter, Caitlín, for always giving me such joy; and my husband, Tony, without whom this book would not have happened. I applaud his wizardry at the computer but, more importantly, depend on his faith.

Maryann Gialanella Valiulis
New Orleans, 1992

N

0 10 20 30 40 50 MLS
0 20 40 60 KM

Londonderry

Donegal

Derry

Antrim

Larne

NORTHERN

Tyrone

Dungannon

Belfast
Lisburn

IRELAND

Fermanagh

Down

Armagh

Monaghan

Newry

Sligo

Leitrim

Cavan

Dundalk

Mayo

Roscommon

Longford

Louth

Drogheda

Meath

Galway

Westmeath

Athlone

Dublin

Galway

Dublin
Kingstown

IRISH
SEA

ATLANTIC
OCEAN

IRISH FREE STATE

Offaly

Kildare

Clare

Laois

Wicklow

Wicklow

Limerick

Carlow

Tralee

Limerick

Tipperary

Kilkenny

Kilkenny

Wexford

Kilmallock

Wexford

Kerry

Clonmel

Cork

Béal na Bláth

Waterford

Cork

Waterford

ST GEORGE'S CHANNEL

Queenstown

IRELAND IN 1922
SHOWING THE
TWENTY-SIX COUNTIES OF THE IRISH FREE STATE AND
THE SIX COUNTIES OF NORTHERN IRELAND

Richard Mulcahy, 1886–1971

Richard Mulcahy was born in Waterford, Ireland, in 1886. He was educated at Mount Sion Christian Brothers' School and began a career in the Post Office at the age of sixteen. He trained as a Post Office engineer and was in Dublin in the Engineering Department when the 1916 Rebellion took place. During Easter Week, he was second in command to Thomas Ashe of the Fingal Volunteers. He and Ashe mounted one of the few successful actions during 1916 at Ashbourne, County Meath, in which a large number of RIC were either captured or killed. After the Rebellion, he was interned in Frongoch. He was released at Christmas, 1916, and quickly rose to leadership positions in the Volunteers as Officer Commanding the 2nd Dublin Battalion and then O/C of the newly formed Dublin Brigade.

With the formation of a General Headquarters Staff in March 1918, Mulcahy was appointed chief of staff of the Irish Volunteers. Working closely with men like Michael Collins, Liam Lynch, and his own staff at GHQ, Mulcahy was responsible for directing the Anglo-Irish war of independence, 1919–1921. He continued as chief of staff during the six months of the Truce up to the time when the Treaty was ratified by Dáil Éireann in January, 1922.

Mulcahy was appointed minister for defence in the post-Treaty Dáil government. When the civil war broke out, he returned to the army as chief of staff. Soon afterwards he asked Michael Collins, who was then chairman of the Provisional Government and virtual leader of the country, to return to the army as commander-in-chief. These two men guided the Free State army through the perils of civil war until Collins was killed on 22 August 1922. Mulcahy then became commander-in-chief as well as minister for defence, assuming the awesome responsibility of ensuring the survival of the Free State. After the civil war, Mulcahy continued as minister for defence in the Free State cabinet until the army mutiny of 1924.

Mulcahy remained in the political wilderness until 1927 when, because of pressure from the rank and file of Cumann na nGaedheal, President Cosgrave appointed him minister for local government and public health. He was Mr Cosgrave's most active lieutenant and assumed the leadership of the party when Cosgrave retired in 1944.

Mulcahy was the moving force behind the formation of the inter-party government in 1948. He organized the coalition and persuaded Mr John Costello to become Taoiseach. The inter-party government was defeated in 1951, but was re-elected in 1954 for a further three-year period. On both occasions Mulcahy was minister for education.

Mulcahy married Mary Josephine Ryan in 1919 and had six children. "Min" Ryan, as she was known, was a member of a prominent nationalist family from Wexford—most of whom were active on the anti-Treaty side and subsequently in the Fianna Fáil party. Mulcahy had five sisters, four of whom became nuns, and two brothers. Paddy Mulcahy was chief of staff of the army from 1955 to 1959. His younger brother, Sam, otherwise known as Dom Columban Mulcahy, established the first post-reformation Cistercian community in Nunraw, Scotland in 1948.

Mulcahy retired from politics in 1959. During his retirement, he spent much of his time annotating and archiving his extensive collection of papers which covered the Anglo-Irish war, the civil war and the early political life of the Free State. He also recorded numerous conversations with contemporaries, family members and historians about the revolutionary period. Mulcahy died in 1971 at the age of eighty-six.

This brief biographical note of Richard Mulcahy is based on a memo written by Professor Michael Hayes in 1962. Professor Hayes was Chairman of the Dáil from the ratification of the Treaty until the change of government in 1932. He was a contemporary and intimate friend of Mulcahy from the time of their first meeting in 1916.

ONE

The Formation of a Revolutionary

I was in the presence of my Commander-in-Chief; both of us in the hands of the British Army authorities; I could be nothing but the most perfect soldier; it was a moment for standing to attention.

Richard Mulcahy, *Recollections of Easter Week*

A Nation cannot be fully free in which even a small section of its people have not freedom. A nation cannot be said fully to live in spirit, or materially, while there is denied to any section of its people a share of the wealth and the riches that God bestowed around them.

Richard Mulcahy, TD, Speech in the Dáil, 21 January 1919

In many ways, Richard Mulcahy was a most appropriate candidate for a leading role in the revolution for Irish independence and in the transformation of Ireland from colony to state. Having grown up in the last years of the 19th century, educated at a Christian Brothers' school and nurtured in the social atmosphere of large provincial towns where his father was a civil servant, Mulcahy typified the mores, beliefs, and limitations of a generation of Irishmen and women who were part of an emerging Catholic middle class.

Mulcahy came of age amid intense cultural and political ferment. Anticipating a Home Rule bill that would grant it a limited form of independence, nationalist Ireland sought to justify its claim to nationhood. As England's first colony, Ireland had known both the benefits and brutalities of British domination. Association with England had forged a political unity unfamiliar to Gaelic Ireland, provided direct participation in the parliamentary tradition of Westminster and, by the turn of the century, had created an internal bureaucracy and local government structure that would be a citadel of stability. However, like so many other colonized people, the Irish also experienced the more destructive aspects of colonialism—the dehumanization, the loss of dignity, the atrophying of indigenous culture and the confusion of identity. Alienated from their own history, the conquered people were stereotyped as inferior, incapable of governing themselves, cursed with a culture which was at best considered quaint, at worst, primitive.[1]

The Irish response to colonialism followed the general historical pattern. A large segment of the Irish responded to British colonialism by becoming blatantly assimilationist. They wished to forget their origins, to cleanse themselves of Irishness. Irish assimilationists willingly embraced British culture and accepted British standards as indicative of a superior way of life; however, a significant segment of nationalist opinion rejected assimilation and saw their task as finding or perhaps recreating their indigenous culture in such a way as to both demonstrate their cultural uniqueness and confer dignity on a conquered people.

Under the pervasive influence of the 19th-century European nationalism, earlier Irish nationalists such as Thomas Davis and Young Ireland had sketched the outline of a viable Irish identity. The imminent expectation of Home Rule, however, compelled the Irish nationalists of Mulcahy's time to color in the details. They drew an ideological portrait which conferred a distinctive identity on a colonized people, an identity that was suitable for an emerging middle class. It was a unique blend of Gaelic culture, Catholicism and Victorianism, a composite of past and present.

Reaching into their pre-colonial past, nationalists affirmed their commitment to Gaelic culture in general and the Irish language in particular. In the criteria of cultural nationalism, language was the key distinction of nationhood, the vital component which distinguished one group from another and justified the quest for political independence. To the resurrection and recreation of Gaelic culture was added the cultural dimension of Catholicism. Once an emblem of inferiority and colonized status, Catholicism now was a badge of identity. To their definition of identity, nationalist Ireland appended elements of Victorianism such as respectability, self-help, and a puritanical zeal and righteousness—qualities that would be suitable for the type of Irish society they envisioned. Despite their protest against Anglicization, they blended elements of middle-class Victorian thought into the ideological background of their collective self-portrait.

Richard Mulcahy was both product and advocate of this definition of identity. His vision of Irish society was formed during this age of intellectual ferment, discovery and rediscovery. His passion for Gaelic culture, his zealous Catholicism, and his belief in the value of Victorian virtues determined and sustained his political and social vision throughout his long political career.

Unquestionably, the most pervasive element in shaping Mulcahy's values and beliefs was Catholicism. His writings and reflections are laced with unselfconscious references to God and the Church. With directness and simplicity, for example, he would write of his early stay in County Wexford, "If Wexford was a kind of a vacuum, it was a restful one where at 6 o'clock every evening there was benediction. I usually went from the office so that the day closed on quite a restful and reverend [*sic*] note before I went home to tea close by."[2] Mulcahy, four of whose five sisters would enter the convent, enjoyed life long friendships with nuns and priests. As was typical for many of his generation—the comparison with de Valera, for example, is strikingly obvious—Catholicism was an integral and integrating facet of his life. More than simply adhering to the teachings of the Church or the dictates of the bishops, it was an ingrained value structure within which the religious doctrine of the Church and the demands of national life coexisted.

As a young man, Mulcahy was also very much the Victorian. His character reflected the virtues of self-help, self-discipline, hard work and personal reserve. His early life was a testimony to diligence, determination and discipline. Although Mulcahy discontinued his formal education in 1902 to embark on a career in the post office, he retained not only a love for learning but a belief that education was a means of social mobility. A self-imposed course of study moved him up the scale of the post office hierarchy to a position in the engineering division. He later remembered how he disciplined himself for "private study and morning work", and recounted how, during one period of his life, he studied from 5 a.m. to 6 a.m. before setting off for a full day's work.[3]

Mulcahy was, however, also part of a broader tradition, heir to a more general historical lineage. In the spirit of 19th-century European nationalism, Mulcahy believed that the nation—its language, its traditions, its spirit, its people as a whole—was an intrinsic good. Each nation, therefore, had a right to determine its own destiny, to make decisions in its own self-interest, to protect that unique character with which it was endowed. These beliefs were the general guiding principles behind Mulcahy's career.

Mulcahy arrived in Dublin in 1908. Here he successfully tutored himself for the matriculation examination, and then enrolled in Kevin Street technical school and, later, Bolton Street School for evening classes. Years after, when he was minister for education, his experience at these technical colleges would influence his attitudes and policies. In 1911, he turned down a College of Science scholarship because the post office would not grant him a three-year leave of absence. Displaying a caution perhaps typical of a type of civil servant mentality, he wrote: "I balked at the prospect which leaving the service in those circumstances might open up, and I continued my night study at the technical school at Bolton Street into 1914."[4] His cautious attitude would change radically, however, when, swept up in nationalist politics, Mulcahy abandoned a respectable career for the position of chief of staff of the Irish Volunteers.

Mulcahy's earliest colleagues in the post office stimulated his interest in the nationalist movement of the day. They introduced him to Arthur Griffith's paper, the *United Irishman*. It was an unlikely publication for the Mulcahy household. Mulcahy remembered his mother allowing him to read it as long as he "did not bother . . . [his] father by letting him see it lying around.[5] He read it thoroughly, its philosophy moulding his ideas, shaping his opinions, keeping him informed of the nationalist perspective on current events. Like many of his generation, Mulcahy looked to Griffith as his ideological mentor:

> It was Griffith who most fully painted in his weekly writings for us the traditions and the resources of Ireland, portrayed its mission, and gave us for practical purposes our dream, our sense of work, and opened for us work's widespreading scope.[6]

Quite typically, Mulcahy's formal introduction to the national movement came via the study of the Irish language and the Gaelic League. He recalled:

> News of the Gaelic League came to Thurles in about the autumn of 1902 when a lay teacher who had been a member of the Croke hurling club in Dublin, and no doubt connected with the language movement in Dublin, came to teach in the Christian Brothers . . . . He was given permission by the Brothers to take classes in Irish in the afternoon and some of us used to go up, and in one of the lower rooms . . . we began a certain amount of instruction in Irish.[7]

Within two years, Thurles had regular Gaelic League classes. Mulcahy applied himself diligently and eventually became fluent in Irish. He remained active in the Gaelic League as he moved from town to town, post office to post office. The Gaelic League offered him more than just a language course. It provided him with the opportunity to participate in a nationalist organization. It also gave him the chance to socialize with a congenial and interesting group of people and established for him "a definite social contact unrelated with mere official work and encouraging in relation to things that were definitely going to [be] an important national and educational influence.[8] His love of the Irish language and his belief that it held the key to Ireland's independence would remain with him throughout his life. It would become, in fact, a dominant theme of his political career.

Despite his growing sense of national involvement, Mulcahy seems to have been almost apolitical in his early years. Once, for example, he came upon a large political meeting at which William O'Brien, the veteran parliamentarian, was speaking and did not even make the effort to find out what it was all about. Years later, he wrote: "It perhaps is not easy to understand at this distance that I didn't go down to see what it was all about or that I didn't feel that it was something to be interested in."[9]

This example illuminates an important fact about Mulcahy. Despite spending the greater portion of his life in politics, Mulcahy was a politician made, not born. Because politics was a duty rather than a vocation of choice, Mulcahy did not seem to possess those intuitive political instincts which enable politicians to be successful. His later career demonstrated this.

He would be outmanoeuvered by his cabinet colleagues and by his political opponents, and he never quite understood why his party accrued such a dismal electoral record. Mulcahy was dedicated, hard-working, and sincere. But he was not a successful politician.

By the time the post office transferred him to Dublin, Mulcahy's nationalist consciousness had clearly been raised, but he was not yet a revolutionary, not yet an advocate of an armed struggle for independence. Eight years before he would participate in the Rising of 1916 and ten years before he would become chief of staff of the Volunteers, Mulcahy was very much the moderate. He remembered believing at that time that the nation was simply fighting for its own parliament, for some kind of home rule.[10] This is clearly not the position of an extremist.

Mulcahy's evolution from moderate to revolutionary was aided by his decision to join the Keating Branch of the Gaelic League in Dublin. It was of the utmost significance in introducing him to advanced nationalist circles. Here he met many of the people who were to play a dominant role in the struggle for independence. Cathal Brugha—destined to be Mulcahy's colleague and then his bitter foe—was president of the Keating Branch. Here also he developed a friendship with Thomas Ashe who gave Mulcahy his chance to participate in the 1916 Rising. Most importantly, here he met Michael Collins, with whom he would work so closely and successfully in the Anglo-Irish war. It was in the Keating Branch that Mulcahy established himself in an active and advanced group, and made the contacts that promulgated him into struggle for independence. It was, in his own words, a "spawning bed". As Mulcahy noted, when the Irish took over the British headquarters in Dublin in 1922, four of the five men who represented the Irish army were former members of the Keating branch of the league— Mulcahy then minister for defence and commander-in-chief; Gearoid O'Sullivan, adjutant-general; Diarmuid O'Hegarty, director of intelligence; and Sean O'Murthuile, quartermaster-general.[11]

Furthermore, soon after he arrived in Dublin, Mulcahy became a member of the Irish Republican Brotherhood—a secret society dedicated to securing complete independence for Ireland. Prior to this, he was only indirectly acquainted with the IRB. He subscribed in 1906 to *The Republic*, then the organ of the IRB, and some of his friends and colleagues in Wexford may have been members of this secret society. He had heard that there was "an organisation that was not Sinn Féin nor the Irish Parliamentary Party, but that was out for the freedom of Ireland".[12] When he inquired about this organisation from a contact he had been sent to see, Mulcahy was told that the organization in question was the IRB. His induction into the secret society was less than inspiring. His contact

. . . put his hand in his waistcoat pocket and took out a small slip of paper which he unfolded and holding it out for me to see said, "and that is the oath they take." When I had looked at it he put it back in his pocket and said that he would get in touch with me again in about a fortnight, and bring me to a meeting of one of the groups or circles. This he did by bringing me to a room in the Irish National Foresters' Hall at 41 Parnell Square, where without any more ceremony than an introduction to the person who was to preside over the meeting, and a welcome as a new member of the meeting, I became a member of the IRB.[13]

While Mulcahy's initiation into the IRB was less disheartening than that of Denis McCullough, who was inducted in the back room of a pub into a circle which consisted of men who drank too much and talked about what might have been, it nevertheless indicated the looseness of the organization.

Mulcahy became a member of the Teeling circle. According to him, during subsequent monthly meetings which rarely lasted more than twenty minutes, members simply paid their dues and suggested other potential members:

There were no matters for discussion, there was no necessity for anything like an agenda, the chairman might have some remarks to make about matters of passing interest. . . . The members had no routine duties nor responsibilities of any kind nor any drilling. On one occasion an elderly member of our circle came one night with a rifle under his topcoat, and explained to us the parts of the rifle and gave us their names.[14]

While the reorganization efforts of IRB leaders Denis McCullough, Bulmer Hobson and the veteran Fenian Tom Clarke would eventually tighten and renew the organization, it would take time before their efforts would produce any significant results in the activities of the rank and file.[15]

Overall, Mulcahy's transfer to Dublin opened up for him an exciting, vibrant world. He remembered feeling that "Dublin in its own very democratic way was for all intents and purposes a university city. Its various institutions great and small and its societies offered spheres of information, instruction and company promising an ever widening field of interest."[16] There was electricity in the air. It was, after all, not only the Dublin of the Gaelic League and the IRB, but also the Dublin of W.B. Yeats, Lady Gregory and the Abbey Theatre; of Arthur Griffith and Sinn Féin; of poet, educator and orator Patrick Pearse and his innovative school, St Enda's; of labour leaders, James Connolly and Jim Larkin and their Citizen Army; of small groups of people who mingled freely, debated hotly and, above all, cared passionately.

The British elections of 1910 increased the intensity of debate and added to the feeling of excitement. These elections left Prime Minister

Asquith's government dependent on the votes of the Irish Parliamentary Party. Home Rule appeared certain. Irish nationalists argued about the powers an Irish parliament would have, about the best terms they could expect. Irish unionists, on the other hand, opposed any Home Rule bill and their opposition crackled into threats of armed rebellion. They openly proclaimed their intention of defying the British parliament if it passed a Home Rule bill for Ireland.

Within three years, the discord reached crisis proportions. Excitement gave way to watching and waiting. Nationalist Ireland watched and waited as the British government lost its will to implement Home Rule for all of Ireland and as John Redmond and his party seemed more and more helpless. Only the unionists remained firm and determined. They marched; they organized; they badgered the government; they threatened rebellion; and perhaps, most importantly, they formed themselves into an army, the Ulster Volunteers, whose sole purpose was to prevent the passage of Home Rule.

For nationalist Ireland not to have reacted to the unionist example would have been strange, indeed. Previously, much of Ireland had been content with the prospect of Home Rule. Leaders such as Arthur Griffith and Patrick Pearse waited to see how encompassing a bill John Redmond could deliver. Such sentiments were so pervasive that the IRB was worried. Die-hard revolutionaries like Tom Clarke believed that a Home Rule bill would preclude all possibility of an armed rebellion against England and total independence would be lost. He need not have been concerned. The failure of the British to carry through such legislation for all of Ireland in 1912 strengthened the position of those who claimed that the constitutional process would never work for Ireland. Threats of treason seemed to persuade the British government while the constitutional politics of the Irish Parliamentary Party failed. As talk of partition floated through the halls of Westminster, the British cabinet equivocated.

Nationalist Ireland tried to strengthen the resolve of the cabinet by forming its own counterpart to the Ulster Volunteers, the Irish Volunteers. While the IRB had previously discussed such a possibility, the public suggestion came from Eoin MacNeill, founder of the Gaelic League and known follower of Redmond. He suggested that the rest of Ireland follow the example of Ulster and create their own Volunteer force. MacNeill's idea met with a welcome response. Not only was the IRB leadership delighted with the idea, but many nationalists, tired of waiting on the sidelines, welcomed the creation of a military force that might influence the political future of Ireland.

This was Mulcahy's position. He was conscious of this sense of waiting, and felt "reduced to an arid patience" until the Volunteer organization was formed. Mulcahy was among the 3,000 who enlisted on 25 November 1913, during a mass meeting at the Rotunda Rink in Dublin. To him, the meeting was "a complete and joyous bursting open of a door, not only to the complete Dublin populace, but to the complete body of the patient, silent, suppressed Nationalist element in Ireland awakening them to their strength and inviting them to instruction".[17]

Irish nationalists now had an army, a "people's army", to press their claim for Home Rule. The establishment of the Volunteers also gave the IRB the opportunity it had been awaiting. IRB stalwarts quickly infiltrated the leadership of the Volunteers and Brotherhood officials instructed their members to join this open and popular movement. Mulcahy remembered the instruction given his circle at their monthly meeting to "join the Volunteers and take your orders from your superior officers". He insisted later that this was the only direction he ever received as a member of the IRB during his entire army career.[18] Mulcahy's assessment is probably accurate. The IRB had so thoroughly infiltrated its men into the officer corps of the Volunteers that there was no need to issue orders outside the regular chain of command. Some believed that the IRB controlled virtually all the important commandant positions in the country. Clearly, the IRB was covertly shaping the new army for its own purpose: armed rebellion against the British.

The establishment of the Volunteers began Mulcahy's career as an "army man". While Mulcahy would be in uniform only until 1924, his experience in the army was a formative one. In career terms, it was his most successful period. He rose to be chief of staff and then minister for defence. As chief of staff, he was instrumental in creating a guerrilla army whose success would force the British to the negotiating table. And, in a time of even greater turmoil and tragedy, as minister for defence, he organized the army of the newly established state to defeat the rebels in the civil war of 1922–23. When he resigned in 1924, he was one of the most prominent leaders in the new State.

In personal terms, the founding of the Volunteers provided Mulcahy with a sense of purpose and belonging which he had never before known. Contacts made in the Gaelic League and the IRB now crystallized into warm and intimate relationships, and this acceptance helped him to overcome a certain shyness and self-consciousness that had plagued him from childhood. Mulcahy recalled, for example, feeling hesitant and unsure when walking as a child through the square in Thurles.[19] Even as a young man in Dublin, he remembered how he often would leave his rooms in the evening to spend some time at the National Library and "turn back at the corner of Nassau Street, too overcome by shyness to think of facing into the big brightly lit reading room".[20] He would never lose his sense of reserve, never be able to engage, for example, in the pranks, in the free and easy camaraderie which characterized Collins' relationship with his friends. But his acceptance in the Volunteers and then the IRA eased his self-consciousness and gave him a feeling of relaxed camaraderie and an important sense of belonging. Mulcahy long remembered this esprit de corps.

In the Volunteers, Mulcahy was a member of C Company of the Dublin Brigade and worked his way through the ranks from corporal to sergeant to second lieutenant. On the eve of the 1916 Rising, he was promoted to first lieutenant. With the skills he developed as an engineer in the post office and his ability to work a telegraph machine, he took charge of instructions in signalling and inter-communication. He worked hard with his company as they tried to form themselves into an organized, disciplined, and trained army. They practised drills. They learned how to handle a rifle. And they marched along city streets and in country lanes until they began to feel and look like an army.

Shortages of arms and ammunition plagued the Volunteers. To meet this problem, the Irish Volunteers once again followed the example of the Ulster Volunteers who had dramatically run guns ashore at Larne. On 26 July 1914, the Volunteers marched to Howth—a seemingly routine outing. It was only when they approached Howth that they were aware that they "were out for something special". Quickly, the men were ordered to form into lines to move the rifles off a boat and "were very soon on . . . [a] sunny march back without any memory but the tumultuous reception of the arms and falling back again into company and route formation".[21]

The return to Dublin was not to be pleasant and uneventful, however. The authorities, who ignored the Ulster Volunteers' gun-running, chose not to ignore this same activity by the Irish Volunteers. The British military blocked the approach of the columns into Dublin. The columns halted. As the Volunteer officers argued and parlayed with their British counterparts, the command was whispered through the ranks for the Volunteers to disperse. They were to hide their guns wherever they could—in gardens, ditches, hedges and homes—and try to collect them later.

Mulcahy hid his rifle close by and returned to Dublin. There he learned that the military had over-reacted and fired into a crowd awaiting the return of the Volunteers. Three people were killed and thirty-eight wounded in what came to be called the Bachelor's Walk massacre. As Mulcahy noted:

> The attempted difference of treatment by the British authorities of the Volunteer gun runners to that of the Unionist gun runners incensed people further. The incompetence and the futility of the move taken by the Authorities made them a laughing stock into the bargain; but the brutality, bringing tragedy, brought the whole episode to a climax that was symbolic of what Nationalist Ireland was faced with. The whole country resounded for days.[22]

Mulcahy returned with a group of Volunteers that evening to collect the hidden rifles. In a humorous note to what was a tragic day, he remembered how they went to collect the rifles in a large taxi and that it was his first drive in a motor car.[23]

The Howth gun-running incident and the Bachelor's Walk shooting clearly illustrated the double standard of the British authorities. One set of rules governed their behavior toward the unionists and another, their behavior toward the nationalists. Coupled with their toleration of treasonous threats from unionist politicians, and their weakening resolve toward a home rule bill, the British cabinet and its military authorities strengthened the position of those who looked to armed rebellion to free Ireland.

Despite the provocative actions of the British government and its representatives, most of the Volunteers still viewed themselves as a defensive force whose primary purpose was to insure passage of a Home Rule bill. Redmond remained the acknowledged political leader of nationalist Ireland. Although he was initially cool to the formation of the Volunteers, he had come to appreciate their strategic importance in his negotiations with the British. In June 1914, he, therefore, publicly threatened that unless twenty-five of his nominees were added to the governing body of the Volunteers, he would create a rival force. To preserve unity, Volunteer leaders acquiesced. But the agreement was short-lived.

With the declaration of war in August of 1914, John Redmond and the Volunteer executive agreed that the Volunteers would defend Ireland so that British troops stationed in Ireland would be free to fight in France. Redmond soon had a change of heart. In a speech at Woodenbridge, in his own Wicklow constituency, on 20 September 1914, he called on the Volunteers to enlist and fight as members of the British forces—an idea totally alien to their spirit and purpose. Redmond's suggestion shattered the precarious unity of the organization. Most of the original members of the Volunteer executive repudiated Redmond's idea. A majority of the rank and file of the Volunteers, however, heeded his call—and many subsequently died in the trenches of France. By splintering the Volunteer movement, Redmond enabled the IRB to more easily control the minority that remained within the original Volunteer organization.

Mulcahy remained loyal to the original executive and, during 1915, became increasingly involved in Volunteer activities. To give themselves practice in simulated fighting conditions, the Volunteers regularly held manoeuvres. To Mulcahy, it seemed as if "we were manoeuvring always from the beginning of 1915 to the beginning of 1916".[24] In September 1915, Mulcahy spent his annual holiday at an officer training camp at Coosan, Athlone—one of three such camps in Ireland.[25]

At Coosan, the first week was devoted to simple drill movements, small tactical exercises, scouting expeditions and communications and signalling. The second week was spent on strenuous route marches and much more vigorous drills and exercises. There was even some real-life drama. One day, after a tenant gave the Volunteers permission to pitch camp, his landlord ordered them off the site. They refused to move and serious sentry duty was required that night to ensure their safety. Interestingly, the Royal Irish Constabulary, while duly observing the actions of the Volunteers, made no move to interfere with their activities. In fact, Mulcahy and his comrades seemed to move about openly in uniform. Uniformed men marching through the countryside and city streets became a fairly common sight. Thus, a Volunteer march through Dublin on Easter Monday, 1916, would attract no undue notice.

A curious situation was developing, however. Volunteers such as Mulcahy were living a split existence. By day, they tended to their jobs. At night, on the weekends and, sometimes, on holidays, they practised being soldiers. But it was not clear where their soldiering would lead them. For Mulcahy:

> This 1915 period of annual leave was dominated entirely by the thought of volunteer activity and training; language matters were entirely in the background. That did not mean, however, that there was any sense of emergency in the atmosphere. I went back to my civil service duties and my ordinary work with C Company of the 2nd Battalion.[26]

In fact, Mulcahy characterized the period from 1913 right up until the Rising of 1916 as one in which the Volunteers were "waiting for the Home Rule situation to develop naturally".[27] Most of the Volunteers, he added, thought they had no other option.[28]

Other options, however, were being considered. As early as 1915, the Supreme Council of the IRB established a military committee to plan, organize and execute a general rising of the Volunteers before the end of the war. Joseph Mary Plunkett, Patrick Pearse, Eamonn Ceannt, Thomas Clarke, and Sean MacDermott comprised the original military committee. Later James Connolly and Thomas MacDonagh were added. They selected Easter Sunday of 1916 as the date for the rising. To thwart the spies and informers that had foiled past efforts, the committee worked in the utmost secrecy. Their clandestine behavior was also necessitated by the fact that they were keeping the plans for a rising from the more moderate faction of the Volunteers, including the chief of staff, Eoin MacNeill. That the IRB could contemplate the staging of a rebellion without the co-operation of the chief of staff indicated its dominance within the movement.

Mulcahy remained on the fringe of the IRB during the Easter Rising. Easter Week, in fact, belonged not to those who would continue the fight for independence in the Anglo-Irish war, but to the military council who had planned, executed and directed this Rising. These men would be executed by the British, and their successors would completely change military tactics. The grand defiance of an uprising would be replaced by the small skirmishes and harassing attacks of a guerrilla war.

The Rising came as a shock to Mulcahy as well as to most of the Volunteers. Mulcahy certainly knew the members of the military council, but had no inkling of their plans until a week before the Rising. He was indeed so far from being suspicious that when Diarmuid Lynch asked him in January 1916, for the names of some telegraph and telephone linemen at the post office, Mulcahy thought nothing of it. He did not see "any reason for attaching any special significance to this request of Lynch's".[29] Mulcahy's own plans for Easter 1916 included a three-day religious retreat and then a holiday with his family in Clare. He intended to skip the proposed Volunteer maneuvers set for that weekend. He felt he needed the rest.

A mere eight days before Easter, Mulcahy was still unaware that rebellion was imminent. Having just been promoted to the rank of first lieutenant, Mulcahy went to the Saturday night meeting of the officers of the Dublin Brigade. He listened as Pearse described the Easter Sunday manoeuvres as especially crucial, and called for all members of the brigade to attend and bring with them any and all military equipment that they owned. In response to a question about those who were scheduled to work on Easter Sunday, Pearse made the prophetic comment that no one who was afraid of losing a job should come. A more realistic caveat would have been that no one who was afraid of losing his or her life should come out on Easter Sunday.[30] Mulcahy accepted it all at face value.

Later that night, however, at a dance cleverly arranged as a cover so that the leaders of the rising could meet their officers, Mulcahy talked to Sean MacDermott. Without giving Mulcahy any background information or explanation, MacDermott asked Mulcahy if he had any plans for blowing up the telegraph system in Dublin. Taken aback, Mulcahy responded that he had not. But then, recalling his January conversation with Lynch, he mentioned that Lynch might have specific plans. MacDermott was not pleased with Mulcahy's response and informed Mulcahy that he would see him the next evening. Mulcahy, however, resisted the temptation to cancel his plans, and confessed to Mac-Dermott that he was going on retreat and would see him when he returned to Dublin on Holy Thursday. By now, he suspected "that there was something up",[31] but nothing so urgent as to require him to meet with MacDermott before Thursday. He went on retreat.

When Mulcahy returned to Dublin, he met with MacDermott and Tom Clarke. They told him about the general plans for the rising and gave him his assignment for Easter Sunday. Mulcahy was to be part of the group whose objective was to destroy the communications system in Dublin. His specific task was the destruction of the communication lines that connected Dublin with Belfast and those at Howth junction that allowed communication with Britain. Mulcahy was to work with two other volunteers from his area and some members of the Citizen Army.[32] All seemed in order.

However, through a series of mishaps and misadventures, the rebels' plans for an Easter Sunday rising went awry. The story is well known. Secrecy was breached. MacNeill, the chief of staff, and those who opposed any offensive action by the Volunteers, discovered what their colleagues had actually planned for Easter Sunday. Arms were lost. MacNeill issued a countermanding order cancelling the Easter maneuvers. Confusion and chaos reigned. Some officers received contradictory sets of orders, one from Pearse and one from MacNeill. Some officers saw only MacNeill's order, which he published in the *Sunday Independent*. Officers, especially those outside of Dublin, floundered. Most did nothing.

Mulcahy experienced this same kind of confusion. Leaving home for his Easter assignment, he was ready to participate in the rising. He left this description of himself:

> . . . a young man . . . stood on the steps of Bayview House, Sutton. He wore the leggings, knee breeches and the uniform of the Irish Volunteers. The cap badge of the Dublin Brigade held the soft leaf of his green hat pinned up to one side. Signalling flags and a long strong handled bayonet together with a satchel were attached to his bicycle. Otherwise he appeared to have no other military equipment. It was 3:20 p.m.[33]

Mulcahy was stopped short by a fellow lodger who showed him MacNeill's order in the *Sunday Independent*. He wavered, then threw off his uniform and headed into the eerie quiet of Sunday in Dublin. After wandering the empty streets, he spotted James Connolly and asked him about further orders. Connolly curtly replied that "if there are further orders you'll get them".[34] Mulcahy believed that he had been indiscreet in asking this question, although, given the confusing state of affairs, it seems both natural and necessary.

On Monday morning, Mulcahy returned to Dublin which had lost its stillness and was now experiencing a certain amount of activity. Mulcahy met MacDonagh, "a military cape hanging from his shoulders", who ordered Mulcahy to be ready to "strike at twelve" that day. Mulcahy set about organizing the destruction of the cables at Howth junction.[35]

Despite the setbacks and confusion, the military council decided to go ahead with the Rising. Hard-liners like Tom Clarke pushed for military action. The poets and the pragmatists agreed. Those, like Pearse and Plunkett, who believed a blood sacrifice was necessary to rejuvenate the spirit of the nation, supported Clarke. Those, like Connolly, who saw the Rising as striking a blow at England and English capitalism, believed that they had gone too far to turn back. To a degree, they were correct.

Dublin Castle, the seat of British rule in Ireland, was simply awaiting final authorization to arrest the leaders of the Volunteers. Despite the overwhelming odds, if the military council was to stage an uprising, it had to act at once. Thus, on Easter Monday, the Volunteers and the Citizen Army occupied strategic points throughout Dublin. At noon, they raised the tricolor over the General Post Office and Pearse read the Proclamation of the Republic establishing Ireland as a free and independent nation. The rebel forces, approximately one thousand men and women, paralysed the city for about a week. It was a heroic albeit futile gesture of defiance and self-sacrifice.

Mulcahy's orders were to report to the GPO after he had completed his work at Howth junction. He never made it back into the city. After meeting MacDonagh, he had hurried to rouse his companions for the Howth assignment. He could contact only two of his group. In a scene which illustrates the inexperience of these revolutionaries, Mulcahy recalled that on their way to Howth Junction, he learned that one of the pair had left his gun at home. Mulcahy sent him back to retrieve it.

Nearing their assignment, Mulcahy's group met two RIC men. Mulcahy positioned his hand on his gun, thinking they were about to be stopped and he would have to fight.[36] The RIC, still oblivious to the impending Rising, were so accustomed to Volunteers marching about, that they passed them by with hardly a glance. After cutting the communications cables, the three Volunteers were unclear as to what to do next. Feeling somewhat exposed in uniform and uncertain as to how events had progressed in Dublin, the two uniformed men sent their civilian-clad colleague into Dublin for news of the Rising.

Upon his return, Mulcahy's companion was mistakenly captured by Thomas Ashe and the Fingal Volunteers of the Fifth Battalion, Dublin Brigade. He informed Ashe that he was looking for Mulcahy who was somewhere in the area. Mulcahy subsequently joined Ashe and his men for one of the most successful encounters of Easter Week. Ashe appointed him second-in-command and together they led their men in an attack on two RIC barracks at Swords and Donabate in County Dublin. They hoped their action would relieve some of the pressure on the men in the city. Under Ashe's direction, the Fingal Volunteers successfully disarmed the police and thus acquired for themselves some much needed arms and ammunition.

The most dramatic encounter of the Fingal Volunteers, however, took place on Friday at the RIC barracks in Ashbourne, County Meath. There Ashe and Mulcahy succeeded in capturing a police force who significantly outnumbered them. Mulcahy and Ashe had divided their force into four sections to enhance their mobility and convey the illusion of far greater numbers. Mulcahy took charge of the sections which were to force the police down towards Ashe in a pincer-type movement. After a heated battle with the police, the Volunteers were successful. Police morale was broken by their commander's death and they agreed to surrender. The encounter at Ashbourne lasted for more than five hours. Two Volunteers and ten policemen died; five Volunteers and eighteen RIC were wounded.[37]

Not only was the fighting at Ashbourne one of the few military successes of Easter Week, it was also important in terms of the subsequent guerrilla campaign. The fighting in Dublin was of a defensive nature. The Volunteers seized buildings and waited until they were attacked. It was a grand gesture which committed all the forces of the Volunteers to action at one time and in traditional fighting positions. Mulcahy observed that in such a conflict, there was little opportunity to display any military strategy or distinction— to do anything, in fact, except "wait for the end".[38] It was also the type of military situation which makes it almost impossible for those with smaller numbers and limited amounts of arms and ammunition to win.

The engagement at Ashbourne, however, prefigured the guerrilla war that the Irish Volunteers would fight in 1919–21. Select troops would fight limited, intermittent battles. Moreover, the Anglo-Irish war began with attacks on RIC barracks to capture arms and ammunition. Ashbourne was the prototype engagement and Mulcahy, who would be the chief of staff during the war of independence, was one of its architects. It is no wonder that one of his colleagues subsequently remarked that Mulcahy was the only one to come out of 1916 with a military reputation.[39]

Although the Fingal Volunteers were successful, the Rising was overall a resounding military defeat. In Dublin, the British poured in troops and sent a gunboat up the Liffey. Buildings were set on fire. Volunteers were forced to yield their positions. The death toll mounted. After a week, concerned over the growing number of deaths and worried about the fate of those still fighting, Pearse gave the order to surrender.

While Pearse was surrendering in Dublin, the men at Ashbourne were still enjoying the feeling of victory engendered by their successes that week. Mulcahy remembered how, just before they heard about the surrender order, Ashe turned to him and said, "I get the smell of victory in the air.'[40] The mood was irreparably destroyed, when, shortly after, word came of Pearse's order to surrender. Mulcahy was sent to Dublin with the police authorities to confirm Pearse's order. Mulcahy has left a vivid, poignant picture of his encounter with Pearse:

> Inside the prison, on the right, the door of the second or third cell was noisily opened by a soldier who shouted harshly "Get up!" Pearse, in his uniform, was lying on bare trestle boards at the back of the cell; on a small table alongside was a glass of water and some biscuits. He arose and moved quietly a few steps toward us. . . . I turned to the officer and said I wished to speak to Commandant

Pearse alone. I was not surprised that this request was refused, and
that in a manner which alerted me to the full realities of the position.
I was in the presence of my Commander-in-Chief; both of us in the
hands of the British Army authorities; I could be nothing but the
most perfect soldier; it was a moment for standing to attention . . . .
"Is this your order, sir?' I asked, as I held it out before him. Pearse
answered "Yes". "Does it refer to Dublin alone or to the whole of
Ireland?" "It refers to the whole of Ireland." "Would it be any use," I
asked, "if a small band of men who had given a good account of
themselves during the week were to hold out any longer?" And Pearse
replied "No." My lips moved to frame a "Beannacht Dé agat" but
the sound was stifled, absorbed in the solemnity of my salute which
closed the scene.[41]

Mulcahy was next taken to British general headquarters to see General
Friend. He refused to give any information about the military situation of
his battalion. General Friend appealed to him to use his influence to stop
the bloodshed, implying that the British had vast forces with which to
quash further resistance. Mulcahy remained noncommittal, but did inquire
as to the procedure to be followed should his commanding officer chose to
surrender. Trying to denigrate the status of the rebels to mere rowdies, one
British officer flippantly suggested they turn themselves in to the nearest
police authority. The barb lost its sting, however, as General Friend was
forced to point out that "Unfortunately the District Inspector has been
killed and the County Inspector is severely wounded."[42] They arranged that
if Ashe agreed to surrender, a cavalry escort would be sent to receive it.
After Mulcahy returned with verification of Pearse's directive, Ashe
surrendered. The Easter Rising of 1916 was over.

The commonly accepted interpretation of 1916 is that the British actions
after the surrender guaranteed its political success. Coming in the midst of
World War I, the British viewed the Rising as treason. They were determined that the Irish would pay a heavy price. After a charade of a court-
martial, they summarily executed the leaders of the Rising at the agonizing
rate of two a day. Horrifying stories swept through Dublin. The known
pacifist, Francis Sheehy-Skeffington, was shot in cold blood by a crazed
British officer. James Connolly, wounded during the fighting, had to be
strapped to a chair in order to be executed. The cumulative effect of these
events was to turn the Irish population, previously hostile, sympathetic.
While the rebels had originally been scorned as they were marched off to
prison, they became, after their deaths, the martyrs and heroes of 1916.
Thus, according to this interpretation, the British actions turned military
failure into political success.

As a participant in the Rising, Mulcahy took a different view of 1916.
He believed that, even though the leaders of the Rising knew by Easter
Sunday they were doomed to defeat,

> . . . they were fully justified in that by all the circumstances of the case [delay of Home Rule]; they were fully justified in the faith that they had that the people would understand and would react to their gesture, and that when they were gone as they expected to go, that the people would be able to carry on without them, both inspired by their gesture . . . and guided by their own instincts—their own initiative—to a post-rising achievement.[43]

Mulcahy believed that it was the example and the sacrifice of the 1916 leaders that inspired its success, not the executions. The drama of 1916 ignited latent, powerful forces into action. For Mulcahy, the Rising "detonated the whole strength of the people".[44]

Mulcahy's interpretation illuminates several factors overlooked in analyses that concentrate solely on the British executions. First, a number of Volunteers who were confused over the conflicting orders for Easter Sunday genuinely regretted their failure to participate in the Rising. For example, the Cork Volunteers, especially someone like Terence MacSwiney, felt the need to atone for their inactivity. Executions notwithstanding, the struggle for independence, for these men at least, would not have ended in 1916. In some form, in some way, it would have continued.

Secondly, before 1916, the work of the various organizations, loosely termed the Irish-Ireland movement, had raised nationalist consciousness. Men and women had mobilized in a spirit of idealism to create the structures that would enable them to regroup after the rising and carry on the fight for independence. Thirdly, eyewitness accounts of the events of Easter Week—most notably those of James Stephens and Ernie O'Malley—confirm that as Easter week wore on, the general population expressed a growing admiration for the rebels' steadfastness and valor. O'Malley himself seems to have been transformed during Easter Week, from an initial scorn of the rebels and a decision to defend Trinity College against the Volunteers, to growing respect and a rather amateurish attempt to engage in the Rising himself.[45] Even the parliamentary leader, John Dillon, admitted that the 1916 revolutionaries fought gallantly.

Obviously, however, the executions of the leaders of 1916 had a significant impact. Revolutions need martyrs and the British conveniently accommodated the Irish—as they did the South Africans in the Boer War and would do the Indians at Amritsar.[46] That, however, is not to say that but for the executions there would have been no struggle for independence. If the British provoked the Irish to armed struggle, they did so by ignoring their own parliamentary rules and traditions. The executed leaders of 1916 would be hallowed and enshrined, models to imitate, heroes to inspire.

However, in focusing on the actions and reactions of the Irish in 1916 rather than the effects of the British executions, Mulcahy makes the development of the Anglo-Irish war far more intelligible. The Volunteers had been inspired by Pearse and Connolly and their comrades in the GPO. Their deaths only quickened the rebels' resolve to regroup and press the demand for independence. In this, they were aided by the fact that a significant portion of the population had been won over by the work of the many pre-Rising nationalist groups.

Whatever the interpretation of 1916, one point remains clear. The Easter Rising signalled the end of the old order. The Volunteers would carry on the work of the leaders of 1916, but they would do it in a different way, in a way which would provide an example for the revolutionary struggles of the 20th century. The post-Rising Volunteers would fight a successful guerrilla war of liberation. This fact, however, was not yet apparent to Irish nationalists as they faced the consequences of the Easter Rising.

The British response to the Rising was swift and harsh. They declared martial law throughout Ireland. Fifteen prisoners were executed in the first weeks after the Rising. Those who escaped the firing squad were sent to prison. Determined to eradicate the spirit of rebellion from the country, the British swept the streets of Ireland clean looking for anyone who was suspected of being either a rebel or sympathetic to the rebels. They arrested 3,340 men and 79 women, of whom five women and 1,832 men would be interned in Britain.[47] Their sweep yielded them a strange and varied mix of prisoners. Some were Volunteers who had fought in the 1916 Rising; some were Volunteers who had missed the Rising; some were not Volunteers at all. It did not seem to matter. The British were determined to demonstrate that rebellion simply did not pay.

For his part in the Rising, Mulcahy was sent to Knutsford and then to Frongoch prisons. After surrendering to the British cavalry at Ashbourne, the Fingal Volunteers were taken to Richmond jail—the gathering place for all those Volunteers who had surrendered. Hauled into a large room, the prisoners were divided into two groups, one of officers or those the British believed to have played a prominent part in the Rising, and another group consisting of the rank and file, the unknown men of the Volunteer corps. Because the British authorities did not know who he was, Mulcahy was placed in this latter group. A search for the officer who had arranged Ashe's surrender with General Friend yielded no positive identification. Mulcahy believed that slouched on the floor, with the beginnings of a beard visible on his face, the authorities simply did not recognize him. Ashe, however, was brought over to the other side of the room. These men would be tried and sentenced and ultimately would serve longer, harder sentences than Mulcahy's group.

Mulcahy was transferred from Richmond to the prison camp at Knutsford. His recollection of the journey through Dublin is not of being surrounded by a hostile population, but rather of groups of people assembled along the route, rather subdued, "their attitude was one of interest giving a feeling that there were more eyes looking out to see whom they could recognise rather than conveying any critical message." Even when the prisoners encountered a much larger crowd, Mulcahy did not sense that it was "unfriendly".[48]

Mulcahy arrived in Knutsford on 3 May 1916. He would spend six weeks there, three in solitary confinement and three under internee conditions. The conditions in the prison were primitive. There were no mattresses and no pillows. Mulcahy remembered being constantly hungry. The prisoners were forced to subsist basically on tea and bread. The cells were cold. Recalling those days, Mulcahy wrote:

> a great dark cloud of gloom necessarily surrounded our solitary confinement period for the first three weeks in Knutsford. Information seeped into the prison that executions had taken place in Dublin, and generally there were many elements in the situation to torture the heart.[49]

Frongoch, however, would be different. On 17 June 1916, Mulcahy was transferred to Frongoch, the prison in Wales which came to be known as the Sinn Féin university. It was here that Mulcahy experienced the type of organization and solidarity which made prison such an important and radicalizing experience for so many of the prisoners. Basically, the Irish prisoners were in charge of organizing their own living conditions—food, clean-up, recreation, and general discipline. As they considered themselves soldiers, they naturally organized along military lines. There was a camp commandant—J.J. O'Connell when Mulcahy first arrived, to be followed by Michael Staines—and the camp was divided into companies and then by huts. Mulcahy was in charge of D Company and later on became O/C of dormitory No. 3.

When it was not in a state of disturbance, life in the camp tended to follow a set routine. The men were required to present themselves for inspection twice a day to the prison authorities and generally spent the rest of their time on either military drills or in work parties. For recreation, they organized various educational classes: in languages (especially in Irish), in Irish history and even in book-keeping and shorthand. The day ended with the men saying the rosary aloud in Irish. Prison life was building military skills and increasing ideological awareness.

By early summer, the British began releasing some of the internees. Mulcahy was not released at this time. According to his prison record, the reason for his continued internment was that he was part of the group which surrendered to the police after the Ashbourne battle. This obviously classified him as a serious rebel, although the British authorities admitted that "really very little is known about him locally".[50] Mulcahy would be fortunate in retaining that anonymity for the next few years. It was one of the keys to his survival and his success.

For those who remained in prison, life quickly became more exciting as the prisoners set about defying the British authorities. There were two main causes for disturbances at Frongoch—the question of what duties the men should perform, and the British attempt to single out Irish prisoners eligible for conscription. In both cases, the Volunteers acted with a solidarity of purpose and a cunning defiance. In both cases, they were victorious.

The organized defiance of the British authorities in particular, and the experience of prison in general, created a close bond among the internees. It gave them the opportunity to establish intimate relations with men from all over Ireland, contacts that would be valuable in the upcoming guerrilla struggle. In a letter from Frongoch, Mulcahy specifically mentions making "new friends from all parts of the country".[51] Thus, the experience in Frongoch was valuable in terms of the solidarity it built among the men, their exposure to military discipline, their experience of constant drilling, and the educational opportunities it provided for expanding and solidifying nationalist sentiments.

Prisoners who were members of the IRB also used the opportunity of prison life to reorganize the Brotherhood. Most notable among them, of course, was Michael Collins. Mulcahy was not involved. While he knew Collins from the latter's brief sojourn in the Keating Branch, he was not part of the IRB clique. Mulcahy regarded himself as an "outsider" to the inner circle of the Brotherhood and assumed that Collins would have regarded him as such also.[52] He was, therefore, not invited to IRB meetings nor was he privy to their plans. It is interesting that the close relationship which would develop between these two men did not start in Frongoch. More significant was the fact that Mulcahy, the man who would be chief of staff of the army, was not consciously thinking in terms of reorganizing the Volunteers. From Mulcahy's experience, there is no evidence to suggest that the Volunteers were contemplating a guerrilla war or even of actively renewing the struggle with the British. Their thoughts were neither that clear nor that farsighted.[53]

Outside of Frongoch, however, those who had either escaped arrest or had been released were indeed trying to reorganize the Volunteers. In November of 1916, Sean O'Murthuile, Diarmuid O'Hegarty and Cathal Brugha called a meeting of about fifty members of the Volunteers from all over Ireland. Brugha, who had been so severely wounded in the Rising that he was not imprisoned, was looked upon as "the principal councillor and adviser in relation to Volunteer matters".[54] At the November meeting, the Volunteers selected a provisional council to try to reassemble their organization. It was an important step in keeping the Volunteer movement alive and together. It gave the scattered group a sense of purpose—a reason to recruit new members and reorganize their ranks. Moreover, when the internees and then later the sentenced prisoners returned home, they would be able to quickly resume their connections with the Volunteers. Thus, when Mulcahy, along with the other internees in Frongoch, was released in December 1916, the Volunteers had an embryonic organization in place.

The return of the internees in December, followed by the release of the sentenced prisoners in June 1917, quickened the pace of political life in Ireland. The men who returned home found a warm and welcoming atmosphere awaiting them. They had become heroes—or at least the associates of heroes. Yet it was a difficult time. On one level, there was much activity. Nationalist groups like the IRB, the Volunteers, the Gaelic League, Sinn Féin were re-grouping and re-forming, trying to replace leaders lost in the Rising and trying to decide on a post-Rising strategy.

On another level, however, there was much ado about nothing. No one knew exactly what the position of nationalist organizations should be and what work needed to be done. They knew their continued existence was essential. It was just not clear why. Even some of the leaders were unclear as to what should happen next. For example, after his release from prison, Mulcahy returned to Dublin and from there, intended to spend some time in the country. Before he left Dublin, he sought the advice of Arthur Griffith as to what he should say about current political developments when asked for his impressions. Griffith's response was indicative of the state of flux of the time:

> Griffith's attitude was that there wasn't really anything that he could usefully say at the moment and I was struck by his statement that he would "have to look back over the newspapers".[55]

The problems of the returning prisoners were, moreover, exacerbated by feelings of personal anxiety, the lack of employment, and concern over an uncertain future. At this time, Mulcahy enrolled as a medical student in University College, Dublin, and subsisted on an student allowance from the Prisoners' Dependants Fund—a fund set up under the hidden auspices of the IRB and administered first by Kathleen Clarke, widow of Tom Clarke, and then by Michael Collins.

For many of the Volunteers, it was a period of contradictions and possibilities. Mulcahy provides a good example of the lack of focus which permeated nationalist organizations of this period. After his return to Dublin, he rejoined his old company, C Company, which was meeting fairly regularly. Almost immediately he became captain of C Company and within a short time, he was O/C of the 2nd Battalion. However, Mulcahy's duties as O/C were not so pressing that he could not leave Dublin for five months to travel around County Cork collecting funds for the Gaelic League. Interestingly enough, Mulcahy makes no mention of doing any work in Cork for the Volunteers. However, whether officially or not, the contacts he made through the Gaelic League would also be contacts for the Volunteers. In light of his meteoric rise through the ranks of the Volunteers to become chief of staff by March 1918, it is reasonable to assume that Mulcahy's work was not simply limited to the language movement. This was certainly the case later on when Mulcahy used his participation in the Sinn Féin elections as a cover for doing Volunteer work.

Throughout 1917, both the military and political wings of the nationalist movement began to coalesce and define themselves. In the political sphere, the events of the Rising transformed Arthur Griffith's Sinn Féin organization. The British had mistakenly but prophetically dubbed 1916 as "the Sinn Féin rising" and it was through the Sinn Féin clubs that the political challenge to the British would be articulated. In a series of by-elections, Sinn Féin candidates defeated the representatives of the Irish Parliamentary Party. What emerged from these electoral victories was the policy of abstention from the British House of Commons—those elected would not take their seats. The election in Clare in July 1917 was particularly significant. It brought to the forefront of the movement Eamon de Valera, destined to be the head of both Sinn Féin and the Volunteers. It secured the status of Sinn Féin as a new national party, confirmed the policy of abstentionism and endorsed the general principles of 1916.

The election in Clare also was significant for the Volunteers. In organizing Sinn Féin branches throughout the country, in many cases the Volunteers were the nucleus around which the organization formed. They were also very active in supporting Sinn Féin candidates in the 1917 by-elections. In fact, the Volunteers were so involved that in May 1917, the Volunteer Executive issued a directive warning of the pitfalls of becoming too involved in the political movement and losing sight of their primary function as soldiers:

> They are at liberty, and are encouraged, to join any other movement that aims at making Ireland a separate and independent nation. They are reminded, however, of what occurred when Parnell induced the Fenians to fall into line with him—a fusion that resulted in the almost complete abandonment of physical force as a policy. They are warned, therefore, against devoting too much time or energy to any movement except their own, but to help them solely for the reason that they may enable them to spread the principles of their own organisation, which is the one to which they owe and must give first allegiance.[56]

When de Valera, however, read the 1916 Proclamation of the Republic during the election campaign, at least some of the reservation disappeared. The Volunteers wholeheartedly participated in the Clare election, marching in the streets, preserving order, and guaranteeing that the Sinn Féin position would receive a hearing.[57] As Mulcahy noted, "by the time the Clare election was over, the Volunteers were the operative part of the election machinery for the new party."[58]

Mulcahy did not participate in the first round of by-elections. He remained absorbed in his fund-raising tour for the Gaelic League. In keeping with his rather apolitical posture, even when he did ostensibly participate in by-election activities in the next few months, he used the occasions to do Volunteer work. The election campaigns provided good cover for meeting with local Volunteers and helping them reorganize.

When Mulcahy returned to Dublin, he immersed himself in Volunteer activities. He was part of a small group which met early in August to plan a Volunteer convention for the fall of 1917. Among those who attended this August meeting were: Eamon de Valera, Cathal Brugha, Thomas Ashe, Diarmuid O'Hegarty, Diarmuid Lynch, Michael Collins and Michael Staines. This group decided to organize a Volunteer convention concurrently with the Sinn Féin convention being planned for October. Volunteer delegates would thus not attract undue notice from the authorities.

Although the leaders of the Volunteers took pains to meet under the cover of the Sinn Féin convention, this emphasis on secrecy was not necessarily indicative of the spirit of the movement generally. Volunteers were, in fact, asking to be noticed by the authorities. Buoyed up by the success of the Clare and Kilkenny by-elections—William T. Cosgrave had been elected in Kilkenny—the Volunteers were no longer content to remain unnoticed and underground. At least some of the Volunteers decided that they would openly defy the authorities and engaged in very public drills and parades. Not only were parades held after Mass on Sunday, but the front of the police barracks was considered ideal for Volunteer drills. On 5 August 1917, the Volunteers planned a series of political meetings, despite the ban on such gatherings. On that day, Volunteer leaders preached their message of defiance and adherence to the principles of 1916 to large unlawful assemblies throughout Ireland. Clearly, there was a new spirit of militancy in the country.

Both the public drilling and the open meetings resulted in the arrests of numerous Volunteers. For example, the Brennan brothers of Clare— destined to be in the advanced action wing of the Volunteers—were arrested as was Thomas Ashe, hero of Ashbourne and leading figure in both the IRB and the Volunteers. The Brennan brothers were arrested first. They defied the authority of the court, refusing to acknowledge the right of the British to try them. When in prison, they opted to go on hunger strike. The Brennan brothers set the example and, in a sense, formulated the policy of the Volunteers. It had progressed from open drilling and marching, to defying the authority of the Court, to hunger strike.

When Thomas Ashe was arrested, he was sent to Mountjoy prison and there, along with his Volunteer companions, demanded prisoner of war status. It was denied. The prisoners went on hunger strike. In September, Ashe died from being forcibly fed by the prison authorities. Ashe's popularity in the Volunteer movement, his youth, his 1916 reputation, and the general climate of defiance, guaranteed that his death would receive a great deal of attention. The Volunteers were determined that Ashe would have a military funeral to rival the 1915 funeral of O'Donovan Rossa at which Pearse gave his famous oration. It would be a testimony to their dead comrade and a statement of rebellion.

Because of his association with Ashe in 1916 and because he was O/C of the 2nd Battalion in Dublin, Mulcahy was placed in charge of the military aspects of the funeral. Volunteers came to Dublin from all over the country. On 30 September 1917, the Volunteers, in uniform and carrying their arms, took over the entire city. In traditional style they escorted Ashe's body to Glasnevin cemetery. Thousands lined the streets and after the Angelus bells had rung, Mulcahy ordered the cortege to begin the journey from Dublin City Hall to Glasnevin cemetery. After three volleys were fired at the graveside, Michael Collins gave a brief funeral oration which Mulcahy described as "echoing in a short sharp symbolic sentence, the volley just fired."[59]

Ashe's funeral was an impressive tribute and a symbolic statement. Ashe's death had deeply stirred the feelings of nationalist Ireland and his funeral provided the Volunteers with the opportunity to test their strength. In general it galvanized the Volunteer movement. It had, moreover, direct specific effects. As a result of their work in the funeral, the Dublin battalions were reorganized and formed into the Dublin Brigade. Because of his direction of the funeral, Mulcahy was elevated to a position of prominence in the Volunteer organization. He became the O/C of the newly formed Dublin Brigade. As a result of his funeral oration, Collins achieved national prominence. And, it was through their co-operation on the Ashe funeral that the friendship and co-operation between Mulcahy and Collins began to grow and develop.

The growth of the Volunteers, as evidenced by the large numbers who participated in the Ashe funeral, indicated that some type of central authority was necessary to bind them together. Following the precedent established at their founding in 1913, the Volunteers held a convention on 27 October 1917, the day after the Sinn Féin convention had met. The Volunteer Convention was much smaller and was held in secret. Most of the delegates to the Volunteer convention had, in fact, attended the Sinn Féin meeting and were those who had been active in the organization in recent months. From the prison camps and from the by-election campaigns the new leadership of the Volunteers emerged.

The Volunteer convention elected a national executive to oversee the movement. Eamon de Valera was selected as president of the organization and Cathal Brugha was chosen as chairman of the resident executive. The other members of the executive were leaders from each of the four provinces and from Dublin. In addition, a number of fields were singled out as needing special attention. Directors were appointed to strengthen these areas. For example, Mulcahy was appointed director of training and Collins, director of organization. The directors would also be members of the executive.[60]

For the most part, the leaders of the Volunteer movement were also active in Sinn Féin. The most obvious example was, of course, de Valera who was elected president of both bodies. In addition, six of the twenty members elected to the Volunteer national executive were also members of the Sinn Féin executive. This overlapping of personnel provided the unity which would give additional strength to the struggle for independence. Mulcahy viewed the two conventions as having "fashioned and planted the two great tap-roots around which the new national movement was to grow—a new national government to speak for the people . . . and an armed military force which would defend its growth and secure and maintain its prestige and authority."[61] They also set a pattern for the military-political relationships which would endure through the formation of the Irish Free State. According to Mulcahy:

> the work done at the two Conventions of 1917 provided the basis of that Government-Army relationship which came so instantaneously and automatically into operation on the establishment of the Dáil and endured so effectively.[62]

The involvement of both the military and political wings of the nationalist movement also helped legitimize the struggle for independence. As a contemporary of the period, Florence O'Donoghue, later observed:

> the nation was given the combined strength of the political and military arms in a manner which was most aptly in accord with the spirit of national unity at that time. In contrast with earlier insurgent movements, which had relied sometimes on arms, sometimes on constitutional or political effort, a combination was forged in 1917 which made possible the mobilisation of the nation's maximum strength, and based the claim for national independence firmly on the consent and approval of the great majority of the population.[63]

The two conventions with their interlocking personnel thus synthesized and blended the constitutional and physical force traditions of Irish nationalism. This synthesis was vital to their success. As the heirs of the Easter Rising, they would soon wage a war of independence; but following the constitutional tradition of leaders like Daniel O'Connell and Charles Stewart Parnell, they would also fight elections and establish a government, thereby legitimizing their military efforts.

It was, however, equally important for future developments that the Volunteers held their own convention and remained a separate and autonomous body. Thus, the political and military wings each retained their own distinctive identity. While participants such as Mulcahy would argue that there was no question but that the military would be subject to government control, this was not true for all members of the Volunteers, nor would the distrust of political interference in the affairs of the military ever totally abate. As the above quoted directive of the Volunteer executive of May 1917 pointed out, the memory of militant physical force nationalists being subsumed and undermined by political, constitutional organizations was still very much present.

The leaders of the Volunteers harbored no deep, dark sinister motives regarding their relationship to politics and politicians. They did, however, have a keen, if not always accurate, historical memory. In their view, parliamentary movements had proven themselves to be weak, compromising and ineffective. The recent history of the Irish Parliamentary Party was just another vivid example. Thus, it was important to them that they retain control of their own organization. However, the question of the relationship of the Volunteers to Dáil Éireann, would not become a burning issue until the civil war. Prior to that, the two bodies existed more or less harmoniously—most often with the Volunteers leading the way. And at this point, the Volunteers were moving the nationalist movement into open conflict with the British authorities.

TWO

Drifting into Rebellion

A Nation cannot be fully free in which even a small section of its people have not freedom. A nation cannot be said to live in spirit, or materially, while there is denied to any section of its people a share of the wealth and the riches that God bestowed around them.

Richard Mulcahy, TD, Speech in the Dáil, 21 January 1919

The common attitude of all guerrillas is material weakness in relation to the army opposed to them. They cannot fight positional warfare; they cannot afford losing battles; they must fight only when there is a prospect of success.

Florence O'Donoghue, Guerrilla Warfare in Ireland[1]

By the end of 1917, the Volunteers had a secure foundation for their organization. Morale was high. Training was progressing. Discipline was being patiently acquired. To coordinate the work of the various units throughout the country, and to provide a central focus for the organization, the directors and members of the resident executive decided to establish a General Headquarters Staff. It was the moment when firm and inspiring leadership

> . . . was most essential if their [Volunteers'] exuberant enthusiasm was to be disciplined, controlled and directed into effective, combined action. It was time to lay down guide lines for their internal problems of organisation, training and arms, and for their relation to the political wing of the movement in which many of them were deeply involved.[2]

Accordingly, in March 1918, the members of the executive met to select a staff. Collins and Mulcahy were the two candidates for the position of chief of staff. Because of his activities during the Easter Rising and his handling of the Ashe funeral, and because he was O/C of the Dublin Brigade and was thus well known in Dublin, Mulcahy was selected for this position. The decision seemed to hinge on the fact that Collins was not well known in Dublin and hence some were concerned about his seemingly impetuous nature.³ Regardless of the accuracy of this assessment of Collins, it was an extremely wise decision. Collins was then left free to undertake the myriad activities that was to mark his leadership in the Anglo-Irish war, while Mulcahy could concentrate on the work at General Headquarters. Each occupied positions for which they were temperamentally well suited. The entire staff that was selected in 1918 was: Mulcahy, chief of staff; Collins, director of organisation and adjutant-general; Sean MacMahon, quartermaster-general; Rory O'Connor, director of engineering, and Dick McKee, director of training as well as Mulcahy's successor as O/C of the Dublin Brigade. While the Volunteer executive remained in control of policy, GHQ was responsible for directing military activities. They began by holding regular meetings, demanding frequent reports from the directors, discussing problems, and encouraging suggestions.

The most pressing issue facing the newly formed GHQ staff, as well as other nationalist leaders, was conscription. Plagued by an ever increasing shortage of men for the war effort, more and more the British talked of extending conscription to Ireland. It became a *cause célèbre* around which all Irish nationalists could unite and had direct consequences for both the Volunteers and Sinn Féin.

The agitation against conscription propelled Sinn Féin into a new respectability and an acknowledged position of leadership in the country. It seemed to vindicate their defiantly anti-British stance. As Sinn Féin's position grew more favorable, that of the Irish Parliamentary Party worsened. They had become increasingly tainted by their association with the British government. Even though the members of the party walked out of the House of Commons when the conscription bill was passed, this move heightened the odium of the alliance.

Sinn Féin leaders profited greatly from the campaign of resistance to conscription which was waged by all the various segments of nationalist Ireland. It was *their* issue. When a huge anti-conscription rally was held in the Mansion House in Dublin on 18 April 1918, Sinn Féin leaders shared a platform with leaders of the Irish Parliamentary Party and the Catholic hierarchy. It was visible proof that former rebels and dissidents were now acknowledged as respectable and responsible leaders. Their status in the anti-conscription campaign would also belie later election propaganda that Sinn Féin was unfit to govern the country.

Prior to the Mansion House Conference, General Headquarters staff met to discuss the policy implications of the conscription threat. Because he was laid up with an attack of lumbago, they met, in fact, in Mulcahy's bedroom. All the members of the General Staff—except Collins then under arrest—were present. De Valera as president of the Volunteers and Cathal Brugha as chairman of the resident executive also attended. The group decided that there was no need to issue any new directives as their policy was that Volunteers were required to take all possible precaution to avoid arrest, and even to avoid creating occasions that invited disorder and the danger of the use of force. If arrested they had orders to be defiant of authority and non-cooperative on detention. If, while in possession of arms their arrest was attempted, the arms should be used in an effort to prevent their loss and to evade being taken into custody.[4]

After the Mansion House meeting, the Volunteers' position was given official clerical sanction. The bishops had openly supported the policy of resistance and this fact strengthened the moral position of the Volunteers. Conscription was being portrayed as tantamount to an open declaration of war on the Irish nation. The only group which was organized, was at least semi-trained and ready to resist any attempt at conscription was the Irish Volunteers. Not surprisingly, their ranks swelled. They, like their political counterparts in Sinn Féin, had acquired new status and stature, new respectability and responsibilities. The anti-conscription campaign provided them with a new focus, a more sharply defined purpose. In this regard, the threat of conscription seemed to Mulcahy to be, "a favourable wind in . . . [the] political sails".[5]

The Volunteers prepared to resist the threat of conscription. They skirmished and manoeuvred and "practised bayonet fighting with brush handles up and down streets".[6] They tried to perfect their skills, in signalling, in establishing their own means and methods of communication and trained themselves in the most efficient way to destroy railroads. Maps were in great demand as were training manuals. Guns and ammunition were, of course, the highest priority. Cartridges were collected and refilled; locksmiths made revolver springs; carpenters made pikes; and the women's organization of Cumann na mBan sewed signalling flags and haversacks, gathered medical supplies and made field dressing kits. There was a hum of activity, complemented by a crescendo of arrests.

This increase in arrests, especially among the officers, caused serious problems for training new recruits and unskilled Volunteers. Experienced officers were much sought after. GHQ tried to shift and shuffle officers around the country to take charge of training. Continuing by-elections provided them with a necessary cover for their activities. Ernie O'Malley left this picture of his interview with Mulcahy whom he went to see about taking on the training of some Volunteers during the by-election in East Tyrone:

> In Dungannon I reported to Dick Mulcahy, Assistant chief of staff [*sic*]. He had been in my class at the medical school; but I had been too much in awe of his rank to speak to him. He was seated at a table in a small, bare room, writing. I saluted: "I have been instructed to report to you, sir."

"By whom?"

"By the Dublin Brigade Adjutant."

"Your name?"

"O'Malley, F Company, First Battalion."

"Can you handle men?"

"I have helped to train a Fianna Company on the North side."

He [Mulcahy] was in grey green uniform. It fitted well. He wore a soft, slouch hat, one side was pinned up by the Fianna Fail badge of the Dublin Brigade. He looked neat and trim, quiet. He had a shrewd cold look. There was little expression on the muscles of his mouth or cheeks when he spoke. He spoke slowly, stressing words nasally. His face was of the thin type, clean-shaven with bushy eyebrows.[7]

O'Malley's recollections, while providing a good insight and description of Mulcahy, are much more formal and structured than Mulcahy's memory of their meeting. Mulcahy remembered meeting O'Malley as he was on his way to Dungannon. O'Malley seemed upset about examinations and somewhat unsettled as to what to do in the immediate future. Mulcahy suggested that he come to Dungannon and work for the Volunteers. It was a much more casual encounter and lacks the sense of formality which O'Malley's picture creates.[8]

Both recollections are valuable. Mulcahy's picture of the meeting between the two men was probably more accurate in depicting the loose informality of the Volunteer organization. O'Malley, on the other hand, was probably correct in assessing Mulcahy's reserved and somewhat formal nature. The actual facts of this particular encounter are not important. What was significant was that this image of Mulcahy was the one which would prevail for the remainder of his military career—a bit aloof, formal and proper. It probably masked his shyness and lack of ease in dealing with strangers, but it would be interpreted negatively by some who did not know him well.

Another of Mulcahy's personality traits, albeit one which would serve him well during this period, was his ability to become totally engrossed in his work, attacking the problems at hand with a great deal of concentration and attention to detail. The tasks which faced the chief of staff and GHQ staff were formidable. The only policy articulated at this time was a negative one. There would not be another rising unless there was hope of success.[9] The commonly held belief was that the Volunteers could be nothing more than a threat to England. It does not seem that most Volunteer leaders were thinking in terms of actual combat with the forces of the British Empire. GHQ, therefore, had to tread the extremely thin line between encouraging the Volunteers to organize, drill, and discipline themselves while not inciting them to be provocative or aggressive. GHQ was concerned about the possibility of loss of life, and wanted to foster prudence and patience without killing the initiative of local units or smothering the spirit of defiance from which the Volunteers drew strength and purpose.

Their job was made more difficult, moreover, by the fact that the authorities were, naturally enough, not content to idly watch the Volunteers defy their prohibitions and restrictions. As one participant noted: "In the year 1918 there were 260 raids by the police or military, 81 baton and bayonet charges, 32 proclamations and suppressions, 973 sentences on men and women for political offences, 6 men murdered, 61 court-martials and 91 persons deported without trial."[10] From the Volunteers' perspective, increasing police and military aggression was a threat to their existence.

On a practical level, GHQ tried to further develop the organizational structure of the Volunteers. They encouraged each group to learn the rudimentary skills of army life, to begin to think and act like soldiers. At this stage, GHQ's thinking was fairly traditional, envisioning an army divided into units, companies, battalions and brigades. In fact, in March 1918, the Volunteers' structure was so imitative of a regular army that British intelligence felt confident that their troops were prepared to handle any outbreak of hostility in the country. The British army, like the Volunteers themselves, foresaw any new crisis or military outburst coming in an old form, another rising.[11] Few, if any, had made the quantum leap to the concept of guerrilla warfare.

But the Volunteers were being pushed, were being forced to confront the contradictions in their own policy. On the one hand, the Volunteer organization came into being in 1913 as a defensive force, to secure the rights and liberties of the Irish people. For men like Mulcahy who had been schooled in the thinking of Arthur Griffith, the key to winning Ireland's freedom lay in the doctrine of passive resistance—not active, aggressive warfare. At the time of the conscription crisis until well into 1919, this was the fundamental outlook of many of the leaders of the national movement.

On the other hand, this was a difficult position, especially for the chief of staff, to maintain indefinitely. Mulcahy was in charge of developing an army, a Volunteer corps which would not only defy the British authorities, but which also was taking on the trappings, the mentality, the structures of a military force. It would be just a matter of time until some Volunteers forced the switch from passive to active resistance, from a defensive to an offensive mentality. By late 1918, *An t-Óglach*, the journal of the Volunteers, was hinting that a change in tactics might become necessary for the Volunteers.[12] Eventually GHQ would alter its position, but the way would have already been paved by local leaders in the Volunteer organization.[13]

British policy, moreover, continued to alienate nationalist Ireland. The blunder of trying to extend conscription to Ireland—an error exacerbated by passing a conscription bill and then not implementing it, having thus the worst of both worlds—was succeeded by the so-called German plot arrests. Charging that Sinn Féin leaders were involved in a new conspiracy with the Germans, Dublin Castle authorities arrested a host of prominent advanced nationalists. The evidence was dubious, at best, but it gave the British the excuse they needed to order mass arrests. The British authorities hoped to break the momentum of the anti-conscription movement and to check the open defiance of the Sinn Féin/Volunteer movements. They succeeded in doing neither. Fortunately for those targeted for arrest, Michael Collins had already begun to establish intelligence contacts inside Dublin Castle and these sources warned him of the impending arrests. This information helped some, such as Mulcahy, Brugha, and Collins himself, escape arrest. Others, however, were not so fortunate. Arthur Griffith and Eamon de Valera, for example, were captured despite Collins' warning.

The momentum of the anti-conscription campaign carried over into the post-war election of December 1918. Volunteers, now seasoned veterans of a number of by-election campaigns, were active in support of Sinn Féin candidates. More importantly, a number of Volunteers were themselves selected to run as candidates. They were political as well as military leaders, their political beliefs—often a fiery, militant defiance of British authority—being responsible for their involvement in Volunteer activities. Thus, when candidates were being slated for nomination, it would have been odd if prominent Volunteers were not among those selected. For example, eleven of the twenty members of the Volunteer executive would be elected in 1918.[14]

Mulcahy was a candidate for Clontarf. His selection was rather an afterthought. The Sinn Féin organization had originally nominated Harry Boland, well-known nationalist and friend of Collins, for the Clontarf constituency. However, later on, the election committee decided that Boland should stand in Roscommon. Mulcahy was then asked to be a candidate. He attributed his selection to "Collins and the IRB element".[15]

After his nomination, Mulcahy began to take a more active role in Sinn Féin. In November, he attended an executive meeting and in the following month he was appointed to a special foreign affairs committee to "prepare Ireland's case for submission to the peace conference and to get in touch with foreign peoples and governments".[16] This committee laid the groundwork for the appeal which would be made for international recognition of the Irish republic.

Mulcahy's involvement with the Sinn Féin executive was important in strengthening the links between that body and the Volunteers. From November 1918 until March 1919, he and Collins alternated in attending meetings of the executive.[17] Thus, the two people most responsible for the military struggle for independence were in regular contact with the political leaders. This allowed for a greater understanding and co-ordination between the two bodies. An interesting early example of the cooperation between the two groups arose over the proposed attempt to secure the release of the German plot prisoners.

In December of 1918, Mulcahy discussed with the Sinn Féin executive the possibility of holding meetings in every town throughout the country to demand the release of the prisoners. Mulcahy feared, however, that these meetings might provoke great resistance and he thought "drastic action" might be necessary if this occurred.[18] It is not clear what he meant by the term "drastic action", although, in context, it would imply armed resistance to any attempt by the authorities to interfere with meetings or make arrests. The question before the Sinn Féin executive was what central authority would control such action, and who would decide the limits to "drastic action". Their decision was that:

> while drastic action should be left to the Volunteers, there should be no action taken without reference to both executives, and there should be always unity of intention and in no case should there be interference with the freedom of action of the Irish Volunteers.[19]

The Sinn Féin executive appointed Harry Boland as their representative. He was to confer with Mulcahy on all matters relating to the release of prisoners. Mulcahy believed that this experience demonstrated the trust that Sinn Féin leaders had in the political judgment of the Volunteers and their willingness to leave a certain amount of power in their hands.[20]

This discussion was important because it explicitly recognized the autonomy of the Volunteers and their right to independently decide military matters. The Sinn Féin Executive simply demanded to be kept informed, and, to this end, established a liaison. It would be the pattern for civilian-military relations throughout the struggle for independence.

Mulcahy was one of the 73 Sinn Féin candidates returned at the 1918 election. Sinn Féin, aided by the anti-conscription campaign and the German plot arrests, annihilated the Irish Parliamentary Party. While it was true that the election did not turn on whether nationalist Ireland should fight a war of independence, it was equally true that the platform of Sinn Féin was an affirmation of the republican ideal, an endorsement of the spirit of 1916. Specifically, the Sinn Féin candidates had promised to abstain from Westminster and create a national assembly, to drive the English out of Ireland by whatever means were necessary, and to appeal to the post-war peace conference for recognition. They struck a responsive chord in the electorate and nationalist Ireland gave them a ringing endorsement. Sinn Féin captured 46.73 per cent of the votes on the register in the 26-county area and 64.86 per cent of the votes actually cast.[21]

Thus, at the beginning of 1919, nationalist Ireland had a duly elected political assembly and a thriving military organization. The presence of a democratically elected parliament—the expression of the will of the people—gave the Volunteers a moral sanction and sustenance which no other revolutionary movement before—or since—could claim. Moreover, once again there was an overlapping of personnel which gave the revolutionary struggle a high degree of unity and harmony. It also obscured important questions as to civilian-military relations.

The first modern Irish parliament, Dáil Éireann, convened on 21 January 1919. Their ranks were depleted by arrests—34 of the representatives were in prison at the time. Nevertheless, the small nucleus of delegates began the task of constructing a government. Their first order of business was to reaffirm the free and independent republic proclaimed on Easter Monday in the Declaration of Independence. This document clearly asserted Ireland's right to independence, characterizing English rule in Ireland as "an invasion of our national right which we will never tolerate" and demanding "the evacuation of our country by the English Garrison".[22] The Declaration could be seen as giving the Volunteers

> . . . a clear mandate and a definite mission. The moral right inherent in all revolt against unjust alien rule became thereafter also for them an explicit duty—the duty of defending national institutions set up by the free will of the people.[23]

Thus, when it became clear that simple proclamations and appeals to international organizations would not bring the Irish independence, the position of those who had argued for armed struggle or had moved away from the idea of passive resistance would be strengthened.

The first meeting of the Dáil also ratified a Constitution and adopted a Democratic Programme. The Constitution of 1919 demonstrated a strong commitment to a democratic parliamentary form of government and reflected the political values of the new leaders. On the other hand, the Democratic Programme, a statement of social and economic policy, was not actually reflective of the type of society a majority of the representatives actually envisioned. The Democratic Programme spoke of the right to all men and women to the land, resources, and wealth of Ireland. It echoed the sentiments expressed in the 1916 Proclamation, a fusion of the ideas of Griffith, Pearse, and Connolly, complemented by traditional historic ideas and sentiments.

The traditional interpretation of the Democratic Programme is that it was passed by the Dáil to enhance the Irish Labour Party's position at an upcoming international socialist conference. The Dáil hoped that the conference would recognize its claim to independence and thus further its bid for international recognition. Moreover, as the actuality of independence would demonstrate, these ideals would not dominate the first government of the Irish Free State. However, the ideas expressed in the Democratic Programme retained a symbolic appeal which extended beyond a particular conference. It represented a kind of utopian vision which some nationalist leaders would cling to. The aspirations expressed in 1919 would, for example, be reflected in the December 1922 policy statement of the newly formed Cumann na nGaedheal Party.

Mulcahy introduced the Democratic Programme. His speech revealed the almost romantic appeal which the ideals expressed in this document had to many of his generation. In his Dáil speech, Mulcahy argued:

> Let us understand, too, that it is this people of ours living in gaiety and peace among the riches that God bestowed on them, and gaining by their industry from those riches their sustenance. And when we set ourselves to regulate by our laws the application of our people's industry to our Country's riches let us do it in such a way as will prevent the spiteful and the robber stealing the riches for themselves to the impoverishment of the People.
>
> A nation cannot be fully free in which even a small section of its people have not freedom. A nation cannot be said fully to live in spirit, or materially, while there is denied to any section of its people a share of the wealth and the riches that God bestowed around them to make them living and to sustain life in them. Therefore, I ask you to accept this programme. Let us enshrine it in our laws, and let us ever remember in our actions our People whom it is our responsibility to teach and to defend.[24]

This speech contained the core of Mulcahy's political philosophy and represented the guiding principles which would inform his political career. Mulcahy had a vague notion of the people—not divided into class but seen as a whole—and a clear belief that what would benefit Irish society would benefit all its members. While Mulcahy can be faulted for a rather unsophisticated analysis of the social and economic conditions which plagued Irish society, his view was consistent with the general thinking of the nationalist movement. Beyond endorsing an ideal, the majority of the leaders of the revolutionary movement were unwilling to involve themselves in social and economic issues. They did not want to alienate the more prosperous members of the community. And they feared that to extend the parameters of the movement beyond political concerns would destroy the fragile unity necessary for success. It was not that they were indifferent to social and economic concerns. They were not. It was simply not their priority. The time to deal with economic and social issues would be after independence had been achieved. Moreover, there persisted in nationalist thinking a belief that the ills which plagued Irish society resulted from British domination and that, when they were free to control their own destiny, these problems would be ameliorated.

To bolster its claim to independence, the Dáil also sent a "Message to the Free Nations of the World". It outlined the Irish claim to independence and called on the international community to recognize and support this claim at the upcoming peace conference. To argue its position, the Dáil selected delegates to go to Paris to speak for the Irish Republic. It was an idealistic and vain hope to assume that the victors of World War I, the countries who had passionately asserted the right of small nations to self-determination during the war, would impose this standard on any but the vanquished. To the American president, Woodrow Wilson, and the rest of the delegates to Paris, Ireland would remain an internal British problem. The failure of the Paris peace conference to acknowledge and support Ireland's claim to independence pushed Irish leaders to a more militant position.

Having justified its existence and provided itself with a theoretical framework, Dáil Éireann began the process of state-building by appointing a temporary ministry under the leadership of Cathal Brugha. Mulcahy was appointed minister for defence in this Cabinet as well as retaining his position as chief of staff. However, weakened by arrests and the threat of arrests, and groping its way through the darkness of inexperience and uncertainty, Dáil Éireann did not became a serious reality until April 1919. At that time de Valera, having escaped from prison, formed his first cabinet. Brugha was chosen as minister for defence and Mulcahy became assistant minister for defence. Brugha, in fact, chose to continue to run his own business and not devote himself completely to his ministerial position. He, therefore, deferred his salary to Mulcahy, enabling him to be a full time chief of staff. It was a welcome source of revenue. Mulcahy's time was increasingly occupied by his concerns as chief of staff and the growing demands of the struggle for independence, the Anglo-Irish war.

If Mulcahy and nationalist Ireland were to wage a successful struggle for independence in 1919, certain changes would have to occur. They would have to reject the legitimacy of British rule. They would have to shift philosophical positions from that of passive resistance to one of active armed defiance. And, they would have to move from the traditional military thinking of the 1916 Rising to the more innovative initiatives of guerrilla struggle.

Various factors converged to make these changes possible. The convening of Dáil Éireann, the selection of a cabinet, and the establishment of certain governmental structures—such as Dáil courts of law—were highly significant. All helped to undermine the legitimacy of British rule in Ireland. The shift away from passive resistance was, in a sense, the result of these changes, of the fact that the nationalists had established themselves as the elected rulers of Ireland. This not only legitimized the struggle for independence, it also made it necessary for the military to defend these political institutions against British harassment and aggression.

The shift from traditional to guerrilla warfare was possible only because Volunteers leaders—both locally and at GHQ—were willing to break the old rules. They had no manuals, no applicable precedent to follow. While the Irish retained some of the trappings, some of the structures of a traditional army, they also adapted themselves to using techniques and methods which would emphasize their strengths. Less the result of a clear-cut decision than a response to the situation at hand, moulded by pressures from within and without, the Anglo-Irish struggle began slowly, picked up in intensity and only reached a fever pitch in 1921. It was an uneven evolutionary journey to a violent political revolution.

In retrospect, a guerrilla war seemed the Volunteers' only recourse. In 1919, there were 38,000 British troops in Ireland and 10,000 armed members of the Royal Irish Constabulary. The RIC occupied over 2,000 barracks scattered throughout the country—in villages, towns and cities. These forces had weapons and access to war material which the Volunteers could never match. Moreover, the British administration in Ireland buttressed the British military presence and conferred upon it a degree of legitimacy.

In military terms, the Volunteers were at a clear disadvantage. Their numbers certainly paled in comparison to those of the British and the RIC, and not all in the Volunteer ranks were trained soldiers who could be called upon to fight. Moreover, despite GHQ's best efforts to equalize the fighting, the country remained uneven both in its ability and desire to fight, thus allowing the British to concentrate their attention on the more bellicose areas. Furthermore, the Volunteers were poorly armed. While the Volunteers did have shotguns, serviceable rifles were rare and machine guns and heavier weapons were virtually unavailable to them in 1919. Ammunition was scarce and training with loaded weapons was a luxury few units could afford. Some fired their first rifle shots during an actual engagement.

The Volunteers did have certain advantages. They had a sense of cohesion and general purpose. For the most part, they fought because of their political commitment to obtaining freedom for Ireland. And they found, according to Mulcahy, "that being driven to take an interest in politics . . . they could only defend themselves as politicians by arming themselves".[25] Mulcahy's view reflects the fact that the Volunteers were, from the beginning, a politicized body, called into being by political aims and ambitions.

The *raison d'être* of the Volunteers was to ensure the favorable outcome of political developments—much like the situation at their founding in 1913. The minister for defence, Brugha, minimized their potential as a military threat. He believed that the Volunteers could only be used to influence the outcome of political events, not actually to fight the British.[26] Mulcahy, on the other hand, foresaw a more active role for the Volunteers. He described them as "an armed military force . . . which would defend the growth of the Parliament and secure and maintain its prestige and authority".[27]

Few observers, however, predicted a full scale war of independence. Mulcahy and his staff awaited political developments. With the notable exception of Michael Collins, GHQ remained off centre stage, intent on developing a Volunteer force, but, as yet, with no clear vision of an armed struggle for independence. This period was dominated, in fact, by individual groups of Volunteers who, having received some rudimentary training and some sense of discipline, acted of their own accord. They moved from parade drills to actual fighting.

The ambush at Soloheadbeg in County Tipperary on 21 January 1919 is usually cited as the opening engagement of the Anglo-Irish war. Led by Dan Breen and Sean Treacy, the Third Tipperary Brigade attacked a Royal Irish Constabulary guard in order to acquire guns and explosives. The RIC resisted and two policemen were shot and killed. The death of the two RIC men caused a great deal of consternation in the press, the pulpit, and the political platform. Interestingly enough, it was not the first time an RIC man had been killed.[28] Perhaps because of the publicity it received, perhaps because the ambush serendipitously coincided with the opening of the Dáil, historically, Soloheadbeg came to be regarded as the opening skirmish in the Volunteers' attacks on the RIC. It typified the type of activities which would dominate the year 1919.

The Soloheadbeg ambush was significant not only for the precedent it established, but also because it illustrated certain important facts about the state of the revolutionary movement. Most important, the ambush was not sanctioned by GHQ, but, as was characteristic of most of the early activities of the Volunteers, was the decision of the local leaders. While a GHQ directive forbade raiding private homes for arms—an order that some counties such as Clare blatantly ignored[29]—it did not expressly prohibit the raiding of RIC barracks. However, GHQ had specifically warned Volunteers against life-threatening encounters.[30] Mulcahy was concerned with preventing injury and loss of life. He understood that killing policemen at this stage of the struggle would have an adverse effect on public support for the Volunteers.

Soloheadbeg was also evidence of the growing impatience of some of the Volunteers. They felt the time had come to stop playing at being soldiers and become a real fighting force. Dan Breen justified Soloheadbeg as being necessary for the morale of his men and he spoke for a number of Volunteers when he asked, ". . . but of what use . . . are men who are soldiers only in name, of guns that are oiled and cleaned but never fired?"[31] This sentiment would surface in Clare, in Cork, and other counties that would bear the brunt of the fighting in the next few years. It was not totally unreasonable.

As chief of staff, Mulcahy's task was to balance the Volunteers' desire for activity with the need to retain the support of the people, making sure "that the struggle wouldn't get beyond the power of the people to withstand."[32] Thus the chief of staff had and continued to have a very cautious attitude toward escalating the struggle. He wanted the Volunteers to move carefully. Mulcahy believed that "the people had to be educated and led gently into open war."[33] That is why he did not approve of Soloheadbeg. Years later he would write of this incident:

> This episode has on the one hand been outrageously propagandised as a leading episode in waking up the country and particularly waking up General Headquarters Staff; it had many regrettable and unwarranted features; it took place on the day the Dáil was being assembled for the first time and a Dáil Government established, . . . bloodshed should have been unnecessary in the light of the type of episode it was; it completely disturbed the general public situation in the area; and it pushed rather turbulent spirits such as Breen and Treacy into the Dublin area from time to time, where their services were not required and their presence was often awkward.[34]

This is an important point. Mulcahy was not against Volunteer activity, but he understood one of the cardinal features of guerrilla warfare—success, to a large extent, would depend on the support of the people.

Soloheadbeg typified the first phase of the independence struggle which would be dominated by raiding for arms and ammunition by the Volunteers. Other attacks soon followed—for example, at Fermoy, at Collinstown airfield, in the Dublin Mountains and in County Meath, to name but a few. In addition to acquiring arms, the Volunteers also had another purpose in mounting attacks against the RIC—to force it to abandon its posts and retreat from the countryside. While the effectiveness of the RIC as a fighting force has been questioned, if not disparaged,[35] it was an important source of information and a symbol of British rule in Ireland. Therefore, attacks on the RIC yielded both practical and symbolic gains.

Histories of this period both glorify and denigrate the first stage of the fight for independence. Participants saw themselves as heroes. Recent historians, on the other hand, have downplayed the conflict, depicting it as a form of "social banditry" rather than as a noble fight for freedom.[36] Both positions seem exaggerated. The RIC was an armed force whose duty was to uphold British rule, enforce British laws and aid in the administration of British justice. The Volunteers very sensibly began their struggle against this foe. If it was inadequately trained, if morale had sagged, if it was, in effect, a "soft target", then it was an obvious place to initiate combat. Strategically, it was a smart decision.

Because Soloheadbeg provoked such widespread condemnation, it forced GHQ to clarify its position on the ongoing clashes between the Volunteers and the police. According to Piaras Beaslai, the editor of *An tÓglach*, Cathal Brugha, acting head of the cabinet and chairman of the resident executive of the Volunteers, met with the General Headquarters staff and together they agreed on a policy statement which appeared in *An tÓglach* as the editorial on 31 January 1919. It argued that the Volunteers were the legitimate army of the Republic entrusted with the responsibility of defending the government. Moreover, it continued, the government had declared that a state of war existed between Ireland and England and the Volunteers were the army which would fight that war. Hence:

> Every Volunteer is entitled, morally and legally, when in the execution of his military duties, to use all legitimate methods of warfare against the soldiers and policemen of the English usurper, and to slay them if it is necessary to do so in order to overcome their resistance. He is not only entitled but bound to resist all attempts to disarm him. In this position he has the authority of the nation behind him, now constituted in concrete form.[37]

Thus, in the face of criticism, GHQ and the Volunteer executive closed ranks and asserted at least their theoretical right to act like an army at war. This would have been Mulcahy's position. He believed that the Volunteers were the legitimate defenders of the Republic. But, being cautious, he would still try to forestall incidents like the Soloheadbeg ambush.

The campaign against the RIC operated not only militarily, but politically as well. In April 1919, the Dáil passed a resolution which called on the Irish people to socially ostracize the RIC. It was a tactic reminiscent of Parnell and his call for a boycott. Ostracizing the RIC was meant to both discourage recruitment and encourage resignations from the force. It was also the political parallel to the Volunteer action and a more accept-able alternative for those who were not yet ready to condone violence.[38]

Numerous political events, however, weakened the position of those who wished to avoid violence. The failure of the Paris peace conference to uphold Ireland's claim to independence was singularly important in this respect. In a sense, it was a pivotal event for Mulcahy and his staff. Massive war propaganda about the rights of small nations and the coming of a new world order gave the Irish hope that the peace conference would recognize their independence. Ireland had a duly elected government with support of the people and an army. It seemed to have all the trappings of an independent state.

Irish-Americans shared the Irish belief that if the victors at Versailles sincerely wished to consider the right of all nations to self-determination, Ireland's voice would be heard. They, therefore, organized an Irish Race Convention in February 1919 and sent a special commission to Paris to try to use their influence to secure a place for Ireland on the agenda. The commission stopped in Ireland for a briefing. Mulcahy was part of the party which met them at Dun Laoghaire on 3 May 1919 and with W.T. Cosgrave, minister for local government, escorted them to Cork and the west.[39] As chief of staff, Mulcahy was called upon to explain the

Volunteers' policy, to document continuing British aggression, and, overall, to argue that Britain held Ireland only through force and against the express will of the people. The commission travelled around the country and "very much stirred up the feelings and the confidence of the people".[40] But, despite the evidence they collected in Ireland, despite being formally received by the Dáil, despite their political "clout", the Irish-American Commission fared no better than did the Irish with Woodrow Wilson. The Irish case was not heard in Paris.

The possibility of a peaceful solution was further eroded by the outlawing of Sinn Féin, the Gaelic League, as well as the Volunteers, in July 1919. This action made political meetings exceedingly difficult and increased the Irish sense of oppression.[41] It also severely weakened the political sector of the nationalist movement and strengthened the military faction.

The situation was exacerbated by the suppression of the Dáil in the autumn. Declared an unlawful organization, Dáil Éireann would now meet only sporadically and at great risk. In Mulcahy's view, "the suppression of the Dáil . . . made it natural that there would be clashes and that gave rise to the necessity and the justification for our organizing aggressive attacks for the purpose of building up our arms supply at the expense of the police."[42] On another occasion, Mulcahy was uncharacteristically blunt in assessing the impact of the suppression of the Dáil: "It was not the continued violence [of the British] that 'ultimately let loose the guns of Volunteers'. What turned passive resistance and defensive tactics into an offensive war was the suppression of the Dáil."[43]

With its suppression, deputies no longer had a forum in which to question the Volunteers' policy. In addition, because it would meet so infrequently, the Dáil was not forced to confront the question of the accountability of the army to parliament. Thus, the relationship between the Volunteers and the Dáil remained shrouded in uncertainty throughout the struggle for independence.

In theory, with the establishment of Dáil Éireann and the formation of a cabinet, control of the Volunteers passed to the minister for defence. However, because the Volunteer executive remained in existence, the degree of power exercised by the minister for defence over the army was unclear. Mulcahy consistently argued that the Volunteers were subordinate to the Dáil and that this was the accepted view throughout the army. He believed that "from the moment the government was appointed, the policy and work of the General Headquarters staff was carried on with ministerial under-standing, approval and control, and with financial support authorized by the Dáil,"[44] adding that there was "complete confidence and closest possible understanding and cooperation between the army and the government".[45] Most likely, Mulcahy was overly optimistic in his assessment. Moreover, what was true for Mulcahy personally or for the majority of the members of

GHQ, was not necessarily true for all members of the Volunteers. De Valera was probably more accurate when he said on 19 April 1919 that "the Minister for Defence is, of course, in close association with the voluntary military forces which are the foundation of the national Army."[46] Close association clearly did not mean control.

As minister for defence, Cathal Brugha did formally try to clarify the relationship between the military and the civilian government. In August 1919, Brugha proposed that all Volunteers swear an oath of allegiance to the Dáil. He argued that, as a standing army, the Volunteers

> should be subject to the Government. . . . The important thing was that the Irish Volunteers under their present Constitution owed allegiance to their own Executive. Since the Dáil had come into existence there had been no Volunteer Convention, but one would be held as soon as possible. It was necessary to have this matter adjusted.[47]

Not everyone agreed with Brugha. Some argued that the Volunteers should remain a separate body.[48] Some, perhaps, understood that Brugha's motives were more complex than his argument revealed. The minister for defence seemingly invoked the issue of the oath in order to try to break the power of the IRB.

Brugha had opposed the continuation of the Brotherhood. He felt that an oath of allegiance to the Dáil would supersede the oath of the IRB and thus he hoped to weaken its influence within the army. If he could diminish the power of the Brotherhood, he could also undermine the prestige and stature of Michael Collins—an effect which Brugha would welcome. Brugha was envious of Collins and a rift was developing between them.

Although the Dáil supported the idea of an oath, a Volunteer convention to enact the constitutional change was never held. It was simply too dangerous to call such a meeting. The Volunteers took the oath individually. There was obviously some delay, because in July, 1920—nearly a year after Brugha's proposal—GHQ issued an order that all Volunteers must swear an oath of allegiance to the Republic and to the government of the Republic. It laid out the procedure to be followed in its administration and ordered the process to be completed by the end of August 1920.[49] The Volunteers had become the army of the Republic, the IRA.[50]

Despite the oath, the Volunteers retained a spirit of autonomy, a spirit that would be most apparent in the days and months following the acceptance of the Treaty with England in 1921. Moreover, the structures of independence remained—the Volunteer executive, for example—which reinforced the idea of association rather than subordination. While the general view is that the Volunteer executive was left to atrophy during the war, a GHQ order dated June 1920, specifically mentioned the executive as a separate, functioning body. According to General Order No. 9, "the General executive of the Irish Volunteers have, therefore, agreed to place at the services of the Dáil, under Officers especially appointed for the purpose, a police force."[51] The order implies that the Volunteer executive could have refused the Dáil's request; its wording supports the view that, while there was a high level of cooperation, the army remained autonomous.

Because of the ambiguity surrounding the association between the Volunteers/IRA and the government, the relationship between the minister of defence and the chief of staff was critically important. However, it too was enveloped in some of the same uncertainty. Brugha was a part-time minister, not involved in the actual day to day planning which took place at GHQ. Mulcahy met informally with Brugha to keep him informed. According to Mulcahy,

> Cathal did not attend meetings of the General Staff which was entirely conducted by myself, but my contacts with him kept him in timely awareness of any policy developments taking place whether from any new planning, thinking, or from force of circumstances. The circumstances were never such as to require his attendance.[52]

Brugha's role in the army remained unclear. In Mulcahy's view, "Brugha did no systematic work in connection with carrying on of the military organization."[53] Years after the Anglo-Irish war had ended, Mulcahy related a story that was obviously exaggerated, but whose essence was probably accurate, at least in the early stages of the guerrilla war:

> If for any particular reason I was getting a group of fellows to Dublin from any particular area to discuss general matters with them on say, a Sunday morning, I would tell Cathal Brugha that I would have the officers from the south Mayo battalion up in Dublin and perhaps he would like to come and talk to them. He would run over after 11:30 Mass for a few minutes and have a talk. The most he would say would be to ask them to stick to the Irish language.[54]

Brugha, however, did seem to take more of an active role in the final phase of the struggle. During that period, there is ample evidence of Mulcahy corresponding with the minister for defence—reporting developments to him, asking for his opinion or requesting a policy decision from the government. The greater frequency of cabinet meetings after de Valera's return from America in December 1920 and the growing pressure on GHQ to give its officers more direction would account for Brugha's increased participation in Army affairs.[55] However, it was also possible that the feud between Brugha and Collins impelled the defence minister to exert his authority more directly and thus try to undermine Collins' dominance. Brugha's jealousy of Collins placed Mulcahy in an awkward position.

Mulcahy, however, refused to allow himself to be used against Collins nor would he consent to having Collins' position in the army weakened:

> His [Brugha's] trouble about me was that I was in a position that he couldn't get at Collins; I was chief of staff and in interfering in any way with Collins or shifting Collins off the Staff, he had me to deal with. I was just a stubborn kind of understanding rock because I couldn't see the organisation of the GHQ Staff at that stage changing in such a way that Collins would move off it.[56]

Brugha became almost obsessive about Collins. For example, during one of the most trying periods of the war, in the early months of 1921, Brugha accused Collins of mishandling money which had been deposited in an account in Scotland for the purchase of arms and ammunition. He demanded a detailed accounting and summoned a full staff meeting to discuss the issue. Mulcahy was horrified. A British raid would wipe out the entire staff. Brugha had insisted that the complete staff convene at a point when Mulcahy, for security reasons, would gather no more than three of his officers together at any one time. Moreover, valuable staff time was diverted to working out the accounts. Mulcahy reported the matter to de Valera, warning that, if Brugha's behavior continued, Mulcahy "could no longer accept responsibility for the morale or the esprit de corps of the Staff". Acknowledging Brugha's jealousy, de Valera was said to have lamented the fact that "a man with the qualities that Cathal undoubtedly has can fall victim to [such] a dirty little vice".[57] Nevertheless, he refused to restrain his minister for defence.

Brugha's jealousy of Collins was, in part, a reaction to his own lack of dominance in the revolutionary struggle. The fact was that the war for independence came to be run by a small revolutionary elite, who occupied military and political positions simultaneously. In the absence of an effective Dáil and a full-time functioning cabinet, they decided policy, made decisions and directed the revolutionary struggle. One historian has gone so far as to say that Collins and Mulcahy ran the IRA as a "private empire".[58] While they were paramount in directing the revolutionary struggle, the connotation of empire building is unfair to both of them. Collins and Mulcahy were zealous, determined, able, and well-positioned in the Volunteers. Hence it was natural for them to assume leadership roles. Nor does it seem unusual that the chief of staff should take the lead in organizing and fighting a guerrilla war. Furthermore, other leaders who could have played a more prominent role were not available. Brugha retained his business; de Valera was first in jail and then abroad; Griffith was often in jail. And, when de Valera was in America and Griffith was in prison, Collins had shouldered the responsibilities of acting head of government. Collins and Mulcahy, with their uncanny ability to stay out of jail, were at the centre of the conflict and, therefore, would dominate the revolutionary movement.

Neither Mulcahy nor Collins tried to construct an empire; both tried, however, to free a nation.

Moreover, Collins' dominant role in the revolutionary struggle was, in part, a result of the fact that he was both a government minister and a member of GHQ. He was a natural liaison between the two bodies. The close relationship between him and Mulcahy obviated the need for stricter control of the army by the Dáil ministry or a more attentive minister for defence. Collins was the ministerial presence in the army and the army's link to the government. Collins' dual roles covered over much of the ambiguity surrounding the relationship between the IRA and the Cabinet. For the rank and file of the IRA, Collins' high-ranking positions in both the government and the army obscured the subordination of the military to the civilian government. To them, Collins and Mulcahy were of paramount importance.

In addition to his position as Minister for Finance and Director of Intelligence, Collins was also president of the Supreme Council of the IRB. He used his IRB contacts extensively. For example, Mulcahy credited de Valera's escape to the United States to Collins' IRB contacts who provided information, sympathetic people to help with details of the escape, and the necessary cover to move de Valera and his rescue team about. Moreover, Mulcahy himself worked with an IRB member to arrange Robert Barton's escape from Mountjoy prison. Barton cut the bars of his cell with the hacksaw Mulcahy gave him.[59] Mulcahy saw IRB contacts as extremely useful in outwitting the authorities.

Despite its effectiveness, or perhaps because of it, the IRB was the subject of much controversy. Mulcahy's position was clear. Not only did he not see a conflict of interest between the IRB and the Volunteers, he, in fact, saw positive value in the mechanism it provided for escapes and the intelligence contacts it established. Some, like Brugha and de Valera, on the other hand, saw it as secret society that had outlived its usefulness and should be discontinued. Some, perhaps like Brugha, objected to it as a source of Collins' power. The Brotherhood had sufficient adherents, however, that it survived at least until 1924.

The IRB's usefulness in the struggle against the British was extremely important to Mulcahy. As chief of staff, Mulcahy faced a host of pressing problems. He had to organize, train and develop an army under very adverse conditions. In the beginning of the struggle, both he and head-quarters staff exercised only limited power. Throughout 1919, most of the clashes between the Volunteers and the police were the result of what Dan Breen called "unofficial policy", and what Mulcahy preferred to call "spontaneous reactions to aggression".[60] Both men recognized that the Volunteers leaders acted autonomously most of the time, clearly limiting the power of headquarters staff. However, when GHQ learned in advance of an unacceptable action, the chief of staff could and did summon the offending officer to Dublin and halt the venture. However grudgingly, Volunteer leaders obeyed. Even the free-spirited Michael Brennan backed down to Mulcahy's "rough handling" and called off his plans.

Mulcahy interceded when his officers were grossly out of line. In Clare, for example, he invited Michael Brennan to step aside and allow Brennan's brother, Austin, to take over as commanding officer. Mulcahy summoned Michael Brennan again to Dublin and

> put before him [Michael Brennan] that my authority in my sphere and his authority in this could not but be exposed to damage by the action taken; that the people's confidence in the army could be impaired at a time of imminent decisions of importance for the army. Again he took up a good soldierly attitude when I put it to him that his brother Austin take up the post of officer commanding again.[61]

Michael Brennan eventually returned to Clare as a column commander.

The relationship between GHQ and its officers remained delicately balanced throughout the struggle. For the most part, the men had elected their own officers without interference from General Headquarters. GHQ simply ratified their selection. For example, according to Dan Breen the Cork officers had, previous to a meeting with Mulcahy, agreed on Seamus Robinson as commandant. At the subsequent meeting, Breen proposed the candidate, the appointment was approved without further discussion and it was ratified by Mulcahy who had gone to Cork for the election.[62] Mulcahy seemed not to have exercised his authority in any direct or provocative manner. As the struggle progressed, however, Mulcahy was more demanding. Memos from GHQ were peppered with references to the need to drum out incompetent officers.

In the beginning, Mulcahy's policy was to exhort his weak officers to be more active and his active officers to be more prudent. He was rather gentle, perhaps too gentle, with his ineffective officers, being careful not to frighten them away from activity. With his strong, dynamic officers, Mulcahy, while counselling restraint, tried not to cramp their initiative and to be sensitive to their concerns and their needs. Mulcahy was aware that those who were fighting had a keener, more acute sense of the tactics and strategies which were necessary for their survival and their success. He knew he had to grant some latitude to his officers in the field. This realization would be balanced, however, by the very real need of GHQ to coordinate strategy among the Volunteers and by the centralizing tendency of GHQ. Both features became more pronounced as the struggle unfolded. It created a dynamic tension appropriate for a chief of staff and a headquarters staff in a guerrilla war of liberation.

Significantly, Mulcahy defined the parameters of action for his officers. In the first stage of the conflict, he was instructing Volunteers to avoid initiating violent, blood-letting conflict. His strategy was to have the

Volunteers appear as the victims of aggression who responded only out of self-defence. Mulcahy knew that any successful struggle would need the support of the people. He believed that this support would come slowly as British aggression intensified. Because the people would have to bear the burden of British reprisals, it was important that the Volunteers not be seen as causing the hostilities, but rather be perceived as protectors of the people as well as defenders of the Republic. If the Volunteers expected the people's cooperation, they would have to win their approval. If the people were seriously divided, it would gravely impair the efforts of the army. Mulcahy's plan: move slowly and educate the people.

The support of the people was critical for the success of the intelligence operations. In the past, Irish revolutionary movements had been plagued by spies and informers. Michael Collins took the lead in reversing this historical trend and developed an intelligence system that would rival that of the British and which would penetrate into the heart of Dublin Castle itself. As director of intelligence, Collins assembled a group of secret agents—called the Squad. Officially, the Squad was attached to GHQ, but, in reality, it owed allegiance and obedience only to Collins. Mulcahy allowed Collins to operate freely and, while this was an effective arrangement during the Anglo-Irish war, it caused difficulties for Mulcahy after Collins' death.

The role of intelligence was twofold: to gather information about enemy movements—threat of arrests, troop strength and deployments—and to prevent the British from infiltrating the revolutionary movement. Such a threat from British spies caused GHQ, in July 1919, to first sanction the use of force against British detectives, "G men". The first detective was shot in that month. It began an unremitting effort by the Volunteers to destroy the men, who if left unchecked, would destroy them. Mulcahy claimed his decision to use force " arose out of a clear conviction that the continued activities of . . . [four especially dangerous detectives] would make it impossible to operate a representative and a constructive political group" and would "involve the disintegration of the people both in mind and attitude".[63] Mulcahy used this same rationale to justify Bloody Sunday a year later.[64]

The work of GHQ was thus divided between the military activities of the Volunteers and intelligence. Mulcahy was in charge of the former and Collins, the latter. In theory, it was neat division; in practice, there was a great deal of overlapping. Collins summoned officers to Dublin, demanded monthly reports from brigade commandants,[65] and organized and coordinated operations. Clearly, he invested his position of director of intelligence with the broadest possible definition of authority. His stature was undoubtedly helped by his standing in the IRB and by his bellicose attitude. According to Dan Breen, Collins was the only person at GHQ who looked favorably on their "unofficial" raids and who "always

promised to continue to push our war policy in the "proper quarters".[66]
Sean O'Murthuile, a friend and colleague of Collins and eventually
quartermaster general under Mulcahy, agreed with Breen. He called Collins
"the recognised military head of the Volunteers, because although there
was a Defence Ministry, Collins as a Volunteer officer was a man of action
and approved and encouraged attacks on the Crown Forces and Police".[67]

Mulcahy would not have seen Collins' activities in this light. He maintained that he and Collins enjoyed a close and harmonious relationship
which enabled them to work together without friction or antagonism:

> I opened and kept open for him all the doors and pathways he
> wanted to travel, and we didn't exchange unnecessary information.
> . . . I had no occasion to be questioning him. Over many matters
> we exercised a constructive and practical Cistercian silence.[68]

Mulcahy admired Collins. There was a bond between them, a sense of
common commitment and shared dreams. On a practical level, Mulcahy
also realized that as director of intelligence, Collins sometimes received
information that required immediate action and that he had to be given
a great deal of latitude.

However, Mulcahy may not have been completely informed about
Collins' activities, even those outside Intelligence—a result perhaps of
the "Cistercian silence". At times, while Mulcahy was urging prudence
and patience, Collins was advising an escalation of operations or at least,
condoning operations that his chief of staff would frown upon.[69] Collins
also may have been fostering and using his IRB contacts in a way in
which Mulcahy was simply unaware. At least twice there appeared to be
a conflict between the Volunteers and the IRB. In one instance, the
brigade commandant from Sligo, suspecting that members of the IRB
may have been involved in an unauthorized bank robbery, asked Collins
to explain "the attitude of the Irish Volunteer organisation to the
IRB".[70] Collins' response befitted a secret society:

> Arising out of your letter of the 4th inst. re attitude of Irish
> Volunteers and another organisation, you will notice that there is
> no difference between the aims and methods of the Irish Volunteer
> Organisation and the other one you mention.[71]

And, in another instance, the adjutant from the Leitrim Brigade wrote to
Collins requesting the names of those who were in the IRB because those
who claimed such membership seemed "to have power over us".[72]

Mulcahy was neither mentioned nor referred to in these communiqués.
Thus, he could stubbornly deny that the IRB interfered in the workings of
the Volunteers simply because he may not have been privy to all of the
details of these kind of events. Mulcahy had a way of becoming totally
absorbed in the tasks which were before him. While this was a very useful

characteristic in that it assured his prompt attention to detail and organization, it sometimes blinded him to what was happening around him. During the Civil War, for example, Mulcahy would be so intent on army matters that he failed to appreciate the concerns of his cabinet colleagues. Years later, when he was minister for education in the inter-party government, Mulcahy would demonstrate the same single mindedness which left him oblivious to tensions in the cabinet. This may have been the case, especially in the early part of the struggle, when he was chief of staff.

At the end of 1919, it was clear that small scale raiding for arms and isolated attacks on RIC barracks were insufficient activities for a group which considered itself an army. Restlessness and discontent festered in areas which longed for action. While GHQ recognized this problem, it was Terence MacSwiney's visit to Dublin that was the catalyst for a policy change at GHQ.

MacSwiney, vice-commandant of the 1st Cork Brigade under Tomas MacCurtain, went to Dublin to explain to his long-time friend, Mulcahy, the frustration which he and his men felt. MacSwiney believed that those in Dublin did not understand these feelings because they had participated in the Rising of 1916. He and his men, however, had missed the Rising and had simply been drilling and marching since 1913—almost six years. They had reached the breaking point. MacSwiney proposed, therefore, that GHQ allow the men in Cork to stage another rising. He estimated that they could last about two weeks and then, he said, another rising could begin in a different part of the country. Mulcahy rejected the idea of a "travelling rising", but proposed instead that MacSwiney

> select three barracks in the brigade area and arrange to attack them all in one night: take every possible precaution that those engaged in the attack will suffer no loss of life and, as far as possible, avoid taking the lives of anyone in the barracks. Let those who engage in the attacks go about their business the following morning as if not a dog had barked in the area.[73]

The goal was to further weaken the RIC and to clear areas of the country of British administration in order that Dáil departments could begin functioning. Amenable to this plan, MacSwiney and MacCurtain mapped out an attack on three police barracks in their area. As it turned out, three barracks were unrealistic. However, on 2 January 1920, the Cork Volunteers successfully attacked and took over the barracks at Carrigtwohill. Mulcahy saw the attack as "the beginning of the nation-wide offensive in reply to the suppression of Dáil Éireann".[74]

There followed a round of systematic attacks on police barracks across the country. Mulcahy learned from the experience in Cork that three barracks a night in the same area was too difficult. He, therefore, scheduled one attack against an RIC post in each of three different areas, launching a series of coordinated strikes against the RIC. A new phase in the struggle for independence had begun.

By June of 1920, the Volunteers had destroyed sixteen occupied barracks and damaged twenty-nine others.[75] The RIC began to abandon a number of its posts—some were damaged, some were deemed indefensible, some were too remote and isolated. Consequently, there were numerous uninhabited barracks throughout the country. Mulcahy ordered a second action—a flaming tribute to Easter Week. He instructed his officers to burn down all empty RIC barracks in the country in one co-ordinated effort. Accordingly, over three or four nights, concerted action by the Volunteers destroyed approximately four hundred deserted police posts. It was, in the words of the chief of staff, a "spectacular and effective operation", that

> . . . freed large areas of the country from police observation. It also destroyed a large number of buildings which otherwise might subsequently have been reoccupied by the British forces for military purposes. The detonation at Carrigtwohill reverberated throughout the whole country and inside three months the roofs had been swept off hundreds of RIC barracks and the police structure and its power in Ireland were seriously disrupted.[76]

These activities were important because they gave GHQ the opportunity to initiate action and coordinate the work of the Volunteers. It also boosted morale and quenched the desire for action. It was Mulcahy's kind of engagement—visible success with low risk of life. Furthermore, as Mulcahy predicted, the writ of Dáil Éireann replaced the writ of the House of Commons and the elusive Republican government became a concrete force wherever the RIC was expelled.

The Volunteers also began to seriously intercept British communications. Collins had established contacts with ordinary people throughout the country who were in positions to give him valuable information. A network of telegraph operators, postal workers and railway employees, for example, deciphered codes and transmitted keys to Collins, information which he relayed to local Volunteers. In this respect, GHQ provided valuable assistance to its subordinates.

Throughout 1920, attacks on RIC patrols became more frequent, the engagements lasted longer and involved more and more men. The Volunteers' assaults on the representatives and rule of the British crown did not go unchallenged. At first, the British army came to the rescue of the RIC, taking over much of the police work and protecting the men themselves. The British government also began recruiting non-Irish soldiers and officers into the RIC. They would come to be commonly known as the Black and Tans and the Auxiliaries. Though their presence would be much more substantial by the end of the year, the first important trickle of recruits began in March of 1920. In addition, the British government ordered the arrest of all known revolutionaries. Searches became a common feature of Irish life—at least in active areas—as the British raided private houses, blocked off streets and ransacked offices. The relatively safe and quiet days of the struggle were over. The stage was set for a year of terror and counter-terror.

Mulcahy himself was on the run. He kept over twenty hideouts and offices scattered all about Dublin. Several times he barely avoided arrest. The British raided his offices. They raided houses where he slept—often Mulcahy escaped through a garden or a window. During one escape, he casually made his way through a cordon of Black and Tans undetected. Despite the pressure, Mulcahy retained a nonchalant air, bicycling around Dublin, holding meetings and running GHQ.[77]

As chief of staff, Mulcahy was responsible for ensuring that his staff remained both free and functioning. Weekly meetings of the entire staff became impossible. Mulcahy organized his officers into small groups and it was he who kept them all generally informed. Mulcahy was the lynch-pin of GHQ, involved in the workings of its every operation, responsible for keeping his officers informed, inspired and working harmoniously together. His challenges and frustrations would increase, however, as the tempo and brutality of the guerrilla war intensified.

THREE

Guiding the Guerrilla War

With organisation and system, we shall win this war.

Richard Mulcahy, chief of staff

No one will suggest that the people as a whole and whole national mind weren't subjected to almost inconceivable terror and murder and destruction in the most agonising condition.

Recollections of Richard Mulcahy

Terror and counter-terror grew more fierce and more frequent through-out 1920. The Black and Tans and Auxiliaries increased their numbers in Ireland; Tomas MacCurtain, Lord Mayor of Cork was murdered in cold blood; his successor, Terence MacSwiney, died on hunger strike in prison. This year also marked the ruthless killings of Bloody Sunday, the wanton burning of Cork city, and a growing number of raids, arrests, executions, and reprisals. Mulcahy, described this year of terror

> There were two elements in the terror, the brutal, malignant conscienceless intent of Lloyd George [the British prime minister] and . . . the murderous brutality of the armed forces introduced into Ireland to achieve . . . the destruction of the people's will and of their [right] to express it. . . . We on our part at GHQ and all down through the ranks of the Volunteers, in the discharge of our own responsibilities, we watched over and sustained the people's will which did not break. No one will suggest that the people as a whole and whole national mind weren't subjected to almost inconceivable terror and murder and destruction in the most agonising condition.[1]

In these adverse conditions, GHQ was hard pressed to keep the threads of the revolutionary struggle loosely woven together. Its overall aim was to affirm its authority, inculcating in its officers a sense of discipline and a sense of professionalism. To this end, in May 1920, it explicitly ordered the Volunteers to refrain from any action not authorized by a superior officer and stated, moreover, that when such authorization was granted, it was limited to the battalion or brigade in which permission was granted.

Authorization in one area did not imply blanket permission for other areas. GHQ explained:

> This order is not intended to restrict in any way the "imperturbable offensive spirit" of our forces, but rather to preserve this spirit by preventing it running riot in hasty action to its own detriment. Success depends on foresight, and careful observation and planning and the offensive of thought and planning must be unceasingly kept up.[2]

General orders set the rules and standards for military engagements, but the degree of power that GHQ could exert was questionable. By November 1920, brigade officers had to submit monthly diaries of their operations plus an account of the operations of the RIC, the Auxiliaries, and the Black and Tans. Through this device, GHQ was kept informed of activity throughout the country and officers would be held accountable for their leadership.

Mulcahy and his staff consciously attempted to lay down the boundaries of the struggle. As the guerrilla war evolved, critical issues had to be decided. Mulcahy took the lead in setting forth the policies of the IRA. GHQ orders for 1920–21, for example, dealt with questions of reprisals, of executions, of penalties for associating with the enemy. Mulcahy advised the government through the minister for defence, and when necessary, sought government policy. But it was headquarters staff who provided the procedures for handling these very sensitive issues.

In general, GHQ acted as a brake to ensure, as far as it was able, that the war of independence would not degenerate into wanton violence, sectarian conflict or personal vengeance or vendettas. Mulcahy specifically warned "that for purposes of . . . reprisals, no one shall be regarded as an Enemy of Ireland, whether they may be described locally as Unionist, Orangeman, etc., except that they are actively anti-Irish in their outlook and in their actions."[3] Headquarters' insistence on procedure, authorization, and gathering evidence was intended to ensure controlled fighting against legitimate targets. By defining what was and was not acceptable, GHQ created at least an atmosphere of restraint.

Most historians of the period have overlooked this role of GHQ. Participants and analysts alike have viewed GHQ as rather ineffective, taking itself too seriously and pretending to a grandeur and power it did not possess.[4] This misconception arose either from the tendency to concentrate on particularized areas of the conflict or from trying to compare GHQ with its British counterpart. As a headquarters for a guerrilla army, GHQ combined flexibility and respect for initiative, while trying to maintain discipline, enforce authority, and provide overall direction. In these respects, it was effective and over time, grew even more effective.

Moreover, in the past, GHQ had been viewed as a body which did not lead, but simply followed the more innovative of its officers in the field, adopting their practices and implementing their ideas. This assessment is largely true, but not necessarily negative. Among its activities, GHQ analyzed those procedures and tactics which developed spontaneously from local conditions, sometimes improved upon them, and then recommend them to the IRA as a whole. It happened on numerous occasions. For example, one chronic problem which plagued the Volunteers was funding. Each brigade was expected to be basically self-supporting with only occasional help from GHQ. Units paid for their own guns and supplies, but with more and more men "on the run" and unable to continue their regular employment, they needed some supplementary income. To help meet this need, GHQ advised each brigade commandant to arrange for a collection in his area. As an example to follow, headquarters staff sent the circular which was used by the Cork Brigade:

> A collection is being made in this area, by the authority of the General Headquarters of our Army, to enable me to carry on the work of arming the Volunteers in this Brigade, and so sustaining and increasing the fight waged against the enemy here.
>
> You are asked to subscribe a fair amount. It is for your own protection, as well as for the national good. The enemy forces are running loose wherever they get an opportunity. They are murdering defenceless people. They are pillaging, burning, outraging, wherever they go. Arms are needed to meet them and to beat them. Money is required to get the arms. That is the plain statement of the case. It is no appeal. It is a just request to every man and woman in Ireland to help the Army of Ireland to carry on the fight.[5]

GHQ then provided a general outline as to how the money should be allocated. It was a typical instance of how GHQ operated. It facilitated the exchange of information and also regularized and standardized procedure.

GHQ worked hard to correct the many deficiencies which plagued the IRA. They knew, for example, that their men were, for the most part, woefully ill-trained. Hence, they set up training camps. Dick McKee, director of training and O/C, Dublin Brigade, ran such a camp, for example, that was considered one of the best. Liam Deasy, one of the premier guerrilla fighters of Cork, allegedly remarked that "the success of west Cork was due entirely to the example, discipline and instruction that Dick had imposed on them in a week's training camp in the summer of 1919."[6]

GHQ increasingly understood what the struggle required and tried to prepare their men. Headquarters sent training officers into the country to instruct the men in the kinds of skills that the struggle was coming to demand—not parade drills, but crawling through wet grass, not how to address an officer but how to learn to spot ambush positions.[7] Organizers from Dublin helped to establish the IRA into brigades, battalions and then divisions. Overall, GHQ issued directives, gave advice, mediated quarrels.

They were a focal point, a central clearing house for ideas and information, orders and instructions.

Moreover, in terms of tactics and strategies, headquarters staff, especially Mulcahy, realized that they could learn much from their officers in the field. He stressed the value and importance of on the spot decisions. For example, he wrote to one of his officers:

> Personally, I have thought until recently that we might allow road repairing to go on, but the importance of keeping them impassable is being realised more and more, *and only you and your officers who are in close touch with the details of the situation in your area, can really decide the matter.*[8] (Emphasis added)

Mulcahy often asked his officers for specific information—how did a particular procedure work, what were the implications of certain decisions they had taken, what were their recommendations. It was one of his strengths and contributed to the success of the IRA.

Mulcahy particularly valued the opinion of Liam Lynch of Cork and depended on him to give informed and realistic advice and to set an example for the other officers of the IRA. For example, on one occasion Mulcahy wrote to Lynch:

> I think, therefore, you should act in your Division without waiting for any other Division to move in the matter; and your tackling of problems in some particular way in your area may help to point the way to other Divisions, as to what they should or could do.[9]

Often, Mulcahy would offer to send a struggling commanding officer a copy of one of Lynch's reports or recommendations which detailed the procedures, methods and techniques Lynch himself used.

Lynch was especially valued because he combined all the characteristics Mulcahy wanted in an officer. He had an excellent sense of guerrilla tactics. He understood the necessity for maintaining order and discipline. His reports were accurate and exact. He maintained regular contact with GHQ. Coupled with all of this, Lynch achieved results. Mulcahy's feelings about Liam Lynch were important in explaining his actions in the beginning of the Civil War. Mulcahy would order Lynch's release from arrest seemingly because he did not believe that Lynch would actually go anti-Treaty and fight against his former colleagues.

The creation of Active Service Units was another example of GHQ listening to, and learning from, its fighting troops In August 1920, the British passed the Restoration of Order Act. The bill was a step removed from martial law, but it gave the British authorities much more latitude in their operations against the IRA. British forces launched a campaign of widespread raiding which, in turn, made it increasingly unsafe for active Volunteers to remain at home or in their usual employment. The result was far from what the British authorities had intended. The Volunteers now had a group of men who would devote themselves solely to fighting the war of independence. The idea of active service units or flying columns developed in some of the "war zone" areas—regions like Clare, Cork and Tipperary—but was seized upon and endorsed by Headquarters' staff. GHQ then issued orders for the formation of active service units throughout the IRA.

The formation of the flying columns ushered in the third and final phase of the struggle for independence which by the end of 1920 had escalated to full-fledged guerrilla warfare. The men of the flying columns with their hit and run tactics were the premier guerrilla fighters. Their mission was:

> . . . continually to harass, kill, capture and destroy the enemy forces; to keep in check his [British] attempts to rebuild his badly shaken civil administration; to guard and protect the building of our own State Institutions and the people who were establishing and using them.[10]

Above all, the flying column had to choose their targets wisely and cautiously.

The flying columns were vital to the survival of the IRA. They gave the Irish a mobile striking force which allowed for greater coordination and more flexibility. Consisting of about thirty men in each brigade, they were the elite units of the IRA who received special training in attack and defence tactics, musketry, map reading, communications, town fighting and security. Mulcahy also saw the flying column as a "training ground" wherein members of the column would convey to others in their unit "the experience and the soldierly training that they have received".[11] Active service units would also test the leadership ability of the officer corps. New leaders would emerge; strong leaders could excel; weak leaders could be weeded out.

Mulcahy believed that leadership was the key to the success of the IRA. In his role as chief of staff—as teacher, critic, analyst and strategist—he insisted on detailed reports from his officers. He then read and annotated every operations report which GHQ received.[12] He learned, and urged his officers to learn, from each encounter with the enemy—be it successful or not.

The chief of staff was lavish in his praise and scathing in his criticism. Both were used frequently in his dealings with his officers. When Mulcahy heard that the IRA had been successful in a particular attack, he took the time to congratulate the officer and men involved. He would, on these occasions, express his admiration "for a magnificent fight" or his appreciation of "the dash and coolness" which the men displayed. Mulcahy knew the value of positive reenforcement. For example, he wrote to the commandant of west Connemara that your "difficulties and the struggle you are making to overcome them are very much appreciated by the various members of GHQ Staff and I want you to convey to each member of your small fighting group that this is so".[13]

Mulcahy was quick to offer both applause and assistance when merited. Once, for example, he credited ten pounds to the West Connemara brigade's account to commend improvement. In addition, Mulcahy promised them the full support of GHQ and offered to send four experienced active service men to help bolster the brigade.[14] However, officers who shirked their duties, who disregarded proper discipline, or failed to provide adequate protection for their men, Mulcahy deemed criminally negligent. Not only did they endanger the lives of their men, they were "tinkering with the honour of the nation".[15] Mulcahy had an abiding concern that the IRA act in a way which would visibly disprove the British view that those who were waging the war of liberation were nothing more than murderers, thugs and common criminals. Thus, he particularly exhorted his officer corps to conduct themselves in a manner becoming to the army of the Republic.

Mulcahy reserved his most vehement criticism for officers who did not even attempt to engage the enemy but simply complained of their ill-luck or lack of guns and ammunition. He pilloried the brigade commandant from Sligo, for example, for his "tendency to poor-mouth and complain" which Mulcahy believed only added to his brigade's problems. Similarly, Mulcahy railed at the Offaly brigade commandant for reports that

> simply represent the continuation of that whole story of incompetency and slovenliness which began by your own missing of the afternoon train. . . . Unless each individual officer . . . shows that he appreciates his responsibilities he shall have to go, and I am taking steps to ensure that a stricter watch will be kept over them in the future.[16]

By 1921, Mulcahy felt confident enough to threaten dismissal for incompetency and to take a much harsher line than he had at the beginning of the struggle.

Mulcahy had to know when to press home his criticism and when to retreat. Some of his officers were under a terrible strain. Others were simply extreme individualists who bristled at the slightest hint of criticism. Some did everything well. Some did nothing but complain. Others fluctuated widely in their moods and attitudes. It was a delicate and difficult task.

In Mulcahy's view, monthly reports were critical. He analyzed, evaluated, and judged the reports of his officers. Officers who sent in incomplete, sloppy or inadequate reports were reprimanded. Mulcahy believed that these reports reflected the state of command in the particular area. He felt very strongly about the matter. A comment which he made to the brigade commandant in Sligo typified his attitude: "The key-note for today must be, that with organisation and system, we shall win this war, if we are left with nothing but picks and shovels to wage it."[17] Some of his officers grumbled. Some complained that Mulcahy was trying to win the war with pen and ink rather than with arms and ammunition. But few, if any, escaped without sending in their monthly diaries.

Mulcahy analyzed seemingly every aspect of the officers' reports, homing in on any unsettling detail, such as the failure of a party of rifleman to inflict any casualties at a distance of 300 yards. He wrote back to the officer pointing out that:

> the shooting seems to have been very bad. . . . There is no excuse for men missing with rifles at 300 yards in the circumstances—i.e. when not interfered with by serious enemy forces. It does not seem as if in this case the rule of giving rifles to the best shots was observed.[18]

In other instances, Mulcahy reprimanded a commandant for an accidental and premature shooting which involved a "serious danger to men's lives and . . . involves our Army in the discredit of a defeat"; or complained that in one encounter the IRA could not succeed in disarming a patrol of six police.[19] He usually had suggestions for difficulties, pointing out ways in which the men could fight more effectively, or particular problems overcome. Mulcahy's basic philosophy was embodied in a letter he sent to the GHQ organizer in North Cavan:

> While we must not magnify our defeats or let them weaken our will to see the present struggle through to the very end, there is nothing to be gained by shutting our eyes to actual facts.[20]

Mulcahy tried to be realistic about the IRA's strengths and weaknesses and develop his strategy accordingly. The monthly reports had provided him with a fairly accurate idea of what he could expect from his men. Major battles against the British forces were reserved for the flying columns. The task for the remainder of the Volunteers was to continually harass the enemy. In particular, he urged them to engage in "small actions", that is, activity sufficient to provide them with experience and confidence. These types of activities would allow the raw recruit to actively participate, required a minimum amount of ability and ammunition, and would keep up the pressure on the British forces. He warned his commanding officers of the folly of undertaking engagements for which their men were not prepared:

> You will, of course, appreciate the fact that until your men have acquired the very necessary training in conducting themselves and co-operating with others in action, it is dangerous and inviting disaster to think of engaging the enemy with large numbers on our side.[21]

Mulcahy continually urged his officers to restrict the movements of the British troops and destroy their communications system—to fell trees, block roads, and destroy bridges. The British would thus not be able to move freely around the country and surprise the IRA camped in the hills or out in the fields. This was particularly important in protecting the flying columns. In the face of random, but frequent, small attacks and sniping, the British would have to be constantly on guard, which would wear down their morale and force them to concentrate their energy on their own survival.

In Mulcahy's view, to allow British troops total mobility imperilled the revolutionary struggle. He hounded his officers on the matter. If roads and bridges were repaired, he ordered his men to destroy them again. If British troops attempted to repair roads or mend bridges, Mulcahy ordered his men to attack. The British responded, however, by forcing civilians to repair what the IRA destroyed. If the IRA fired on the repair crews, they risked shooting their own supporters. One tactic the IRA employed was to fire over the heads of road repairing parties to deter civilians from being caught so easily to do such work.[22]

In June 1920, Mulcahy asked the Dáil administration for a proclamation forbidding citizens to work on the roads. He believed that if the civil population en masse refused to work in this capacity, the British would be thwarted. In a letter to the minister for defence, Mulcahy pointed out that repairing the roads for the British added considerably to the work load of his men and, therefore, was "a danger to the Army as well as to the people as a whole".[23] In a draft memorandum of the desired proclamation, Mulcahy called on the people "to face resolutely the terror and violence of the Enemy, and to steadfastly refuse to be used as forced labour".[24] More and more, the people of Ireland were being caught in the guerrilla struggle and called upon to make sacrifices, endure hardships and take a definite stand.

The dock workers and railway workers, in particular, responded to this challenge and helped to restrict the mobility of the British troops. In the spring of 1920, the dock workers refused to unload munitions and the railway men refused to carry munitions, troops and supplies of the enemy. The British were forced to run the trains themselves to transport goods or men from one area to another. They had to tie up troops running the railroad and, therefore, had fewer men to send on searches and raids. The strike had another effect as well: "It [the strike] broadened the Republican campaign and heightened the atmosphere of resistance; it was a true example of civil resistance."[25]

Eventually, in order to preclude attacks, the British travelled with civilian passengers on mined trains. This made it impossible for the IRA to attack the trains. Too much harm would be done to the civil population. It was a tactic the British had learned to use effectively in the Boer war.

If the IRA could not attack the trains, they could damage or destroy railroad tracks. They had to be selective, however. Destruction of the railway would isolate certain areas of the country and make the transport of food supplies more difficult. The IRA carefully considered the degree of danger and difficulty to the civilian population as well as the availability of suitable alternative roads on which to move supplies before they undertook any action.[26]

The British troops, on the other hand, had little concern for the hardships which the closing down of railroads or blocking of roads inflicted on a population which sheltered, fed and abetted the IRA. In fact, it was an effective means of reprisals. For example, according to a report submitted by the Kerry No. 2 Brigade, after an IRA ambush at Glenbeigh,

> The train service to Cahirciveen was suspended on Saturday, April 30th. . . . This had an immediate and detrimental effect on the civil population; it being the sole means of export and import. The farm produce as a result is now 3 weeks on the people's hands and is getting bad . . . boats are unable to bring supplies owing to coal shortages. The potato crop of last year was practically a failure and the people are more or less dependent on imports. As a result of the above, food supplies are running scarce, there being only about 120 tons of flour presently in town. . . . The fishing industry is at a standstill and those so employed are now idle. Labour is practically nil there being very little employment. Since Friday last (13th) people going into town for supplies are turned back by police owing to their being ambushed on that night and since successfully sniped.[27]

The divisional adjutant wrote to Mulcahy asking for immediate relief for the district and for help from the Dáil or the minister for home affairs. The British, he believed, were trying "to reduce a portion of the civil population, and thus break the morale of our people". At Mulcahy's request, the department of home affairs tried to provide some remedy for the district.[28]

In his correspondence with the department of home affairs over the Cahirciveen matter, Mulcahy suggested that civil bodies start shouldering some of the responsibilities which had hitherto fallen on the army. Mulcahy believed that the IRA was being called upon to perform duties not strictly within their purview which distracted them from their role as soldiers. Specifically, he was concerned about the establishment of a Dáil police force under the supervision of the minister for home affairs, Austin Stack.

As was noted, in June 1920, the IRA had agreed to recruit a police force from among its ranks to replace the vanishing RIC and enforce the decisions of the Dáil courts. The police would retain their status as Volunteers and be under the direction of their IRA officers. This was to be a temporary measure, in effect until a proper police force could be formed. GHQ's priorities remained clear, however. According to General Order No. 12 issued in November 1920, GHQ advised the IRA that 'while it must be realised that the police will require some good men from the Army, the Army should not be *unduly* impoverished of good men in the forming of the Police. Very suitable men for Police work may be found in persons who have not actually been Volunteers."[29]

Eventually, the department of home affairs began functioning. Friction developed between the police and the army because of the overlapping of activity. Tension was exacerbated, however, because Austin Stack, like Brugha, had developed a hostile attitude toward Collins. Mulcahy and his staff, firmly committed to Collins, felt the animosity as well. An IRA cattle stealing incident in June 1921 illuminates the tension which existed between the two departments. The minister for home affairs harassed the adjutant-General about this matter, complaining that he had been ignored, and that, when he finally learned of the incident, it took him months to receive a report which, in the end, was unacceptable and unsatisfactory.[30] The adjutant-general appealed to Mulcahy. He believed that the time had come when GHQ should cease interfering with local matters and "if an Officer has done wrong when working for some other Department, that other Department must deal with him."[31]

As the Curragh cattle stealing incident revealed, the IRA was involved in more than just military affairs. In many instances, they were looked upon as the law in the community. Whether it was a question of cattle stealing or a question of confiscation of land, the IRA would be called upon to resolve the matter. And, if the IRA were involved, GHQ would be involved, often becoming entangled in conflicts with other departments. The tension between the police and the army, between GHQ and the department of home affairs was a prime example of this type of entanglement. It was not resolved during the Anglo-Irish war and would be paralleled in the civil war by the tension which existed between Mulcahy and the department of defence, and Kevin O'Higgins and the department of home affairs.

Mulcahy's position was that GHQ had consistently tried not to interfere in civilian matters, but that they were forced to because of the incompetence of other departments. To a certain extent, he was correct. Some departments had just begun to organize themselves and were neither effective or efficient. Some lacked strong leadership. Stack's ability as administrator, for example, has been seriously questioned. Moreover, Mulcahy did try to rein in the powers of the IRA which had grown extensively as the guerrilla struggle progressed. For example, he did not want the army to have the power to execute civilians or involve themselves in land matters. Above all, Mulcahy did not want it to appear that the army was running the country.

However, the truth was that, for all intents and purposes, the army was running some parts of the country and, in a number of other areas, the IRA was a conspicuous presence. Because of its paramount position, the IRA was an obvious target for criticism. Mulcahy resented these condemnations and defended his men against charges from other departments. He was exceedingly, perhaps excessively, loyal to his men. Moreover, it seemed to him that in some cases, the IRA had been doing all the work and now were being censured by those who had just arrived on the scene.

Mulcahy's feelings are understandable. For the most part, the political wing of the revolutionary movement had been being quiet and quiescent. In January 1921, the Dáil held one of its few debates on the nature and conduct of the war. A few deputies criticized the policy of the IRA. De Valera, while not overly critical, did suggest a "delaying policy" by which the IRA would reduce attacks on the enemy so as to lighten the burden on the people.[32] Mulcahy did not engage in the policy debate. However, fearful that talk of easing the conflict might demoralize his men, that rumors and half-truths would breed confusion, Mulcahy reminded the deputies that any decisions regarding the course of the war would be transmitted to the army by the minister for defence through GHQ. He also warned his Dáil colleagues of the impropriety of discussing these matters with his officers.[33] While he would implement Dáil and cabinet decisions concerning the army, he did not want individuals interfering with the authority and chain of command of the IRA.

Mulcahy's contribution to the debate in the Dáil revealed his complex, almost contradictory, attitude toward civilian-military relations. There is no question but that he believed the army was subordinate to the government. His resignation in 1924 was proof of that commitment. However, he interpreted that principle very broadly. He believed that after it had decided general policy, the government should leave the actual working out of strategies and tactics to headquarters. Mulcahy resented what he characterized as "a looking over the shoulder", that is, political interference in what were properly military matters.[34] It would be a recurring problem.

On questions of policy, however, Mulcahy frequently sought the opinion and direction of the Minister for Defence and the government. Most of the correspondence relating to policy occurred after the Dáil had formally assumed responsibility for the war of independence in March 1921. Perhaps Mulcahy felt that after such an acknowledgment, policy should be articulated formally rather than on an ad hoc basis. Moreover, de Valera's return from America and the resulting increase in cabinet meetings, coupled with Brugha's renewed interest in army affairs, portended increased contact between the political and military factions. Finally, as the conflict accelerated in the first six months of 1921, policy decisions became imperative.

Simply put, the war had become much more brutal. There were a number of factors responsible for this change. The recruitment of improperly trained non-Irish troops to bolster the RIC clearly changed the character of the war. Also, the fighting men of the IRA changed. As the violence escalated, the unthinkable became thinkable and was deemed necessary. Certainly, there were aspects of self-preservation involved. But, what is significant is that killing had become an accepted part of the struggle. Mulcahy need no longer worry about the reaction of the Irish people as he had following the ambush at Soloheadbeg. The killing of two policemen paled as combat intensified. If violence and brutality were not commonplace, they were at least not shocking. Mulcahy was forced to confront the changing nature of the war and consult the government on questions of reprisals, executing spies and prisoners of war, desertion and emigration. These issues would become commonplace during subsequent guerrilla struggles. The venue would change repeatedly, but the problems would remain basically the same.

Furthermore, the changing role of GHQ necessitated that policy decisions be made on critical questions. Increasingly, GHQ had centralized the workings of the IRA and had established itself as a decision making body which set standards and procedures. Although some officers would continue to inform GHQ about actions and decisions *ex post facto*, change was evident. Officers now looked to GHQ for guidance and for direction.

Two of the most pressing issues which Mulcahy had to contend with concerned deserters and potential émigrés. IRA men who were unable or unwilling to continue fighting often attempted to emigrate to America. Moreover, not only were deserters trying to leave the country, but young men eligible to serve in the IRA were instead departing for New York or Boston. During World War I, because emigration was impossible, the ranks of the Volunteers had swelled. The coming of peace, however, had opened the ports once again. The British, moreover, exploited emigration to lure away possible IRA recruits or even active members.

By June 1920, it was clearly a serious problem. Brigades were asking GHQ if the IRA had the power to prevent emigration of men of military age even though they were not members of the IRA.[35] GHQ informed its officers that an act of the Dáil was necessary to prevent eligible men from leaving the country and cautioned against coercion.[36] GHQ specifically ordered, however, that "the booming of emigration and the touting for emigrants by Emigration Agents shall not be allowed, all cases of this occurring shall be reported at once to Headquarters." Moreover, according to this same order, emigration "at the present time must be regarded as desertion in the face of the enemy", and no Volunteer would be allowed to leave the country without special permission from headquarters.[37]

Apparently this order was not sufficient to stop the flow of Volunteers out of the country. While anyone who wished to emigrate was required to obtain a permit from the Republican authorities, the system was not very effective. Permits were forged or simply ignored by the Volunteers and the civilian population alike.

GHQ searched for solutions. In an intra-office memorandum, it advocated "systematic action" against emigration agents and proposed an anti-emigration crusade. This campaign would include enlisting the aid of the younger clergy to discourage those who were thinking of leaving Ireland, applying pressure on families who sent men of military age out of Ireland, and even "raiding American letters in the districts where emigration is rampant." The crusade could, moreover, be extended to the United States under the slogan "Stay at Home and Fight" in an attempt to stop the flow of money for boat tickets. Finally, the memo proposed "exemplary punitive measures" against deserters. In machiavellian fashion, it suggested that the men shot not be advertised as deserters per se, but rather let the impression spread that they were killed for emigrating. The memo concluded that "the type of man who runs away now will be very amenable to such reasoning".[38]

Similar sentiments were echoed by the Cork No. 1 Brigade. In March 1921, it wrote to GHQ suggesting

> that public notices be issued in all Brigade areas that after a certain date all Volunteers emigrating without permission will be shot as deserters, and all civilians emigrating without a permit from the Dáil be arrested and dealt with severely.[39]

Pressure was mounting for a more aggressive policy. At the end of March, 1921, Mulcahy wrote the minister for defence pointing out the seriousness of the matter:

> It is certainly hard for men fighting in the country to see a wave of emigration developing around them, and the matter should perhaps get careful consideration, to see what we can do in addition to what has been done already to check it. In my opinion, it is impossible to deal with it at the ports.[40]

On 8 April 1921, a Dáil order prohibited emigration without a printed permit signed by the minister of home affairs and affixed with the seal of the Republic. Violators would be deemed to have committed a grave offence against the State in time of war and would be dealt with accordingly.[41]

Emigration implied desertion and GHQ fumbled for appropriate disciplinary measures. In March 1921, a staff memo urged that the death penalty be imposed on deserters:

> The death penalty should be inflicted for the grave class of crimes if the situation calls for it. Quite lately there have been some cases of Desertion, and unless disciplinary measures are taken there is a good prospect of large numbers running away in the Western areas. It is absolutely essential to stop this rot. Drumming out is of no use in such a case—the type of man concerned would only welcome it. Flogging has never been done in the case of Irish troops and should not be started now.[42]

In fact, GHQ eventually decided on a much softer position. According to General Order No. 18, issued on 2 April 1921, men were permitted to leave the army if they so chose. The only restriction was that they preserve silence about IRA activities and that they "be made fully aware of the penalty they are liable to suffer for refusal to surrender their arms or for conduct prejudicial to the discipline of the Army".[43]

The issue of reprisals and counter-reprisals also grew more pressing as the war intensified. While Mulcahy and headquarters staff continued to insist that the IRA not engage in wanton behavior, the increasingly provocative conduct of the British troops made this more difficult to ensure. The British military authorities in Ireland themselves admitted that

> the troops are getting out of control, taking the law into their own hands, and that besides clumsy and indiscriminate destruction, actual thieving and looting as well as drunkenness and gross disorder are occurring.[44]

Not only were individual houses burnt, but the economic life of the country was imperilled by the destruction of shops and creameries and portions of towns—the most infamous being the burning of Cork city. Unofficial sanction by the British government of these kinds of actions by its army gave way to the official sanctioning of reprisals in January 1921. At first, this policy of official reprisals was limited to areas under martial law, but within two months it spread beyond the proclaimed area of Munster. Thus, with the official endorsement of a policy of retaliation by the British government and with the increasingly disorderly conduct of the Black and Tans and Auxiliaries, the issue became more pressing for Mulcahy.

Until May, Mulcahy had given limited endorsement to reprisals and counter-reprisals, but no formal sanction. Decisions were made on an individual basis. In certain cases, he had given general permission to commanding officers to counter-retaliate against enemy property when spontaneous action was necessary. For example, the brigade commandant in Belfast received such permission, with Mulcahy adding the caveat that such action be "a thoroughly efficient and intelligently directed blow".[45]

In mid-May, Mulcahy decided to give formal sanction to a reprisals policy. He proposed that the IRA engage in counter-reprisals in instances where British troops carried out reprisals against Republican supporters. If the British further retaliated, the burning for burning would continue until the district concerned was entirely cleared of loyalists. Mulcahy further proposed that the commanding officer inform GHQ of British reprisals so that headquarters might organize similar action abroad. The IRA had, in a limited way, extended the war to Britain and Mulcahy proposed that this campaign be used to include reprisals. In keeping with his own standards, Mulcahy did insist that owners of houses involved in the reprisals be duly notified. However, he also believed that they should be ordered out of the country and their land confiscated. They would be allowed to dispose of their stock.[46]

These ideas were subsequently embodied in General Order No. 26 issued on 22 June 1921 but with two significant changes. GHQ itself would approve all orders to deport and confiscate land.[47] Such a delicate matter was not to be left in the hands of subordinate officers. Secondly, the section on extending reprisals to Britain was omitted. Instead, the order simply stated that GHQ would consider possible further action.[48]

Mulcahy's move to issue an official policy came rather late in the struggle, nearly four months after the British declaration. The timing was interesting. It may have signalled Mulcahy's concern about the escalating scale of terrorism and the need to set guidelines. Or Mulcahy may have been worried about the continued ability of the people to endure the terrorist tactics of the British forces. It may also have been related to his growing concern about the ability of the IRA to maintain the struggle. Or finally, with a truce and negotiations a distinct possibility, Mulcahy may have designed this policy to notify Lloyd George that the IRA was not in retreat and that the price of continuing the war would become higher and higher. Most likely, it was a mixture of all these motives.

The IRA burnt houses not only as a reprisal, but also to prevent the British forces from occupying large homes and mansions. Dotted over the countryside, were a number of these houses which the Black and Tans could use as a base from which to conduct raids, collect information, and intimidate the local population. Mulcahy seemed to condone the IRA's destruction of these types of dwellings. In some cases, his permission was sought. In others, he simply noted and approved such actions.

Another issue which Mulcahy had to resolve was the question of association with the enemy. Those who housed Crown forces or engaged in business with British troops were potential targets for counter-reprisals. Mulcahy, for example, pointed out to a man who complained that he had been threatened by an IRA officer, that, while any threat was unauthorized, it must be understood that "property of the Crown forces is always liable to seizure and confiscation by us; and that it is regretted that he cannot be guaranteed any immunity in this matter."[49] In wartime, those who chose to deal with the enemy had to accept the consequences of their action.

Civilians who conducted business with the British forces certainly challenged the spirit of the fight for independence. Some officers in Cork wanted an economic boycott of Crown forces:

> It is time we get the Irish people, no matter who they are, not to freely supply the enemy. Several people have large contracts for meat, oats and dozens of other important supplies. It seems ridiculous to have the civil population supplying the enemy, while the army is on the field to cut off supplies, etc. If they force supplies from the people, it is alright, but then it will take time and men to do it.[50]

Mulcahy, however, did not believe that a general order forbidding firms to work for the Crown or sell supplies to the British troops would be effective on a nation-wide scale. In a rather pessimistic evaluation—especially in comparison with his later description of the support and unity of the people—he noted his own dissatisfaction with the response of some areas to the request of the Dáil to boycott the police. He felt that an order forbidding the furnishing of supplies to the British would fare even worse. Despite his pessimism, Mulcahy applied to the Ministry "for power to delegate to the O/C of any particular area, authority to forbid supplies of materials of any kind to Enemy forces in his area, in such circumstances and at such time as GHQ Staff was agreed to be necessary."[51] By June 1921, the IRA had begun attacking enemy ordnance stores. Policy seemed to be drifting toward complementing military activity with attempts to deprive the British troops of essential materials. This would be a significant advance for the IRA because it would raise the economic and psychological costs for the British to stay in Ireland.

"Association with the enemy" was a problem which bedevilled GHQ and which appeared numerous times in monthly reports to GHQ from the field. In ordinary social exchanges, important information was often, unwittingly, conveyed to the British forces. As one report noted, "people here are very much inclined to talk among themselves, and the story keeps going till the enemy hears it. It is very hard to know who brings the information directly."[52]

With the declaration of martial law in the most bellicose areas of Munster in December 1920, and the large-scale searches in Dublin, the IRA was feeling pressured. It was imperative that all leaks to the enemy cease. Discussion ensued as to how to best stop the flow of information to the enemy. On 26 March 1921, Cork No. 1 Brigade Council recommended to GHQ "that public notices be issued in all Brigade areas that after a certain date, all persons associating voluntarily in any way with the armed forces of the enemy will be regarded as traitors and treated as such."[53]

Mulcahy wrote to Brugha urging the government to issue a proclamation on associating with the enemy. GHQ felt the problem required it to issue a general order. This would allow headquarters to set out guidelines and procedures for its men in the field. On 20 April 1921, GHQ issued General Order No. 19 under which those who continued to communicate with the British forces and who were, therefore, endangering the lives of members of the IRA, would be warned by the brigade commandant that "such association cannot be allowed to continue with impunity; that it is not desired to molest or inflict punishment or inconvenience unnecessarily upon any person but . . . if this dangerous association continues, action shall have to be taken." Those who ignored these warnings would be referred to the adjutant-general, GHQ.[54]

Apparently the problem persisted because within two months headquarters issued another order. General Order No. 24 was more explicit:

> The communication to the Enemy of information concerning the work or personnel of the Army or of the Civil Administration of the Republic, is an offence against the life of the Nation, and in the ultimate is punishable by death.[55]

This order acknowledged degrees of offences and provided for lesser punishments—for example, the payment of a fine—in cases where the information was unimportant or where there were mitigating circumstances. Always there was to be a court of inquiry, sentences to be ratified by the brigade commandant and reports submitted to the adjutant-general. Mulcahy detailed the procedure to be followed at headquarters. When GHQ received the reports, the adjutant-general would pass them to the director of information and to the chief of staff. Mulcahy, moreover, retained the right of final authorization in cases which needed a ruling from GHQ.[56] This typified Mulcahy's approach to critical issues. He wanted to ensure that proper procedures were followed. At the local level, senior officers would make the decisions and at GHQ, Mulcahy himself was to be informed of, and involved in, the decision making process.

Actual spying was handled in the same way. GHQ approved the execution of spies whose information had led to the capture or death of IRA soldiers. According to General Order No. 20, "a convicted spy shall not be executed until his conviction and sentence have been ratified by the brigade commandant concerned," and all cases were to be reported to the adjutant-general.[57] Mulcahy repeatedly insisted that evidence be gathered and a trial conducted to determine guilt or innocence. Only in the most extreme circumstances would this be waived. He rebuked his senior officers for allowing their junior officers to execute spies and, time and time again, informed them that questionable cases were to be referred back to GHQ.

There were obvious difficulties in following these procedures. Often times it was difficult to obtain evidence and IRA officers acted on allegations and assumptions. Certain areas of Cork, in particular, were reputed to be especially quick to shoot spies. Interestingly enough, the officers involved felt this allegation damaging enough to write to GHQ professing their adherence to procedures in dealing with spies.[58] Moreover, in some cases, people were killed by the British and then marked with a sign that said "executed by the IRA". In these cases, Mulcahy demanded a speedy investigation and report.[59]

Women spies presented a more delicate challenge. General Order No. 13 instructed brigade commandants to follow the same procedure in holding a court of enquiry. A woman found guilty:

> . . . shall then be advised accordingly, and except in the case of an Irishwoman, be ordered to leave the country within 7 days. It shall be intimated to her that only consideration of her sex prevents the infliction of the statutory punishment of death. A formal public statement of the fact of the conviction shall be issued in poster or leaflet

form or both . . . as a warning and a preventative. Ordinarily it is not proposed to deport Irishwomen, it being hoped that the bringing of publicity on the actions of such will neutralise them. In dangerous and insistent cases of this kind, however, full particulars should be placed before GHQ and instructions sought.[60]

Although Mulcahy sometimes authorized the destruction of property belonging to women spies, he shied away from execution. Mulcahy knew such action would make good propaganda for the British. Even in the passion of the 1916 Rising, the British had not executed Countess Markievicz, but rather commuted her sentence. Some of Mulcahy's officers disagreed and argued for the execution of women spies. The commanding officer from south Roscommon, for example, wrote that a number of IRA men were almost captured because of the work of a woman spy, but for a "miraculous escape in a hail of bullets. Had we fallen the whole brigade organization was gone."[61]

In another instance, the IRA actually executed a woman thought to be a spy. A Mrs Noble's house had been raided and a letter from the head constable arranging a meeting with her had been found. Witnesses had seen her going into the police barracks four or five times and claimed to have seen her handing a list of names of the Volunteers to the head constable. Mrs Noble was arrested by the IRA and, according to her captors, "admitted guilt on all the charges. She was fortified with the Rites of the Church before being executed."[62]

There was, moreover, at least one case where a woman spy was executed and GHQ not informed. The elderly Mrs Lindsay had given information to the British that led to the killing of two IRA men and the capture of ten others. In response, the 1st Southern Division kidnapped and shot her. At the time of the truce, the chief of staff ordered her release only to learn that "this lady had been executed long ago."[63]

Shooting prisoners of war presented another thorny issue for Mulcahy and his staff. As a guerrilla army, the IRA had neither the facilities or the personnel suitable for keeping prisoners of war. Men detailed to look after prisoners were soldiers lost to combat. Numerous prisoners, moreover, had escaped and provided information which allowed the British to score a number of successful raids and capture IRA men. For their part, the British had killed a number of IRA men in captivity, the typical explanation: "shot while trying to escape". Dick McKee and Peadar Clancy were but two of the more well-known examples of IRA men who were killed during interrogation. In response to this practice, there was a growing sentiment among the IRA for an official statement that those taken as prisoners of war would be shot as retaliation for IRA men who were killed while in custody.

On 4 May 1921, Liam Lynch wrote to Mulcahy suggesting that, in the future, the IRA shoot a local loyalist for each prisoner shot. "It is proposed to notify the loyalists to this effect, and by doing so we hope to get them to prevent the enemy from shooting our prisoners." Mulcahy rejected Lynch's suggestion for the moment, questioning the ability of loyalists to influence British policy. Lynch persevered, placing the matter before the chief of staff again in June:

> If the enemy continue shooting our prisoners then we should shoot theirs *all round* and they should be told so. If a day is fixed for such action and the whole Army act together from that [time] forward, I am sure the enemy will quickly change its policy. All lives must be considered sacred, and indeed we would all wish to be chivalrous but when the enemy continue such an outrage, let it be a barbarous war all round.[64]

The coming of the Truce less than a month later precluded any official policy decision on this matter. However, unofficially British officers who were captured in certain areas were executed in retaliation for IRA men killed. For example, in June, 1921, GHQ received an official report from Headquarters Tipperary No.3 Brigade on the capture and execution of three military officers.[65]

The discussions surrounding these policy issues are important because they reveal something of the delicacy of Mulcahy's task as chief of staff of a guerrilla struggle. His correspondence and GHQ's general orders demonstrate that Mulcahy was navigating a fine line between the demands of the struggle and the need to impose some moral limits. Because of the uniqueness of the struggle, Mulcahy had few if any precedents to fall back on. As chief of staff, he was forced to make judgments and decide issues as best he could in the circumstances. He certainly was not always correct. However, despite British propaganda to the contrary, neither he nor his officers were blood-thirsty criminals who delighted in killing. Mulcahy did not glorify violence in the tradition of Pearse. But he did believe it was necessary and effective. He would meet violence with violence and ruthlessness with ruthlessness. While it was not clear that Mulcahy thought the IRA could win, he certainly did not want them to lose the fight for independence.

By the beginning of 1921, GHQ was increasingly pressured by threats of arrests. Lloyd George had publicly declared that his government now had "murder by the throat" and a new, more intense British initiative seemed imminent. Large-scale searches and concentrated patrolling by the British forces led them to a series of successful raids, including the discovery of the office of the minister for home affairs. These activities affirmed that their intelligence system was improving and foretold more harassment and arrests for the IRA.

Mulcahy knew that he had to ensure that the fight would continue, regardless of arrests. Thus, he opted for decentralizing the IRA, forming them into divisions:

we never knew when the blow would come and that GHQ might be wiped out. . . . We therefore set out from the beginning of 1921 to divisionalize the country—that is we took the brigades of Kerry, Cork and Waterford and we put them under a divisional group and the same way we had about 15 divisional areas where we knew there was military capacity among the people there to provide 15 GHQ Staffs so that if Headquarters here was wiped out there would be sufficient authority and prestige attached to local groups to do the same thing. Our idea was that they could get on if they were driven to get on without us and we organised for that purpose.[66]

Divisionalization also served another purpose. GHQ had become increasingly aware of the need to co-ordinate IRA activities. Mulcahy had received complaints from some officers in his more active areas that they were receiving no help from their neighbors. Cork No. 2 Brigade, for example, complained that "individual brigades are often hard-pressed by the enemy, while neighbouring Brigades are listening to the guns and do nothing, often perhaps allowing enemy reinforcements to pass through unmolested."[67] There was little GHQ could do about this type of situation.

Creating divisions would thus ensure the continued survival of the IRA, enhance cooperation between adjacent areas, and, in general, facilitate co-ordination. Furthermore, creating divisions would reduce the number of commanding officers GHQ would oversee. This would allow the chief of staff and his officers to give more attention to the main problems of an individual area and to devise a more unified strategy.[68] GHQ could concentrate on putting the fighting into a broader perspective, analyzing strengths and weaknesses, assets and liabilities not simply of a brigade but of an entire division. After divisionalization was under way, Mulcahy, in fact, began to draw up a directive for each area. He analysed their overall position within the guerrilla struggle, pointed out what their particular contribution could be and suggested tactics and strategies for carrying on the fight.[69]

On 8 March 1921, Mulcahy wrote to Liam Lynch to explain the idea of divisionalization and to appoint him commander of the first division of the IRA—the 1st Southern Division.[70] GHQ was forced to proceed slowly toward its goal of approximately sixteen divisions throughout the country. Good officers were scarce; some were reluctant to give up their autonomy and become part of a division; some brigade commandants were hesitant to yield good officers to a divisional staff. However, by the time of the truce in July of 1921, GHQ had established nine divisions with functioning staffs.

Divisionalization obviously decentralized the structure and control of the army. According to GHQ instructions, the divisional staff was to replicate the central staff in Dublin. They now would have to decide many matters which were formerly referred to Dublin. Indeed, GHQ conferred on the divisional staff a "grave and solemn responsibility—nothing less than the absolute military control of two or three counties".[71]

GHQ hoped that having divisions would draw the more quiescent areas into the fight and would, by virtue of the divisional commander's greater accessibility, increase local initiative and the spontaneity with which actions could be planned and executed.[72] GHQ planned to issue only general directives to the officers commanding the divisions, allowing the divisional officers a wide degree of discretion in implementing their orders.

Divisional officers were instructed to keep in close contact with their brigades, to develop initiative among their subordinate officers and to prune their staffs of any inefficient or incompetent officer. The monthly reports previously submitted to GHQ would now go to the divisional staff, who would forward them to Dublin. Except in rare cases, GHQ would only deal with divisional commandants.[73] All in all, GHQ intended that

> Each Division must come more and more to regard itself as a definite Unit capable of carrying on a formidable campaign unaided, and capable, also, of organising and administering its own Units. The Division is an army in miniature and should regard its problems from that point of view.[74]

Divisionalization was not without its critics or disadvantages. At a meeting of brigade commandants to discuss the formation of the first Southern division, the idea met with both criticism and hostility. According to reports of the meeting, officers like Tom Barry and Sean O'Hegarty opposed the formation of divisions on the grounds that the division encompassed too large an area to operate effectively in a guerrilla struggle. The IRA did not have the communications equipment necessary for the immediate transmission of instructions. Thus, opportunities would be lost as messages slowly made their way around the division. Moreover, Barry, for one, questioned the actual power which the divisional staff would possess, pointing out that they would not be able to supply arms, ammunition, or equipment to the Brigades. More importantly, Barry argued that:

> Although it [the IRA] was highly disciplined, its members would resent the removal of officers by an authority outside the Brigade, unless very good cause existed, and a Brigade might easily be disrupted by such action . . . and it would not be capable of enforcing an order to transfer material from a strong unit to a weaker one, unless the Brigade Officers agreed to the suggestion.[75]

However, the brigade commandants did believe that more cooperation and coordination among the brigades was necessary.[76] Despite objections, the brigade commandants did eventually agree to forming a division.

Divisionalization was not the only topic discussed at this meeting of brigade commandants. These officers used the opportunity of the meeting with Ernie O'Malley, headquarter's representative, to vent their anger at both GHQ and the prevailing conditions. Why, they demanded, had not

Mulcahy or Collins come to discuss this idea with them in person? They argued that GHQ could not understand the fighting conditions in the country if they always remained in Dublin. Moreover, some were scornful of the document—replete with military jargon—which O'Malley read to them. The officers wanted guns and ammunition, wanted GHQ to relieve the mounting British pressure on them by extending the struggle to other areas, not fancy phrases. Some viewed the Headquarters document as totally removed from the realities of the guerrilla war.[77]

The criticism which the officers levelled at Mulcahy and Collins was born out of the frustrations of the situation and the limitations inherent in a guerrilla war. They did not know, for example, the efforts that GHQ was making to procure arms and ammunition. They only knew they were constantly in short supply. Nor did they make clear what more headquarters could do to induce quiet areas to pick up the fight. The disgruntled officers could not understand the conditions and limitations under which GHQ functioned. Their complaints, while understandable, were more in the nature of "grousing" than legitimate criticism. Furthermore, it would have been fool hardy for Mulcahy as chief of staff or Collins as minister for finance—those who in the popular mind seemed to symbolize the war for independence—to venture into the country in the current climate. The risks were too great. Not only would the central control of the army have been seriously weakened by their capture, but it would have been a shattering psychological blow for the IRA.

However, the criticism does speak to an important perception which developed among some of the officers. Some officers believed that they were taking all the risks, doing all the fighting, bearing the brunt of the struggle, while those in Dublin sat at desks and wrote memoranda. GHQ exacerbated this perception by using military terminology which, in the light of the conditions, could seem both pompous and pretentious. Mulcahy was a prime offender and probably set the tone for the rest of his staff. But Mulcahy was not simply indulging himself. His writing style reflected and reinforced his determination that the IRA act and feel like an army. While his style may have alienated some of his officers, it impressed others and, more importantly, "increased the credibility of the Republican counter-state as a whole. . . . To some extent the most substantive function of GHQ was one of political propaganda."[78]

Despite these criticisms, Mulcahy was a popular chief of staff. In particular, officers appreciated the fact that Mulcahy did whatever he could to help them and their men, replying promptly to their requests. For example, in a request for a book on explosives, the O/C of the 3rd Southern Division wrote to Mulcahy, "I know that it is not proper to communicate with you for literature etc., but I feel that no other officer at GHQ would pay such immediate attention to a matter of this kind." His faith was well placed; he received a reply within a week.[79]

Mulcahy's concern for his officers and his men was readily apparent in his communications with them. His caution frustrated some; his insistence on procedure annoyed others. But he patiently reiterated the reasons for his actions, and even those who disagreed, had to admit that he wanted to understand their point of view, their concerns, their problems. Tom Barry, who frequently battled with GHQ, gave this impression of Mulcahy:

> I had several lengthy interviews with the Chief of Staff, Richard Mulcahy. This calm, unhurried man was meticulous in seeking out details, and probed me on questions affecting the organisation, discipline, training and tactics of the IRA in the South. . . . Throughout those talks the Chief of Staff was courteous, friendly and interested.[80]

However, Mulcahy suffered from the fact that he did not have the flair of someone like Collins nor the bravado which came to be associated with the stereotypical "rebel gunman". He remained quiet, rather reserved, and certainly preoccupied with his work. Sean O'Murthuile captured the image of Mulcahy and his staff when he wrote:

> My school was that of Collins. . . . We were a happy carefree lot, who, in the hardest of times could be found carelessly congregated at one or another of our various haunts. . . . Of Mulcahy and MacMahon [quartermaster-general, later to be chief of staff] and their work I knew practically all there was to know, but I had come to regard them as *stern silent workers who scorned pleasure and frivolity and who had enslaved themselves to their respective tasks.* . . . once I had begun to work and live with [them] . . . I realised the greatness of their outlook, their tireless devotion to their great task, and their fairness to all within the limits of their responsibilities.[81] (Emphasis added.)

Some of his opponents and critics never had the opportunity to see, or could not appreciate, that side of Mulcahy.

Especially at this point, popularity would not be one of Mulcahy's primary concerns. As the summer of 1921 approached, long hours of daylight gave the British a definite advantage in guerrilla fighting. Moreover, a large number of IRA men had been arrested and Mulcahy needed time to train their replacements. His greatest worry, however, was the safety of the flying columns.

Mulcahy knew that the flying columns were his primary fighting force, the key to the IRA's struggle. He fretted over their safety and security. Some of his officers, however, did not show the same concern. In May 1921, Mulcahy sent a memo to all of his officers defining the paramount position of the flying columns. He stated quite clearly that "the fighting men must be protected at any cost," and that the responsibility for this fell directly on each company. Mulcahy minced no words in spelling out the consequences for failure to give the necessary protection:

> The penalty for negligence in this matter is Death, and if any members of the Column lose their lives, through negligence, this Penalty will be rigidly enforced against the men responsible.[82]

As later revolutionaries would also come to discover, the chief of staff had grasped the basic fact that, if the struggle against the British were to continue, the flying columns must never be destroyed.

It was a paradoxical situation. During the months of May and June, one fourth of all Crown casualties occurred, and the number of IRA attacks, ambushes, and engagements reached a new high. Yet pressure from the British, especially from Dublin Castle, continued to increase. The home where Mulcahy was sleeping one night was raided. Though Mulcahy himself escaped, climbing along rooftops still in his nightclothes, he left behind a large stack of papers. It provided the British with detailed information on proposed IRA attacks in England, in particular, an operation in Manchester. The attack had to be cancelled.[83]

Collins, too, lost papers and files. Neither he nor Mulcahy could afford to spend more than one night in any house. Collins' men inside Dublin Castle were vanishing through arrest and dismissal and, with them, the system which had virtually guaranteed the safety of GHQ.

The lack of arms and ammunition continued to bedevil the IRA. It was a chronic complaint. Typically, the IRA replenished its supply of ammunition from what it captured from the British. Some also was smuggled in from Britain or the United States. Attempts were even made at manufacturing at home. But the IRA never had an abundance of arms and ammunition. In the monthly reports throughout 1921, from all over the country, officers complained of having "very little stuff".

There was not much Mulcahy could do. He tried to ensure that active areas had priority in any shipment which GHQ received. He also exerted pressure on those responsible for supplying weapons to the IRA. For example, Mulcahy reprimanded the director of purchasing for his reported failure to buy ammunition because of lack of money. If the allegation were true, he said, it was "an appalling state of affairs". And, probably remembering all those reports which complained about the lack of arms and ammunition, added, "there are people in the country who would lynch us if they thought that we were in any way responsible for missing stuff like this." He demanded a full financial accounting.[84] Mulcahy also directed his director of munitions to concentrate all his resources on manufacturing grenades, land mines and buck shot cartridges—items which they had both the facility and the ability to produce. It was, in his view, too serious a situation to divert attention to anything else.[85]

In May, however, the IRA did score a coup with the purchase of a number of Thompson machine guns from the United States. GHQ believed the machine gun would offer relief to hard pressed areas by increasing their defensive power. For less active areas, headquarters had great hopes that it would "make opportunities for its own employment".[86] While GHQ may have overestimated its effectiveness, it was definitely a morale booster:

> They [the Thompson guns] were not ideal from a guerrilla point of view, as they used heavy and bulky .45 ammunition, and had a slow rate of fire and limited range. None the less, "the rattle of the Thompson gun" was to become a much-loved sound among rebels; while the British military authorities acknowledged that "such a weapon cannot be ignored", and that its possession "undoubtedly makes the IRA a more formidable organization from the military point of view".[87]

As the IRA experimented with their new weapon, whispers of a truce and peace negotiations once more filled the Dublin air. Lloyd George's policy seemed to fluctuate with his moods. In his conciliatory mood, he sent a number of representatives to Dublin to try to negotiate a truce. All failed. Just as the Irish would agree on general terms, the prime minister would switch into his bellicose frame of mind and decide that the British could actually quell the rebellion. In an ironic way, this impression impelled the IRA to greater activity. Collins, for one, believed that only keeping up the struggle would force the British to peace terms. Anything else would be construed as a sign of weakness.[88]

Perhaps it was this assumption that motivated Collins, Mulcahy and GHQ to agree to one of the most costly and most spectacular engagements of the Anglo-Irish war, the burning of the Custom House. Perhaps they believed they needed a grand gesture of defiance. This was de Valera's view, at any rate. Since his return from America, de Valera had been uncomfortable with the guerrilla tactics of the IRA. He disliked what he characterized as the odd shooting of a policeman now and then. What the IRA needed, he said, was one good battle a month with about five hundred men on each side. It was clear that de Valera was out of touch with the military situation in Ireland and with the new methods of fighting which the IRA had developed. He was still thinking in terms of the 1916 approach.

But de Valera exerted a great deal of influence and he apparently convinced the senior officers of the army to try his idea. Their aim was to deliver a significant blow at English rule in Ireland. The target was the Custom House. It seemed to be the kind of high-risk operation that Mulcahy would have been unwilling to endorse—especially in light of his concerns at this time about the IRA. Indeed his own later explanations are contradictory. Mulcahy claimed that neither he nor his staff argued against the attack nor hesitated in helping to plan and organize it.[89] However, Mulcahy was also later extremely critical of the event and accused de Valera of letting political concerns interfere with military affairs.[90]

Mulcahy's inconsistencies in this case are glaring. On the one hand, he wanted to portray GHQ as the humble servant of the government, loyally carrying out instructions. On the other hand, he seemed to forget that he and his senior officers had an obligation to argue against a major military initiative about which they had doubts. Most likely, Mulcahy opposed the operation, but was overruled by de Valera, Brugha and possibly Collins. Once it was decided upon, however, GHQ cooperated. But it was clearly not their operation. The Dublin Brigade organized and executed the event without undue involvement from GHQ.

The burning of the Custom House was a military disaster: six IRA men were killed, twelve were wounded, and about seventy were captured. As a propaganda ploy, however, it proved that the IRA was capable of more than small-scale attacks and ambushes. As a political stroke, it destroyed the tax records of the British and further hampered their administration of the country.

Moreover, the burning of the Custom House most likely helped Lloyd George take the prospect of a truce more seriously. Even more convincing, however, was the report from the British chief of staff in Ireland that British troops were under considerable stress and strain and that the fighting must cease by the next autumn. His men could not endure another winter campaign. Serious negotiations ensued and on 11 July 1921, a truce between Ireland and England ended the state of war—a war which the British had refused to formally acknowledge, but which the Irish had slowly but unceasingly forced them to fight.

FOUR

Time of Truce and Uncertainty

"This thing must stop. We must have either Truce or War, and whoever, by any want of discipline, reopens the War prematurely will have to be held strictly accountable for it."

Richard Mulcahy, chief of staff

On Saturday, 9 July 1921, General Mulcahy issued the following communication to all his officers:

In view of the conversations now being entered into by our Government with the Government of Great Britain, and in pursuance of mutual understandings to suspend hostilities during these conversations, active operations by our troops will be suspended as from Noon, Monday, July Eleventh.[1]

War would soon be over—at least for a time. Neither side, however, would let the hostilities cease without one last outburst of violence. Before the Truce came into effect, the IRA received word that the British forces would attempt one final action. In Cork, for example, the "entire company [was] warned about reprisals by crown forces on the night previous to the Truce and all left their homes with few exceptions." The reason for the contemplated action by the Crown Forces was that six soldiers were captured and shot on about 9 July 1921.[2] In addition, records indicate that 11 spies were executed by the IRA just prior to the advent of the truce.[3] If the British government needed evidence that the IRA was not beaten, the IRA gave it to them. If proof were needed either by the Dáil or the English parliament that the IRA was an organized and determined army, that also was provided.

While talk of a truce had been in the air for some time, the actual declaration came with unexpected suddenness. No one was quite sure what it meant or how long it would last. Ernie O'Malley remembered receiving the chief of staff's note with a sense of bewilderment: "We sat down to talk about the news in wonder. What did it mean? And why had senior officers no other information than a bald message? Would the Truce last a week, or perhaps two weeks?"[4] No one, either at GHQ or in the field, could know the answers to O'Malley's questions. The Truce would last as long as the politicians talked. If an agreement was reached, it would become permanent. If not, war would resume. Both armies were to endure this uncertainty for almost six months.

The IRA was not particularly optimistic about the Truce. To many, it was only a respite—a lull in the fighting which would give both sides time to rest and regroup after the last six months of gruelling hostilities. Liam Deasy, O/C Cork No. 3 Brigade, described it as "a breathing space which might last for three or four weeks" during which the IRA would be able to reorganize their forces.[5]

Mulcahy and GHQ were under no illusions about the volatile nature of the Truce. Mulcahy was "very uncertain [as to] how long present conditions will last",[6] and pointed out rather emphatically that "a truce is nothing but a truce and is not a final settlement of the object we fight for."[7] Michael Brennan of Clare, who visited Dublin on the day after the truce, left with this same impression of GHQ:

> I . . . reported to GHQ. Collins, Mulcahy, Gearoid O'Sullivan and others all emphasized that they didn't expect the Truce to last very long and that it must be used to improve our organisation and training. I left them quite convinced that we had only got a breathing space and that a resumption of the fighting was an absolute certainty.[8]

Neither Mulcahy nor GHQ were directly involved in negotiating the terms of the truce, although they had considerable influence as to the terms which the IRA would accept. Two commandants, Barton and Duggan, represented the Irish army in arranging a truce. This was partially a response to the British refusal to recognize the IRA as a legitimate army and partially a precautionary measure on the part of GHQ. It was not yet time for the leaders of the army to come out in the open.[9] Mulcahy later recalled:

> It may seem funny to think that the discussion which led to an agreement to have a Truce was conducted, as far as the Irish side was concerned, entirely at the political level, although it was with Macready, who was the general officer commanding the British troops in Ireland. . . . As far as I can recall, at the meeting with Macready at the Mansion House, de Valera and Brugha were there and I think Duggan and Barton. I was told by Cathal Brugha that it wasn't necessary for me to attend (we may have been kept "under cover") and I waited at Mrs. Stopford Green's house in St. Stephen's Green for news as to the termination of a truce.[10]

Later, probably influenced by the events of the Treaty debate and the Civil War, Mulcahy would be critical of the choice of Barton. According to Mulcahy, Barton's selection was incomprehensible given that he had only recently been released from prison and elevated to the rank of commandant. Duggan, on the other hand, seemed to Mulcahy to be a more logical negotiator. He was associated with Collins in the Intelligence department and was a solicitor whose legal background could be useful in dealing with the British.[11] In any event, it seemed as if the chief of staff had little to say about the selection of the two representatives.

According to the agreement reached between the Irish and the British representatives, both sides agreed that:

> 1. No incoming troops, R.I.C., and Auxiliary Police and Munitions and no movements for military purposes of troops and munitions, except maintenance drafts.

> 2. No provocative display of forces, armed or unarmed.

> 3. It is understood that all provisions of this truce apply to the martial law area equally with the rest of Ireland.

> 4. No pursuit of Irish officers or men or war material or military stores.

> 5. No secret agents, noting description or movements, and no interference with the movements of Irish persons, military or civil, and no attempts to discover the haunts or habits of Irish officers and men.

> 6. No pursuit or observance of lines of communication or connection.

On behalf of the Irish Army, it was agreed that:

> a. Attacks on Crown Forces and civilians to cease.

> b. No provocative displays of force, armed or unarmed.

> c. No interference with Government or private property.

> d. To discountenance and prevent any action likely to cause disturbance of the peace which might necessitate military interference.[12]

If the truce were terminated, seventy-two hours notice would be given to each side.

The Truce was a political decision. It was a prelude to negotiations between the two sides, a military agreement which would enable politicians to make their way to the bargaining table. Progress was slow, however, as de Valera and Lloyd George engaged in verbal combat and in a war of letters for the next two and a half months. Each side vied for position. The British offered limited dominion status. The Irish spoke of independence and self-determination. Finally, in the fall, they agreed to begin negotiations on "how the association of Ireland with the community of nations known as the British Empire may best be reconciled with Irish national aspirations".[13]

The cessation of hostilities raised, and continues to raise, basic questions:

Who profited from the truce? Why was it agreed to by the respective leaders? From the British point of view, the truce reflected the desire of the government to come to a political settlement. Lloyd George and his cabinet had come under increasing pressure to stop the war in Ireland. His own military leaders were pessimistic about defeating the IRA without the influx of more men and war material, and more sweeping powers. The British prime minister recoiled from this step and sought instead a negotiated solution.

Because of the controversy surrounding the acceptance of the Treaty and the subsequent Civil War, the Irish position *vis-à-vis* the Truce is more difficult to assess. One point seems clear. There was growing political sentiment for negotiations among some members of the government and the Dáil. While this desire predated de Valera's coming back to Ireland from America, it certainly gained considerable support with his return. De Valera thought in political, not military terms—as evidenced by his advice on how the IRA should fight the war of independence. Moreover, he, as well as others, questioned how much longer the Irish people could endure the disruption in their lives. This was a particular concern in the martial law districts where the war created severe hardships.

Beyond this, however, the issues are not clear. Questions abound: What was the actual condition of the IRA at the time of the Truce? Was their supply of ammunition so low as to jeopardize their continuing the struggle? Was British intelligence actually regaining a foothold and were Irish intelligence sources diminishing? More importantly, what were the perceptions of the chief of staff, GHQ, and the officers in the field about their status at the time of the truce?

The answers to these questions are shaded and colored by the controversy over the Treaty. Those, like Mulcahy, Collins and the majority of GHQ who supported the Treaty, tended to be pessimistic in their evaluation of the ability of the IRA to continue or resume the fight with the British. Those, like Liam Lynch, Ernie O'Malley, and Tom Barry who opposed the Treaty, argued that the IRA could have continued the struggle and could have won an independent republic. Each side found factual evidence to support its claim.

From a historical perspective, it seems that, militarily, the IRA was in trouble. Arrests were becoming a serious problem. A number of officers and men had been captured and the IRA was facing a shortage of experienced fighting forces. And, as noted, GHQ itself was concerned about its own ability to avoid arrests. Moreover, GHQ had not been very successful in trying to relieve the pressure on the martial law area. One or two other areas showed some signs of life, but how long or how intensely they would fight was problematic. And, as always, there was a lack of ammunition. While it was a perennial problem, and while it alone would not have necessitated a truce, the fact that soldiers had to worry about how many rounds of ammunition they expended during any one engagement, could not have made any officer feel completely confident about the prospect of a long military struggle.

Interestingly, a British intelligence report of September 1921 substantiated the claim of those who believed the IRA was facing serious difficulties at the time of the truce:

> the rebel organisation throughout the country was in a precarious condition, and the future from the Sinn Féin point of view may be said to have been well nigh desperate. The Flying Columns and active service units into which the Rebels have been forced, by the search for prominent individuals, to form themselves, were being harried and chased from pillar to post, and were being constantly defeated and broken up; the Headquarters of the IRA was functioning under the greatest difficulty, many of its Officers having being [*sic*] captured . . .[14]

Obviously, this was an interesting reversal from what the upper echelon of the British military had been saying to Lloyd George previous to the Truce. Their explanation—however lame—was that they had simply miscalculated.[15]

Regardless of the actual condition of the IRA in July 1921, it seems obvious that, once a truce was agreed to and the fighting stopped, resuming the struggle would be difficult. First of all, the IRA had lost one its most effective weapons—secrecy. In Collins' apt phrase, they would be "like rabbits coming out from their holes; and pot shots for the 'farmers' should the truce ever fail".[16] This fact was not lost on the British who urged their troops to "keep your ears and eyes open but your mouth shut and don't forget to report what you hear and see". This advice was reinforced by examples of how effective intelligence could be garnered from the most innocuous situations. For example,

> The fact that a youth was seen a few days ago to salute certain civilians in the town and to hand over to them papers has definitely proved that he is a member of the IRA—a fact that was not certain before the Truce.[17]

Second, the momentum of the struggle had been broken. It would be difficult to re-establish it and regain the intensity of June 1921. As the truce dragged on, both civilians and soldiers grew accustomed to peace. Third, unless there were extremely good grounds, it would be difficult to ask the people to resume the state of war. The news of the truce had been greeted with sighs of relief and shouts of joy. If England offered the Irish a serious settlement, it would be difficult to convince the majority of the people that they should turn it down and resume the war.

While both Mulcahy and GHQ were aware of these problems and pitfalls, they had to work on the assumption that negotiations might fail and hostilities resume. The IRA had to be prepared for this eventuality. Headquarters used the Truce as an opportunity to improve the military position of the IRA. Both Collins and Mulcahy visited various divisions to see for themselves the actual conditions of their soldiers, assessing strengths, noting weaknesses, and discussing problems. During this time, headquarters set out to rectify the shortage in arms and ammunition, to strengthen the organization of the army, and to establish training camps to further the development of their officers.

The question of arms and ammunition was, of course, paramount. At the outset of the Truce, a memo was circulated at GHQ on the problem of munitions output. It argued that:

> The period of Truce should be utilised to the fullest possible extent for developing the Munitions supply. There should be no question of Vacation or Half-time work on the part of anybody engaged in this department. In the event of a renewal of hostilities, it is of vital consequence for us to have a liberal supply of War Material of all procurable kinds.[18]

The memo went on to suggest that home output should be intensified in every way and that foreign purchases should be fully re-organized to put it on a regular and dependable basis.

The Irish did not believe that importing arms and ammunition was a violation of the Truce. The British disagreed. During the subsequent negotiations in London, the Irish delegation—led by Arthur Griffith and Michael Collins—acquiesced to the British interpretation. In October, they recommended that the Dáil government agree to refrain from importing war material.[19] It is not clear why the Irish negotiators, especially Collins, would agree to such a demand. Perhaps by October, he believed that they had purchased as many arms or as much ammunition as they were likely to acquire. Perhaps Collins believed he could circumvent this restraint by using secret IRB contacts. More likely, he believed that it was not worth jeopardizing the success of the conference over this issue. The chief of staff dutifully ordered his quartermaster-general to take the necessary steps to have the agreement faithfully carried out and insisted that it should be "very strictly and honourably adhered to".[20]

There is, however, some indication that GHQ continued to import arms and ammunition. A report from the quartermaster-general in December of 1921 offered evidence that the IRA did import as well as manufacture munitions during the Truce. According to this report, the IRA had made some progress in acquiring munitions abroad, having purchased machine guns, rifles, various kinds of ammunition and explosives. This detailed list, apparently written in response to criticism of the department, pointed out the difficulties involved in importing munitions—noting, for example, the problems in transporting the material to Ireland and then landing, storing, and distributing the purchases. No mention was made in this document of stopping purchases as of October and, indeed, the dates of the report run from the time of the truce to the middle of December 1921.[21] It would seem that, regardless of any agreement, GHQ continued its policy of importing munitions. Perhaps, they believed the situation critical enough to warrant this obvious violation.

Moreover, in addition to acquiring arms, GHQ took the opportunity afforded by the Truce to begin a recruitment campaign to fill the units depleted by arrests. In terms of numbers, it was an extremely successful campaign. The IRA grew in size, if not in quality. The men who joined the IRA at this time came to be known as the "trucileers". In some cases, they were "sunshine soldiers"—to use Collins' phrase—men who had been absent during the fighting but now were more than eager to share in the acclaim. As Ernie O'Malley noted:

> The Irish Republican Army was in danger of becoming popular; recruits came in large numbers. Some men appeared in uniform who had never shown much anxiety to run special risks when courage was needed.[22]

The hero status the IRA acquired and the influx of recruits posed difficult problems for GHQ. It made it more difficult to enforce discipline and, in the long term, created a potentially dangerous situation.

During the Truce, GHQ set up officer training camps. The purpose was two fold. GHQ wanted to train sufficient officers to fill the gaps which massive arrests had created in their leadership. They needed to find new talent to shoulder the responsibilities of divisional and brigade staffs. GHQ also used the opportunity presented by the Truce to reorganize its staff. This entailed shifting officers who, regardless of their talent and dedication, simply were unable to inspire their men. As Mulcahy noted in a letter to one of his disgruntled officers:

> I am quite sure, however, that you will understand, in view of the perhaps, very long and hard struggle in front of us, it is absolutely necessary to throw responsibility upon younger men, even though, by doing so, we suffer some present loss. Unless responsibility is thrown upon younger men now they will not develop as rapidly as it is necessary they should . . .[23]

In general, the mission of the training camps was to instruct and inspire the officer corps, and to prepare them for possible post-Truce fighting with the British. Ernie O'Malley left this description of the training camp of the 2nd Southern Division:

> We trained the men in administration, organization, scouting, field sketching, engineering; we rehearsed imaginary barracks assaults, and ambushes, taught them the use of explosives and land mines, and how to manoeuvre.

Nor was it all drudgery or devoid of humor. O'Malley's description continues:

> One day on manoeuvres a position up the hill was being attacked; machine-gun fire was maintained by beating tin cans to make the attackers realize that they could not advance rashly. I was an umpire, mounted on a horse that seemed to reach the heavens, he was so high. I came upon one of the defenders in the angle of a hedged field, sitting down, smoking. "Why the deuce don't you open fire?" I demanded. The officer pointed to his large tin can. "It's a new make of machine," he said, smiling, "and I think it's jammed. I can't strip it."[24]

Mulcahy received regular reports on the camps, detailing the particular level of instruction and evaluating the knowledge, ability, and efficiency of the officers enrolled. It was a mixed review. Some, like the training camp of the 3rd Southern Division, received nothing but praise:

> . . . I have never seen any system of training work out as well as the one used in this camp. The men simply eat up the work. It opened up an entirely new field of work to all officers and showed up the proper working of the company in concrete form.[25]

Other camps, while clearly beneficial to the participants, revealed that the men came to camp with a very low level of military knowledge and training. As one report noted:

> The men of the camp are very keen and desirous of being trained, but on starting it was evident that they were totally ignorant of drill or discipline in any shape or form. At present they show a very marked improvement, and the Instructors will spare no time or trouble in still furthering and maintaining the present situation shown by all ranks.[26]

In these cases, basic instructions were given in the traditional topics—for example, drilling, musketry, signalling and map reading. In other cases, however, the training camps reflected the changing conditions of the IRA at the time of the truce. Instructions were given in the use of the Thompson machine gun and more emphasis was placed on having a trained officer to supervise the manufacture of grenades and the ammunition.

Mulcahy enthusiastically supported these camps, authorizing grants to subsidize them and making a point of visiting some of them. While he clearly appreciated their value in providing instruction to his officers, he also saw them as a way of holding the IRA together during the Truce. In his evaluation of the training camp in south Wexford, for example, he noted:

> The function of the Camp up to the present has been to pull them out of themselves and give them something like the appearance and bearing of soldiers. It has given them some idea of what their work should be.[27]

This function of the training camps became especially important as the Truce lasted longer and longer and it became harder and harder to maintain control over the army.

Difficulties with discipline were exacerbated by notices that the resumption of hostilities was imminent. The IRA would be informed at various times during the period from July to December to prepare for the termination of the Truce. Officers and men geared up to resume the war, only to be told that it was a false alarm. For example, on 7 September, President de Valera ordered his ministers to prepare to resume their activities on a war time basis. The minister for defence informed the army. And, on 20 September 1921, the adjutant-general noted that "At the moment this GHQ is of the opinion that the truce period is coming to an end."[28]

GHQ had prepared its officers as to the actions they should take immediately on the resumption of hostilities: camps were to be demobilized; all officers and men were to report to their units and cease appearing in public; stores were to be dumped; and, special precautions peculiar to each unit were to be undertaken to ensure the safety of the officers and men.[29]

Obviously, talk of termination of the Truce roughly corresponded with the course of the political negotiations. In October, when the two sides were trying to resolve issues involving alleged truce violations, there was a crisis. The British were worried that negotiations would break down on this point. Captured intelligence documents revealed that British forces in Ireland were informed that the situation was "somewhat critical" and advised "to be on the alert".[30] Moreover, while an Irish military memo of 9 November 1921, spoke of a likelihood of a further two months truce,[31] the completion of a draft treaty on 24 November impelled de Valera to issue another alarm to his ministers. Again they were advised "to prepare for an immediate breakdown in the peace negotiations".[32]

These changing and unsettling conditions imposed a severe strain on all those connected with the army. For six months, they lived on the verge of war, in a state of readiness yet not knowing when, if ever, they would be called upon to resume the fighting. This tension coupled with the relaxation of hostilities meant that differences of opinion, personality clashes, and political disagreements—which had been submerged during the war—would all surface. Not only was the Truce a time of training, it was also a time of accusations, recriminations, and complaining.

Most significantly, the atmosphere engendered by the Truce, an atmosphere permeated with antagonism, hostility, and vituperation, would be a factor in the outbreak of Civil War. Grievances, real or imagined, festered and poisoned the relations among members of the IRA. The unity and solidarity which seemed so real in the early months of 1921 gave way to bitterness and recriminations. Thus, when the time came to debate the merits of the Treaty, the exchanges were sharp and wounding. And, when a section of the army drifted into open revolt against the government, it was not quite as difficult for some to characterize their former colleagues as traitors or to imagine fighting against them. It was all made easier by the atmosphere which had developed during the Truce.

Mulcahy himself later agreed that the Truce had a deleterious effect on the army, but refused to recognize that it was a direct link to the Civil War:

> It is true that the prolonged Truce was very bad in every way, and that excesses of one kind or another arose out of the relaxation of strain, and that a certain amount of demoralisation took place, but don't let us think that there was anything in the situation of that particular kind that would not have been completely arrested and corrected at the time of the signing of the Treaty, if even at that late hour de Valera had accepted and supported the Treaty signed by Griffith and Collins. That checking would have been much more secure if the country was in the position of realising from the start that he [de Valera] was leading the delegation of plenipotentiaries to London himself.[33]

Mulcahy's analysis reflected his obsession with de Valera's responsibility for the Civil War—an obsession which would be a dominant motif for the remainder of his life and which obscured from him the fact that, despite a degree of culpability on the part of de Valera, a section of the army was determined to revolt.

Most of the antagonism expressed during the Truce was, in one way or another, channelled through, or even directed at, the chief of staff. Overall, there were three types of situations that Mulcahy had to deal with: 1) those which involved complaints from his own officers about the running of the army; 2) those which were directed at him by the minister of defence and his governmental colleagues; and 3) those which were directed at the IRA and which resulted in a series of complaints from members of the community to the president, the minister for defence and the chief of staff himself. In this last case especially, Mulcahy was caught in the middle between the demands of his political colleagues and the feelings of frustration of his officers and men. While he would defend his men to the government, he would also insist that complaints be examined, and if necessary, explained. It was not a popular position.

In dealing with the complaints and accusations which were levelled at the IRA, Mulcahy's basic position was that, above all, the honor of the army must be upheld. He reiterated this theme countless times in his correspondence with his officers, and urged them to take particular care not to tarnish their image. This emphasis was in keeping with Mulcahy's general outlook throughout the struggle. The army must act in a way which would bring credit to Ireland. It must be respectable. And, as he did during the struggle for independence, Mulcahy continued to try to impose ethical limits on the IRA, to set standards for behavior which would insure that the IRA would act, and would appear to act, as a disciplined and dignified army.

It was not an easy time for Mulcahy. His office was inundated with complaints. Some were serious. Some were petty. Some were the result of misunderstandings. Some were not even true. The chief of staff dealt with all of them. While Mulcahy understood the adverse effect the barrage of complaints was having on the army, his own sense of propriety demanded that they be investigated. Perhaps he would have been wiser to demand some proof of the accusations before asking his officers for an explanation. The constant demand for inquiries was straining relations between GHQ and its officer corps. For example, Liam Lynch clearly was showing signs of aggravation in his correspondence with the chief of staff and even the soothing tone which Mulcahy always employed with Lynch could not completely assuage the increasingly irate commandant.

Mulcahy also knew that some of the complaints about the IRA were simply not justified, were simply not true. The Truce seemed to create a situation where anyone felt free to complain about the army. For example, there was a complaint about an officer "joy-riding" in a car. Upon investigation, it emerged that it would have been impossible for the officer to use the particular car mentioned because it was at headquarters being rebuilt.[34] That was a minor incident, but it is indicative of the very easy way charges were levelled against the IRA. As one officer so accurately stated:

> It is high time to realise what a nuisance this type of polished Irishman is—a staunch friend of the enemy during the critical stages and naturally as a result was not lacking in preventing the forward movement of our local Unit. Now that he no longer from a business point of view deal with the enemy he would like to misrepresent for obvious reasons the local O.C.[35]

Mulcahy himself objected to the "army of complainers" who emerged during the Truce and came to the conclusion that "if a person listens civilly to them it is equal to saying to them 'oh this is a most serious thing and you should have complained about it long ago.'"[36] At least to his officers, he advised that they "avoid listening to these people's yarns and simply refer them to their proper authority".[37]

However, some of the accusations against the IRA were serious. For example, one type of complaint concerned intimidation of civilians by members of the IRA. Letters indicated that, in some areas, the Volunteers were throwing their weight around in the local communities. They commandeered cars and bicycles. They took over dances. They poached on private property. They appropriated houses. In general, these complaints emphasized the fact that some IRA men were exceeding their authority and taking advantage of their status.

One of the primary causes of this type of behavior was excessive drinking. During the war, there was very little indication that over-consumption of alcohol was a problem. Save for an occasional case, the evidence does not indicate that this was a problem. According to Ernie O'Malley, for example, during the war of independence "the familiar stage Irishman had disappeared. One met now a young man who did not drink, who had developed a sense of duty and of responsibility, and whose bearing showed it."[38]

However, with the cessation of hostilities discipline sagged. Now, thinking of themselves as victors of the war of independence, some became excessively self-indulgent. Complaints abounded—both from civilians and from officers who were having a difficult time controlling their men. For example, at a Sinn Féin convention, one priest complained to Mulcahy that in "nearly the whole of west Limerick there was universal drinking among Volunteers".[39] And, the chief of police complained to the chief of staff:

> While realising the reaction and natural tendency on the part of the men who have been fighting for the past few years to enjoy themselves during the truce, it is very plain that quite a number of men in the Army, and in some cases officers, are indulging in excesses which do not tend to maintain the good name of the Irish Army.[40]

Even Liam Lynch complained of the "demoralising and poisoning" of some of his forces by drink—in this case the illegal brewing of poteen— and asked that the government take some action.[41]

The complaints about excessive IRA drinking reached the ears of the cabinet. At a meeting on 21 October 1921, the cabinet instructed the minister for defence to issue a general order to the army on the matter.[42] Three days later, the minister wrote to the chief of staff instructing him to issue an order on excessive drinking:

> Some very serious complaints were made at the last meeting of the Ministry about excessive drinking by the Volunteers—both officers and men. The complaints are coming from districts so wide apart as Meath, Kerry, N. Roscommon, Tipperary, Wexford and Dublin. The President requests that you send out an order on this matter calling upon the O/C's in each district to use stern disciplinary methods to have this thing stamped out. It will be necessary, however, to have this order carefully worded so that the enemy will not be provided with material for their propaganda.[43]

GHQ responded very quickly to this directive and in early November, issued a general order which provided for reduction in rank and subsequent dismissal from the IRA for an officer found guilty of "continued indulgence in drink" and dismissal after a warning for ordinary Volunteers convicted on the same offence.[44]

The second most common and wide spread problem with which GHQ had to contend involved the collection of money from the local community to support the IRA. For the most part, the IRA was still self-supporting and the needs and expenses of individual brigades had to be met by appealing to the local population. It put the army in an awkward position. As Michael Brennan, O/C, 1st Western Division, noted:

> We are very much handicapped by lack of funds but I daresay we are no worse off than most other areas, as this I believe applies fairly generally all over Ireland. It seems rather a pity all the same that in view of the position in which the Army has put the country, Officers and men should not alone give their whole time free but that they should still have to provide the means of paying all their own expenses and the expenses of the Army. I quite realise all the difficulties, but I can't help feeling and knowing that while the army is so dependent on the goodwill of individuals we can never have proper efficiency.[45]

However, while the IRA was depended on the community for support, under the terms of the truce, it was forbidden to impose levies, that is, a mandatory assessment of money from people in their district. Instead, they had to depend on voluntary contributions. The difference between the two was subtle, not always clear either to those making the collection or those being asked for funds. Mulcahy instructed his officers to take great pains to explain the voluntary nature of the contribution and not allow it to appear that people were being forced to give money or threatened if they refused. He urged them to be sensitive to public opinion and avoid unnecessary irritation or annoyance.[46]

The problem continued throughout the Truce. By the end of September, apparently aggravated with the number of complaints he was receiving, Mulcahy instructed one of his commandants:

> Will you please take steps to have it hammered into the heads of all O/Cs that Truce time collections must be collections pure and simple and neither loans nor extortions.[47]

One of his officers in dealing with a subordinate was even more blunt: "Men can do far better work by gentle persuasion towards selling tickets than by terrorism. When an opportunity for terrorising Auxiliaries occurred during the hostilities those men did very little of it."[48]

However, to those who complained of the IRA's collections, Mulcahy politely pointed out their obligation:

> . . . and I have to say that it is no doubt, quite correct that a collection is being made in your area for the administration of the Volunteers. Commandant [Frank] Barrett, of Ennis, would have authority to organise such a collection. It is found necessary in the work of the Volunteers to rely on each particular district, not only to provide its quota of Volunteers for the Army, but to provide also such administration expenses as are necessary, to have properly carried out its organisation and training.[49]

While insisting that the IRA seek only voluntary contributions, he also insisted that the people in general realize their obligation to support the army. He had no sympathy for those people who wanted a republic, but wanted it free of charge.

Despite the best efforts of GHQ to keep the distinction between levies and collections clear to their officers, the problem continued. It became an issue at the negotiating table in London and sparked correspondence between Mulcahy and Collins on the matter.[50] In October, the chief of staff issued a special order which reiterated that all IRA collections must be voluntary and added, characteristically: "Our National reputation for honour and discipline is involved in this matter."[51]

The problem of collections was exacerbated by the fact that, for the most part, the men of the IRA were not paid by the government. As of July 1921, salaries were paid only to full time divisional officers to enable them to devote themselves totally to army work. Headquarters realized the importance of paying at least some of their officers and was very insistent on this point. For example, when one of the officers balked at accepting a salary, GHQ made it clear to him that it was more than simply accepting four pounds:

> As regards your not accepting a salary, you at least shall be paid direct from here. You are our Officer and represent GHQ in No.2 Division. I believe that GHQ must insist that all the Divisional Officers who devote their whole time to responsible Army work, accept an allowance as decided by GHQ. You will therefore forward a covering address.[52]

GHQ did its best to ease the financial plight of its men. A special fund was established from which struggling districts could borrow money.[53] In certain cases, grants were made to enable a division to continue functioning or to meet special needs as they arose. For example, Collins and Mulcahy proposed that a grant be made to the No. 1 Brigade, 1st Northern Division to prevent some of the best officers and men from migrating to Scotland for seasonal employment. In his appeal to GHQ, the O/C of the 1st Northern Division provided an insight into the socio-economic conditions in the area which affected both the IRA and the population in general:

> You are probably aware that up here the holdings are all uneconomic and every year the young men migrate to the mines and other works in Scotland while the older men and young boys and girls go to the potatoe [sic] digging in the same country. The end of the Summer and all the Autumn is for us a bad time of year as during that period the numbers of the organisation are very small and generally the best men are absent. . . . The Batt. and Coy. Officers are often absent for six months so that the Coys. have to be reorganised periodically. Could you suggest anything to hold on the existing officers?[54]

Collins responded to this particular situation by authorizing £2,500 to keep the "bulk of the necessary Officers and men at home".[55]

The problem with unemployment was indeed widespread. A number of IRA men found themselves without jobs after the war ended. Some found that their previous positions had been filled during their absence and they were now unable to support themselves and their families. Some lost their jobs because their employers looked unfavorably on the IRA or because as soldiers they had to take time off of work to attend meetings, parades or drills.[56] Mulcahy was concerned about the problem of unemployment and suggested that, at least in the Dublin area, contact be made through the brigade with the Labour Bureau in hopes of finding jobs for their unemployed men.[57]

Mulcahy had good reason to be concerned. Unemployment was cited as one of the chief reasons for disorderly conduct on the part of the IRA.[58] Having spent time in the service of their country, unemployed soldiers felt cheated by their inability to find a job, by their lack of money, and lack of prospects. As Sean Moylan of Cork, poignantly but pointedly stated:

> We took men away from their employments . . . and got them ready to fight. . . . Those men have been out of employment, without a smoke, ill-shod, badly clad and—we are not all Pusseyfooters— in want of a drink too. . . . I have always seized every opportunity I could get to try and get comforts for my men.[59]

It was not a healthy situation and certainly contributed to the tension which the Truce generated.

The question of collections in particular and complaints about the IRA in general during the Truce raised issues of class conflict and divergent nationalist perspectives. Some of the complaints levelled against the army were from British sympathizers who simply were striking out at the IRA. During the Truce, they wrote to various ministers, especially the minister for defence, but also to the chief of staff, to complain about their treatment at the hands of the IRA. On the other hand, some of the actions of the IRA were directed against people they believed to be anti-national or who supported the British in the war of independence.

In Clare, for example, the IRA boycotted a shopkeeper who freely associated with the Black and Tans. The family protested to the minister for defence. The O/C's response to Mulcahy about the complaint was enlightening—illustrating the degree of resentment and antagonism which existed in the community between those who supported the IRA and those who did not:

> I had an interview with the Keanes on the 20th inst.[November 1921], at which I informed them that if I had been in charge of West Clare before the Truce, at least the son would have been shot, but that as he had not been, the Government had decided that the

financial loss which had been inflicted on him met the case at the moment and that the boycott would now be raised. . . . I pointed out that if a few of the worst offenders like the Keane family had been executed, such a good example might have shown the others the error of their ways, and that when the war started again the slightest infringement of the International regulations covering association with the enemy would be punished by death.[60]

While sympathetic to the feelings of frustration of their officers, Mulcahy and the government tried to keep the situation under tight control. The government pointedly reminded the army that "no matter what their [citizens'] private politics may be, or their hostile associations, as citizens of this State they are entitled to share in all protections and benefits until such time as they are put outside the Pale as declared public enemies."[61]

In Cork, on the other hand, a boycott was the result of the merging of issues of class and nationalist outlook:

The state of things when I took charge was that the Volunteer movement was ridiculed by farmers' sons in this area. The movement was good enough for the labouring class but beneath them. The tax was imposed by the local Captain according to means. This was ignored. They would not pay neither would they fight. A remark of one of them was that he would not be made a cock-shot of. The only means we had of getting the tax was to make a black list and give this list to owners of threshing machines with instructions not to thresh for anybody on the list. The majority paid up but a few refused and I think those have not threshed yet. Mr. Thomas Linehan (the ex-J.P., ex-Land Commissioner, ex-etc.) the protector of the cowardly farmer's sons of Whitechurch has four fine sons. He gave three of these to help the empire but can't afford a few pounds to the Republic . . .[62]

Issues of class and nationalist outlook also surfaced in the various labour disputes that the IRA were involved in during the Truce. In general, labour leaders accused the IRA of being anti-union, of thwarting the just claims of the working class. For example, the Irish Transport and General Workers Union charged:

In most cases it is a matter of farmers' sons taking unjustified action to obstruct the claims of labourers to better treatment; in practically all it is a matter of employers making use of the IRA to protect their petty interests against their employees, under the pretence of safeguarding National interests.[63]

Some in the IRA disagreed with this assessment. Liam Lynch, whose 1st Southern division was involved in a number of disputes, took issue with the union's analysis:

> in my opinion there is no grounds for insinuation that employers and farmer's sons are using the Army for their petty interests. There are instances, especially in Waterford where the I.T.W. Union Organisers are antagonistic to Ireland's National demands. . . . We cannot allow any civil organisation [to] interfere with the Army, especially at a time when the Enemy is making desperate efforts to crush us. My experience is that certain organisers try to put Labour above Freedom. . . .[64]

While both sides oversimplified the issue, what did emerge was that the government and GHQ had no qualms about using its resources, including the IRA, to protect persons and property. This held true even when IRA members were involved in the strike. For example, when labour leaders organized an unemployment demonstration, the minister for home affairs authorized the chief of police to "take necessary steps to protect persons and property threatened and to maintain order".[65] The minister for defence added his support. He wrote to the chief of staff requesting that he order the O/C, Dublin Brigade, to give the chief of police any help he may need in maintaining order.[66] There is no recorded objection by the chief of staff. The government's revolutionary zeal did not extend to disturbing the social order. They would countenance only a respectable political revolution. Mulcahy had no difficulty with that position.

This lack of social radicalism was also evidenced in the political and military leaders' attitude toward land redistribution. In the beginning of the struggle, some officers used the eagerness for men to obtain land to involve them in the national struggle. Michael Brennan recalled that although he himself

> hadn't the slightest interest in the land agitation . . . I had every interest in using it as a means to an end, the end being, to get these fellows into the Volunteers, and once they were in you could do something with them. Up to that they were just an unorganised mob . . .[67]

During the Truce, the land issue was again raised, but the government would countenance no widespread confiscation of land. Mulcahy again agreed with this decision and was generally in harmony with the socially conservative nature of the government.

One issue which the authorities had to contend with concerned the land belonging to executed spies or those who were accused of being spies and left the country. These lands were confiscated in the name of the Republic by the Volunteers and were worked by local members of the IRA. With the truce, the question of disposal of these lands became more pressing. Mulcahy was reluctant to delve into the question, preferring not to disturb the existing arrangements. He understood the volatile nature of the land question and did not want to cause any more friction within the army.

However, the issue could not be completely avoided and Mulcahy's recommendations on the redistribution of land were consistent with his social conservatism and his general values and outlook. His primary concern seemed to be that the army authorities not become involved. Land questions, he argued, were the responsibility of the department of home affairs. In particular, he did not want it said that the army was sanctioning land grabbing or rewarding its soldiers with gifts of land. He also recommended that in cases where the legitimate owners of the land wanted to sell their property, they should be allowed to do so in an unrestricted manner and:

> Where such a sale takes place any furniture or other effects, seized and held by Volunteers and any proceeds of sales in hands of Volunteers should be returned in total to the owner.[68]

Thus, the sacrosanct rights of private property would not be violated, the property owners would have no grievance against the republic, and the IRA could not be seen as profiting in any way from accusing people of spying.

The last reason was, of course, important in assuring that there was no incentive to unjustly accuse and convict someone of spying just to lay claim to their land. It was consistent with Mulcahy's view that parameters must be placed on the struggle. However, the decision not to reward soldiers who fought for independence with land and not to inflict any financial loss on those involved in spying was much less tenable. It seems to have been a product of Mulcahy's middle class mores and his desire that the new state be regarded as respectable.

Questions of land and labour relations not only raised issues of class and nationalist perspective, but, along with other issues, they brought the IRA into areas which were, strictly speaking, within the purview of the republican police. Because the republican police force was not fully functioning in some areas and because, at times, the IRA either overstepped its authority or was guilty of civil offenses, conflict between the two bodies continued. It was not a situation which could be resolved by a general directive or a hard and fast rule. Sometimes the IRA was needed; sometimes, not. Sometimes its members were guilty of offenses; sometimes, not. The result was that the chief of staff had lengthy communications with the chief of police and minister for home affairs about relations between the two groups.[69]

In fact, relations between the civilian and army administration had become a constant source of tension. Volunteers who committed crimes sometimes refused to recognize the right of civil courts to try them. This was in direct contradiction to GHQ's order that Volunteers who committed crimes while not acting as members of the army were to be tried by civil courts.[70] This problem inevitably generated much correspondence and, to an extent, a degree of ill-will.

Tension also resulted from those instances where the IRA tried to interfere with local boards to secure the appointment of someone they favored. This happened, for example, in the case of a teacher at Milltown Infants

School and the complaint to GHQ was calculated to upset Mulcahy no end:

> Rumour has it that the act was unauthorised, but it has done much towards unbalancing people's confidence. It is taken as an indication of the trend of affairs under new management.[71]

Quite simply, the IRA had intimidated the civilian authorities. To Mulcahy, this meant that the image of the army had been tarnished and the government's desire to appear fair and impartial undermined.

In a similar instance, the IRA of Limerick used its power to have a medical doctor who was a member of the army appointed to the county hospital. They gave two reasons for their actions. The first was that they "adopted the practice general in all counties of exercising their influence on behalf of the candidate who served in the war as against the candidate who did not".[72] Second, the Mid-Limerick Brigade believed that if fighting were resumed, it would be important to have a sympathetic doctor in that position.

While understanding the feelings of his men, Mulcahy did not believe that their action was justified. Not only was it an explicit violation of orders which prohibited interference in matters of civil administration, it was also calculated to stir up feelings of ill-will against the army:

> We can afford to miss placing a Volunteer in any key position here and there in public life, but we cannot afford that public representatives would feel that the Army were interfering in this way with their special function. . . . The greatest possible care must be taken, therefore, that in none of their actions shall Volunteers lay themselves open to any such charge.[73]

There were, however, cases which made it difficult for the IRA to remain aloof. For example, in Youghal, County Cork, the civilian authorities appointed as town clerk a man who was a deserter from the IRA during the war of independence. Mulcahy wrote to the minister for defence protesting this appointment. He pointed out that not only was a deserter not proper material for such an appointment, but that it would also undermine the confidence of the army in the civil administration.[74]

It also, of course, increased the likelihood that the IRA would feel justified in involving themselves in these matters. Despite the claim of the men of mid-Limerick that it was general practice for the IRA to use its influence in civil appointments, it is not clear just how widespread was this type of intervention. What did seem to be a problem was that some members of the IRA were increasingly of the opinion that those with sound republican principles were involved with the army, while those who filled the civil positions were, in the words of Liam Lynch, "the shoneens".[75] Appointments such as the Youghal town clerk bred the feeling that somehow the IRA's work, all that it had achieved by fighting, was being undone. This sentiment gained strength during the drift into civil war and would also surface again during the mutiny of 1924.

Relations with the civilian population were further strained, albeit in an entirely different manner, by complaints from Sinn Féin. Their complaint was not that the IRA was interfering, but rather that it was not responsive enough or interested enough in the political work of the organization. At times, it did seem that the IRA was caught in a "no win" situation.

Mulcahy's attitude towards charges against the IRA was exemplified in his handling of a complaint from Sinn Féin officials. In this instance, the accusation was that the IRA was not helping its political wing. The details of the complaint were passed along to the division in question for inquiry and explanation. The divisional O/C replied that the IRA was not making the work of Sinn Féin more difficult, but that they were indeed holding themselves aloof from the organisation. This, he explained, was because "the majority of the leading lights of Sinn Féin in the division instead of having ever in any way assisted the Volunteers, have treated them with contempt and in the majority of cases are either secretly hostile or openly indifferent."[76]

Mulcahy's response was twofold. In the first place, he took the charge seriously enough to discuss it with his officers in a weekly memorandum. The memo reiterated the complaints which had been received in a general fashion. Mulcahy then explained that, while war conditions still prevailed, the work of the army had to be given over-riding consideration, but that it was important for the members of the IRA to remember that:

> the ultimate object of the Army work is the building up of Social and Civil life of our country as an independent country; that the Sinn Féin clubs are the medium through which proper Republican representatives in the Civil sphere are selected and secured; and that unless this very important work is efficiently and vigorously done our work can only be regarded as being half done, and the efforts of the Army shall be stultified.[77]

Having thus taken his soldiers gently to task, Mulcahy, on the other hand, protested to the minister for defence about "the system of simply 'passing on' complaints of this kind", claiming that it led nowhere and should really be investigated at the local level by those involved. He went on to defend his officers and men, claiming that they:

> understand at least as well as and perhaps, better than most non-Volunteer workers, the necessity for an efficient Civil Administration, and it cannot but be irritating to them to know that complaints are being frequently made against them here, which are, perhaps, unfounded; or which, even if there was any foundation for, can best be settled by having the complaint definitely formulated and examined locally.[78]

It would be interesting to know the response of some of his more disgruntled officers to Mulcahy's defence of them. Some would indeed have been surprised.

Not only was Mulcahy irritated at the indiscriminate manner in which accusations reached his desk, he also believed that the British were involved in trying to create complaints about the IRA. The IRA had intercepted a wireless message which suggested that the British were "not content with simply receiving complaints with regard to Truce-breaking . . . [but were] going around actively looking for such and endeavouring to create complaints."[79]

Mulcahy also had to contend with charges from the British of alleged truce violations and problems with the liaison officers. Each side accused the other. The British charged the IRA with flagrantly breaking the truce by drilling, training, carrying arms, levying rates, holding Sinn Féin courts, commandeering houses, vehicles, and lodgings, importing arms and boycotting those friendly to the British.[80] The Irish countered with their own accusations: wanton brutality to the people, systematic interference with those driving motor cars, especially members of the IRA, interference with meetings, fairs, and creameries, removal of republican flags, provocative conduct, carrying arms and mistreatment of prisoners in jails and internment camps.[81] At times, the antagonism between the two sides flared into open violence. In Galway, for example, a British soldier was killed and a member of the RIC wounded in an exchange of gunfire at a dance in the town hall.[82] By October, Mulcahy was writing to his chief liaison officer that the truce was in danger:

> The Enemy Liaison Officer should be given to understand that a persistent petty aggression by individual members of the RIC cannot be allowed to grow in the manner in which, apparently, it is growing, without involving a danger of very serious breaking of the Truce.[83]

And, in November, Collins complained from London that it seemed "there is more and more laxity creeping in the observance of the Truce on the part of our people—could anything be done to tighten up matters?" He also stressed the importance of reporting British truce violations to the delegation. Collins noted that "when we met them this evening we had practically nothing to put against them, whereas they had several important cases against us."[84]

Mulcahy's problems just seemed to multiply. Not only was he having difficulty with harassment from the British, he was having trouble with his own liaison officers. There were problems with the liaison officers from the beginning of the truce. At first, there were serious disagreements between the Irish officers and the British military authorities. The British military refused to recognize the liaison officers of the martial law districts as representatives of the IRA. They insisted instead in referring to Commandant

Barry, chief liaison officer of the martial law area, as Mr Barry, Mr de Valera's representative in Cork.[85] Mulcahy protested that they were army officers and were to be treated as such.[86]

The situation, however, continued to deteriorate. It was particularly bad in Cork. There were conflicts over the treatment of prisoners, especially at Berehaven and Spike Island. Charges were made. Protests were filed. Inquiries were promised. After three months, it appears that Barry and his fellow liaison officers lost faith in the ability of the Irish chief liaison officer to fairly represent their position. In October, Barry and his colleagues resigned their positions.[87] The liaison situation had important repercussions. Mulcahy believed that it led Cork to turn against GHQ and against the Treaty:

> A lot of it was due to the Barry spirit and a lot of it was due to the snobbish insolent intransigent spirit of the Cork British commander during the truce that made things very difficult there and a lot of it was due to the kind of spirit that developed in the internment camps in Spike Island and Berehaven, etc., where things were quite unsatisfactory; the British spirit rubbed the prisoners the wrong way and they were so long in there they felt that people in Dublin were having a gay time during the truce—and they were in Berehaven for August, September, October, November and December while the discussions were going on and all kinds of irritations arose there.[88]

Barry's resignation—which he subsequently rescinded—sparked an interesting and revealing exchange. Not only did Barry resign as liaison officer in his area, he also resigned as deputy commandant and training officer of the 1st Southern Division. Lynch, his divisional O/C, apparently only learned of his resignation after notice had been sent both to GHQ and brigades in the area. It was a most irregular procedure. Barry claimed that Lynch was not satisfied with his work and that neither of them wanted to work with the other. Lynch, for his part, disputed Barry's statements, arguing that he was satisfied with Barry's work and had gone to great pains to show his appreciation. Mulcahy retained full confidence in Lynch. In his view, Barry was the problem, especially for what Mulcahy considered his "vanity" and "petulant and childish" nature.[89]

Barry's resignation demonstrated the growing friction which was developing among various officers of the IRA. There were clear difficulties in Cork. There were also difficulties for GHQ in Limerick, in Clare, in Kerry and in South Roscommon.[90] These personality clashes would have direct repercussions in the civil war. For example, Paddy Cahill and his followers who had a long dispute with GHQ went against the Treaty. Part of the reason was probably the hostility they felt over the dismissal of Cahill. And, although ultimately Lynch and Barry would fight against the government, there was obvious antagonism between the two men in the beginning and Lynch was originally not part of the executive which took over the anti-Treaty forces. Part of this was an outgrowth of the atmosphere of the Truce period. Lynch aptly summarized the effect of the truce on the IRA when he said:

> The sooner *all* our Officers realise they are nothing more than the ordinary fighting man, the better for the Army as a whole, especially during Truce period. . . . Since Truce, it is about four times harder to run the Division owing to different complications . . .[91]

The effect of the Truce on the IRA raises an important question. Were the accusations and complaints levelled against the IRA indicative of a wide spread disorder and a growing lack of discipline among members of the army? Historians have traditionally interpreted the tru.ce period as a time when the IRA developed the tendency "to domineer over civilians and despise politicians".[92] The ultimate expression of this would be the refusal of a section of the army to honor the Dáil's acceptance of the Treaty. Some blamed it on the trucileers who could be brave against unarmed civilians if not against the Black and Tans.[93] To a degree, this interpretation is valid. Clearly, there were problems with the IRA. Some members took advantage of the Truce to do whatever they liked to whomever they pleased. The numerous complaints testify to the difficulties which plagued the army.

However, this traditional explanation must be qualified. In the first place, the numerous complaints must be scrutinized more closely. As noted, not all were legitimate or serious accusations. The small section of the civilian population who indiscriminately hurled charges against the IRA must be blamed for contributing to the sense of alienation which some in the army felt. If there was a certain frustration in dealing with civilians, this may have been caused by the tendency among a part of the population to object to any interference or disruption in their lives. While there is absolutely no excuse for the army to domineer over or intimidate the people, the civilian population had to share in the responsibilities of establishing the government that they themselves had elected.

Second, the Truce was an important factor in leading to the civil war, not because of the attitude which the IRA developed toward civilians, but because of the friction which grew among some of the officers and their men. What has been overlooked is the effect of the complaints on the IRA. Officers and men had to answer charges that almost anyone cared to bring against them. Mulcahy cannot truly be faulted for examining these complaints, but it did diminish support for himself and GHQ. Moreover, the seeming willingness of ministers and Dáil deputies to demand explanations from the army authorities must have appeared as if the politicians were siding with those who complained before they even evaluated the evidence, presuming the IRA guilty until proven innocent. This could only diminish respect for political leaders among the IRA.

Lastly, even if the behavior of the IRA lacked discipline or respect for civilians, it does not necessarily follow that this led the army into civil war. A number of the officers who rejected the Dáil's decision were those—like Liam Lynch—who insisted on the highest standards of discipline and conduct. Moreover, the bulk of the divisions who went against the Treaty came from the areas of Ireland which had fought the hardest in the Tan war. It is hard to imagine that these officers and men were influenced by "sunshine soldiers". It was something much more than braggadocio or lack of discipline which led to the Four Courts and the outbreak of the civil war.

The truce had additional consequences. It was devastating to the relations between Mulcahy and Brugha. Twice during the Truce period, the minister for defence fired his chief of staff. In neither case was it more than a passing dismissal. Mulcahy's dismissals, however, reflected the now obvious split within the cabinet. Stack and Brugha were openly antagonistic to Collins. And, as had been true right along, Mulcahy was solidly in the Collins camp.

During the Truce, Brugha took an increasingly active role in the army. He resented the fact that Collins and Mulcahy were the two men associated in the public mind with the IRA. This was especially true in the publicity which Collins received during the truce. Brugha may have decided that it was time to break their hold on the army. Hence he became more possessive of his role as minister for defence and more determined to assert himself in army affairs. Moreover, the number of complaints which poured into his office, and the type of policy issues which had to be decided upon, gave Brugha more opportunity to become involved. Certainly, the voluminous correspondence of the Truce period testified to the fact that Brugha was now active in army affairs.

Mulcahy believed that Brugha used the opportunity afforded him by the truce to increase his standing among the members of the IRA:

> Cathal took advantage of the freedom of the Truce to be in public and to meet people and . . . to take a greater control in Defence affairs. He was able to listen to their complaints about arms and things like that, and he began to take an active and an interfering part in dealing with arms questions, and indeed with Defence matters generally.[94]

Mulcahy's observation was substantiated by Michael Brennan's experience. He remembered that he and Brugha

> had long talks on the organisation and arming of the 1st Western Division. He was annoyed when he learned that the Mid Clare Brigade was still not formally included in the Division under my orders, as he said he had given a direction (as Minister for Defence) for its inclusion some time previously. He noted my anxiety about arms and ammunition and he asked if I had any hopes of being

able to get some myself. I thought I could if I had money, but our small funds were now almost finished. He said he might be able to help and I promised to call and see him before I left town. . . . I saw Cathal Brugha and he gave me a cheque for a thousand pounds to help in getting arms.[95]

One inference that can be drawn from Mulcahy's observation and Brennan's experience is that Brugha was using his position as minister for defence during the truce to bolster his status among the officers in particular and in the army in general. A sympathetic minister to listen to the grievances of the officers would be a popular role. Or a bountiful minister who could produce money for arms and ammunition would win the gratitude of men who expected the war to resume at any moment. Perhaps this judgment is too harsh and Brugha was not consciously trying to curry favor or win popularity in the army. At the very least, it is curious that the minister for defence could produce £1,000 for the 1st Western and that this was not done through the authorized channels of GHQ.

Moreover, Brugha seemed even more determined to undermine Collins' role in the army and degrade his accomplishments. These attacks naturally spilled over and affected the relationship of Brugha with Mulcahy and the general workings of GHQ. Minor problems and difficulties escalated into threats and dismissals. For example, a man named Robbie of the Yost typewriter company was forced to leave the country by the Volunteers on insufficient and inaccurate information. As director of information, Collins' office was involved in the mistake. During the Truce, Brugha and Mulcahy agreed that Robbie should be allowed back into the country and be free to resume work. The information was conveyed to Collins and his staff.

When this information was not acted upon immediately, Brugha issued a spirited denunciation of Collins' department:

> The handling of this case from start to finish—even to yesterday's letter signed I/O GHQ displays an amateurishness that I thought we had long ago outgrown. On the chief of staff's return, I intend to see about putting our Department of Information on such a footing that things of this kind cannot occur in future.[96]

Mulcahy's reply to Brugha was, in a word, insolent. It was the culmination of a long, drawn out controversy, and Mulcahy obviously lost his temper with his minister. Mulcahy informed Brugha that he considered:

> . . . the tone of your letter of 30th July is very unfortunate and must have a very destructive influence on the harmony and discipline of the Staff, and unless something can be done to eliminate the tendency to revert to this tone when differences arise, I cannot be responsible for retaining harmony and discipline among the Staff.[97]

Brugha quite properly replied with a threat to suspend or fire Mulcahy if he ever wrote to him in that vein again. Furthermore, he added:

What good purpose was served by your writing thus 5 weeks after the event is probably best known to yourself. To me it seems a further development of that presumption on your part that prompted you to ignore for some months past the duly appointed deputy chief of staff [Stack]. However, before you are very much older, my friend, I shall show you that I have as little intention of taking dictation from you as to how I should reprove inefficiency or negligence on the part of yourself or the D/I, as I have of allowing you to appoint a deputy chief of staff of your own choosing.

In regard to your inability to maintain harmony and discipline among the Staff, it was scarcely necessary to remind me of the fact, as your shortcomings in that respect—so far at least as controlling the particular member already mentioned [Collins] is concerned—have been quite apparent for a considerable time.[98]

Brugha, however, was not content to let the matter rest with a verbal reprimand. In the following week, he demanded that Mulcahy provide him with the particulars on how the Yost typewriting case had developed within twenty-four hours or else threatened him with suspension.[99] It was an unreasonable demand. Mulcahy obviously failed to reply in time because the next day, Brugha informed him that "until further notice your services will not be required by this Department". Mulcahy was instructed to "hand over to the Deputy Chief of Staff all monies, papers, books, and any other property of the Department in your possession".[100]

Despite the fact that his earlier letter was written in a tone wholly inappropriate for an officer to use with the minister for defence, Mulcahy appealed to President de Valera to intervene in this matter and to curb his minister for defence. He wrote:

The continuance of the present relationship between the Minister for Defence and myself must, I fear, lead to the destruction in a very short time of the vigour and discipline of the Staff, and I feel it my duty to ask that the position be estimated and adjusted without delay. The matter is one of very great urgency in view of the critical nature of the present time. I cannot usefully discuss any matter with the Minister for Defence, and . . . I cannot accede to his request to preside at or be present at any meeting of the Staff.[101]

Mulcahy later explained his position. The minister of defence was

welcome to summon and meet and interview and talk to the staff whenever he wanted, but from my point of view, meetings of the staff were for the purpose of doing work and I did not want the actual doing of work to be invaded by some of the considerations that Cathal might insist on introducing into staff discussions and work.[102]

De Valera could not resolve the dispute, but probably intervened so that Mulcahy was not forced to resign.

This incident, in September 1921, was followed by a similar one in October. This time Brugha and Mulcahy were bickering over staff appointments. Brugha claimed ignorance of certain appointments which had been made over a year ago and protested against the appointment of J.J. O'Connell as assistant chief of staff. The minister for defence believed that this position was the same as deputy chief of staff and was already held by Austin Stack. He demanded an explanation from Mulcahy as to why Stack had not been summoned to staff meetings and ordered his chief of staff to make sure that he was included in all future meetings.[103] Mulcahy again protested to de Valera about Brugha's attitude:

> I send you herewith a copy of correspondence now arising between myself and the Minister for Defence. It arises purely in a nagging spirit. It must be clear to you that its tendency must be devitalising and degrading. I again protest to you against this attitude of the Minister for Defence.[104]

A meeting among the three failed to ameliorate the basis of the controversy and it continued to simmer throughout the Truce period.[105]

Stack's appointment became a *cause célèbre* for Brugha. It was a continuing source of friction between him and Mulcahy and a symbol to each of them. To Brugha, it was a constant reminder of how his authority been flouted by his chief of staff. To Mulcahy, it was an example of malicious interference in military affairs.

In Brugha's eyes, the matter was simple. Stack had been appointed deputy chief of staff in the early days of the Volunteers. Despite the fact that he had never functioned as such, Brugha still believed he was the legitimate heir to the chief of staff. To Mulcahy, on the other hand, Stack's appointment had been simply a casual suggestion which he himself made. Stack was arrested soon afterwards and never actually held a position on GHQ staff. Mulcahy believed it would destroy the harmony and efficiency of GHQ to introduce a foreign and contentious element at this point. Stack's hostility to Collins was well known and, as minister for home affairs, he had some difficult dealings with members of GHQ.

The controversy over Stack was intimately tied up in the formation of what has been called the "new army". According to this plan, the IRA was to be reconstituted as the official army of the State under the control of the civilian authorities. This would clarify the ambiguous relationship between the two bodies and eradicate the theoretically autonomous position which the Volunteers/IRA had enjoyed since their inception. The minister for defence gave the IRA the following explanation:

> In view of the possibility of further fighting and in order to put the Army in an unequivocal position as the legal defence force of the Nation under the control of the Civil Government, the Cabinet has decided to issue fresh commissions to Officers, and to offer re-enlistment to all ranks.[106]

Although it was discussed at a cabinet meeting on 15 September 1921, new commissions were not issued until November. The new army was planned to come into existence on 25 November, the eighth anniversary of the founding of the Volunteers in 1913.

The idea for creating the new army did not emanate from GHQ but rather from the civilian government, most notably Brugha and de Valera. Possibly they believed that reconstituting the army would strengthen their position within the IRA. If that were so, the initial response of the officers had to be disappointing to them. Most officers were surprised when they received the notice from the minister for defence. Dan Hogan of the 5th Northern Division had a typical reaction. On being offered his commission, he wrote to the minister for defence that:

> as your communication is the only intimation I have had of the formation of a New Army, I consider it necessary for me to communicate with the chief of staff on the matter. Subject to the approval of GHQ, I am prepared to accept any position which I am considered capable to fill.[107]

This type of response was a testimony to the respect and loyalty which Mulcahy and his staff enjoyed.

To alleviate the confusion which Brugha's letter caused, GHQ sent a note to all their officers verifying the validity and authenticity of the new commissions and indicating that it could be signed. Confusion should not have been unexpected because as Frank Aiken, O/C, 4th Northern Division, pointed out the "circular was the first we ever received from the Minister for Defence".[108]

Mulcahy was offered a new commission as chief of staff. Before he accepted, he raised two questions. The first concerned the power and authority of the position of the chief of staff. In particular, he wanted to know if he would have the power to select his own staff. Mulcahy recommended to the minister for defence those officers whom he would like to have on staff. Basically, he proposed to keep the same people at GHQ as were there previously.[109] The sticking point was that Mulcahy had appointed Eoin O'Duffy as deputy chief of staff and Brugha was, not unexpectedly, insisting on Austin Stack.

On 16 November, Mulcahy wrote to the minister for defence inquiring if the position of chief of staff was invested with "such powers in the matter of the selection and placing of the members of the General Staff that an appointment to a position on the General Staff should not be made against his judgment and without his concurrence," and, furthermore, asked Brugha if he accepted his recommendations for staffing at GHQ.[110]

Brugha replied that the position of chief of staff had more limited authority vested in it. According to the Minister, the chief of staff's advice would be sought and considered, "but both himself and the whole

General Staff will be appointed by the Cabinet on the recommendations of the minister for defence." Brugha went on to say that he accepted all of Mulcahy's appointments except for two. He would recommend Stack for deputy chief of staff and O'Duffy for director of organisation.

Mulcahy's response to Brugha was as predictable as Brugha's answer. Mulcahy informed the minister that his acceptance of the position of chief of staff was contingent on the cabinet's accepting all of his recommendations. He reiterated the position he had taken earlier, that is, that "if the Ministry decide to make an appointment to such an important Staff position against my judgment, I cannot accept the responsibility attaching to any position on the Staff."[111] Once again, Brugha and Mulcahy were at a stalemate position.

Mulcahy had a great deal of support for his position. Liam Lynch, for example, took Mulcahy's view of the situation and declined to accept his commission under the present circumstances. He wrote to the minister for defence:

> I feel that the Commander-in-Chief and his Staff cannot do their duty when they are not placed in a position to do so. I may have the wrong views of the duties of a Commander-in-Chief and Minister for Defence, if so I will put up with the result. I painfully realise the consequences of the present relations between Cabinet and GHQ Staff, therefore I cannot act blindly in the matter and be responsible for waging war in the most active area of Ireland. I hold GHQ Staff responsible for directing general operation policy, at the present moment when war may be resumed at short notice . . . .[112]

Lynch's attitude, as well as the response of a number of other officers, demonstrated not only a basic loyalty to GHQ but also a reluctance to tamper with a formula that worked. In light of the subsequent civil war, it would be easy, but misleading, to see the officer's response to the new army as indicative of hostility to civilian direction. In the circumstances of the times, it would be more accurate to see it as an indication that the IRA believed that war would eventually be resumed and they did not want to fight under a divided or untried staff. Moreover, they were concerned—as Lynch pointed out—that the interference by the cabinet was having a deleterious effect on the workings of GHQ. It appeared as if the minister for defence was determined to insist that someone with no experience, Stack, be designated as the deputy chief of staff while trying to oust Collins who not only had a great deal of experience but also inspired trust and confidence in the officers. Brugha seemed insistent on having his own way at the expense of the efficiency and efficacy of the army. Under such circumstances, it was no wonder that there was opposition and threatened resignations.

The second issue which Mulcahy raised with Brugha concerned the status of officers at GHQ. Until the formation of the new army, officers at GHQ had ranked higher than divisional commandants. The new scheme of organization proposed to change that and directors on the general staff would have ranks subordinate to divisional commandants. Mulcahy and some of his officers both at GHQ and in the divisions thought this proposal raised serious difficulties.

In order to clarify the situation, Mulcahy asked that the Cabinet arrange to meet with the GHQ staff of the old army and explain the proposals to them. He also noted that at this meeting the Cabinet could acknowledge the work which GHQ had done in the past few years.[113] It was indicative of the state of affairs that Mulcahy had to remind the cabinet that his staff deserved a vote of thanks, a statement of gratitude.

The meeting which Mulcahy requested was duly held on 25 November 1921. According to Mulcahy's accounts, it was a stormy encounter. Prior to meeting the entire GHQ staff, Mulcahy met with cabinet. The chief of staff voiced the objections he had previously made to Brugha. He objected to Stack both on practical grounds and because of the implications that this type of decision would have. His position was that the chief of staff should have the officers of his choosing. De Valera tried for a compromise. He suggested that O'Duffy, Mulcahy's choice, could be deputy chief of staff and act for Mulcahy, while Stack could be "Cathal's ghost on the Staff".[114]

After the discussion had continued for a while, the rest of the staff were called into the room. Mulcahy remembered that:

> They [the staff] sat around the walls of the drawing room in the Mansion House where de Valera sat at a small table near one end of the centre with his Ministers sitting around him. He explained he wanted to reform the Staff, and having spoken shortly about it he asked their opinion. One after another, starting from the left the members of the Staff gave their opinion against the contemplated changes. The general tone was expressed by Ginger O'Connell who said that "the General Headquarters Staff had been a band of brothers." And the objection went all round the room until it reached O'Duffy who was the second last on the right. O'Duffy stood up and his voice became a little bit shrill as he characterised this as being an insult and a criticism to himself. A slight touch of hysteria in O'Duffy's approach to the subject reacted on De Valera in the chair, and after a very short time Dev rose excitedly in his chair, pushed the small table in front of him and declared in a half-scream, half-shout "ye may mutiny if ye like, but Ireland will give me another Army," and he dismissed the whole lot of us from his sight.
>
> I came down the steps of the Mansion House with Sean Russell. Sean—always very highly strung—was very white and, in a rather tense kind of whisper, he said "I didn't think that there was a man in Ireland that would speak like that to my Chief." That is, he didn't think that Dev would speak to me like that.[115]

The question of reforming the IRA into the new army brought to the fore the dissension between some members of the cabinet and the army about civilian-military relations. One historian has argued that "de Valera's plans for a 'new' or re-commissioned army emphasised the supremacy of the cabinet and government over the army, at the head of which stood the minister for defence as the cabinet's own representative."[116] Another historian has chastised Mulcahy for his refusal to work with the "official Deputy Chief of Staff appointed by Brugha".[117] In both these interpretations, Mulcahy and the GHQ staff are pictured as thwarting the legitimate claim of the civilian government to control the army.

On a theoretical level, these interpretations are correct. Certainly the ambiguity surrounding the relationship of the army to the government needed to be clarified. Left unresolved in 1921, it would not be decided finally until 1924. Moreover, because of the nature of the guerrilla war which the IRA fought, and because neither de Valera—due to absence in America—nor Brugha took an active role in the early stages of the army's development, the chief of staff and GHQ remained fairly free of outside control. And, of course, Collins' presence in the army gave it ministerial sanction of some kind.

However, the "new army" episode must also be interpreted within the particular context in which it developed. Brugha's desire to oust Collins from the army was unconscionable. Moreover, Brugha can be faulted for insisting on Stack's appointment—a man who had no previous association with the army, who had not demonstrated impressive administrative skills as minister for home affairs, and who was openly antagonistic to some of the staff members. It was not a wise choice and said a great deal about Brugha's personal animosity and his judgment as minister for defence. Moreover, although de Valera's attempt at compromise was perhaps well-intentioned, in this instance, he did not provide strong leadership. He was aware of the hostility in his cabinet and to allow such a divisive appointment would have seriously weakened the effectiveness of the army. If war resumed, the IRA would be handicapped by a divided and antagonistic central staff. If, as has been argued, de Valera wanted "his people" intimately associated with the army, he was willing to pay a very high price for it.[118]

Moreover, the question of the "new army" taken in conjunction with all the events of the Truce period provides evidence of a clear anti-IRA feeling among civilian politicians. It was more than just a desire to regularize government relations with the army. It was more than just dissatisfaction with the IRA overstepping its boundaries at times. Rather de Valera and some of his civilian colleagues seemed threatened by the popularity and prestige which not only Collins but Mulcahy, GHQ and the IRA in general enjoyed. Personal issues of power and control seemed to color their actions and influence their decisions.

Mulcahy, on the other hand, was wrong in demanding complete control over staff appointments. Ultimate power had to be vested in the minister for defence. However, Mulcahy was on firmer ground in resisting the appointment of Stack. His arguments on that issue were sound and his decision not to accept re-appointment if Stack were appointed instead of O'Duffy was a legitimate response. He could not effectively lead a divided staff nor one infected by partisan politics.

The entire question, however, became somewhat muted as the attention of both the political and the military leaders focused on the Treaty which the plenipotentiaries signed on 6 December. It is, however, interesting to note that those who seemingly were invoking the idea of civilian control of the military would rebel against the wishes of the Dáil, while many of those who were protesting against the "new army" would uphold the right of the Dáil to decide issues of war and peace.

The Treaty immediately became the centre of attention of the cabinet, the Dáil, the army and the people. It was far from a perfect document. It offered the substance of freedom—dominion status within the British commonwealth of nations. In practical terms, it meant the evacuation of the British army and control over domestic affairs such as finance and education. But the Treaty included an oath of allegiance to the king of England. It legitimized partition, cutting off the six counties of the North from the rest of Ireland. Most significantly for those involved in the debate, it did not fulfil what some saw as the basic demand of the Irish revolution—an independent republic.

Mulcahy was accompanying de Valera and Brugha on a tour of the army when news reached them the Treaty had been signed. The chief of staff took the telephone call from the adjutant-general, Gearoid O'Sullivan, and informed the President that an agreement had been reached. According to Mulcahy, de Valera "took the message quite unmoved or even quite unsurprised, and said 'no' to my query as to whether he would like to speak to Gearoid on the 'phone". But Mulcahy also recalled that there was "no uplift in the air" as they journeyed back to Dublin.[119]

The terms of the Treaty were published in the press on 7 of December. De Valera publicly rejected them before the plenipotentiaries had a chance to explain their position or, perhaps more accurately, defend themselves. Mulcahy later described de Valera's public repudiation as "an infamous performance . . . tantamount to his meeting Griffith as the boat at Dun Laoghaire and slapping him publicly across the face."[120]

It was worse than that. Some even wanted the plenipotentiaries arrested as traitors. And, despite de Valera's assurances that "the army as such is of course not affected by the political situation,"[121] there were, in fact, ominous rumblings from some sections of the army. They had declared for a republic and would accept nothing less. The situation was fraught with difficulties. Would there be a "terrible and immediate war" which Lloyd

George had threatened if the agreement was not signed? Or would there be a war more tragic, more vicious and more destructive than any struggle against the British, a civil war? And, what would be the attitude of the chief of staff?

Theoretically, however, it was not the army's decision to accept or reject the Treaty. The Dáil would decide. Attention now shifted away from training camps, truce violations, and munitions supplies to the Treaty debate in the Dáil.

FIVE

The Elusive Quest
for Army Unity

"I see no solid spot of ground upon which the Irish people can put its political feet but upon that Treaty."

Richard Mulcahy, TD

"Political friction has been forced into the Army from outside."

Richard Mulcahy, minister for defence

It was a trying time. The days between the announcement of the terms of the Treaty on 7 December 1921 and the actual debate on the Treaty which began on 14 December was a period of confusion and uncertainty. Positions on the Treaty changed during the week interval. Positions also hardened. Many looked to the leaders who had guided them throughout the struggle for advice. But there was no unanimity.

The cabinet was divided. The Dáil was divided. The IRB was divided.[1] And, most significantly, the IRA was divided. The veil of war-time unity, tattered during the Truce, was now publicly rent apart to reveal grave divisions. Sometimes, the attitude of the local officers determined whether IRA members would accept or reject the Treaty. Others simply followed the lead of nationally recognized leaders—Collins or Mulcahy, Lynch or O'Malley. Sometimes, it was a question of personal relationships or old grievances. The irritations and antagonisms built up during the Truce period clearly did not help in preserving the unity of the army.

Mulcahy favored the Treaty, but did not delude himself that it was in any way a perfect or final settlement. Frank Aiken later claimed that Mulcahy's initial reaction to the settlement was negative and that he only later went over to the Treaty side.[2] Dr Jim Ryan, however, remembered Mulcahy's reaction as quite the opposite. Ryan believed that the chief of staff supported the Treaty because Collins had convinced him of its merits. Ryan claimed Mulcahy countered objections to the Treaty with "Wait until you see Collins." In fact, Ryan argued that:

No matter what Mick Collins said, Dick Mulcahy thought he was right. Mulcahy himself took no credit for anything. Always Mick was the big man with him.[3]

Regardless of his personal feelings, Mulcahy knew he would have trouble selling the agreement to the army. Most likely, he was counting on the loyalty of the army and hoped his and Collins' influence would smooth over the difficulties.[4]

Collins and Mulcahy did have the majority of officers at GHQ on their side.[5] This was made clear at a meeting which de Valera had with the general staff. Probably in an effort to convince him to change his mind, Griffith had urged de Valera to meet the members of GHQ before he embarked on a course which Griffith believed would lead to a renewal of the war with Britain.[6] According to the president's subsequent account of the meeting to the Dáil, that was the purpose of the meeting:

> With reference to my meeting with the Headquarters staff, I want to make it clear—I didn't ask them for their political opinions. I brought the chiefs of staff to find out from them . . . how they stood as regards the strength of the army. I asked would you be for continuing or not. It was only in that particular way that the question of Treaty or anything like it came in. I didn't discuss the Treaty. . . . I called that as my duty to know the strength and to find out the fighting strength of the army.[7]

Mulcahy's recollection, however, was slightly different. According to him, the central question of the meeting was: What would be the position of GHQ if de Valera carried the vote in the Dáil against the Treaty. As chief of staff, Mulcahy was the first to respond:

> I said that if he won the vote in the Dáil, as far as I was concerned [I was] with him in any position in which I could be of the greatest service; that I thought I would, however, in my discussion of the Treaty proposal in the Dáil, have to make statements of a kind that would preclude me in the public mind from being reasonably looked on as the man to be entrusted with the command of the army in the new circumstances. De Valera's answer was the "Oh, it would be grand to have us all together in the same old way." As regards the general position that might arise, if . . . we went back into a war situation, I felt that our strength and morale was such that we might possibly carry on in the way in which we were carrying on at the period immediately before the truce for, say, another period of six months.[8]

The other members of the staff answered in turn. Collins stated that he would accept a position as an ordinary soldier, but would have to decline responsibility of any other kind. All the other members of GHQ assured the president that they would place their full services at his disposal if he were to form a new government.[9]

While members of GHQ had assured de Valera of their loyalty, it quickly became obvious that the key issue was not going to be what the army would do if the Treaty were defeated. Rather the major concern was what the IRA would do if the Treaty were approved. While those against the Treaty were in a minority on headquarters staff, they had strong backing from divisional commandants like Liam Lynch and Ernie O'Malley. Sections of the IRA were, in fact, seething with discontent.

It became clear almost immediately that there would be serious difficulties in convincing some members of the IRA to accept the Treaty. For example, upon learning of the terms of the Treaty, Ernie O'Malley remembered being angry at "the men who had betrayed us", and warning Ginger O'Connell, the assistant chief of staff, that the supporters of the Treaty would have to fight his division, if they broke their oath to the Republic.[10]

More significantly, even before the Dáil debates began, there was organized protest from within the IRA. On 10 December, the 1st Southern Division held a meeting of the divisional staff officers and all brigade commandants. They passed the following resolution unanimously:

> The Treaty as it is drafted is not acceptable to us as representing the Army in the 1st Divisional Area, and we urge its rejection by the Government.[11]

In their explanation, the officers of the 1st Southern highlighted the key issues which would divide the Dáil as well as the army. They objected to inclusion in the Commonwealth, the oath of allegiance, the presence of a British governor-general, the continuing use by Britain of Irish ports, and partition.

The Dáil discussions focused primarily on these same points: the oath of allegiance to the Crown, inclusion in the British empire, the nature of dominion status and the abandonment of the Irish Republic. Significantly, deputies said little about partition.

The Treaty debates were saturated with passion, emotion and personal hostility. Deputies were being forced to choose between the ideal of the liberation struggle and the practical realities of the political climate. Friendships dissolved. Former comrades who had trusted each other with their lives found themselves hurling epithets at one another. It was a bitter time. Each side felt betrayed and this feeling of betrayal would give both the debates and the civil war which followed a ferocity and intensity which would scar the body politic for years to come.

The arguments about the Treaty are well-known. To Griffith, it represented the capstone of his life's work. In his view, it gave Ireland the essential freedom needed to control the future. For Collins, it was a stepping stone, the opportunity to build and rebuild the national life. In the eyes of those who opposed the Treaty, however, the document had no such merits. To de Valera, it was an imperfect imitation of his own solution,

External Association. As outlined in what came to be called Document No. 2, this made Ireland an independent republic within the Commonwealth. To die-hard Republicans, it was a forfeiture of the national ideal, a betrayal of the revolution.

Mulcahy basically endorsed Collins' position. The Treaty could be used to achieve total and complete freedom. Most critical, he believed, was the need for reconciliation. He urged his colleagues to reconcile their differences, and he himself devoted a great deal of time and energy in the upcoming days to trying to effect a rapprochement between the pro- and anti-Treatyites.

Mulcahy opened his speech to the Dáil by asking his fellow deputies what had become of his suggestion that members on both sides come together to find a way out of the impasse which the Treaty had created:

> What we are looking for is not arguments, but alternatives. None of us want this Treaty. None of us want our harbours occupied by enemy forces; and none of us want what is said to be partition; and we want no arguments against any of these things. But we want an alternative. We want the road open to us to show how we can avoid this Treaty. . . . I, personally, see no alternative to the acceptance of this Treaty. I see no solid spot of ground upon which the Irish people can put its political feet but upon that Treaty.[12]

Interestingly enough, in light of the bitterness which later characterized his feelings toward de Valera, Mulcahy chastised his colleagues for not treating the president and his proposed alternative (Document No. 2) fairly. But more than anything else, Mulcahy wanted the Dáil to restore unity and stop the drift to political chaos.

The Treaty, Mulcahy argued, had merit. Above all, it gave the Irish people full executive and administrative powers upon which to build their future. Mulcahy voiced a strong faith in the people of Ireland to take the freedom which the Treaty offered—"full control over legislation, over order, over peace, over the whole internal life and resources of the country"—and use it to its maximum potential.[13] Mulcahy did not deny the shortcomings of the Treaty, but he believed that they were not as significant as some of his colleagues both in the army and in the Dáil claimed.

As chief of staff, Mulcahy's opinion on the military aspects of the Treaty were of special significance. Under the terms of the Treaty, Ireland had to cede to England the right to use its ports, a right, which some argued, clearly circumscribed Irish sovereignty. On the question of the ports, Mulcahy argued that:

> . . . we are not in a position of force, either military or otherwise, to drive the enemy from our ports. We have not . . . been able to drive the enemy from anything but from a fairly good-sized police barracks. We have not that power; and with regard to the ports, I doubt if anybody in this assembly at the present moment—visualising

the necessity for coastal and external defence . . . would be able to point to the mark we are aiming at as regards the necessity for defence and the financial aspect of it. When we have established a police force that will do the internal work of the country, and when we have established such small internal defence forces as is necessary . . . we will be coming to a point of intelligence at which we can decide what our external defences should be like.[14]

Contained within this section of Mulcahy's speech is his most often quoted statement that "we have not been able to drive the enemy from anything but a fairly good-sized police barracks". Traditionally, this phrase has been interpreted to mean that Mulcahy accepted the Treaty because of military necessity. While valid to a degree, this interpretation slants his speech in a way that does not do justice to Mulcahy's basic reasons for accepting the Treaty. Mulcahy was not denigrating the IRA's ability to fight or its record in the previous struggle. This would have been totally out of character. He was simply saying that, realistically, the IRA could not hope to achieve a total military victory over the British forces. He was, in fact, giving voice to one of the basic precepts of guerrilla warfare. The aim of a guerrilla struggle is not complete military victory. Rather it is to harass and hound the enemy so that they are forced to bargain, to concede the political demands of the guerrilla leaders. This was what the IRA had accomplished. The Treaty was the result of their bargaining.

Nor was Mulcahy saying that the IRA could not resume war with England. In fact, at one point, he said very clearly, that if the choice was political chaos with war or without war, "I would rather go into political chaos with war, than to go into political chaos in Ireland at the present time without war."[15] Mulcahy preferred a resumption of the war with England rather than anarchy under the Treaty. While he did not deny that the IRA could resume the war and hold out against the British troops for quite a while, Mulcahy did not believe they were strong enough to actually win "even a war of internal liberation". Years later, Mulcahy explained that he believed that the British army "had never exerted their force before the truce," and that, if the Irish had rejected the Treaty, the IRA would have had to fight the British army directly, not merely those units of Auxiliaries or Black and Tans who were assisting the RIC.[16]

Reaction to Mulcahy's speech was mixed. From his political constituency (Dublin, North West), he received a ringing endorsement. One member of his constituency wrote to congratulate him "for the brave stand you took in An Dáil" and assured the chief of staff "that your action in An Dáil will be endorsed by the vast majority of your supporters here." The letter went on to proclaim that even if President de Valera stood against Mulcahy in an election in that area, Mulcahy would win.[17]

Not all shared this opinion, however. One letter asked him if he had forgotten his principles.[18] Another came from a veteran of 1916 who perceptively characterized Mulcahy's endorsement of the Treaty as "very reluctant and luke warm," and then went on to urge Mulcahy not to support the Treaty:

> If you read so far, you will say there's nothing of the alternative you're looking for here, but there is, at the back of it, the fact that people who did the work which made any negotiations possible are willing to continue to do so rather than barter their birthright for such a mess of pottage.[19]

The mixed reaction which Mulcahy's speech evoked was typical. The IRA men who were also members of the Dáil were divided. A number agreed with Mulcahy's and Collins' position on the Treaty. In general, they argued that from a military point of view, the Treaty meant the evacuation of the British forces. And, the Treaty provided them with the opportunity to establish a proper Irish army. Overall, it gave them the substance of what they had been fighting for.

Those who opposed the Treaty claimed that it was not what they had fought for. Dan Breen expressed the sentiments of a number of men of the IRA, both inside and out of the Dáil, when he wrote to Seán McKeon taking issue with his pro-Treaty position:

> I wish to point out to you that you are reported to have stated in An Dáil to-day that this Treaty brings the freedom that is necessary and for which we are all ready to die. You also are reported to have previously stated that this Treaty gives you what you and your comrades have fought for.
>
> As one of your comrades I say that I would never have handled a gun or fired a shot nor would I have asked any of my comrades living or dead to raise a hand to obtain this Treaty.[20]

Anti-Treaty deputies were equally as forceful inside the Dáil. To Sean Moylan, it was not a question of peace or war, it was a question of right or wrong. And, in his view, the Treaty was wrong.[21] Liam Mellows of GHQ made one of the most impassioned and moving speeches against the Treaty. To him, the words, actions and elections of the Irish people and the IRA had established a republic which they had no right to dismember. There was no need to talk about stepping stones to total freedom. In Mellows' view:

> the Republic does exist. It is a living tangible thing, something for which men gave their lives, for which men were hanged, for which men are in jail, for which the people suffered, and for which men are still prepared to give their lives. It was not a question so far as I am aware, before any of us, or the people of Ireland, that the Irish heifer was going to be sold in the fair and that we were asking a high price so that we would get something less. There was no question of making a bargain over this thing, over the honour of Ireland, because I hold that the honour of Ireland is too sacred a thing to make a bargain over.[22]

But it was not only a question of honor. Practical considerations also had to be taken into account. Lloyd George had prophesied "terrible and immediate war" if the Treaty were rejected. Could the IRA successfully resume the war with Britain? Mulcahy had articulated the position of those IRA deputies who favored the Treaty. The IRA could resume the fight, but it was totally unrealistic to think in terms of a complete military victory. Other deputies added particulars to his argument. Sean McKeon, for example, pointed out that, despite an increase in numbers and better training, certain problems remained. The IRA was still plagued by a shortage of arms and ammunition. To impress upon the deputies the seriousness of the situation, McKeon gave some figures for his area:

> I know perfectly well I have charge of four thousand men. I do not hesitate to say that number. But of that four thousand I have a rifle for every fifty. Now that is the position as far as I am concerned and I may add that there is about as much ammunition as would last them about fifty minutes for that one rifle.[23]

As would be expected, those who opposed the Treaty argued that IRA could resume war. Cathal Brugha stated that the army was "in a much better position to fight now than when the Truce started."[24] Some even talked of winning the war.

There was no question but that the IRA felt itself intimately involved in deciding whether to accept or reject the Treaty. Realistically, it could not have been otherwise. The IRA was a people's army, called into being on a political issue to fight for a political cause. To pretend otherwise, was to deny the very nature and *raison d'être* of the IRA.[25] The men of the republican army were citizen-soldiers, motivated to fight by their ideals and beliefs, successors to the men of 1916 and guardians of the Republic. As Seamus Robinson, commandant of the Tipperary Brigade and T.D. for Waterford, said: "If we had no political outlook, we would not be soldiers at all."[26] President de Valera's statement that the army was not affected by the debate on the Treaty was unrealistic, given the history and development of the army. As one army officer and subsequent analyst noted:

> The army, because of its spirit and character, because of the very factors that had made it an effective weapon of liberation, could not be insulated against the storms of passion and controversy which began to rage around the question of the Treaty.[27]

There was also no question but that the views of the IRA would influence the general community. It was no accident that Sean McKeon, legendary hero of the Black and Tan war, seconded the motion to approve the Treaty. Nor did it hurt the pro-Treaty position that most members of GHQ in the Dáil spoke in its favor. In fact, to counter this influence, those commandants who opposed the Treaty sent a notice to the Dáil, expressing their unqualified hostility to any such compromise and making their opposition public:

> In view of the false rumours that have been circulated about Dublin to the effect that we, the undersigned, have declared ourselves favourable to the acceptance of the proposed Treaty . . . we desire, first, to enter our emphatic protest against the use of our Division of the Army to influence public opinion and the opinion of members of Dáil Éireann in the direction favourable to the Treaty; and we desire, secondly, to state that we maintain unimpaired our allegiance to the Irish Republic and it alone.[28]

The document was signed by Liam Lynch, Ernie O'Malley, Oscar Traynor, O/C Dublin Brigade, and Michael MacCormaic, O/C 3rd Southern Division.

No one denied the right of the members of the IRA to their opinions on the Treaty. The concern was that some in the army might attempt to dictate to the Dáil, to enforce their views with arms. The underlying question tormenting the deputies was whether the army would accept the dictates of the Dáil, regardless of the outcome of the vote on the Treaty. Having abdicated responsibility for the struggle for independence, the Dáil was unsure whether it could now establish control.

Some sections of the army gave Deputies little reason to think that they could impose their will on the IRA. Deputies were subjected to intimidation and threatened by soldiers. For example, the senior deputy for Cork city was given the following notice:

> To all T.D.s in Cork No.1 Area: (1) On December 10th the Staff of the First Southern Division and all Brigade Commandants met and sent forward to GHQ a unanimous demand for the rejection of the Treaty proposals. (2) You are reminded it is your duty to support this demand. (3) To act otherwise would be treason to the Republic to which we have sworn allegiance.[29]

More explicitly, Mr Fahy of Galway claimed: "I was approached by a member of the IRA as I came here today and told if I voted for the Treaty I would be shot."[30]

Everyone condemned the threats of violence. The president, the minister for defence and the chief of staff all gave public assurances that the strictest discipline would be maintained in the army.[31] Cathal Brugha promised that he would maintain the highest standards of discipline. And de Valera threatened that "if the army as a national army does not obey the Government and until the Dáil is dissolved any man who does not obey the Government, if there is any scrap of an army left to arrest him, he will be arrested."[32] There is an inherent irony in these assurances given by leaders who eventually took up arms against the government in the civil war.

As chief of staff, it was up to Mulcahy to explain the army's behavior and intentions to concerned deputies. With what would be a characteristic insensitivity to the fears of those not directly involved with the military, Mulcahy stated: "I don't know what undercurrent of irritation is troubling people in regard to the army."[33] He dismissed the threats and warnings of the IRA as simply the expression of opinion of soldier-citizens. Regarding the note from the southern divisions, he argued that "the tone and spirit of that note was such that nobody could take exception to it".[34] His defence of Lynch was in keeping with the very warm relationship which existed between the two men and the very high opinion Mulcahy had of him:

> The officer who wrote that note [Lynch] has been the man who was perhaps so far as I personally was concerned at any rate an education and an inspiration in the army. . . . he submitted that note which I submit was eminently reasonable.[35]

Mulcahy did acknowledge that he was surprised at the threatening notice from the Cork No. 1 Brigade, but he assured the Dáil that when the O/C realized the lack of discipline which the note implied, he would understand the impropriety of his action. Mulcahy concluded his remarks with an appraisal which was more a reflection of what he wanted to believe than the existing reality:

> the Dáil may be perfectly satisfied that the First Southern Division will stand as soldiers with the generosity of service that the country has always got from them.[36]

Despite Mulcahy's seeming dismissal of IRA threats and warnings to the Dáil, he was worried. It was typical of the way he approached matters. Publicly, he would support the army. Privately, he would reprimand his officers, pointing out to them the irregular nature of their behavior. This was the tactic he employed in the truce; he would also use it, though with some modification, during the rest of his military career. The results were the same—no one was satisfied.

Mulcahy voiced his private concerns to the O/C, Cork No. 1 Brigade and asked him for an apology. The brigade commandant, O'Hegarty, replied that he would neither apologize nor withdraw the notice he sent to the T.D.s in his area. He felt it was important that the deputies be informed "in plain terms of our attitude toward these proposals." O'Hegarty went on to explain:

> The suggestion that the issuing of this document was "a most irregular interference" I repudiate—with all respect to the chief of staff. The circumstances cannot be judged as the ordinary political variations of a settled country. Here is no ordinary political change. What is contemplated in these proposals in more than that. It is the upsetting of the Constitution—the betrayal of the Republic. Who

better than these who fought to maintain it have a right in this crisis to uphold the Republic; to make clear to those who have the decisions in this matter what their duty is.[37]

O'Hegarty's reply captured the essence of the attitude of those in the IRA who dissented from the Treaty. It was not, however, particularly pleasing to either the chief of staff or the minister for defence. Brugha wrote to Mulcahy advising him to deal with O'Hegarty directly and forcefully:

> It is evident from the reply of the O/C Cork No.1 Brigade that this officer requires some enlightening as to the scope of his duties. You will now kindly define those duties for him and inform him that sending reminders to public representatives pointing out what he, or those under him, consider those representatives should do in crises like the present is not one of them. One would think that a person holding the rank of Brigade Commandant should know this without having to be told it. It is intolerable that military men as such should interfere in matters of this kind. This officer should be severely reprimanded.[38]

Mulcahy, however, would not be so direct, so confrontational. The balance in the army was very delicate and it was not clear just how severe Mulcahy could afford to be with O'Hegarty without upsetting the entire 1st Southern Division.

Nor did the situation in Cork improve. There were other complaints. The men of the Cork No. 1 Brigade disrupted a meeting of pro-Treaty farmers who were in the process of passing a resolution calling on the Dáil to accept the Treaty. The IRA barged into the meeting, interrupted the speakers, confiscated the notes of those from the press and informed them that they were not to report on the results of the meeting.[39]

The chief of staff demanded an explanation. Lynch sent on to GHQ a copy of the O/C's report which he, as divisional commandant, had received. His only comment to Mulcahy was that the report "speaks for itself".[40] And clearly, on a certain level, it did. According to the Brigade commandant's report:

> I have to-day had dispersed and reporters' notes seized at a meeting of farmers . . . call[ed] for the ratification of the Treaty. This meeting, had it been allowed to have been held would have been splashed as a meeting of Co. Cork Farmers—of whom it could not have been representative and could only have served a mischievous purpose. Those present (about 30 people) were all the reactionary pro-English type, opposed to the Republic and an utterly useless class. They included one suspect and one professor in the National University.
>
> I have also to report that I have instructed my O/C's to prevent the holding of similar meetings called in their areas and to turn back reporters who may come to report them. In every case such meetings have been called by open enemies to the Republic; or useless non-committals.[41]

Once again, O'Hegarty's comments captured the essence of feelings—the hostility and betrayal which members of the IRA were experiencing. Once again, the chief of staff was in a dilemma.

It must have seemed to Mulcahy that the difficulties would never end—a feeling that would only grow during the upcoming months. The Cork No. 1 Brigade continued to act as a law unto itself and destroyed all copies of a pamphlet written by Professor O'Rahilly of the National University entitled "The Case for the Treaty". They even destroyed the printing type. O'Hegarty's justification was that "the pamphlet contained a statement in reference to the Army which was unauthorised and at variance with the truth. In my opinion too, the publication of this pamphlet was intended to press for us [*sic*] repudiation of the Irish Republic."[42]

O'Hegarty's actions formed a pattern. What was more interesting was Lynch's evaluation of his officer's attitude and action. Writing to Mulcahy concerning the O'Rahilly pamphlet, he pointedly stated that if O'Hegarty's statements about the contents of the pamphlet were true, he agreed with his O/C's action and:

> If O'Rahilly persists in his attitude . . . action will have to be taken to prevent him from making Army publications. I would suggest that O'Rahilly be made aware that at least this Command is yet a Unit of the IRA and will take action now as in the past to put down all actions against the Republic.

If this were not clear enough, Lynch offered Mulcahy the following advice:

> I would advise that the action of suspension and disarming be not decided or insisted on as GHQ should be highly pleased that they have not far more serious reasons to complain. Officers and men here realise that the Government, GHQ Staff and the Army in the rest of Ireland outside the Southern Division and Dublin Brigade have outrageously let them down. When the Free State comes into existence GHQ can be responsible for discipline which I have grave fears will be hard to maintain.[43]

Mulcahy's response to the difficulties in Cork were tempered by Lynch's evaluation. The chief of staff was intent on holding the army together. He did not want to provoke any of his officers into precipitous action. Perhaps Mulcahy should have acted more firmly, more quickly and more decisively. But Mulcahy obviously did not know that his efforts to preserve unity would be in vain, and to avoid a civil war he was prepared to gamble. Unfortunately, he lost.

After a recess for the Christmas holidays, the Dáil resumed its debate on the Treaty. Speeches continued through the first week of January, but it had now degenerated into bitter accusations and personal recriminations. Cathal Brugha's vicious denunciation of Michael Collins as a fraud, a war hero only in the annals of the press—a speech described by Mulcahy as a "death rattle"[44]—was but one extreme example of the poisonous atmosphere permeating the Dáil. Finally, on 7 January 1922, the Speaker called the roll and Dáil Éireann approved the Articles of Agreement between Great Britain and Ireland, 64 to 57, a margin of merely seven votes. Immediately following the vote, the minister for defence, Cathal Brugha, said: "So far as I am concerned I will see, at any rate, that discipline is kept in the army."[45]

The vote on the Treaty permanently split the Irish nationalist movement apart. For the next six months, the country drifted almost inexorably towards civil war. The politicians were peripheral to this process, unable to agree among themselves, unable to do anything but obstruct and obfuscate. Their war of words, verbal attacks as stinging as bullets, only exacerbated the already volatile temper of the army. But it was the IRA who were once again the main actors. It was the IRA who would decide the question of peace or war.

From the beginning of the split in the IRA over the Treaty, certain points were very clear. In the first place, there were a number of extremists who did not seem to flinch at the thought of fighting their former comrades. They were, however, a minority. Most of the members of the IRA hoped for and worked for a compromise. They believed that they could find a way out of the dilemma. To this end, they held seemingly endless meetings, circulated documents and position papers, and tried desperately to hammer out a compromise. Although it eventually all came to nought, the representatives of the army spent six months trying to find the elusive formula that would prevent civil war. The politicians were impotent. The army at least tried. The army led. The politicians followed.

On 9 January 1922, Arthur Griffith succeeded de Valera as president of the Dáil. He formed his new ministry—the Dáil government—the next day. Mulcahy became minister for defence. Immediately, de Valera asked about the position of the army. Mulcahy's reply was that the army would be kept intact, that it would occupy the same position in the same spirit as it had under de Valera's government. De Valera claimed this was an ambiguous reply. Mulcahy clarified his remarks with a clear and direct statement:

> it has been suggested I avoided saying what could have been said very simply. It is suggested I avoided saying the Army will continue to be the Army of the Irish Republic. If any assurance is required—the Army will remain the Army of the Irish Republic.[46]

Mulcahy was subsequently criticized for making this statement. Some claimed that, while it was calculated to ease the tension in the army, it ultimately was not a wise statement. Mulcahy could not fulfil this promise. Moreover, his response was a personal statement, not a governmental decision.[47]

Mulcahy's statement, in fact, was absolutely necessary. In the course of the debate, deputies expressed their concern about maintaining and enforcing discipline in the army. Had Mulcahy said anything less, it might have provoked out and out rebellion at a time when the new government was one day old and the loyalty of much of its army was questionable. But there was another reason Mulcahy gave the Dáil and indirectly, the army, the assurance he did. His statement most likely reflected his belief that somehow, through constitutional manoeuvring and jesuitical machinations, the army could remain the army of the Republic under a treaty based government. He would spend the next six months trying to effect that impossible compromise. His patient and methodical personality would serve him well in this quest.

Once he became minister for defence, Mulcahy resigned his position as chief of staff and was succeeded by Eoin O'Duffy. As minister, Mulcahy immediately took steps to prevent the army from splintering. According to Frank Aiken, on the same evening that his appointment was ratified by the Dáil, Mulcahy held a meeting at the Mansion House of nearly all of his staff at GHQ and officers commanding divisions and independent brigades. Notably absent were Cathal Brugha, Liam Mellows, Rory O'Connor and Ernie O'Malley. According to Aiken's account, Mulcahy arrived late and within a few minutes called the officers to attention as de Valera entered the room. Mulcahy insisted that the former president be accorded the same respect as always.

During the meeting, de Valera asked the minister for defence to keep the army intact and appealed to Mulcahy not to allow anything to happen that would cause any uneasiness among the members of the IRA. Mulcahy reiterated the pledge which he had given that afternoon in the Dáil. The army would remain the army of the Republic. Because of this pledge, De Valera called upon the officers to give the new minister for defence their full allegiance.[48]

Discussion continued about the Treaty. Most likely, each side reiterated its arguments—putting forth positions that were by now well-known but yet hoping that through dialogue some type of accommodation could be reached. It must have been a very emotional encounter. Aiken recorded that Lynch was "very deeply moved and broke down", declaring once again that the Treaty was not what he had fought for and telling his old chief of staff that he could no longer take orders from GHQ. Mulcahy would not let the meeting close on that note. He asked Lynch and the other officers who had spoken so vehemently against the Treaty to remain after the meeting "so that he might have a chat with them".[49] Afterwards, Mulcahy seemingly convinced Lynch at least not to formally and publicly break away from GHQ and to continue the efforts to find a way out of the dilemma which the Treaty created.

Despite the minister for defence's relative success in holding the army together and despite his assurances, the anti-Treaty section of the IRA was still worried that the new government would subvert the army of the republic. On 11 January 1922, therefore, they wrote to Mulcahy requesting an army convention. This convention would consider the following resolution:

> That the Army reaffirms its allegiance to the Irish Republic. That it shall be maintained as the Army of the Irish Republic, under an Executive appointed by the Convention. That the Army shall be under the Supreme control of such Executive, which shall draft a constitution for submission to a subsequent Convention.[50]

Obviously, if this resolution were passed, the army would be a sovereign, independent body—not accountable to any civilian authority. Mulcahy responded to each of the signatories by saying:

> 1. That the Dáil as a whole is the elected Government of the Irish Republic and that the supreme control of the Army is vested in it, and 2. That the proposal contained in the resolution to change the supreme control of the Army is entirely outside the constitutional powers vested in the Dáil Executive by the Dáil.[51]

The minister for defence did not dismiss the idea of the convention *per se*. He rather stressed the point that the army had to remain under the direct control of the Dáil—a position which he would gently try to circumvent as the months went on and the situation became more critical.

Mulcahy also tried to meet personally with those officers who requested a convention. His aim was to convince them either to drop the idea of a convention or at least delay it. In a note which reflected the pathos and tragedy inherent in the situation, Liam Lynch wrote to Mulcahy:

> No purpose will be served by meeting me after 10.30 tomorrow as I must then take united action with signatories.[52]

This rejection coupled with Lynch's moving yet firm rejection of the Treaty hurt and upset Mulcahy deeply. It also impressed upon him more forcefully—if that were possible—the gravity of the situation. Lynch was not even one of the extremists.

Mulcahy needed time. He hoped that once the anti-Treaty officers saw that the British troops were actually evacuating their barracks throughout Ireland, they would realize the value of the Treaty. He did not expect them ever to like the agreement, but perhaps a majority of those opposed to the Treaty could be convinced not to oppose it. Mulcahy hoped to isolate the moderates from their more extremist colleagues. To achieve this, he needed proof that the Treaty could work to Ireland's benefit. British evacuation was part of this proof.

Mulcahy's strategy was aided by the rapidity of events. On 14 January 1922, the Provisional Government was formed under the direction of

Michael Collins to supervise the transfer of power from British to Irish rule. Mulcahy was not part of this government. Most likely, this was decided upon to preserve the illusion that the army would remain the army of the Republic. However, by 17 February 1922, Mulcahy was attending meetings to allow the provisional government "closer touch with the Defence Department".[53]

The long-awaited evacuation by the British started almost immediately. On 16 January, Collins, on behalf of the provisional government, took over Dublin Castle—for centuries the symbol of British rule. Collins gave voice to a momentary outburst of delight in an otherwise gloomy situation when he announced to Griffith that "The Castle has fallen!"[54]

This note of triumph was not shared by the anti-Treaty officers. Alarmed at what seemed to them the further entrenchment of the Griffith-Collins faction, they were threatening to call an army convention on their own and repudiate the authority of GHQ. On 18 January, the anti-Treaty officers notified the chief of staff, Eoin O'Duffy, of their intention.

The letter which O'Duffy received stated quite bluntly that since the minister for defence and his associates at GHQ would not agree to a convention of the entire army, those anti-Treaty officers who had previously requested such a meeting would themselves call a convention. The letter went on to add that while the anti-Treaty officers would co-operate with GHQ staff in hastening the evacuation of the British, they would only act on O'Duffy's orders if they were countersigned by Rory O'Connor. O'Connor signed himself as Chairman, Acting Military Council, IRA.[55] Obviously, this was a direct challenge to the authority of the minister for defence, the chief of staff and GHQ.

Once again, the army seemed poised to break into factions. A number of officers appealed to Mulcahy to try yet another meeting to prevent the staging of an irregular convention which would put a section of the army beyond the pale. That meeting was duly held on 18 January 1922.[56] The critical issue was whether a Volunteer convention should be held to allow the army to evaluate the current national position.

Those who pushed for a convention urged that their earlier resolutions be adopted. These resolutions reaffirmed the army as the army of the Republic and set up an army executive to see that the IRA remained just that. Their justification was:

> that the action of the majority of the Dáil in supporting the Treaty involving the setting up of an Irish Free State was a subversion of the Republic and relieved the Army from its allegiance to An Dáil, hence the necessity for a Convention to consider [the] above resolutions.[57]

Those who opposed the idea of a convention argued for the principle of civilian control over the army—a basic assumption of democratic government. On a practical level, they countered the idea of a convention with the

argument that it would have "a disrupting effect on the army as the differences which now exist would probably then take definite shape involving
a split".[58] They pointed out that there was no definite army policy to put
before a convention and thus the officers should wait until the constitution
of the Free State was drafted before they undertook to define the army's
position.[59]

According to Ernie O'Malley's recollection, the anti-Treatyites withdrew
from the meeting to discuss the issues. He claimed that the majority of
them were in favor of forming an independent headquarters. Liam Lynch,
however, refused to go along with that suggestion and his opposition
swayed the others. O'Malley explained that this was because his division
was the strongest numerically, was better armed and had the largest
territory.[60] O'Malley was not being totally candid. Lynch's personal stature
also had something to do with his ability to influence his colleagues.

Moderation eventually prevailed. A compromise was reached. The officers unanimously agreed to postpone the army convention for two months.
They also agreed to set up a council of four, a watching committee, which
would ensure that GHQ, Beggars Bush—as Mulcahy's staff came to be
called—would not subvert the Republic. The officers concluded their meeting by issuing a statement on the necessity for maintaining discipline and
preserving order:

> Now that unanimous agreement has been reached providing for the
> control and direction of the IRA pending a Convention, it is
> incumbent on officers and men of all ranks to co-operate in
> ensuring that the splendid discipline which hitherto characterized
> the IRA be rigidly maintained, that the enemy be facilitated in
> evacuating, and that the occupation of the different positions by
> our troops be carried out in an orderly and military manner. While
> the British forces are evacuating, the responsibility for public order
> and public safety in this country devolves very largely on the IRA,
> and the people of the Nation as a whole expect and are entitled to
> the protection of our Army.[61]

On one level, the 18 January 1922 meeting was significant. It demonstrated that within the anti-Treaty ranks, there were moderates who seemed
to recoil from the thought of civil war. Thus, Mulcahy's strategy of trying to
cultivate and appease that moderate faction had some basis for optimism.

Second, the argument advanced by those who opposed the convention
that the army wait until the new constitution was drafted was a major
element in Collins' strategy. Just as Mulcahy hoped to find a way to keep
the IRA as the army of the Republic under the Free State, Collins hoped to
write a constitution that would establish a republic under the Treaty.
Neither was being very realistic. But both were straining to prevent the
political and military wings of the nationalist movement from irrevocably
dividing. Both were willing to agree to compromises that their civilian

colleagues would have difficulty accepting. And, perhaps, both Collins and Mulcahy, at this point, found these compromise positions closer to their own ideological leanings or at least to their own wishes and desires.

The pro-Treaty position was strengthened as the British troops actually began to leave Ireland. On the last day in January, the Irish Republican Army marched into Beggars Bush Barracks to occupy their new headquarters. Sean O' Murthuile left this picture of the event:

> Beggars Bush Barracks was handed over, and became the Head-quarters of the new State Army; it was first occupied by less than 50 members of the "Dublin Guards", who marched in uniform through the City to take it over, and Collins looked proudly on from the City Hall as they passed that building under the Command of Brig. T. Daly, who had been one of the foremost Dublin Officers in the War against the Crown Forces in Dublin.[62]

Mulcahy's, Collins' and GHQ's pride on this occasion must have been tempered by the knowledge that so many of their closest colleagues and valued officers were unable or unwilling to share in their triumph.

British withdrawal, however, raised a difficult issue for Mulcahy: Who would take over the barracks that the British evacuated? Would it be his policy to allow only those who favored the Treaty to occupy these important positions or would the barracks be handed over to local units of the IRA regardless of their loyalty to the new government?

Mulcahy opted for the latter policy. He has been subsequently criticized for this decision, but, at the time, it was not clear that he had any other choice. GHQ did not have enough loyal men to take over all the barracks. Moreover, to make any other decision would have been to undermine his promise that the army would remain the army of the Republic. That would have strengthened the extremists. Finally, it would have contradicted his belief that once the anti-Treaty officers actually saw that the British were leaving Ireland—at least the 26 counties of the south—it would make the agreement more palatable.

However compelling his reasons were for adopting this policy, Mulcahy was not entirely comfortable with sharing them with the Dáil. In fact, Mulcahy's statement to the Dáil on 1 March 1922 concerning the occupation of barracks was ambiguous, if not misleading. On that day, he told the Dáil that while the IRA was taking control of the posts evacuated by the British:

> The Provisional Government is given an assurance that troops occupying such posts shall not use their power to interfere with the expression of the people's will at the pending General Election, and will not turn their arms against any Government elected by the people at that election.[63]

This was more Mulcahy's own personal guarantee based on his faith in the army rather than a statement of fact. It was not at all clear that, in the early months of the evacuations, Mulcahy had received such an assurance from local IRA units.[64] Certainly in the dispute over who would occupy the barracks at Templemore, GHQ did not seem to have required such a promise. It took all their energy and diplomacy simply to effect a compromise whereby their troops were briefly housed in the barracks and then ordered out again almost immediately.[65]

By May, however, Mulcahy was making just such demands. He wrote to Sean O'Hegarty, O/C, Cork No. 1 Brigade requesting such assurances before allowing him to take over barracks in his area.[66] The ongoing negotiations for army unity, the changing political climate as well as the particular notoriety achieved by this brigade all may have influenced this change.

Moreover, Mulcahy was taking steps to strengthen his position. During this time of crisis, Mulcahy ordered his staff to begin recruiting for a national army, an army that would be loyal to the new state. Their uniforms were the uniforms of the Volunteers, their insignia was that of the Republic, their members were pre-Truce veterans. But, despite these similarities, it was a new army. As one historian has noted:

> From its inception, the Free State [Beggar's Bush] army followed regular military procedure. Its soldiers wore uniforms, lived in barracks, learned drill and standard tactics, and were armed with British-supplied weapons. Organizational progress was slow at first. Trained staff officers and instructors were scarce; so were arms, uniforms, and equipment; and strict discipline could not be instilled in guerrilla warriors in a week or two. There were small-scale mutinies in the new force and a number of soldiers resigned, deserted, or were dismissed. Slowly but steadily, however, the army grew as loyal troops underwent training at Beggar's Bush and returned to their home districts.[67]

Mulcahy would have been irresponsible not to have organized a new army. It was one thing to work and hope that the old IRA would survive the present crisis intact. It was quite another not to prepare to defend the state in case it did not.

Anti-Treaty officers were clearly displeased with GHQ's efforts to recruit a new army. Liam Mellows described it as "a paid, mercenary army".[68] The anti-Treaty officers also knew that their positions, their place would be taken by others, unless they accepted the Treaty or fought the new government.

Fissures began to appear. In early February, Ernie O'Malley and the 2nd Southern Division formally broke away from GHQ. O'Malley said at the time that he voted to break away from GHQ because "he thought it would bring about unity in his Division and so tend to effective control and discipline within his area." O'Malley, in fact, had confessed "absolute failure to control his Division".[69] Thus, it appeared in this case that the divisional officer was following—albeit not unwillingly—the lead of his men.

The decision of the 2nd Southern division had immediate reverberations. Included within their area of command was the Mid-Limerick brigade under the command of Liam Forde. Along with his comrades in the 2nd Southern, Forde had repudiated GHQ. His action was of particular importance because of the strategic value of Limerick—commanding access to both the south and the west of Ireland. Hence, when the British decided to evacuate the barracks in Limerick city, the question of who would occupy them took on an added significance. Within weeks, the Limerick crisis threatened to bring about civil war. As Mulcahy later noted in the Dáil:

> The Limerick episode disclosed the extent to which even as early as the beginning of February the movement to split the Army had gone and the extent to which those who were driving this split were prepared to go.[70]

Because of the importance of Limerick and because of the open repudiation of the mid-Limerick Brigade, GHQ departed from its previous policy of handing over barracks to the local IRA unit regardless of their position on the Treaty. It instructed the nearest responsible officer, the O/C of the 1st Western Division, Commandant Brennan, "to occupy these Barracks until such time as the rank and file in Limerick and such officers there as remained loyal to GHQ could be organised to occupy them."[71] Brennan marched into Limerick. The Republicans described it as "the invasion of Limerick". Quite soon, the anti-Treatyites sent in their own reinforcements. Troops were everywhere, housed in asylums, hotels, as well as in barracks. The stage was set for confrontation.

Mulcahy travelled to Limerick. Ernie O'Malley, an active participant in the crisis, claimed the minister for defence and his chief of staff, O'Duffy, went to Limerick to assess the situation. The mayor of Limerick, O'Mara, on the other hand, said that Mulcahy and Gearoid O'Sullivan, the adjutant-general, were there to attend a commemoration ceremony. Both, however, agreed on Mulcahy's mood. O'Malley remembered:

> Mulcahy and O'Duffy had arrived in Limerick, I learned when I reached the city. The officers at our headquarters refused to visit them in the Castle barracks. And they declined to visit our officers on neutral grounds. I surmised from stray remarks that the conversation on the phone was not as polite as it might have been, as they returned to Dublin highly incensed.[72]

The mayor of Limerick substantiated O'Malley's impression. He claimed that when he telephoned the minister for defence to offer his services in any way he could to ease the crisis, the only response he received was a curt thank you. The mayor believed that "Mulcahy probably thought he [the mayor] was being used as a tool by the mid-Limerick Brigade."[73]

The minister for defence was obviously in no mood to cater to the disaffected officers. He must have been angered by the provocative repudiation of GHQ by the 2nd Southern Division in general and annoyed with the mid-Limerick officers in particular. They had been a source of irritation during the Truce, quarrelling among themselves, and now were acting up again.[74] In addition, Mulcahy was most likely concerned that his position as minister for defence not be tarnished. It was one thing to meet with senior officers in the Mansion House in Dublin. It was another to parley with unrepentant officers who had repudiated his authority in the middle of a crisis. Perhaps also, as one historian has suggested, his actual physical presence in Limerick—as opposed to simply receiving reports in Dublin—hardened his attitude.[75]

In any event, the situation in Limerick in the early days of March was highly explosive. On 8 March, Brennan wrote to GHQ informing them that he expected an ultimatum from the anti-Treatyites giving the Beggars Bush forces twenty-four hours to clear out. He asked for a variety of arms, ammunition and equipment. More significantly, he asked that 100 of McKeon's men from the Longford area be sent to Limerick at once. Claiming that 80% of his men were untrained and that, on the other hand, the "mutineers"—as Brennan called them—were all trained, he tried to impress upon GHQ the urgency of this request.[76]

There was, however, another highly significant reason for Brennan's urgent appeal for McKeon's men. In another report to GHQ, he wrote:

> Some of my men here have too many old associations with the mutineers to be properly reliable, hence my anxiety to get 100 good men from McKeon. The 3rd Southern is too near them to be thoroughly reliable.[77]

It was not at all clear who would follow orders if it came to bloodshed. Brennan himself was reported to have said: "I don't see how serious fighting can take place here, our men have nothing against the other lads."[78] Even Ernie O'Malley admitted that the friendliness and camaraderie between the two sides had not yet dissipated, although he himself seemed perfectly willing to fight.[79] In general, most of the soldiers seemed anxious to avoid firing the first shot.[80]

The crisis in Limerick manifested the inherent tragedy of the civil war, of comrade against comrade. However, these events also demonstrated that neither side as yet had a real desire to fight. Fortunately, each side had their "compromisers". But, then each side also had their "hard-liners".

The "hard-liners" were those who felt that a showdown between the two sides was necessary. On the Treaty side, Arthur Griffith took a very stern line toward the anti-Treaty forces in Limerick. In an interview with the mayor of Limerick—who was most anxious that his city not be turned into a battle ground—Griffith refused to concede an inch. Mayor O'Mara articulated his concern that the crisis would lead to civil war and asked that the majority and minority parties of the Dáil come together with the staff of GHQ and try to settle the dispute. Griffith disagreed, saying:

> This is a matter for the Cabinet of Dáil Éireann, and G.H. Staff. IRA troops went in there in accordance with the Treaty and occupied positions. They went in because the mid-Limerick Brigade repudiated the authority of Dáil Éireann. In accordance with the arrangement between Dáil Éireann Cabinet and the Provisional Govt., the Barracks will continue to be occupied by IRA until (Irregular) troops withdraw, when the forces will be reduced to care and maintenance parties.[81]

Needless to say, O'Mara found little comfort in Griffith's words. He wondered aloud if it would not be better to burn the barracks rather than let the crisis continue. Griffith replied to this idea with a verbal slap on the wrist:

> That would not solve the difficulty, which is that these men challenge our authority and right. A section of the army are in mutiny, and those who have incited to mutiny will be responsible. A worse disaster than a continuation of the present situation would be the overthrow of the Dáil and the Provisional Government.[82]

For Griffith, civil war was preferable to abdicating the authority of the Provisional Government and repudiating the Treaty.

Mulcahy did not see it that way. Despite his initial anger, once again, Mulcahy opted for compromise. If he needed any prodding, the minister for defence received just that in an appeal from former President de Valera. On 6 March 1922, de Valera wrote to Mulcahy urging him to take some action to settle the Limerick affair without bloodshed. De Valera argued that if left unattended, the crisis "may well be the beginning of a civil war and a general break up of the army and the defensive forces of the nation". De Valera mentioned that he had heard that Mulcahy had made up his mind not to take any action. The former president characterized this decision as "fatal". He then suggested that Gearoid O'Sullivan and Rory O'Connor be sent to Limerick to jointly investigate the situation and to find an amicable solution.[83]

De Valera's letter to Mulcahy was important for two reasons. It places the former president in an entirely different light from his public utterances on the necessity of fighting and wading through the blood of former comrades. Both his private correspondence and his public concern about retaining discipline in the army, reveal a more complex portrait than his Free State opponents, especially Mulcahy, would allow for.

Moreover, de Valera's appeal most probably had an impact on Mulcahy, strengthening that side of him which abhorred the thought of civil war, weakening the side of him which was influenced by Griffith. Like de Valera, Mulcahy's actions and beliefs were not always consistent during this period. He wavered about Limerick, but in the end, he compromised.

In order to effect a compromise, on 10 March Mulcahy summoned Liam Lynch and Oscar Traynor, O/C, Dublin Brigade, to a meeting at Beggars Bush with himself, Michael Collins, and Eoin O'Duffy. He asked them to proceed to Limerick to work out a solution to the worsening crisis. They did. Under the agreement hammered out by Lynch and Traynor—and one suspects that it took a great deal of hammering—the Republican troops from outside of Limerick left the city, the Beggars Bush troops were confined to barracks and then evacuated, and the mid-Limerick Brigade was left in control.[84]

The Limerick compromise avoided bloodshed, avoided the outbreak of civil war. But Mulcahy and GHQ paid a heavy price. Griffith and a majority of the cabinet opposed the compromise. Griffith believed that if a clash with the Republicans were to come, it was better to face up to it immediately. At a cabinet meeting, he informed his colleagues that if they failed to act, they would be known as "greatest poltroons in Irish history".[85] For Griffith, the honor of the country was at stake.

At first even Collins supported Griffith's militant stand. Mulcahy stood alone in urging compromise. His arguments were weighty, however. The new army was in no condition to fight—either militarily or psychologically. Brennan had sensed this in his men in Limerick. They had just begun the process of trying to create a regular national army. Asking soldiers to fight a civil war would put a horrible strain even on the most disciplined of troops. The implicit assumption was that the minister for defence could not guarantee that the army could or would fight. Collins swung over. The rest of the cabinet backed down. The disagreement over the Limerick crisis opened a wedge, barely perceptible, between Mulcahy and his civilian colleagues. This wedge would, however, become bigger and bigger as civil war became a reality and the army assumed more and more power.

Moreover, at least to some anti-Treaty forces, the compromise was not a compromise but "a victory over GHQ".[86] Ernie O'Malley certainly saw it that way. He wrote: "We had won without firing a shot. We maintained our rights."[87] Some pro-Treaty officers agreed with this interpretation. The story is told that Michael Brennan was so upset that he rushed to Dublin to hand in his resignation.[88] Only the wrath of Collins and Brennan's own realization that it was more personal pride than military sense which was at work made him reconsider.

The Limerick compromise also caused manifest discontent among some of the members of the army who remained loyal to GHQ. At a meeting held at the Gresham Hotel on 12 March 1922, a group of mostly junior officers protested the decision of the minister for defence and GHQ in accepting the Limerick compromise. It was a most irregular meeting for those who clothed their document in terms of loyalty and subordination of the army to the Dáil.

These officers described the Limerick agreement as "something nearly approaching capitulation to the mutineers", and claimed that it had a demoralizing effect on units loyal to GHQ. They had other grievances. They protested the presence of officers who were not members of head-quarters staff at GHQ meetings. In addition, they urged the adoption of a policy that would allow any member of GHQ staff the right to refer a particular decision to the Dáil cabinet.[89] These officers obviously felt that the majority of the staff at GHQ were not to be trusted. The document was another challenge to the authority and role of the minister for defence and a vote of no confidence in GHQ staff as a whole. Liam Lynch described this protest as a mutiny of the junior officers of the old GHQ against the senior officers.[90] Significantly, many of the officers involved in this protest would be also take part in the army mutiny of 1924.

Ginger O'Connell, assistant chief of staff, was one of the few senior officers involved in this affair. He saw the Limerick crisis as capitulation on the part of Mulcahy and GHQ to Lynch and his followers. On a more general level, O'Connell was critical of Mulcahy's attitude toward the anti-Treaty officers. He objected to officers from all parts of the country calling in at GHQ and was particularly incensed at the esteem in which Mulcahy and some of his staff held Liam Lynch. O'Connell subsequently blamed the influence of the IRB for Lynch's popularity and spoke in shrouded terms of a "mental reserve" among members of GHQ.[91] O'Connell's charges are not substantiated. While there were meetings of the Supreme Council during this period, there was no need to blame the hidden hand of the IRB for Lynch's access to GHQ members.[92] Lynch's position was due to his stature as a one of the best fighting officers in the IRA and Mulcahy's hope that Lynch would use his influence to moderate his more extreme colleagues. However, O'Connell's suspicions about the IRB were typical of those who were critical of the Brotherhood. What was not readily understandable or apparent, was blamed on the IRB. It was a convenient scapegoat, an easy answer.

It should have been obvious to O'Connell that Mulcahy needed Lynch. The minister for defence, in fact, needed all the support he could muster as preparations for the promised army convention continued. A meeting of divisional and brigade commandants on 24 February had selected the date for the convention as 26 March. They had also decided to meet again on 15 March to set the agenda for the convention. The officers agreed on two very important points:

> . . . delegates would be selected for the Convention, simply as such, without reference to any particular resolutions, and that no

resolutions other than the resolutions to be agreed on at the meeting of 15th March be accepted from any Unit of the Army.[93]

Mulcahy was trying to ensure as best he could that the moderates dominated the convention and that it could not be disrupted from the floor.

Mulcahy had informed the cabinet on the 27 February that a "Volunteer Convention" was to be held. He thought he had the cabinet's approval. However, as a note from George Gavan Duffy, his colleague in foreign affairs, pointed out, this was not quite the case. Gavan Duffy challenged Mulcahy's statement that the Cabinet had accepted his recommendation that the Convention proceed. Rather his recollection was:

> when you raised the matter, it was decided not to bring it before the Dáil in view of the Free State Bill then passing through the British Parliament, which might have been jeopardised by giving publicity to this matter, but that no decision was come to as to proceeding with the Convention, and in fact that matter was not raised otherwise than incidentally; . . . I fancy you consulted the leading members of the Cabinet privately, but that is a different thing from a Cabinet decision. You will recollect that there was considerable rush when you raised the matter on February 27th., as the Dáil was meeting next day.[94]

Gavan Duffy's irritation was obvious, but the significance of the memo lies in the fact that such an important decision was left in a rather ambiguous state.

Mulcahy and his staff, however, proceeded on the assumption that the convention would be held. The Watching Council of Four sent out election guidelines and IRA units throughout Ireland elected delegates to the proposed 26 March convention.

Mulcahy did not like the idea of a convention. He must have known that, regardless of the safeguards he tried to impose, he could not control it. His rationale, as well as his doubts and his fears, were all expressed in a memo he had prepared for the Dáil meeting on 28 February. In this document, Mulcahy freely admitted that the purpose of the convention was to elect an army executive which would control the army. The executive would draft a constitution which would spell out the relationship of the army to the state. This proposal, Mulcahy noted,

> reverts the control of the Army back to the days before the disbandment of the Volunteer executive. The object of this is to restore to the Army a control which shall be expressive of their feelings, and in which the Army as a whole may expect to have confidence.

He concluded his memo by justifying or rationalizing the setting up an independent army executive:

The setting up of an Executive in this way does not in actual fact take the Army away from the control of the Dáil. It but secures that, just as in the earlier days of the recent operations, the work of the Army shall be along lines agreed to, not only by the Dáil, but by its own Executive.[95]

For a minister for defence, it was an extraordinary admission. Simply put, the Dáil would not control the army. Mulcahy was compromising with the basic concept of civilian control of the army. He himself would not have framed it in those terms. Most likely, Mulcahy believed that he was fashioning a way to accommodate both the Dáil and the proposed army executive. It was a position, however, from which he would soon retreat.

The Limerick crisis, coupled with the allegations that delegates were being elected to the convention on the basis of their attitude to the Treaty—a violation of the agreement worked out at the 24 February meeting—and the rumored threat that the army would interfere in the upcoming election on the Treaty, all caused the government to reconsider allowing the convention to proceed. Mulcahy himself was obviously having second thoughts on the matter. During the afternoon of 15 March, just before the cabinet meeting, he and Gearoid O'Sullivan met Lynch. They discussed the possibility of putting an alternative resolution before the Convention—one which affirmed the allegiance of the army to the Dáil, disclaimed any intention on the part of the army to establish a military dictatorship and resolved to associate the IRA with whatever government would be set up after the elections. Lynch's response was that "it wouldn't do". He said:

> that the Convention will insist right away on an Executive controlling the Army, but that they will not interfere with the Provisional Government or any Government elected by the people.[96]

Lynch's response seems to have convinced Mulcahy that he could not recommend the Convention to the cabinet. Therefore, at that afternoon's meeting, Mulcahy informed his colleagues that "he could not guarantee that if this convention was held there would not be set up a body regarding itself as a military government not responsible to the people."[97] Nor could Mulcahy see any hope of passing a resolution disclaiming military government and pledging the loyalty of the IRA to whatever government the people elected. In response, the cabinet rescinded its previous decision and on 15 March proscribed the convention on the grounds that

> while the Dáil continued to exist it is the sole body in supreme control of the Army and that any effort to set up another body in control would be tantamount to an attempt to establish a Military Dictatorship.[98]

To ensure compliance with this prohibition, the Cabinet also decided that only officers who remained loyal and obeyed the orders of the Provisional Government would receive financial support.[99] This was an extension of an earlier decision of 27 February 1922, which stated that "no funds or other assistance would be given to any unit which did not guarantee not to interfere with an election and . . . [which] would support the Government elected."[100] Through the power of the purse, the cabinet was trying to force recalcitrant members of the IRA to behave themselves.

After the cabinet meeting, Mulcahy held a meeting with the divisional commandants. He informed them of the cabinet's decision. Mulcahy tried to convince them it was for the best, arguing "that the present arrangements as operating for the last couple of months made for strength in any contingency".[101] The southern divisions complained that promises were not being kept, but overall the reaction was, as one historian has aptly noted, discontented but muted.[102] Although President's Griffith's order prohibiting the convention was published the next day, Mulcahy still did not despair of reaching an accord over the convention. As had become a habit with him at this point, the minister for defence looked to Lynch and the 1st Southern for help.

On 20 March, Mulcahy attended a meeting of the officers of the 1st Southern Division. He proposed that yet another meeting of all brigade and divisional commandants be arranged and that at this meeting, they select a council of eight. This council would frame "definite proposals for associating the IRA with the Government elected by the Irish people".[103] This would, of course, circumvent any threat of a military dictatorship or any repudiation of a duly elected government.

The officers of the 1st Southern agreed to this proposal, but on two conditions: 1) that the convention be rescheduled for 16 April—the delay allowing the cabinet a graceful retreat; and 2) that recruiting for the civic guard be discontinued. The anti-Treatyites considered the civic guard, the police force, to be the paramilitary arm of the provisional government. These conditions were unacceptable to the cabinet and, once again, the magic formula for unity eluded the minister for defence.

Unity seemed even more precarious when the Republican Military Council—consisting of five divisional commandants and 29 brigade commandants—openly defied the cabinet's ban. On 23 March, the Council summoned members of the IRA to a convention. Mulcahy was now forced to act. He could not ignore this blatant challenge to the authority of the government which he represented as minister for defence.

In response to the calling of the convention, Mulcahy drafted a notice for the chief of staff to distribute to the army. He was obviously pained and distressed at the way in which events developed. Writing in a most conciliatory fashion, Mulcahy began:

All ranks will understand the intensity with which, in the face of our present very grave National position, means have been sought to avoid any definite breach in the solidarity and the organization of the Army, and in that wonderful brotherhood of the Army which has been its true solidarity and the real framework of its organisation. The calling of the sectional Convention against the orders of GHQ Staff breaks definitely, to some extent, this solidarity and this organisation, but it does not and must not break to any degree the brotherhood of those who in the past have worked and borne responsibility together.[104]

Mindful of his responsibilities as minister for defence, however, Mulcahy informed the chief of staff that anyone who attended this "sectional convention" will sever his connection with the IRA. Even this he softened, however, cautioning those officers in charge of issuing the ordered suspensions to "take the greatest pains to avoid any actions or expressions that would tend to create antagonisms amongst those who have been in the Army". Mulcahy ended with an appeal for unity:

Political friction has been forced into the Army from outside, but in face of the grave issues before our country we must anticipate that this friction will pass and that the fundamental unity of the Army will reassert itself.[105]

Somehow, despite all obvious signs to the contrary, Mulcahy clung to the belief that the army would hold together, that the army would overcome the political influences which threatened to destroy it.

In his interpretation of events since the signing of the Treaty, Mulcahy refused to recognize the role of the radical wing in the army in provoking the current crisis. He blamed the politicians. Mulcahy censured them for not reaching some agreement among themselves, for not finding a political compromise, and, by their failure, for causing disaffection in the army. Later, he would develop this theme more fully. He would indict the politicians for inciting the army to rebellion. Most especially, he would blame de Valera.

Mulcahy has been criticized for not allowing the convention to go forward as planned. By banning the meeting, he ensured that only anti-Treaty members of the IRA would be present and that they would control the proceedings and the resolutions. This argument has some merit. The convention which eventually did take place was solidly anti-Treaty and its decisions were a challenge to the provisional government and a repudiation of civilian control of the government. Had they attended, pro-Treaty delegates may have been able to ally themselves with the moderate Republican faction and perhaps temper the ultimate outcome.

On the other hand, those who attended the convention represented over half of the IRA. Thus, unless they were sure of gaining the support of some of the anti-Treaty delegates, the pro-Treaty representatives would have been outvoted. Mulcahy was aware of this possibility, claiming later that to have allowed a free convention would have given the disaffected section of the IRA the moral weight of claiming that they spoke for the entire army.[106] Moreover, it was not at all clear that the pro-Treaty delegates could be counted on not to change their position. Finally and most importantly, as minister for defence, Mulcahy had a responsibility to inform his cabinet colleagues of the very real danger that a convention posed. As hard as he tried, Mulcahy could not guarantee the outcome of such a convention, and it was his duty to make this point clear to the government.

The sectional or rump convention of the army took place on 26 March 1922. It was attended by 223 anti-Treaty delegates, representing 60 per cent of the army. There were no surprises. The delegates reaffirmed their allegiance to the Republic, denounced the Treaty, and elected an executive of 16 in whom they vested supreme control of the army. The executive repudiated the authority of the minister for defence and the chief of staff and most significantly, repudiated the authority of Dáil Éireann. Mulcahy's fear that a convention would formalize differences and lead to an open split had, unfortunately, been realized. So had his apprehensions about the convention disavowing the authority of the government.

While there was talk at the convention of seizing government funds, commandeering cars, and threats against the civic guards, the government was most concerned about the report that the executive forces intended "to declare the elections abortive or prevent them from being held".[107] There was speculation that the executive would try to impose a military dictatorship and overthrow the civilian government. Rory O'Connor fuelled this speculation with comments about the executive forces setting up its own government. When asked, he did not disclaim the idea of a military dictatorship.[108] When the executive forces destroyed the premises of the *Freeman's Journal* because they claimed it had distorted the proceedings of the convention in its articles, there were those who feared that rule by a rump military executive was underway.

It was not that decisive, however. The convention had brought all the anti-Treaty segments of the IRA together, but they themselves were not united. Nor was their next step obvious even to the most extreme among them. They argued and debated. And they set a date for a future meeting.

On 9 April, a second meeting of the convention delegates was held. Events now began to move dangerously fast. The delegates ratified a constitution and appointed a new headquarters staff. Liam Lynch was selected as chief of staff. On 13 April, Liam Mellows submitted an ultimatum to the Dáil cabinet setting out conditions for reunification of the army. In it, he demanded that the existing Republic be maintained under a republican Dáil government, that the IRA be controlled by an independent executive, that the IRA be financed by the Dáil, that the policing of the country be carried out by the IRA and the civic guard disbanded, and that no elections take place on the Treaty while the threat of war with England exists.[109] Obviously, these conditions were unacceptable to the Dáil cabinet.

On 14 April, a section of the executive forces occupied the Four Courts building. This was followed by the occupation of other buildings in Dublin. The parallel to 1916 was both obvious and striking. The Four Courts executive had both literally and symbolically challenged the government.

The government's initial response was to ignore the challenge. How long it could afford this posture, however, was unclear. Violence was spreading through the country—North and South. Ambushes were numerous. Robberies and raids were frequent. Dublin itself, quiet since the Truce, now rang with the sound of gunfire and shook from the force of explosives. If this were not civil war, it was a very good imitation of it.

The occupation of the Four Courts marked an important break for the IRA. Mulcahy's efforts to save the unity of the army had come to nought. His policy of courting the moderate faction of the opposition IRA had failed to prevent open confrontation. While negotiations would continue after 14 April, the decision to occupy the Four Courts strengthened the position of the more radical faction on each side. Mellows, O'Connor, and O'Malley were now in possession of a military headquarters and offered the IRA a clear choice in deciding who it would follow. On the government's side, the arguments of those who believed that no compromise was possible and who wanted to fight the Republicans immediately were immeasurably strengthened by this provocative action. It was becoming harder and harder to argue for patience and compromise. It was becoming more and more difficult to counsel moderation.

SIX

The End of a Dream

I want to suggest that we depart from all the little points of argument, on this, our 47th debate on the Treaty . . . .

Richard Mulcahy, TD

To The Men of the Army:
Stand calmly by your posts. Bend bravely and undaunted to your work. Let no cruel act of reprisal blemish your bright honour.

General Richard Mulcahy, Address to the Army on the Death of
Michael Collins

Throughout the spring of 1922, the violence intensified. In his report to the Dáil of 26 April, Mulcahy noted that the forces under the control of the Four Courts executive had "interfered with our officers and men in their work of organisation by: Attacks on persons, shootings of persons, Seizure of posts, Attacks on our transport, Systematic attacks on our military posts, Seizure of stores."[1] It must have been difficult for him to publicly acknowledge that discipline and order had broken down. But he would not allow the army to take the blame alone. There was an element of bitterness in Mulcahy's words as he went on to also indict the politicians who opposed the Treaty. The minister for defence argued that, despite their gross misconduct and frequent use of violence, the rump section of the IRA was still being lionized by the opposition. They were, in fact, being portrayed by these politicians "as the only true followers in Pearse's footsteps".[2] In Mulcahy's view, this made these politicians culpable and at least partially responsible for the disorder.

The violence, moreover, was not simply confined to the 26 counties of the South. The six counties of the North were plagued by rioting and dis-order as sectarian conflict escalated once again. In an effort to protect Northern Catholics, Collins had concluded a pact with James Craig, leader of the six counties. It was not working. Northern Catholics continued to be at risk. IRA leaders fretted and tried to figure out a way to help their co-religionists.

On 24 March, Mulcahy had written a memorandum to Arthur Griffith expressing his concern about the continuing violence in the six counties and the role of the British government in supporting and financing those who were responsible for the "extensive campaign of murder and violence". Mulcahy questioned the sincerity of British intentions and saw the situation in the North as so grave as to force him "to consider the re-setting of . . . [his] attitude with regard to the whole present political situation".[3]

Neither Collins nor Mulcahy could sit idly by as their co-religionists were victimized by a sectarian police force. Officially, they could do nothing. Unofficially, however, they could act. Accordingly, Mulcahy, O'Duffy and Lynch met with Frank Aiken, O/C of the 4th Northern Division to plan a strategy of defence. As a result of this meeting, arrangements were made to send men and to ship guns from the South to be used to defend Northern Catholics.[4] Apparently, Mulcahy arranged with Lynch to transfer arms. Unable to send arms directly from the national army—these were purchased from the British and could easily be identified—Mulcahy gave the Lynch faction weapons in return for which his IRA arms were shipped North.[5] It was a politically risky venture which, nevertheless, was an open secret among officers of the upper echelon of the army. Speaking in the Dáil, Liam Mellows, for example, openly stated that arms were to be shipped North.[6]

While the planned offensive in the North never really materialized, the fact that Mulcahy and by implication, Collins, were willing to take such a risk was highly significant. As historians have rightly noted, if discovered, this Northern venture could have wrecked the Treaty. The traditional interpretation is that Collins was so tormented by the sufferings of Catholics in the North and Mulcahy was so obsessed with the unity of the army that both men were prepared to take the gamble involved.[7] To these motives must be added the idea that the state supported violence against Northern Catholics seemed to Mulcahy, at least, to belie British sincerity and good will. In light of British intransigence over interpreting the terms of the treaty and their refusal to allow the pro-Treatyites some space from which to negotiate with their Republican colleagues, British complicity in the North must have been particularly galling. And, as one historian has noted, the joint planning on the North gave the pro-Treaty forces the opportunity to prove their faith and good will to the Four Courts executive.[8]

What is also very interesting about this whole affair is the amount of trust which Mulcahy and GHQ—and again indirectly Collins—placed in their disaffected colleagues. At any time, Lynch or any member of the Four Courts executive could have publicly disclosed in a detailed manner the plans for the North. While Liam Mellows spoke of the exchange of weapons in the Dáil, he mentioned it as yet another example of the broken promises of GHQ. Nor did Mellows name names or provide the particulars which would give his account credibility. In fact, he rather mentioned it in passing.[9] Perhaps there was still some loyalty and trust left among the officer corps of the IRA.

But bonds of affection were quickly vanishing. By early May, skirmishes between the two opposing armies had left 8 dead and 49 wounded. It looked as if a new round of killing was about to commence. As a result, everyone became involved in the business of putting forward peace proposals: the Bishops, the Labour Party, the IRB. Everyone, that is, except the members of the Dáil who continued to debate the Treaty *ad nauseam*. All these efforts failed.

Once again, it was left to the army officers, most of whom were members of the IRB, to find a formula to avert more death and open civil war. Officers from both sides once again came together to try to find a way to stop the violence. In fact, negotiations had never really ceased. In mid-April, an IRB effort to find a solution to the dilemma floundered.[10] Later that month, on 21 April, Sean Moylan of the Republican side, had put together suggestions which he thought might alleviate the crisis. His emphasis was on framing a Republican constitution regardless of what the British thought.[11] This was followed the next week by a proposal from Paddy Daly for a meeting of concerned IRA officers. He wrote to his colleagues that he believed that:

> Owing to the present State of our Country and where it is about to drift, if the present conditions prevail, I am convinced if sensible men on both sides come together it cannot but be possible to arrive at some solution . . .[12]

Daly's attitude was now prevalent among a number of IRA officers. There seemed to be a renewed belief in the power of negotiations. Collins had been meeting some of the Four Courts officers, and, in what appears to be a rather dramatic about face, Sean O'Hegarty, O/C, Cork No. 1 Brigade, spoke to both Collins and Mulcahy about possible suggestions for reunification of the army.[13]

All these conferences culminated in a meeting of ten officers—five from each side—on 1 May. Mulcahy was there. So was Collins. O'Hegarty, destined to play a major public roll in the next few days, participated, as did Dan Breen.[14] Basically, the officers felt that if something was not done, "a conflict of comrades is inevitable." This, they believed, would be "the greatest calamity in Irish history and would leave Ireland broken for generations". The gravity of the situation, therefore, demanded that the IRA close ranks and come together. Displaying a realism which was notably absent in many of their colleagues, the officers noted that the majority of the people accepted the Treaty, a fact all had to acknowledge. Thus, they proposed that there be an agreed election which would result in a government enjoying the confidence of the whole country and a reunification of the army based on the these points.[15]

The officers then took the extraordinary step of addressing the Dáil. A deputation of officers led by Commandant Sean O'Hegarty spoke to the deputies on 3 May. O'Hegarty was passionate but brutal. He left the Dáil under no illusions as to what he thought they had been doing or where the results of their lack of leadership was leading the country. Nor did he mince words in describing the Dáil sessions he had attended:

> What did I find? I found an atmosphere of absolute hostility, personalities indulged in across the room and . . . . utter irresponsibility as to what the country was like and the conditions in it.[16]

Neither side, moreover, was blameless. Each had to accept responsibility for the current state of affairs.

O'Hegarty stressed the need for the Dáil to exert some leadership. "The army two days ago was drifting," he said, "but it is now driving to destruction." If this drive continued, if the South became involved, there would be no way to stop it.

O'Hegarty concluded his address to the Dáil with a moving yet reasonable appeal to his Republican colleagues. What good would it do to insist on a Republic at the cost of civil war, he asked them. Civil war would destroy everything in its wake—Provisional Government, Free State and Republic. What did it matter what they named the government? He argued that

> when a crisis occurs in a country it is not the name of the Government that counts. It is the men. And if you can get the best men in Ireland into the Government, it does not matter under what auspices you put them when the crisis comes, because when the opportunity comes to setup a Republic it can be set up.[17]

O'Hegarty, the officer who had sent the threatening notices to TDs, who had authorized the destruction of the O'Rahilly pamphlet and intimidated the farmers, had come full circle.

The Dáil responded to O'Hegarty's address by setting up its own committee to try to negotiate a settlement. To spur them to any action, O'Hegarty had to be persistent. They quibbled about the terms of the motion. They ignored his request that the Dáil ask the army to effect a truce—a matter which he considered extremely urgent. In an exasperated manner, he turned on them and said:

> If this Committee [the Dáil peace committee] is going to do anything, there must be a truce between the two armies. I have a report now that there is heavy fighting going on in Kilkenny and that 18 have been killed. That is a good start—is it not? *And people are sitting down here discussing whether they will compromise themselves by stopping it.*[18] [Emphasis added.]

The Dáil never did act on the truce, but rather left it up to its peace committee to resolve.

Unlike the Dáil, the officers' committee realized the urgency of the situation and was intent upon stopping the "drive" to civil war. Accordingly, the committee brought together another group of officers—this one including Lynch, O'Connor, Mellows, Mulcahy, Collins and O'Duffy. On 4 May, these men successfully negotiated a truce. The purpose of this truce was to stop the violence so that negotiations for army unification could proceed in a more conducive atmosphere. Both sides agreed to co-operate to maintain order and prevent acts of aggression. The order was signed by the respective chiefs of staff, Lynch and O'Duffy.[19]

Mulcahy must have breathed a little bit easier at the signing of the truce. Not only did the truce give them time to negotiate, it pulled both armies back from the brink of civil war. O'Hegarty had verbalized Mulcahy's continuing nightmare—the rebellion of the South. Most likely, Mulcahy knew at this point, May 1922, that he would have to confront the "impossible people" in the Four Courts. That was different than fighting a full scale civil war. Mulcahy's aim was to insure that the South would not take up arms and join the forces of the Four Courts executive. He did not want to push them together through precipitous military action. The truce decreased pressure on the government forces to take action against their Four Courts colleagues.

But Mulcahy had to know that he was playing fast and loose with the whole concept of civilian control of the army. Once again, he was trying to juggle the demands of the Republicans with his responsibility to the civilian government. Two documents from the end of April indicate that this question was on his mind. The first document, although unsigned, appears to have been written by Mulcahy in an effort to justify the independent position of the army which the Four Courts executive was demanding. This argument provided Mulcahy with a way around the issue by arguing that members of the IRA took risks far beyond that of the ordinary citizen. And, as the citizen expressed his voice through the ballot box, "a citizen accepting soldier responsibilities should have a voice to something like the same percentage in the government of the Army."[20] While not terribly convincing, it could be a way out of the thorny issue of an elected army executive and was, most likely, a rationale with which Mulcahy was toying. This argument was important because in the negotiations which took place throughout the month of May, the question of an elected executive and an elected minister for defence would be key points.

The second document ran along similar lines. In what appears to be an intelligence report, the position of those in the Four Courts was explained. According to this document, the IRA could justify its demands for basically an independent army because:

the army was never really the army of the government. That Defence was simply a connective link with the Cabinet. That army executive planned the war and carried their plan—whether Cabinet was willing or not and that the Cabinet and Dáil were often most unwilling. That Cabinet refused to accept responsibility for shooting of police early on, particularly Arthur Griffith. That the mutineers simply want to revert to the old control which was not scrapped until September 1921.[21]

While Mulcahy would not totally agree with this interpretation, it certainly gave him some room to maneuver intellectually around the question of the relationship of the army to the government.

The minister for defence would need to be mentally agile and adept in the following weeks. After the truce was concluded, proposals and counter-proposals flowed freely—flowed like wine at the wedding at Cana. But unlike that event, there was no miracle, there was no one to turn the water of the Treaty into the wine of the Republic.

GHQ and the Four Courts executive began exchanging proposals for reunification. These proposals were premised on the assumption that some political arrangement would be worked out by the Dáil conciliation committee for an agreed election. At first, it did not look very promising. The Dáil conciliation committee failed to reach a compromise. While both sides would theoretically agree to a coalition government, talks broke down over the allocation of seats and the implicit recognition of the Treaty contained in various documents.[22] The politicians resorted to bickering again.

On 19 May, Mulcahy stood in the Dáil and made one of his most perceptive and persuasive speeches. In it, he protested against the "futility" of the debate and "the inclination to return to bitterness, which is getting back into this House". He reminded his colleagues of their responsibility to the country and of the "dangers, and disasters, and disorders that have been gathering day by day, month by month for the past three or four months". He asked for clear and direct information about the points which were dividing the two sides and warned against their indulging in oratory and rhetoric. Collins and de Valera had been negotiating. Mulcahy asked specifically that the House be informed as to what particular points divided them. They needed to discuss ways of overcoming these differences. And, very wisely, he suggested that the deputies "depart from all the little points of argument, on this, our 47th debate on the Treaty".[23]

Mulcahy was completely correct. His colleagues had been engaging in self-indulgent rhetoric at a time when the issues demanded restraint and good-will. Moreover, the Dáil was plagued by procedural difficulties and uncertainties, exacerbated by an atmosphere of distrust. No one seemed quite sure how to proceed. And, each side was jockeying for position.

Mulcahy's suggestion did bear fruit. Before adjourning that evening, the Dáil directed the former president and the minister for finance to submit reports on their conversations. An eleventh hour agreement secured a compromise. According to the Collins-de Valera pact, the two sides agreed to jointly contest the upcoming election as a Sinn Fein panel with the number for each side being their present strength in the Dáil. After the election, a coalition government would be formed with a president, a minister for defence, representing the army, and nine other ministers—five from the majority party and four from the minority party.

The agreement made elections possible. Despite its much discussed shortcomings, it provided the only chance for holding an election in anything resembling an orderly manner. Many did not like it—Griffith's response was angry acquiescence—but without it, a vote on the Treaty would have been impossible.[24] Despite the strained relations which would exist between de Valera and Mulcahy in the future, at this time de Valera claimed to have suggested that he, Stack, Mulcahy and MacNeill go to the South and speak on behalf of the panel candidates. De Valera thought that Collins and Griffith prevented them from going. The former president believed that this group of four could have agreed upon a "common line of action . . . worked the Pact and beaten England by it".[25] De Valera was probably correct in seeing in Mulcahy a less than an enthusiastic attachment to the treaty. He did, however, underestimate Mulcahy's loyalty to Collins.

Allowing the elections to proceed freely was a primary concern of those involved in both the political and military negotiations. Once that was agreed to, the key issue for Mulcahy was reunification of the army under a joint general staff and a minister for defence mutually agreeable to both sides. Under the terms of the Collins-de Valera agreement, the minister for defence would represent the army. The question was who would select the minister for defence.

Both sides exchanged proposals. Mulcahy and his staff suggested the election of an army council which would have the power to approve, by majority vote, the nominations of the minister for defence and the chief of staff. The government would appoint the minister and the minister would appoint the chief of staff.[26] Thus, the army would have a say in the selection but the regular process of ministerial appointments would be kept intact.

The initial response of the Four Courts executive as outlined by Liam Lynch was not very promising. They harkened back to the idea that the army must remain the army of the Republic under the control of an independent executive.[27] On 12 May, Lynch sent a letter to O'Duffy stating that no satisfactory progress had been made toward unification and that, if after a meeting on the 15th, a definite understanding was not reached, negotiations would cease. Lynch blamed the lack of progress on the fact that the government's officers were not "willing to discuss the vital matters at issue".[28]

However, Lynch's hard line position was being undermined—either wittingly or unwittingly—by O'Hegarty and his group. They indicated that Lynch's ultimatum was not "at all indicative of the frame of mind of the Four Courts people generally—that their mental attitude is that a settlement is coming about."[29] O'Hegarty seemed to be acting as an intermediary between the two sides at this point. During a conference with Mulcahy on 13 May, he discussed the possibility of Mulcahy conferring with Lynch and on the next day, the meeting took place. In his diary, Mulcahy recorded that he and Collins met Lynch and Deasy and that they had a "long talk as if there was no difficulties". It must have seemed like old times. When, however, they did discuss the current situation, it was quite pessimistic— "Statement that things can only last 24 hours."[30] This most likely referred to the truce, to the numerous accusations on both sides of violations, and to the growing sense of futility about the negotiations.[31]

There is some indication that Lynch was increasingly frustrated with his colleagues—a condition which would have cheered Mulcahy and raised his hopes for a settlement. According to a note from O'Hegarty to Mulcahy, the former had heard from one of the Four Courts negotiators, Sean Moylan, that "O'Connor was impossible and that Lynch is fed up".[32] The letter was not dated. However, according to Mulcahy's diary entries, O'Hegarty was in Dublin on 13 May 1922. This letter from the Cork commandant would appear to have been written a few days after this and is in keeping with Lynch's mood in his meeting with Mulcahy and Collins on 14 May. It was significant because it would strengthen Mulcahy's belief that he could isolate O'Connor and his diehard Republican comrades in the Four Courts.

Clearly, Mulcahy seemed to be enjoying a good relationship with O'Hegarty—something that was not always true during the war and the truce. This was particularly evident in the correspondence which passed between them concerning the takeover of barracks in the Cork area.

On 12 May, Mulcahy wrote to O'Hegarty that he desired the evacuation of the Cork Barracks (Ballincollig, Victoria, and Youghal) at the earliest possible moment and "as explained verbally, with a view to this we would be glad to have them handed over for occupation by members of the Cork No. 1 Brigade."[33] As noted earlier, Mulcahy asked for a guarantee that the brigade maintain order and try to allow the election to proceed as smoothly as possible.

Mulcahy's attitude was particularly noteworthy for its optimism. He was convinced that both sections of the army could be reunited and asked O'Hegarty to oversee "the satisfactory fusion of the men who have come over to GHQ within the last three or four months". He added the important proviso that difficulties were to be overcome in a "generous spirit and disciplinary matters made bygones". Moreover, Mulcahy ended his instructions to O'Hegarty with one of his most positive comments:

> Generally, I am satisfied as a result of our various talks here that
> all that is wanted is an agreement to work harmoniously and
> unsuspiciously, and to face any difficulties and suspicions that arise,
> calmly, and in some kind of a detached way.[34]

Mulcahy's optimism was not hard to understand. Peace negotiations
were underway on both the political and military fronts. His dealings with
O'Hegarty had probably strengthened his belief that he could avoid a full
scale civil war by, at the very least, keeping the south neutral. Moreover, if
Lynch and O'Hegarty could bring pressure on their colleagues in the Four
Courts, perhaps the entire issue could be negotiated quietly and without
recourse to arms.

There were still difficulties to be overcome, problems to be resolved,
however. First of all, there were complications with the transfer of barracks
in Cork. The segment of the IRA which had remained loyal to GHQ
strongly protested against the take over of the barracks by anti-Treaty
forces. One loyal officer viewed Mulcahy's decision as the "greatest blow I
ever got in my life". In an angry letter, he informed the Dublin command
that their decision had cost them the support of a great number of their
followers and had humiliated them in the community:

> We are sneered at by our enemies and scowled at by all the friends
> whom we unwittingly made idiots of. All this may not bother you
> people in Dublin, but it means the h-l of a lot to us down South. I
> wish GHQ knew the situation as it really is, but I daresay it is
> criminal to even suggest anything to them. Our Organisers are
> being threatened, assaulted and kidnapped every other day with no
> redress. We must only grin and bear it I presume.[35]

Another officer wrote to O'Duffy that he had been promised Victoria
Barracks and told to "be ready", but now was being completely ignored.
His pride was also wounded, feeling that he and his men were the
"laughing stock of our enemies". He was willing to send his men to up
to Dublin to Beggars Bush, but they lacked the train fare and were
waiting for vouchers from the adjutant-general. If at least this would
come through, he felt the situation would be improved.[36] The chief of
staff, O'Duffy, agreed with these officers. At the very least, he argued,
loyal officers should be given control of the barracks at Youghal.[37]

The fact that the second letter spoke of the financial distress of a number
of men of the IRA was significant. This distress would be alleviated if GHQ
sanctioned their taking over of barracks. Then the men were paid as well as
housed and fed. It was an important consideration. In the early days of the
split, Liam Lynch had alluded to the financial factor when he wrote to
Mulcahy asking him what he was suppose to do "with those thousands of
men who have sacrificed everything during the war. The Nation I am sure
will not allow this situation to continue."[38] But the situation did continue
and, in fact, deteriorated.

1 Richard Mulcahy, commander-in-chief, November 1922

2 A photograph taken at Coosan Camp near Athlone, Co. Westmeath, in
1915. All were members of the Irish Volunteers who had broken with
Redmond at the start of the first World War. Mulcahy is second from the left.

3 Prisoners leaving Knutsford Gaol under military escort and led by Denis
McCullough, the President of the IRB until shortly before the 1916 rebellion. The
prisoners, among whom were Mulcahy, were on their way to Frongoch (Wales).

4 Thomas Ashe,
a photograph taken
after the Rising

5 An early photograph
of Eamon de Valera

MICHAEL COLLINS, M.P.

RICHARD MULCAHY, M.P.

Special note is to be made of these men's features by all ranks. + if they are recognised it should be reported at **ANY** officer or the earliest opportunity. If no officer available to Civil Police.

6 British Intelligence notice issued during the War of Independence, reading: "Special note is to be made of these men's features by all ranks and if they are recognised it should be reported at any officer at the earliest opportunity. If no officer available to Civil Police."

7 (left to right) Seán MacEoin, Richard Mulcahy, Seán Moylan and Eóin O'Duffy during the Truce, 1921

8 Auxiliaries in a Truce Day scene in Dublin

9 Arthur Griffith and Eamonn Duggan

10 General Michael Collins and General Richard Mulcahy leading the Army at the funeral of Arthur Griffith, Dublin, August 1922

11 A painting by Leo Whelan of the General Headquarters Staff at the time of the Truce, July 1921. Seated (from left): Michael Collins, director of intelligence; Richard Mulcahy, chief of staff; Gearoid O'Sullivan, adjutant-general; Eamonn Price, director of organization; Rory O'Connor, director of engineering; Eóin O'Duffy, deputy chief of staff; Sean Russell, director of

munitions; Seán McMahon, quartermaster-general. Standing (from left): J.J.
O'Connell, assistant chief of staff; Emmet Dalton, director of training; Seamus
O'Donovan, director of chemical; Liam Mellows, director of purchases, and
Piaras Beaslai, editor of *An tÓglach*. The original is on loan to the Irish Army
from the Mulcahy family.

12

13

12 Mulcahy inspecting the guard of honour at Collins Barracks, the last barracks taken over from the British (December 1922)

13 An army patrol with its Crossley tender, on active duty during the Civil War

14 An Irregular column (Brian McNeill's) in Sligo during the Civil War

15 An Irish Free State army patrol on active duty during the Civil War

16 Mulcahy, commander-in-chief, with officers of the National Army
in Kilkenny, in the fall of 1922

17 Liam Lynch,
chief of staff of the IRA,
killed in action
at Knockfallen, Co. Tipperary,
10 April 1923

▽**18** General Richard Mulcahy,
commander-in-chief of the Irish
Army and minister for defence,
hoisting the tricolour over GHQ,
Parkgate, Dublin, on St Patrick's
Day 1923. He is assisted by
Major-general Daniel Hogan, O/C
Dublin Command at that time.
Father Seán Piggot was then
Chaplain to the Forces.

19 A German newspaper report on the 1923 election, showing Mulcahy at the hustings

20 The founding of the Army School of Music. Standing (left to right) Professor John Larchet, Commandant F. Sauerzweig, Denis McCullough; seated: Mrs Richard Mulcahy, Col. Fritz Brasé, Richard Mulcahy, Mrs Larchet

21 Mulcahy, minister for defence, at his desk, 1924

22 Mulcahy leaving his family to conduct a nationwide campaign before the 1948 election and the setting up the first inter-party government: (left to right) Neillí, now Mrs Thomas Bacon; Risteárd; Mrs Mulcahy; and Elizabeth, now Mrs Gerard Berney

Part of the reason for the growing disorder and crime rate was that those units of the IRA who did not accept GHQ's authority were not receiving any form of support. To maintain themselves, therefore, they commandeered supplies, raided post offices for money, and survived as best they could through illegal means. As one historian has rightly noted the unrest in the period leading up to the formal outbreak of civil was:

> as much the result of local rivalry, dissatisfaction with the provisions made by headquarters for the welfare of the men, anxiety about the future, physical and financial distress, indiscipline amongst certain brigades, as it was about the allegiance to the republic.[39]

The events in Cork support this interpretation.

By the end of May, prospects for army unity were much brighter. An agreed election with a coalition government and the promise of a republican Constitution all seemed to point to an end to the division in the army. In addition, Mulcahy and Collins had come to an agreement with the Four Courts executive that resulted in the evacuation of all buildings in Dublin except for the Four Courts. Moreover, a tentative army council was set to consider the question of unity of command. Mulcahy saw this as an important step. He felt that the army council would be able "to issue whatever Public Notices are necessary to re-assure people generally".[40]

The chief of staff shared his feelings. So optimistic was O'Duffy about the reunification of the army that on 22 May 1922, he asked Mulcahy to relieve him of his position of chief of staff. O'Duffy noted that he had only agreed to serve because he felt it was his duty to do everything he could to secure unity. Now he believed that there was a good prospect of army unification and hoped "that the army situation . . . [would] be definitely settled up say by 1 July". Therefore, he asked that his resignation be accepted by that date.[41]

It all seemed so close. Mulcahy and O'Duffy were arranging with Lynch for a joint command at GHQ, deciding on the allotment of offices. It appeared as if both sides had accepted certain basic premises and that all that was left was to work out the details. Mulcahy, for his part, was working on the assumption that the minister for defence and the chief of staff would be from the government's party. He had agreed to an army convention to be held on 10 July. The convention would elect an army council which would oversee army affairs as well as approve, by majority vote, the selection of minister for defence and chief of staff. According to Mulcahy's scheme, Lynch would be appointed deputy chief of staff with responsibility for reorganizing the army. Thus, GHQ would have the chief of staff, the adjutant-general and the quartermaster-general. The Four Courts executive would nominate the deputy chief of staff, the director of intelligence and the director of training.[42]

Mulcahy had gone as far as he was able or willing to go. On 5 June, he had informed the provisional government that he had agreed to an army council of eight. It was to consist of himself, O'Duffy, O'Sullivan, Florrie O'Donoghue, Mellows, Lynch, O'Connor and Sean Moylan. The cabinet insisted that the government side be bolstered by the addition of Diarmuid O'Hegarty. There was obviously not total agreement and "further consideration of this matter was deferred."[43]

The next day, Mulcahy wrote to Sean O'Hegarty about the progress of the negotiations. Mulcahy noted that he expected Lynch to arrange for him to meet the executive of the Four Courts. More significantly, Mulcahy admitted to O'Hegarty that he was having some difficulty with the Cabinet:

> I, meantime, have created consternation amongst the Government by letting them know I have more or less agreed to an agreed Army Council the majority of whom were more or less in arms against the Government until a day or two ago; and of whose general attitude they have absolutely no guarantee at the moment.[44]

However, Mulcahy did not anticipate serious trouble from his cabinet colleagues. He was more concerned that negotiations would falter. He feared that he would be forced to call a meeting of all divisional and brigade commandants and ". . . [put] the situation up-to-date before them, in order to force the hand of some of the more impossible people."[45]

His fear was well grounded. The Four Courts executive could not accept his distribution of positions. In particular, they objected to the government's representative occupying the position of chief of staff. On 7 June, Lynch informed Mulcahy that:

> we are agreeable to present M/D until sanctioned or otherwise by next Convention. Executive insists on C/S, but are prepared to give Beggar's Bush Forces D/C/S/, Q/M/G, D/Publicity, and an agreed A/General.[46]

He added that the executive of the Four Courts was pressing for another convention immediately and, unless this proposal were agreed to, they would call one for the 18 June 1922.

Later that same day, Mulcahy informed the cabinet that the executive forces had insisted that they nominate the chief of staff. The cabinet decided "that this proposal could not be entertained".[47] The matter did not end there, however. There was obviously additional contact between Lynch and Mulcahy because on 8 June, Lynch gave a guarantee that if he were appointed the chief of staff, he would do his utmost to maintain the stability of the army and would not "endeavour to overthrow the administration of the Government to be formed as a result of the elections on June 16th even though Mr. De Valera or any of his party do not become members of that Government. . . ."[48] The guarantee was signed in the presence of Sean O'Hegarty and Florrie O'Donoghue, neither of whom were part of the radical wing of the executive forces.

This arrangement was seemingly worked out between Mulcahy and Lynch and not with the full executive of the Four Courts. Thus Ernie O'Malley wrote to Mulcahy on 10 June 1922, reiterating the executive's demand for the position of chief of staff and informing the minister for defence that "the appointments allotted to the IRA executive [will] be filled by that executive".[49] The Four Courts faction, moreover, had decided that the negotiations had gone on long enough and stated that they would not continue the talks after noon on 12 June.

Allegedly, there was some disagreement among the members of the Four Courts executive. At their meeting of 11 June 1922, they debated the merits of accepting the government's right to appoint the minister for defence and the chief of staff, thus effectively guaranteeing them control of the army. The executive rejected the motion by fourteen votes to four. After this defeat for the moderates, Tom Barry called for a convention to consider the question of resuming the war against Britain.[50]

Mulcahy himself could go no further in the negotiations. He responded to O'Malley's letter by pointing out that he and his colleagues had made numerous and wide-ranging concessions so as to try every possible means for a rapprochement. They had hoped that their proposals would have been met "in a spirit not less generous than our own". This was not the case. Moreover, Mulcahy added that he believed that:

> Our proposals go beyond what I, personally, would consider we were entitled to go to in the absence of such a spirit, and considering the very great national responsibility that rests upon us.[51]

The minister for defence then bowed out of all further negotiations. Responsibility would be left to the new Coalition government when it assumed power. That same day, the cabinet decided that private negotiations should cease.[52]

Mulcahy's letter to O'Malley was somewhat curious. It seems that Mulcahy believed that he had risked the displeasure of his cabinet colleagues, had, in fact, made concessions he should not have, only to have these rejected by the executive. It was like a slap in the face. Hence, in the first paragraph of the letter, he made a detailed point of noting that the allotment of staff positions was not really a "suggestion per se", but simply an indication of what the positions on staff would probably be. In addition, he added his disclaimer that the negotiations went beyond terms with which he himself was comfortable. Mulcahy was apparently stung by the rejection of what he considered generous terms. He was also probably covering his political flank.

Mulcahy realized that there were important considerations about civilian control of the army at stake in these negotiations. He had already agreed to have the government's choice for minister for defence ratified by an army council. It was a major concession. Moreover, inherent in all the reunification proposals and explicitly stated in the Collins–de Valera pact was the assumption that the minister for defence was a representative of the army and its interests. It was another major concession—one which, in fact, would have seriously undermined the subservience of the army to the government. Both Collins and Mulcahy were taking great risks, believing that once the army had been reunited, they could control its independent spirit and harness it to the government. Interestingly enough, later on, Mulcahy himself would be accused of just such a charge, of representing the army in the cabinet. Certainly, Mulcahy's perception of his functions and his role as minister for defence must have been influenced by the discussions and events of this period.

The exchange of documents was not quite over. The last thrust was left to the Four Courts executive. On 15 June, O'Connor and O'Malley handed Mulcahy a copy of the resolutions passed at their executive meeting the day before. It stated that negotiations must cease, that the executive forces would take "whatever action may be necessary to maintain the Republic against British aggression," but that no offensive action would be taken against Beggars Bush (government) troops.[53]

In reality, this ended the negotiations to reunify the army. All the work, time, energy, and patience had come to nought. From GHQ's perspective, they had exhausted all possible alternatives. They also knew, however, that they had made good use of the time to begin establishing a national army. From the die-hard Republican viewpoint, the time spent in negotiations was worse than wasted. They also knew that GHQ was establishing its own army which they believed was aimed at undermining the IRA. They were determined to stop that erosion.

On 18 June, the Four Courts executive summoned a convention. Tom Barry proposed his motion that the IRA declare war on Britain; Lynch argued for Mulcahy's compromise. Barry's motion was won. A recount was demanded. The second time it lost. Those who supported Barry's measure left the convention after they were defeated. They retreated to the Four Courts, closing the doors, literally and figuratively, against those who opposed them. The IRA split again. The Four Courts executive deposed Lynch as chief of staff and elected McKelvey as his successor. Lynch took up headquarters at the Clarence hotel in Dublin as head of that segment of the IRA who opposed Barry's motion.

The split in the Four Courts forces was soon overshadowed by political events. On the eve of the election, the constitution was completed. Collins' hope of a Republican constitution was dashed upon the rocks of British intransigence. For their own reasons, the British government forced the Irish to adhere strictly to the terms of the Treaty and its legal restrictions. The slim hope that somehow a constitution could be constructed which would blend the concepts of a Free State and a Republic in a form acceptable to both the British, on the one hand, and the Republicans, on the other, were dashed. It was never a very realistic option, but was rather a daring gamble by Collins to preserve national unity. The promise of a Republican constitution was also, as Mulcahy allegedly later remarked, "finessing a little too much with honour".[54]

Under the constitution, there was no way that those who supported the Treaty and those who supported an unfettered Republic could co-exist in one government. Collins repudiated the Pact. It did not matter. As both Treatyites and Republicans had known all along, the people supported the agreement with England. The Irish people voted for peace, but four days after the results of the election were announced, they would again be at war.[55]

The election gave the government a moral authority which it previously lacked. Now they could claim a mandate from the people to implement the Treaty and establish the Free State. The elections ended an agonizing hiatus. It strengthened the position of those who believed that a duly elected government—despite the Pact or claims of an outdated register—could not tolerate rebellion in its midst.

If the provisional government was strengthened by the election, it was undermined by ensuing events. On 22 June 1922, two London IRA men shot and killed Sir Henry Wilson. Wilson had been an anathema to Irish nationalists, identified with the persecution and murder of Catholics in the North and with the forces who frustrated nationalist ambitions for a unified 32-county state. No one knew who had ordered the attack, but the British blamed the men in the Four Courts.[56] Wilson's death gave the British an excuse to exert additional pressure on the provisional government to move against the Four Courts. This had been their aim from the beginning. The British believed that if the government were serious about the Treaty, they would have to rid themselves of the Four Courts executive. Certainly, the events of the 18 June army convention did not dissuade them from this analysis. Wilson's murder was simply another weapon with which they could badger the Irish government.

It was not external pressure from the British, however, which caused the final rupture and an open declaration of war by the Provisional government. It was rather the pressure of internal events. On 26 June, in retaliation for the arrest of one of their officers, the Four Courts executive kidnapped Ginger O'Connell, assistant chief of staff. According to Ernie O'Malley, the Four Courts executive had considered kidnapping either Collins, Mulcahy or O'Connell. They settled on O'Connell.[57] The Four Courts executive sent a message to the chief of staff that O'Connell was being held as a hostage pending the release of their officer, Henderson.[58] They thought it would be a simple exchange of prisoners. The provisional government did not view it that way. This was a direct affront to their dignity as well as to their authority.

The cabinet convened that afternoon. They discussed the situation—Wilson's murder, the kidnapping, the threat to attack the British. The ledger was piling up on the side of those who wanted action. Yet, they deferred a definite decision, delaying what now seemed inevitable for just a bit longer. At the end of the meeting, Collins is alleged to have remarked to Mulcahy, "I think we'll have to fight these fellows." To which Mulcahy replied that while he was certain Collins was right, the decision was better left to the morning.[59] Most likely, Collins was referring only to the men in the Four Courts. Both he and Mulcahy knew of the split between Lynch and the Four Courts men. This would have made the decision more palatable. It certainly made the course they were embarking on seem more circumscribed, more limited.

On the next day, 27 June, the provisional government issued a formal notice to the Four Courts executive to evacuate the law building and all other buildings in Dublin and to surrender their arms and property. Refusal to comply with this demand would result in the government taking the "necessary military action".[60] Ernie O'Malley claimed that the men in the Four Courts did not take the ultimatum seriously.[61] They should have. The drift to civil war had stopped. The much dreaded and talked about nightmare had become a reality.

The attack on the Four Courts began in the early morning of Wednesday, 28 June 1922. Borrowing heavy artillery from the British, the government's army bombarded the Four Courts. There could be no mistaking the similarity to 1916. Instead of vacating the Four Courts and reverting to the type of fighting that had served them so well in the war of independence, the Republicans modelled themselves on the Easter Rising. To the men in the Four Courts, it was a replay of 1916, only the uniforms had been changed. Their proclamation made this explicit by invoking the "sacred spirit of the illustrious Dead" and claiming that their motto, like that of the men of 1916 was "Death before Dishonour".[62] The men of the Four Courts believed they were fighting to uphold an ideal against the tyranny of the majority. Like the men of 1916, they would be forced to surrender their positions. But unlike the men of 1916, their rebellion did not spark the people to another fight. The Republicans may have viewed the government as simply the British in green uniforms. The people, however, did not. This was the critical difference.

Both sides knew that, as in the war of independence, the support of the people would be critical. The Four Courts executive had forced the government into firing the first shot. The government did its best to justify its position. In its official statement, the government explained that it had warned the "lawless and irresponsible" element in the Four Courts that "having received an emphatic mandate from the Irish people, [the government] would no longer tolerate any interference with their liberty and property." They claimed the Republicans "insolently defied" this warning.

And, when the assistant chief of staff was kidnapped, the government argued that it had no choice but to respond to this "direct challenge to its authority" and order the army to take action. The government's statement ended with a denial of the "false and malicious" rumors that British troops were helping the army shell the Four Courts and stated that:

> None but the regular Irish forces—with the co-operation of the citizens who are loyally and enthusiastically supporting the Government—are engaged in putting down the disorderly elements who attempt to tyrannise over the people and defy their will.[63]

This was the theme which the government would pound home time and time again. It was fighting a war to vindicate the principles of democratic government and majority rule. In its view, a section of the army had mutinied against Dáil Eireann and repudiated the expressed will of the people. Both the Dáil and the people had voted for the Treaty. Now it was the responsibility of the government to uphold that vote and quell the rebellion. To counteract the Republican view that they were carrying on the fight of the men of 1916, the cabinet argued that:

> The Irish Army, therefore, is fighting for the same principle as that for which we fought the British: the right of the Irish People to be masters in their own country, to decide for themselves the way in which they shall live, and the system by which they shall be governed. For that principle they have made, and are prepared to make further sacrifices. Many have died, many have been wounded. They have died and are suffering that the people of Ireland may be free.[64]

The war of words, the war to win the hearts of the people, was now also underway. No one would win. Despite extensive use of propaganda of both sides, the horror of civil war would mark both the victors and the vanquished.

In the beginning, the army saw its task as putting down the "disorderly elements", not as fighting full-scale hostilities. Neither Collins nor Mulcahy saw it as the beginning of civil war. Collins, at one point, referred to the operations in Dublin as teaching the Republicans a lesson.[65] While acknowledging that additional lessons might be necessary, Collins' thinking seemed to be running along the lines of defeating the Four Courts executive in Dublin and perhaps fighting in isolated instances elsewhere.

Mulcahy's treatment of Lynch can be explained only on this basis. During the bombardment of the Four Courts, Lynch was arrested as he was leaving Dublin to head for the south. He was released on Mulcahy's order. Mulcahy did not realize that Lynch and his followers had mended their ties with the Four Courts executive. The minister for defence was still hoping that Lynch could be a force for peace by keeping the south neutral. It was a serious error in judgment. As Mulcahy himself stated:

> Liam Lynch was to Cork from a military point of view what de
> Valera was on the political side. *That is the thing couldn't have been
> what it was without him.*[66] (Emphasis added.)

Mulcahy later admitted his mistake in ordering Lynch's release without
personally talking to him.[67] Had he spoken to him, Mulcahy would have
realized that the Free State's attack on the Four Courts had unified the
Republicans and swung Lynch over to the position that he would have to
fight the government.[68] As Liam Deasy aptly noted, the attack marked "the
end of a dream".[69]

The bombardment of the Four Courts lasted two days. Under the command of General Daly, the Dublin Guards—the nucleus of whom came
from Collins' old Squad and his active service unit—organized and executed the attack against the Republican forces. They repeatedly shelled the
law courts. The Four Courts garrison held out until 30 June. The national
army demanded unconditional surrender. Rory O'Connor, Liam Mellows,
Joseph McKelvey and Ernie O'Malley were among the Irregular leaders
taken as prisoners. Of these four, only O'Malley managed to escape.

Although the Four Courts garrison surrendered, fighting continued to
rage in other parts of Dublin, especially in O'Connell Street. The government ordered the attack on the other Republican strongholds to be
"vigorously continued".[70] Casualties mounted and the list of deaths grew.
Cathal Brugha, for example, charged out of a burning hotel, revolvers
blazing, and was shot to death. The fighting left the capital city scarred and
deformed, an omen of things to come. For approximately one week of
fighting, the cost of damages was estimated at between three million and
four million pounds. The cost in human life was much higher, much more
dear, 65 killed and 281 wounded.[71] Civil war was a grim reality.

Collins' thoughts turned to avoiding further bloodshed. In a memo prepared in the early days of July, he noted the importance of keeping open
some avenue to peace, of giving the Republicans a chance to surrender
their arms and keep their principles—providing they would agree to engage
in only constitutional opposition. He was willing to afford them every
opportunity to win the people to their point of view, if only they would
accept the authority of the government. His concern to avoid further
fighting was obvious when he wrote: "If they don't accept [our] offer, any
further blood is on their shoulders. The onus [is] placed unmistakably on
their shoulders."[72]

The Republicans saw it differently. The government had fired the first
shots. They would defend themselves in Dublin and throughout the country. Lynch returned to the south and established the Republic of Munster.
Neither side had any general plan of campaign in the early days. But still
the fighting continued.

There was an atmosphere of chilling uncertainty. No one knew how
long the fighting would last or how extensive it would be. No one was

sure of anyone's loyalties. Soldiers and officers switched sides openly or helped the opposing side covertly. Once Lynch joined in the fight, it was clear that the south would be a center of resistance. Some of the best, most experienced IRA men were from that area and out against the government. Moreover, the O/C and all the battalion commanders in Dublin and most of the officers of the Western Division took up arms against the government.

One division which remained neutral in the beginning was the 4th Northern Division under the command of Frank Aiken. Aiken had been a voice for moderation, urging his comrades to wait for the constitution before they held an army convention—a position quite close to Mulcahy's. Once it became clear that the constitution would not offer the Republicans any loopholes, Aiken and his officers insisted that the provisional government provide a constitutional way for the Republican party to carry on towards a Republic. Up until the middle of July, the 4th Northern did not take part in the fighting, although technically they were under the control of the government. Aiken had assured Mulcahy that he would not fight against the government because a civil war would "only ruin the country without gaining any ground for the Republic".[73]

There were, however, a series of misunderstandings about, and difficulties with, the neutrality of the 4th Northern. Mulcahy was informed that, at a meeting of the officers of the 4th Northern, they decided not to give any moral or material support to the government if it did not act on their recommendation that the Republicans be provided with a constitutional alternative. They suggested that the cabinet withdraw the oath as a condition for being admitted into the parliament and again resurrected the idea of unifying the IRA under an elected army council.

More importantly, GHQ heard that at this same meeting the 4th Northern had rescinded its neutrality and decided to attack government troops. The national army, therefore, attacked and took over their barracks at Dundalk. Aiken claimed that GHQ's information was wrong.[74] Mulcahy offered to release the arrested officers if they would sign an assurance that they would not wage war against the government. Aiken gave him a verbal assurance, but balked at any written guarantee. Mulcahy must have known that the demands of the 4th Northern officers were untenable and that sooner or later it would put them into the Republican camp. He acted first and had Aiken arrested. Perhaps remembering his mistake with Lynch, Mulcahy took no chances.

Aiken accused him of duplicity. He wondered what had become of his former comrade since he had become minister for defence. Aiken claimed that Mulcahy had changed and that his old friend had not realized this, that "some of us were brought by our love and respect for Dick Mulcahy our old chief of staff to agree with some actions of the minister for defence that we did not think quite right." He pleaded with Mulcahy not to force

the oath of allegiance on either the army or the country. Aiken suggested
that Mulcahy "cast off governmental entanglements and literally take an
hour to himself with my letter on a mountain at least 1,000 feet high and
get the fresh air about him".[75] Obviously, he felt that Mulcahy had to clear
his head of the corrosive and corrupting notions which the Treaty had
foisted on him. There is no evidence that Mulcahy ever took Aiken's
advice. However, the evidence does show that the 4th Division did not
remain neutral but rather joined the ranks of the Republicans. Aiken and
his men escaped, returned and recaptured the barracks. Aiken, of course,
went on to be one of the leading figures of the Republican movement.

Both sides courted neutrals like Frank Aiken. Both sides also tried to
influence the press in order to garner support for their position—a lesson
they learned from the Anglo-Irish war. With the attack on the Four
Courts, the government had begun to censor reports of which it did not
approve. At a cabinet meeting on 28 June 1922, the ministers decided that
references in newspapers to the military situation in Dublin should be
censored by the government.[76] The military, in particular, was worried by
the tendency of the press in early July to announce the end of the fighting
in Dublin or throughout the country. This, they probably reasoned, would
raise false hopes and expectations.[77] The press did not respond the way the
government had hoped. Not satisfied with the results, the cabinet further
decided that representatives of the Dublin newspapers should "be
summoned for an interview at regular intervals, with a view to putting the
situation clearly before them". While the cabinet saw immediate results in
both the *Freeman's Journal* and the *Irish Times*, the *Irish Independent* still
remained unsatisfactory. The cabinet decided that if this paper persisted in
their attitude—characterized as an "unsatisfactory attitude toward the
Government"—"drastic action would be necessary".[78]

The Irregulars, on the other hand, took a more direct approach. They
obstructed the delivery of hostile newspapers and thus large quantities of
newspapers simply never made it to their destination. Moreover, because
their strength was in the south, in particular in Cork, they looked to that
area's dominant newspaper for support. As a report to GHQ on the
situation in Cork pointed out:

> Propaganda has played a large part in deciding "whichway" for
> many. The *Examiner* is doing incalculable harm in this respect
> amongst the people in the country.[79]

The Irregulars also made extensive use of handbills, and pamphlets.
Erskine Childers was the original director of Irregular publicity. His facility
with words in the propaganda war made him a prime target for the wrath
of some in the government. In addition, the Irregulars took the propaganda
war abroad. To counter the government's influence in the United States,
they decided in August 1922 to send two of their men to America both to

solicit funds and to explain the Republican position to Irish-American groups.[80]

The printed attacks from both sides grew more vicious. At one point, Collins objected to the tone which the government press was adopting toward active Irregulars and political opponents. He wrote to Cosgrave— the acting chairman of the provisional government—protesting the fact that much of the criticism of their opponents had degenerated into abuse. This he found objectionable. While he admitted that many of the leaders on the opposing side deserved to be abused, he pointed out that:

> The men who are prepared to go to the extreme limit are misguided, but practically all of them are sincere. Our propaganda should be on a more solid and permanent basis even if what may look to be advantages have to be sacrificed. . . . we must avoid anything that savours of personal abuse.[81]

It was statesman-like advice.

War news was not the army's prime concern, however. Once it became clear that there was to be serious military opposition against the government, the national army had to be prepared to fight. To help ensure their success, Mulcahy believed it was essential that Collins be clearly associated with the army:

> Collins had such a name in the army that I felt that he had to be brought into the active military command and the obvious place for him as chairman of the Provisional Government was that he would come in as the commander-in-chief of the army and that I would come back into the army and act as his chief of staff to deal with real war situation.[82]

Thus, on 12 July, Collins announced the changes in the army to the cabinet. He himself would become general commander-in-chief, and Mulcahy would be general chief of staff and minister for defence. Because of his new role, Collins resigned from his ministerial positions, and William T. Cosgrave was appointed acting head of the provisional government and minister for finance. In addition, Collins informed his colleagues that a War Council of Three had been established, consisting of himself, Mulcahy and O'Duffy, now general in command South Western Division.[83]

The leaders of the army faced a monumental task. First of all, the size of the army had to be increased. On 6 July, the provisional government issued a call to arms in the guise of a victory statement. While claiming that "the valor and patriotism of our National Army have broken the conspiracy to override the will of the nation and subject the people to a despotism based on brigandage," the government, nonetheless, called for men to join the army.[84] Within three weeks, the government had approved Collins' request for an army of 15,000 regulars and of 20,000 reservists.[85]

Mulcahy and Collins resumed their old partnership at Portobello Barracks. It served them well in the months ahead. Their complementary personalities, their common methodical attention to detail and their mutual insistence on rigorous organization gave the national army a dynamic combination at its very core. Mulcahy, for example, would have understood perfectly Collins' impatience with Ginger O'Connell's report which, the commander-in-chief pointed out and underlined for emphasis, was not timed and contained vague references.[86] The chief of staff could have written the criticism himself with no difficulty. Moreover, Mulcahy very likely agreed with Collins' suggestion that GHQ receive a daily report from each of the O/C's on conditions in their command.[87] This would give GHQ a detailed knowledge of the military situation throughout Ireland almost immediately and enable them to make decisions and plans from a more knowledgeable and broader perspective. In utilizing this approach, both Collins and Mulcahy reverted back to the tactics and techniques which had worked so successfully in the Anglo-Irish war.

By August, it was absolutely vital to have the kind of detail which Collins and Mulcahy insisted upon. Because they knew the forms, the language and the type of communications which the national army used, Irregular leaders could send bogus orders to the government's troops. Departing from his insistence during the Anglo-Irish war on anonymity, Mulcahy now insisted that all communications from any army department be signed with a full name, rank and staff, command or unit. Also, every communication was to dated and timed exactly—when it was received or when it was dispatched.[88] It was a necessary precaution.

Mulcahy and Collins also seemed to have devised a very satisfactory arrangement for dividing responsibility. They conferred at length together and with their officers about strategy. Then each would take on the task for which he was most suited. For example, when it came to dealing with the problem of Cork, Collins and Mulcahy jointly decided on a sea landing. But it was Collins who followed up on the organization of the attack—locating the ship, for example, or seeing about supplies.[89] This division certainly facilitated the work which had to be accomplished.

Mulcahy's job was to direct the army from headquarters. Not only did he work very closely with Collins on issues of strategy and tactics, he also worked with the GHQ staff to oversee the development of the army which was rapidly coming into being. Starting with a nucleus of about 4,000 men, GHQ began to raise, train and equip a professional army. The national army would be quite different from the guerrilla units of the IRA.

The decision to increase the size of the army placed an immediate burden on GHQ. Not only did this new force have to be trained and equipped, it had to be clothed, housed and fed. Given the fact that the national army was so hastily assembled and under the strained conditions of civil war, the work of Mulcahy and GHQ deserves much praise. That is not to say, however, that there were not serious problems. There were.

Mulcahy received a flood of complaints about the various problems the army was experiencing. There were bombs which did not explode; men who were not paid and accounts which were not taken care of; and, of course, rifles that were not there but urgently needed. Some men did not have the proper clothing and some men had almost no clothing at all.⁹⁰ Most of the difficulties resulted from lack of staff, from the inability of GHQ to deal with the large number of items which were required, and from the existence of war-time conditions. Not only did GHQ have to finds the necessary goods in the numbers required, these articles had to be transported to the designated areas. Because of the guerrilla tactics which the Republicans employed in the country, this was a slow and arduous process. Mulcahy and his staff must have had a sense of *déjà vu*. Despite real and significant differences, it all had a ring of familiarity about it. Sadly, it was like starting over again.

These types of difficulties were serious, but manageable. A more threatening situation was the problem of discipline and disorder among members of the army. In an intensive recruiting drive, GHQ enlisted masses of the unemployed throughout Ireland. Most were raw recruits who had no experience of army life. Even loyal IRA veterans, moreover, had little or no experience in the discipline and conduct of a regular army. However, their contribution, especially in the early days of the fighting, cannot be overestimated. At first, due to the pressures of war, training merely consisted of basic instructions. New brigades were formed to replace those which had gone Irregular. To help them sculpture an army, GHQ also recruited Irishmen who had served in the British army, especially those with professional skills. It was a decision which gave the Republicans a useful propaganda weapon and would eventually cause much consternation among members of the army.⁹¹

Overall, discipline was uneven and irregular. There was a problem with drinking. In August, the quartermaster-general forbade the sale of spirits in all canteens.⁹² At times, the officers simply could not control their men. O'Duffy, for example, described the situation in July in Limerick to Mulcahy in appalling terms:

> We had to get work out of a disorganised, indisciplined and cowardly crowd. Arms were handed over wholesale to the enemy, sentries were drunk at their Posts, and when a whole garrison was put in the clink owing to insubordination, etc., the garrison sent to replace them often turned out to be worse, . . . 300 "duds" were sent here from the Curragh, who never handled a rifle until they came here. Half of these are now in [the] clink, or have deserted altogether.⁹³

Sometimes it was the fault of the officers. A memo from the adjutant-general's office in August regretfully pointed out that many officers were not performing their work in a disciplined and orderly manner and were not conducting themselves properly in public. The situation was grave enough so that the adjutant-general felt compelled to warn

> that any Officer against whom any charge of lack of dignity, or of discipline, or of order prejudicial to the reputation of the Army as a whole and to its internal discipline can be sustained, shall not be retained in a Commissioned Rank.[94]

This was qualitatively different from the problems which GHQ encountered during the war of independence. It was to be expected. During the war of independence, the men of the IRA were fighting for a cause, for an ideal, against a traditional, identifiable enemy. The men of the new national army enlisted for a variety of reasons ranging from a belief that they were fighting for the existence of a democratic state to lack of employment. Moreover, the enemy was now their own countrymen and women. It made it worse—more brutal and more savage.

Mulcahy and GHQ attempted to compensate for its dependence on raw recruits with the centralized, co-ordinated strategy it had begun to develop during the Anglo-Irish war and by trying to utilize its superiority in equipment and armaments to its maximum advantage. Now, GHQ had access to war material from the British. During the battle for the Four Courts, for example, the national army relied extensively on heavy armaments to shell the building. It was the Irregulars who would now complain about the lack of "stuff".[95] In addition, the fighting prowess of the national army was greatly enhanced by GHQ's policy of deploying small groups of men from the Dublin Brigade who had remained loyal to Collins to various units throughout the country. These men were experienced soldiers whose presence bolstered the recruits, inspiring both confidence and discipline.

While Mulcahy as chief of the general staff was deeply involved in developing strategies to break Republican resistance and in raising an army to carry out these plans, he also held the position of minister for defence. In reality, he did not actually fill this role and function as the government's voice in army affairs. If anyone did, it was Collins. Just as Collins' dual role as minister and member of GHQ had obviated the need for formal relations between the army and the cabinet during the war of independence, so now as commander-in-chief, he deflected the need for the minister for defence to function as such. It was not a deliberate attempt to thwart or overshadow Mulcahy. Partially, it was a function of the fact that Mulcahy was both chief of staff and minister for defence. As chief of staff, the pressing needs of the army consumed all his energy and time. More significantly, as the former chairman of the provisional government, it was natural that it was Collins who communicated with and informed the government. His resignation as chairman, it must be remembered, was only seen as temporary, for the duration of the struggle.

Collins, with Mulcahy's help, undertook to keep the government informed. Mulcahy channelled the information from various members of GHQ to Collins, providing him with details on such questions as the strength of the army, the number of casualties suffered and the situation with those who had been taken as prisoners. Collins would then convey this information to the government.

The cabinet had to wait for reports, however. The first weeks of the civil war were extremely hectic for both Collins and Mulcahy and they had little time to spare for anything not directly relevant to the actual fighting. Despite their intention to keep the government informed, it took a while before the cabinet received the detailed information it desired.

The cabinet was to be increasingly frustrated by its lack of knowledge about the army and the military situation. At first, Collins' stature prevented any serious problem. He was the obvious successor to Griffith as leader of the government and inspired both admiration and loyalty. When Collins' was killed, Mulcahy had to step into his place. He would occupy the positions of minister for defence and commander-in-chief. In many ways, he continued the pattern established by Collins. But Dick Mulcahy was not Michael Collins and the cabinet increasingly balked at what they considered his high-handed ways, his aloofness. What they might tolerate from Collins, they would denounce from Mulcahy. Partly, this was in response to the changing conditions in the country and a growing uneasiness with the army. Partly, however, it was because Mulcahy simply did not have Collins' stature, prestige and charisma. Increasingly, Mulcahy would become an outsider among his cabinet colleagues.

To see for himself the condition of the army, in July, Mulcahy toured military barracks throughout the State. He made a detailed and scrupulous tour, noting everything from a post where he found 21 men in bed at 8.45 a.m., to recruits who had not been medically examined, to the sympathies of the local population.[96] Mulcahy's tour did not escape the notice of the Republicans. In a note of 25 July 1922, the Irregular staff ominously noted that "Dick Mulcahy is going South."[97] As Beal na Blath would tragically demonstrate, it was a dangerous undertaking. Perhaps Mulcahy felt it was necessary to bolster the morale of the troops. Perhaps he was responding to the criticism of the Southern divisions in the Anglo-Irish war that he never visited them. At any rate, Mulcahy survived the tour and was able to provide first hand information to Collins and the cabinet.

The report which Collins eventually sent to the cabinet on 26 July was optimistic about conditions in the country. Collins believed that they had reason to congratulate themselves that "everything has turned out so well, particularly in the case of the Army, and this notwithstanding all our difficulties and troubles." The government now had an army. Interestingly,

Collins saw this as possibly significant in their future dealings with Britain or the North-East. Of more immediate importance, however, was the fact that the army now had actual combat training which increased their confidence. Their victories, moreover, had taught the rebels a lesson which "we absolutely failed to teach them in our peaceful dealings with their leaders."[98]

Collins believed that the Irregulars had shown themselves to be "without an objective, without faith in their cause". He pictured the Republican leaders as sitting around waiting for something to turn up, adhering to a policy of material ruin, simply bent upon destruction. It was, he felt, "pitiful" and every effort had to be made "to save the good fighting men of Cork from the barrenness of their supposed leaders". Collins was outraged at the human and material waste which the civil war was causing. And, he worried about the future:

> We must keep the issue clearly before the public. This is no time for arguing as to who did right and who did wrong in the last six months—that course is fruitless. What matters is not the past six months but the present position and the future six months, and after the future six months the entire future. The question to be asked is what is the position today and what are we going to do for our country today and tomorrow? The rebel leaders never faced this question. We must face it, and we must keep it before the people.[99]

Both Collins and Mulcahy were concerned about the deleterious effects the civil war could have on the new state. As the war went on—and this would be increasingly true as the civil war dragged into 1923—the ferocity and savageness of the violence increased. The ruthless brutality that was just beginning to emerge in the closing days of 1921, surfaced much quicker in the civil war. Much has been made of the reluctance of the men of the old IRA to shoot former comrades. One historian characterized this attitude as a "lack of heart" which resulted in "flights of bullets hurtled through the air harmlessly as migrating birds".[100] While this may have been true in the very beginning, it soon turned into serious hunting. Both the Republican and the government troops made some attempt to persuade former comrades to join their particular side. But when words failed, they resorted to arms. Moreover, most of the members of the national army were not veterans of the IRA and thus not inhibited by such bonds and ties.

As he did during the Anglo-Irish war, Mulcahy tried to navigate a moderate course. There would, of course, be glaring exceptions to this general rule, but, for the most part, both he and Collins tried to rein in the army. They knew that they were dealing in the main with inexperienced soldiers under considerable strain. It made regulations, discipline, and order even more important. In addition, they also had to try to restrain their government colleagues. Interestingly, the cabinet appeared much more ruthless than their military counterparts and much more willing to expand and extend the powers of the army.

The government was eager for victory and sometimes their eagerness clouded their judgment. At times, moreover, their collective lack of military experience led them to suggest alternatives that would be potentially very dangerous. For example, on 27 July Cosgrave wrote to Collins suggesting that the government issue a proclamation warning all those concerned that:

> the troops have orders to shoot persons found sniping, ambushing or in possession of bombs, or interfering with Railway or Road communications, in areas in which military operations have ceased.[101]

Collins was horrified at the idea. In a memo to the government, he said that, while it was ultimately their decision and the army would loyally follow their orders, he opposed this idea. To him, it was tantamount to giving the army the authority to shoot unarmed men. Drastic action was one thing. Shooting unarmed men was quite another. Collins did mention that there were exceptions to this rule: "This would not, naturally, refer to a man who deliberately shoots a soldier and then throws down his rifle and puts up his hands. Numerous specific instances of this are known to us."[102]

By the beginning of August, the government troops were in a strong position. The army had grown significantly. As of 5 August 1922, it was composed of approximately 14,000 regular soldiers and 5,000 reservists, with another 6,000 reservists already signed up but not processed. More significantly, it had decisively beaten the Irregular challenge in most of the country.

From a military point of view, both Collins and Mulcahy should have been pleased with the progress which the national army made in the first six weeks of the war. There were a string of victories. The national army soon secured the east, the north and most of the west. The Republicans were forced to retreat into the south, making their stand in the Republic of Munster. Town after town fell, partly due to the policy of the Irregulars themselves. They would occupy towns and then abandon them, leaving the local barracks gutted by fire and of no use to either the national army or the civic guards. The Irregulars would then flee to the hills and mountains to resume the old guerrilla warfare of the Black and Tan era, to revert as Oscar Traynor said, "to the tactics which made us invincible formerly".[103]

While there were some problems remaining in the Western area, in general, there was no serious military difficulties outside the Waterford-Cork-Kerry-Limerick area. And, even in these areas, the national army was making progress. They had made a successful sea landing in North Kerry and, in the early days of August, had broken the Limerick-Waterford line.

In the south, according to the general strategy mapped out by Collins and Mulcahy, the major objective was not a military defeat of the Irregulars but rather establishing the army in principal points in the area. This would, they believed, shake the "domination held over the ordinary people by the Irregulars". With government troops in evidence, GHQ hoped for:

the resurgence of the people from their present cowed condition, and the realisation by the Irregulars that they had lost their grip on the people and that they could not hope to last. An immediate demoralisation of the Irregular rank and file would be the result.[104]

Thus, as the national army successfully captured towns in this area, it would not only be a victory for the military, but a political and economic triumph for the government as well.

The army followed up its success in north Kerry with an advance on the Irregular stronghold of Cork. Intelligence reports had given them a fairly clear idea of what their troops would encounter. Although most of the experienced fighting men in this area went Irregular, intelligence believed that some of the rest of the forces would fight only "*half-heartedly*; with such men it is a case of *bread and butter*. Many of these would have joined the National Army had they the opportunity of doing so."[105]

Intelligence sources also warned GHQ that the Irregulars had prepared for a government assault. Roads and bridges as well as part of the upper harbour had been mined. With these warnings in mind, Collins and Mulcahy planned their next move. Despite the problem with the harbor, they decided on a sea landing in Cork. It was successful. Government troops swept through the major areas so that by 11 August, the Republicans had evacuated the last two towns they controlled in the area. The war in the field was over.[106] The Republicans had lost—they simply did not know it.

Intelligence reports on Cork had accurately predicted that the Irregulars would turn to guerrilla tactics in Cork and Kerry.[107] Forced to retreat into the hills, Lynch and his followers adopted the practices which they knew so well and which some of their comrades in other areas of the country had already been advocating and using. Traynor had held this view since the battle of the Four Courts. He had opposed defending the law courts and buildings in Dublin, fighting fixed battles from fixed positions. Increasingly, Lynch and the Irregulars adopted his point of view. In July, Sean Moylan had advocated that the Irregulars adopt guerrilla tactics. He shrewdly analyzed their situation. They were without a base, transport, food or intelligence. The only strategy which would not destroy their morale was to fight from the hills.[108] Lynch was forced to concur, especially after the Republican evacuation of Cork. By 24 August 1922, Lynch was reporting "that guerrilla tactics are developing splendidly. [The] enemy will soon find out the futility of his campaign."[109] The adoption of guerrilla tactics insured that it would be a long, drawn out fight.

The tactics used by the Republicans were ones with which both Mulcahy and Collins were only too familiar—ambushes, sniping, destruction of roads, blowing up bridges and breaking railway lines. The task which the army thus faced from mid-August on was to prevent the guerrilla tactics from destroying the economic life and social fabric of the country.

It was truly more difficult than staging battles, positioning troops, and capturing towns. It would also take much longer. The national army had beaten the Republicans in the field in approximately six to eight weeks. Yet the civil war itself would dribble on through the spring of 1923. Everyone's patience would grow thin, especially in government.

Guerrilla war increased the necessity for Collins and Mulcahy to devise ways of keeping control of their own army and restraining their troops in provocative times. It was difficult, for example, to curb men who were attacked with exploding bullets. In one case, the commandant simply switched bullets and forced his prisoners to fight showdown style in an open field against the officer in charge of the national army. The result was that the two Irregular prisoners were killed and the officer slightly wounded.[110] Mulcahy and Collins pondered this unpleasant situation. Although they decided that Mulcahy would prepare an order on the matter, they knew that orders alone would not cover these situations. To supplement and complement their directives, they had to inculcate in their men a sense of "proper action".[111]

Another issue concerned general searches for weapons in areas where the violence continued. The army had apparently asked the cabinet for its opinion on the matter. The government, however, had decided that it would:

> support the Military Authorities in whatever steps they may consider necessary to restore order in districts where military operations have ceased but in which outbreaks of violence still continue.[112]

The question was, in effect, thrown back into the military's lap, or as Collins more politely put it in a note to Mulcahy: "I am afraid it is not very helpful to us, and we shall therefore have to frame proposals to be sanctioned by Government."[113]

Collins suggested that they issue a notice asking those in possession of weapons to turn them over to the authorities within a certain time. After that time, the area would be liable for a general search. Mulcahy agreed that there should be a definite order concerning the possession of arms and ammunition. He suggested that the people have the opportunity to report their holdings to the local commander and explain to him the purpose for which the arms were held. After a certain date, those who had unreported arms and ammunition would be subject to clearly defined punishments.

On the question of general searches in an area, Mulcahy disagreed with Collins. Mulcahy was concerned that such general permission would lead to serious abuse of the civilian population. He believed that only specific areas which had been under observation beforehand—that is, where there was probable cause—should be subjected to a search. Otherwise, he argued, their troops "would get themselves into very serious difficulties in anything like general searching".[114]

Moreover, displaying a political sensitivity that was not always evident in his dealings with his civilian colleagues, Mulcahy suggested to Collins that they take precautions not to alienate the civilian population. In any area where the army authorities were thinking of undertaking these searches, Mulcahy felt that it would be useful:

> If the Officers in each Command were put in a position to make a statement of the approximate amount of the actual damage done in each County in his area, and an approximation of the consequential loss to the area, and make a simple statement of the military intention in restoring order in the country . . . it might provide a suitable introduction to a request to give this particular co-operation, [handing in and locating arms and ammunition] and it would put him in a position to approach intelligently, prominent and pivotal people in the different portions of his area, and privately solicit their active co-operation in this matter.[115]

It was a perceptive and shrewd approach to a situation which had the potential to become ugly.

Collins and Mulcahy moved steadily along, dismayed at the price they were being forced to pay, but, nonetheless, confident of victory. The army was reclaiming the country and the writ of the government was extending farther and farther. The stability of the government, however, was seriously shaken by the events in August. On the 12th of that month, Arthur Griffith died of a cerebral hemorrhage. Collins led the funeral procession. The nation mourned. Ten days later, on 22 August, Michael Collins was killed in an ambush at Beal na Blath, County Cork, his home territory. It was an overwhelming tragedy, the force of which words could not express.

Mulcahy received the news of Collins' death in the early hours of the morning. One can only imagine the grief and sorrow which he felt. But Mulcahy would not allow his emotions to surface. His natural restraint and reserve were probably augmented by the knowledge that he was now the dominant military leader and there was much to be done. Within a short time after hearing the news of his friend's death, he sent cars to bring ministers to a special meeting of the government and issued an address to the army.

Mulcahy pleaded with the army to remain calm:

> Stand calmly by your posts. Bend bravely and undaunted to your work. Let no cruel act of reprisal blemish your bright honour. Every dark hour that Michael Collins met since 1916 seemed but to steel that bright strength of his and temper his gay bravery. You are left each inheritors of that strength and of that bravery. To each of you falls his unfinished work. No darkness in the hour—no loss of comrades will daunt you at it. Ireland! The Army serves— strengthened by its sorrow.[116]

Mulcahy also issued a statement to the people. In it, he informed them that "the greatest and bravest of our countrymen has been snatched from us", at a time when they could just begin to see the victory for which Collins dedicated his life come to fruition. Mulcahy concluded his address on a note of hope:

> He has been slain to our unutterable grief and loss, but he cannot die. He will live in the rule of the people which he gave his great best to assert and confirm and which his colleagues now undertake as a solemn charge to maintain.[117]

To its credit and to Mulcahy's credit, the army basically remained calm. Both sides it seemed were too stunned to do anything else. Tom Barry remembered how when the news of Collins' death reached the prisoners, they knelt down on their knees and said the rosary. Whether true or not, it captures something of the effect this tragedy had on the Irish people.

Liam Lynch's response to Collins' death remains enigmatic. In commending his officer on the successful ambush at Beal na Blath, Lynch very coolly critiqued the engagement—asking for example why they had not laid mines beforehand—and then went on to comment:

> Nothing could bring home more forcefully the awful, unfortunate National Situation at present than the fact that it has become necessary for Irishmen and former comrades to shoot such men as M. Collins, who rendered such splendid service to the Republic in the late war against England. It is to be hoped our present Enemies will realise the folly of trying to crush the Republic before it is too late.[118]

In light of the strong friendship that had previously existed between the two men, Lynch's comment was incredibly detached. One historian has characterized Lynch's comments as patronizing and sanctimonious, concluding that Lynch was succumbing to the lure of power.[119] Perhaps. Perhaps he was restraining his grief. His comments seem to be a studied effort to downplay the tragedy. Perhaps it was a way of quieting his own doubts or justifying his own choices.

Mulcahy marched at the head of the cortege as it made its way through Dublin to Glasnevin cemetery. As he walked along, he could not fail to notice the rough scribbling on the walls: "Move over, Mick, make room for Dick." It was not something that he did not already know. He was probably too numb from grief to give it much thought. Mulcahy gave the graveside address. He spoke simply and directly about his friend and comrade's virtues, aspirations and influence. What emerged was a warm, moving and human picture of Collins which was a most fitting eulogy. In Mulcahy's eyes and in the eyes of many of his contemporaries, Collins was a great hero, already a legend.[120] And, it was now up to Mulcahy to pick up the mantle of this towering figure and lead the army and the nation to victory in the civil war.

23.8.22

To the Men

3.15 am

of the Army —

Stand calmly by your posts.

Bend bravely and undaunted to your work

Let no cruel act of reprisal blemish your bright honour.

Every dark hour that Michael Collins met since 1916 served but to steel that bright strength of his and temper his gay bravery

You are left each, inheritors of that strength, and of that bravery

To each of you falls his unfinished work

No darkness in the hour — no loss of comrade will daunt you at it.

Ireland ! the Army serves — strengthened by its sorrow.

Risteárd Ua Maolchatha
Chief of the General Staff

23 A facsimile of Mulcahy's Address to the Army on the Death of Michael Collins

To the men of the army.
Stand calmly by your posts.
Bend bravely and undaunted
to your work.
Let no cruel act of reprisal
blemish your bright honour.
Every dark hour that Michael
Collins met since 1916 seemed but
to steel that bright strength of
his and temper his gay bravery
You are left each inheritors of
that strength and of that bravery
To each of you falls his unfinished work
No darkness in the hour — no
loss of comrades will daunt you
at it.
      Ireland! The army serves—
strengthened by its sorrow.
                    Risteárd Ua Maolcáta
                    Chief of General Staff
                            3.15 a.m.
                    August 23 1922.

E.C.yeats
cuala.

24 A Cuala Press edition of the address shown in ill. 23

SEVEN

The Price of Victory

. . . there are forces working round us today, more vicious, more insidious, and more striking than Britain ever employed against representative government in Ireland.

Richard Mulcahy, commander-in-chief,
8 December 1922, on the Mountjoy Executions.

The death of Michael Collins had far reaching consequences. William T. Cosgrave succeeded Collins as chairman of the government. His selection was not totally unanimous.[1] O'Higgins, for example, favored Mulcahy as Collins' successor—an interesting twist given the antagonism that would develop between the two men. Mulcahy remembered that:

O'Higgins idea was that I [Mulcahy] should be the head of the government but there was no move to discuss that and as far as I was concerned the position with regard to the army was that I didn't believe that the army could be handled by anyone except myself after Collins's death. Therefore, the question of my taking over the government would be an utter impossibility at that time.[2]

The election of Cosgrave as head of the government, in fact, was the occasion of O'Higgins' caustic remark that a Dublin corporator would make Ireland a nation once again.[3]

Mulcahy did not seem to harbor any ambitions to become head of government—a trait which would re-surface years later when he voluntarily relinquished his claim to be Taoiseach in the first inter-party government. He was content to remain as head of the army and indeed considered that to be his primary responsibility. On the day after Collins' death, he was appointed commander-in-chief of the army on as well as minister for defence.[4] It was and remained an uneasy combination. When his appointment was announced in the Dáil in September, some deputies questioned the wisdom of combining the two offices. The arguments against it were cogent, reasonable and totally out of touch with the reality of the situation. As noted above, Collins had functioned as both the commander-in-chief and the liaison with the government.[5] Mulcahy's appointment simply made formal what was already a reality. The objections which surfaced in the Dáil, especially among Labour deputies, did, however, prefigure the growing anti-military sentiment which would become more evident as the civil war dragged on.

More significant, however, than the shuffling of ministerial positions was the shift in the attitude of the cabinet—a change which would become more apparent in the next few years. The political split in Sinn Féin over the Treaty had obviously seriously weakened the political movement. It meant that the government which was responsible for implementing the Treaty and the Constitution, and which was to guide the birth of the new Free State, was denuded of valuable political talent. The death of Collins and Griffith further exacerbated this problem.

Moreover, the men who were left to run the Free State were, for the most part, of a qualitatively different political ideology than those associated with the traditional nationalist movement. The leaders of Sinn Féin who ran the first Dáil government were, like Mulcahy, weaned on the ideas of Arthur Griffith and the Irish-Ireland movement. While, with only a few glaring exceptions, they were far from being social radicals, they had a vision of Ireland which was significantly different from the present reality. In a rather simplistic sense, they envisioned an Ireland which was predominantly rural, Irish-speaking and self-sufficient, an Ireland which was a united whole, undivided by class, and utilizing its resources for the benefit of the whole society. Although they shied away from the socialist ideals of Connolly and Mellows, they had a sense that Ireland possessed an abundance of resources which, when properly used, would allow a decent life for each of its citizens. This was basically Mulcahy's position and, in the early years of the nationalist movement, he was in the majority.

With the reformation of the cabinet after Collins' death, however, he was in a minority. Cosgrave and O'Higgins typified the new leaders of the state. Conservative, anti-army, not terribly committed to the ideals of a Gaelic Ireland, they seemed more willing to mould the new State in the image of British society—with token gestures thrown to those who clung to the old ideals. This was one reason why Mulcahy found himself increasingly isolated in the cabinet throughout the 1922–24 period.

However, when Mulcahy assumed the role of commander-in-chief, far from being isolated, he was at the peak of his career in terms of power and influence. Mulcahy was now responsible for directing the army in its fight against the Republicans. If the government was to survive, if indeed the new state were to survive, it would be because of the work of the army. The responsibility was tremendous. Mulcahy knew that, as in the war he himself had directed against the British, the Republicans did not have to win. All they had to do was sufficiently disrupt the life of the country so that the government could not function. This would lead to widespread chaos and the demise of the Free State. Possibly the British would return and then the Republicans believed that they could reunite the country against this new invasion. Or, perhaps, they simply believed that they could seize power and declare Ireland a republic.

In any event, it was up to the new commander-in-chief and his staff to deal with the threat from the Irregulars. Some still believed that a peace settlement could be negotiated. Even after the attack on the Four Courts, peace feelers continued to circulate. And, as the national army swept from victory to victory in the first six months of the war, there was some hope that the Republicans might give up the fight and limit themselves to constitutional opposition. By the end of July 1922, Collins and Mulcahy were apparently considering a cessation of hostilities to give the political and military leaders of the Republicans a chance to consider the acceptance of terms. It is not clear from whom the idea originated. Both Tom Barry from the Republican side and P.S. O'Hegarty from the government's side were preparing terms which would form the basis of the negotiations, including acceptance of the government's proposals for army unification and no victimization of any officer for his political beliefs. There was also some vague unofficial talk of another election on the Treaty.[6]

In addition, after the operations in Cork, a group of citizens from that area approached Collins through Major-General Dalton to try to arrange for a week's truce. During that time the Republican leaders would discuss terms for peace which would include surrender of arms and a general amnesty, as well as the acceptance in the national army of Republican military leaders at their due rank, or the option to return to civilian life without penalty or molestation. After Collins' death, there was a renewed attempt to find a negotiated settlement, but nothing came of it.[7]

It was against this background of sporadic yet continuing attempts to seek an end to the hostilities that Mulcahy secretly met de Valera on 6 September 1922. According to Mulcahy's account, Monsignor Ryan of San Francisco had implored him to meet de Valera whom the priest assured Mulcahy was a "changed man". The priest's repeated requests put Mulcahy in a difficult position. Concerned about the various attempts to negotiate peace without the government's explicit approval, on 5 September 1922, the cabinet had decided that it was necessary for all its members to strictly adhere to the principle of collective cabinet responsibility.[8] If Mulcahy met de Valera, he would be violating the spirit, if not the letter, of the cabinet's decision. If he did not, he might be throwing away a significant opportunity to achieve peace. When Monsignor Ryan first approached Mulcahy, apparently, the minister's response was quite simply that "Mr de Valera could stop the civil war by writing a letter to the *Evening Mail*." However, a few days later when the monsignor again appeared with the same request, Mulcahy reacted "impulsively" and acquiesced.[9]

Mulcahy had not mentioned Monsignor Ryan's appeal to anyone else. He claimed that, at first, he did not take it seriously enough even to discuss it with his colleagues. Then he found himself in the position of having agreed to a meeting without consulting other members of the cabinet. On the afternoon prior to the scheduled meeting, he went to discuss the situation with his colleague, MacNeill, claiming that if MacNeill vetoed the meeting with de Valera, he would cancel the arrangement. MacNeill obviously did not, because the meeting took place the following evening. Mulcahy's recollection of the meeting was that, after receiving a blessing from the monsignor, the priest departed and left the two men alone:

> We met one another standing and remained standing. I took the initiative in saying that the position in Ireland was that [there] are two things to my mind that were important: 1. That somebody should be allowed [to] work the Treaty, and 2. That if there was to be an army in Ireland it should be subject to parliament. Given these two things I didn't care who ruled this country as long as they were representative elected Irish men and women, and I came to a full stop. The "changed man" still standing in front of me said, "some men are led by faith and some men are led by reason. Personally, I would tend to be led by reason, but as long as there are men of faith like Rory O'Connor taking the stand that he is taking, I am an humble soldier following after them." My mission was over. I knew where I stood; I knew where de Valera stood. It wasn't necessary for me to say it or to mention it. There was no room for discussion.[10]

De Valera's account of the meeting differed in emphasis, but not in substance. Writing to the Irish-American leader, Joe McGarrity, he stated:

> I met Mulcahy the other evening. Rather amusing. We gave mutual safe conducts to each other for the meeting. We got nowhere in discussion, however, for I made revision of the Treaty the basis, whilst he insisted on the acceptance of the Treaty as the basis. Of course that means "quit" for the Republicans, and if it has to be done, it is much better [to] do it boldly without any camouflage.[11]

The next day, Mulcahy reported his meeting to the cabinet. They were not pleased that Mulcahy had met de Valera secretly. Nor were they heartened by Mulcahy's report of what occurred—or more to the point, what change had not occurred. Mulcahy later claimed that it was only after his meeting with de Valera that the policy of executions was seriously considered.[12]

The meeting with de Valera would, however, have strengthened Mulcahy's conviction that the Republicans were not going to admit defeat, but rather were going to try to drag the country into the mire of chaos and anarchy. To combat this threat, on 15 September 1922,

Mulcahy asked the cabinet to substantially extend the powers of the army.[13] The cabinet agreed and the necessary legislation, the Emergency Powers Bill, was drafted and presented to the Dáil later that month.

The Emergency Powers Bill gave the army almost *carte blanche* in dealing with the Republicans. The act established military courts with the power to impose the death penalty for such offences as aiding or abetting attacks on the army, looting, arson, destruction or seizure or damage to property, or unauthorized possession of weapons and explosives.[14] According to the military, these awesome powers were necessary if the Army was going to establish the authority of the government throughout the country.

In the Dáil, the government justified this extraordinary measure as necessary to save the life of the nation. President Cosgrave opened the debate by pointing out the injury which the nation was sustaining as a result of the rebellion:

> It restricts trade, it attempts to destroy the industry of the nation, it delays the progress of public administration, it destroys life, damages public and private property, it shakes public security, it defames our nation, injures the people's health, and endangers the future generation as it helps to destroy the people's peace . . .[15]

The government, Cosgrave continued, had hoped to crush the rebellion without resorting to such measures as outlined in the Emergency Powers Act. However, "the absolute disregard of life and of suffering that is evidenced by the continuance of the irregular attacks plainly indicated to the government that protection is due to their soldiers" and these resolutions would give the army that protection. The President vowed that "those who persist in those murderous attacks must learn that they have got to pay the penalty for them", a penalty far greater than mere internment.[16]

Mulcahy elaborated on this theme:

> It is a necessity that these people in the country who are committing murder, who are committing arson, looting and destroying the life of this country, should know that they shall forfeit their lives if they continue to do that work, and the Government must set up the machinery for taking that forfeiture. The Army . . . is prepared to do the work of executing these people . . . it is the servant of the Government.[17]

Mulcahy emphatically made the point that the army was asking for such powers because the civil courts were not functioning and that the army would exercise such power only until the proper civil machinery of justice could function.

The minister for defence also had another reason for asking for such power for the army. Not only must the Republicans know that they faced death if they continued to engage in violence; the members of the National forces must also know that the Irregulars faced death for their crimes. Unless the power of execution were legally and formally given to army, Mulcahy was afraid that discipline would break down even more than it had, and there would be a spree of illegal executions. He publicly admitted to the Dáil that discipline was not what it should be in the army and that there were problems in controlling the troops. He cited an instance of a soldier, having seen his comrades blown up, refusing to take the surrender of a prisoner and killing him. He cited other instances of Irregulars who "sniggered and laughed, showing an almost fiendish delight at the fact that one of our men was killed", and of an attack on a group of National troops who were on their way to Mass.[18] Mulcahy pointedly asked the Dáil how he could say to his men that those who killed members of the National Army would face nothing more than internment. Already there were growing tales of torture, execution, and reprisals. The Emergency Powers Act was necessary

> in order to prevent men from taking upon themselves authority to execute people in an unauthorized way, and the dangers that without this legislation such executions will take place is great. They have happened in one or two instances and they would happen in thousands of instances if the men of the Army had not the control over themselves which the vast majority of the Army has.[19]

This reasoning was in keeping with Mulcahy's general belief—as evidenced earlier in the Black and Tan war—that reprisals or executions, if necessary, must be done in a proper and legal manner by those who had the authority to do so. What Mulcahy wanted to avoid—and he was not entirely successful in this—was a general bloodbath in which the army felt it had no recourse but to take matters into its own hands. If this legislation were passed,

> Then our men will have some chance, even among the very difficult and dangerous circumstances under which they work, of being chivalrous soldiers, who will continue to show, to those who are fighting in such an ugly fashion against them, and against the country, the chivalry and kindness and the manly disposition they have shown to them invariably, in the past few months.[20]

There was, of course, opposition to the Emergency Powers legislation. Some deputies were not persuaded that the army actually needed such power. Others, like Cathal O'Shannon of the Labour Party, spoke of a growing revulsion against all armies—Republican or Free State:

> We have denounced militarism, and we have told you the root cause of the militarism in Ireland. The military spirit is as deep in one section of the Army as it is in another, and the reason is that both came with prestige out of the guerrilla warfare against England,

and they have got such swelled heads that the only authority they
have is the authority of the gun.[21]

O'Shannon's sentiments prefigured the increasing antagonism against the
military which would surface after the civil war.

At this point, the politicians could do little but give the army the power
they felt they needed. To allay criticism, the government announced that
they would delay implementing the act in order to issue an amnesty
proclamation pardoning all who would lay down their arms and cease to
participate in the rebellion. The cabinet ordered that the proclamation be
given the widest publicity, with copies circulated in all the papers, distributed
by airplane, sent to all the clergy, and displayed at every post office.[22]
The amnesty proclamation met with little success. However, it eased the
conscience of those who had doubts about the army's new powers and
strengthened the conviction of those who did not.

The first military court under the Emergency Powers Act was held on 3
November 1922. Within less than two weeks, twelve cases had come before
the military courts, all concerning those accused of having possession
without proper authority, of a revolver, or rifle or ammunition. As of 15
November, only one sentence had been handed down and confirmed by
army authorities. It was for a year's imprisonment with hard labour.

The punishment escalated rapidly. On 17 November, four men charged
with possession of illegal weapons were executed. There was an outcry in
the Dáil. Deputies were shocked that the army had taken the extreme
penalty against these young men who were neither part of the leadership
of the Republican movement nor arrested after committing an actual act
of violence. The men who were executed "were found on the streets of
Dublin at night, carrying loaded revolvers, and waiting to take the lives
of other men", according to the minister for defence.[23]

The government defended the army's action. Mulcahy agreed with
Tom Johnson, the leader of the Labour Party, that the executions were a
shock, but believed that the country had to be jolted into realizing the
gravity of the situation. He further argued that, while the army regretted
that these executions were necessary, they had a responsibility—a word
which all members of the government bandied about with increasing
frequency during this period—to save the country. Mulcahy maintained
that unless the government and the army demonstrated conclusively that
they were determined to "throw back the tide of lawlessness and the tide
of lust and loot that some mad political leaders have stirred up in their
train in this country", the nation would perish. He concluded his speech
with the warning that

> anybody who goes around with a loaded revolver in his pocket on
> the street seeking to take the lives of other men must be made [to]
> face the fact that by doing so he forfeits his own life.[24]

Other members of the government lent their support. Kevin O'Higgins argued that the execution of four average ordinary young men was necessary to send the message that those who set about to kill others would pay a heavy price. It did not matter that they were not notorious or accused of an especially heinous crime. It was enough that they conspired to thwart the will of the majority and threatened the very life of the nation.[25]

O'Higgins explained to the Dáil that the policy of executions was undertaken as a deterrent and was not taken in any vindicative or hasty manner. Both he and Ernest Blythe, minister for finance, pointed out that the government had exhausted all attempts at persuasion, at reasoning, at compromise. All had failed. Blythe argued that the time had come "to take all the measures that may be necessary to bring the state of affairs which exist in the country at the present time to the speediest close. We will not prevent bloodshed by shirking stern measures now," by falling victim to "sloppy sentiment".[26]

Blythe also criticized the parliamentary opposition, most notably Labour, for raising their voices in protest only when the government took some "drastic and severe" measure. When, however, "actions as severe as killings that have no justification are done by people on the other side," only "the mildest expression of disapproval" was articulated.[27] Blythe's accusation accurately reflected the feeling in the cabinet, but it was unfair. As the leading opposition party in the Dáil, it was Labour's responsibility to criticize the actions of the government when necessary. Members of the government were extremely sensitive and intolerant of any criticism. They used the civil war as an impregnable defence to cover all questionable practices. Cabinet members charged treason when there was legitimate criticism, spoke more to justify themselves to the renegade half of their own party than to the Dáil, and did not really consult the Dáil but rather used it, in large measure, to endorse and legitimize their previous actions.

Indeed the government was subsequently in for a great deal more criticism as they relentlessly pursued their policy of executions. Two particular judgments were very controversial. The first was the execution of Erskine Childers on 24 November 1922 and the second was the Mountjoy executions of 8 December.

Erskine Childers was captured by national army troops in his family home in Wicklow, having in his possession a small revolver allegedly given to him by Michael Collins. He was tried by a military court for possession of a revolver, found guilty and executed. Gavan Duffy raised the matter in the Dáil. In a moving and emotional speech, he paid tribute to Childers' contributions to Ireland and demanded an explanation from the government.

There were various issues involved in this particular execution. One was the question of putting a man to death for simply possessing a revolver.

The second issue revolved around the fact that Childers had been secretary to the Treaty delegation but had spoken persuasively against the agreement. There was no love lost between Childers and Griffith and this animosity increased during the debates to the point where Griffith referred to Childers as "that damned Englishman". O'Higgins allegedly shared this antipathy to Childers. Much was made of his statement concerning the first four executions that no one could say any of these was executed because he was an Englishman—a statement made on the day Childers was arrested. O'Higgins later claimed that it was an innocent remark. It probably was not. Apprised of the fact that Childers was arrested and in possession of a weapon, O'Higgins knew that the death penalty was at least a possibility. Had Childers been the first person executed, it could have been construed as anti-English gesture.

However, too much has been made of the fact that Childers was English and that there was antipathy between him and Griffith and possibly other members of the government. Childers was executed because he was one of the leaders of the Republicans whom the cabinet believed led others astray. If there was particular animosity towards Childers, it had less to do with his nationality than with the fact that, although he was secretary to the Irish delegation which negotiated the Treaty, he argued persuasively against it. It also had to do with the fact Childers was an extremely skilful propagandist whose barbs stung the government on numerous occasions. While O'Higgins might talk about Englishmen who come to Ireland looking for adventure, this was simply the coating to the argument. Childers' rejection of the Treaty and his subsequent propaganda for the Republican cause were the more basic reasons for any feelings against him in the cabinet.

In the eyes of the cabinet, Childers' position of leadership within the Republican movement made it imperative that he be treated harshly. It would have been inconsistent to execute the followers and not the leaders of the movement. The government held the leaders of the Republican movement responsible for leading trusting and naive men and women into a civil war—as evidenced by their constant use of the term "dupes" to refer to the rank and file of the Republican cause. It was also a constant theme of Collins and Mulcahy. Certainly there is no evidence that Mulcahy hated Childers because of his background. He did, however, believe that it was necessary to take action against the leaders of the Republican movement. They would not escape unscathed while those in the field paid the price with their lives.

Not surprisingly, the Republicans decided to seek revenge for Childers' death. Liam Lynch issued a warning that all who had voted for the Emergency Powers Act and all who actively supported the Free State would be at risk, would be treated in the same way that the government was treating his forces. The Republicans made good their threat on 7 December when, on their way to a meeting of the Dáil, Deputy Sean Hales was assassinated and Deputy Padraic O Maille was wounded. The country was shocked. Sean Hales had been an active popular soldier in the Anglo-Irish war. His family had seemed to embody the tragedy inherent in the civil war. His brother had sided with the Republicans and was, at the time of Sean Hales' death, a prisoner of the Free State government.

When the Ministers announced the news to the Dáil, newspaper reports indicate that both Cosgrave and Mulcahy were visibly shaken and angry. In the Dáil, Mulcahy's speech rang with bitterness as he contrasted the orderly and more humane manner in which even the executed prisoners were treated as opposed to those who were assassinated, gunned down in the streets. According to the *Irish Times*:

> The Minister for Defence remarked bitterly in the Dáil before the members, who stood silently as a token of their sympathy, "There was no Press present. They were not asked would they like to see their relatives, or would they like to see a clergyman, or had they any private business of their own that they would like to transact."[28]

The government's response was swift and brutal. The cabinet decided to retaliate by summarily executing four of the prisoners held since the surrender of the Four Courts the previous June. It was not an easy decision nor was it necessarily a wise one in the long run. But it was the action of a cabinet which felt that the heart of representative government was being threatened. They were determined to respond in such a way so as to make the price of a repeat occurrence much too high to pay.

On the evening of 7 December, Rory O'Connor, Liam Mellows, Joseph McKelvey and Richard Barrett received a notice that they would be executed the following morning. The chilling quality of the announcement has survived the years:

> You _____ are hereby notified that, being a person taken in arms against the Government, you will be executed at 8 a.m. on Friday 8th December as a reprisal for the assassination of Brigadier Sean Hales, T.D. in Dublin on the 7th December, on his way to a meeting of Dáil Éireann and as a solemn warning to those associated [with] you who are engaged in a conspiracy of assassination against the representatives of the Irish people.[29]

The notice was signed by Mulcahy as commander-in-chief on behalf of the army council. The "Mountjoy executions" had no pretence of legality, but were rather a calculated attempt to stop the terror of assassination.

There were vehement denunciations in the Dáil. Deputies had only been informed of the cabinet's decision after the executions had taken place. Labour was outraged. To them, it was murder. Cathal O'Shannon charged: "You murdered these men—nothing short of murder were the executions of these men this morning."[30] Thomas Johnson was no less forceful, characterizing the executions as "most foul, bloody and unnatural . . . . I am almost forced to say you have killed the new State at its birth."[31]

The response of the cabinet to these charges was direct and uncompromising. To them, the issue was clear: either the Dáil would continue to function in a free and unfettered manner or it would be the object of assassination attacks and would eventually cease to function. Mulcahy drew a parallel to the British decision to declare Dáil Éireann an illegal body in 1919. Just as they fought the British over their right to have their own representatives meeting freely, so would they now fight the Irregulars for this very same reason—to preserve their right to representative government.[32]

The government unabashedly stated that the Mountjoy executions were both a reprisal for the death of Sean Hales and a warning to the Irregulars that this particular form of violence would be dealt with most vigorously and most harshly. The decision was not taken in anger nor was it an act of vengeance. As Mulcahy movingly told the Dáil:

> We have too long borne the responsibilities that are on us. We have too long held our hands and our hearts and our minds sacrificially in the flames, like the warrior of old, and gone steadily and straightforwardly through our duties, to act in anger, to know very much about temptation. The action that was taken this morning was taken as a deterrent action—taken to secure that this country shall not be destroyed and thrown into chaos . . .[33]

Outside the Dáil, there was also a negative, if somewhat more muted response, to the executions. Possibly because of the government's censorship policy, the newspapers of the day were mild in their criticism of the government's action. For example, the *Irish Independent* spent more time on the death of Sean Hales—which it had also covered the day before-than on the executions. Concerning the death of the four men in Mountjoy, the *Independent* simply said:

> Yesterday morning four prisoners in Mountjoy jail were executed according to the official report, as a reprisal and a warning. If we deprecate such a proceeding it is because we wish to aid, and not to embarrass the Government in its endeavour to make secure for the nation the rights it has won. May we echo the words of Deputy Fitzgibbon, himself a staunch supporter of the Government, in hoping that what happened yesterday morning may not occur again.[34]

While censorship may have protected the cabinet from feeling the full blast of criticism from the press, it did not protect them from the stern reprimand they received privately from the some of the bishops. For example, Archbishop Byrne of Dublin wrote to his friend, President Cosgrave, condemning the policy of reprisals on both moral and pragmatic grounds as:

. . . not only unwise but entirely unjustifiable from the moral point of view. That one man should be punished for another's crime seems to me to be absolutely unjust. Moreover, such a policy is bound to alienate many friends of the Government, and it requires all the sympathy it can get.[35]

It has recently been argued the archbishop of Dublin's intervention was effective in moderating government policy.[36] While this may well be true, without more conclusive evidence, it would seem that adverse ecclesiastical opinion was only one factor, albeit an important factor, in moderating the government's official policy on reprisals. Two other factors are also important. No other deputies were assassinated and hence the government did not have to employ any more direct reprisals. And, some executions took place throughout the country which may have certainly been reprisals, but were simply not called by that name.

The Mountjoy executions must be distinguished from the government's policy of executions. The executions were carried out in an orderly and legal manner for specific crimes under the authority given the military by the Dáil. The Mountjoy executions, on the other hand, had little semblance of legality. Prisoners who had been in jail since the opening days of the civil war and could not have participated in the assassination of Sean Hales were taken out and shot as a reprisal and a deterrent.

However, both the executions and the deaths of the Mountjoy prisoners resulted from the same frame of mind on the part of the government. They were afraid that they could not weather the threat from the Irregulars and the gains which they had secured in the Treaty would be lost. O'Higgins' well-known but telling description of the government as a group of young and inexperienced men groping in the darkness with wild men screaming through the key hole captures the sense of insecurity which must have affected members of the government.

The decision to execute the four Mountjoy prisoners, moreover, must be evaluated in the light of the escalating violence of that period. It was not only the assassination of Sean Hales which led to the Mountjoy executions. That event was the proverbial last straw. It was also the result of a sense that things were simply getting out of control. For example, a month before the Mountjoy executions and the death of Sean Hales, on 3 November, in an attempt to assassinate the commander-in-chief, Mulcahy's residence, Lissenfield House, was attacked by armed men. A shoot-out followed and one of the attackers was killed. Allegedly, a bomb was thrown into the grounds but failed to explode.[37] Mulcahy and his family were unharmed.

Unfortunately, the government's policy was not effective in stopping the general violence. While there were no other assassinations of Dáil deputies, other types of violence escalated. In response to the Mountjoy executions, the Irregulars struck out against members of the Oireachtas, burning the houses of four members.[38] In the case of Sean McGarry, a child was burnt to death in the attack. Less than two weeks later, a former member of the Dáil and the man who was secretary of the June Peace Committee of Ten was shot dead in his shop in Rathmines.[39] On 14 January 1923, President Cosgrave's home was destroyed by burning. On 13 February, Kevin O'Higgins' father was killed, shot dead in his own house. The civil war was becoming more heinous, more deplorable.

Executions continued throughout the civil war. From 17 November 1922 to 2 May 1923, the government executed approximately 77 people, including 5 members of the Free State army convicted of treacherously aiding and abetting the Irregulars.[40] The efficacy of this policy is difficult to evaluate and any assessment must take into account both short term and long term effects. As noted above, in the short term, the government's policy was successful in at least protecting sitting deputies from assassination. It also possibly demoralized its opponents by the display of what the government would call determination and its opponents would call "dishonorable tactics".[41] Moreover, in the aftermath of the executions, the government enjoyed a great deal of popularity among the supporters of the Free State. For example, in the election of 1923, Mulcahy, the man who was intimately identified with the executions, won an overwhelming number of votes in his constituency.[42] Mulcahy could only have taken this as an endorsement of his policy.

In the long run, however, the executions harmed both the government and the country. It created a spirit of bitterness which made the horror of civil war even more difficult to overcome, which took more than fifty years to dilute. Moreover, it tainted the Cosgrave government with the image of being vindictive, mean spirited and spiteful. After the threat from the Irregulars had receded, what would remain—thanks in part to Irregular propaganda—was the memory of the executions, especially the Mountjoy killings. This would subsequently hurt the government and would be one factor in the declining popularity of the Cosgrave government and the government's party, Cumann na nGaedheal.

During the civil war, Mulcahy did not hesitate to take full responsibility for the executions. He believed they were necessary and he stood by his decision. In later years, however, while he did not retreat from his decision, Mulcahy expressed anger at being put into a situation where such executions were necessary, and he blamed de Valera for making them necessary. For example, at one point in his recollections, Mulcahy refused to deal with the question of the executions and instead insisted on dealing with the more general question of "killing at any time during the period". He posed a series of questions about the validity of ordering engagements in which it was likely that those involved would lose their lives. Not surprisingly, Mulcahy used two examples associated with de Valera: the

Custom House attack wherein the IRA suffered heavy casualties, and de Valera's suggestion of pitched battles with 500 men on each side. Mulcahy wondered aloud how many men might have been killed if de Valera's idea had been accepted by GHQ.[43] Mulcahy linked these engagements to the actual executions. While the connection is, at best, nebulous, it reflects Mulcahy's adamant belief that de Valera had to bear direct responsibility for the violence.

Moreover, in another recollection, Mulcahy cited the policy of de Valera and Lynch as being related to, if not responsible for, the executions. When Republican propaganda characterized the Free Staters as traitors to the Republic, it invited violence against them. More significantly, when the Republican command issued a list of names of all those who voted for the Emergency Powers Bill, it bore a striking resemblance to a death list. These actions, Mulcahy argued, pushed the government into executing the Irregulars.[44] Mulcahy realized, however, that what people remembered was not Lynch's or de Valera's threats against the Free State officials, but rather the executions.

Despite the criticism of the executions, the mood of the army was optimistic. The army's progress against the Irregulars was having noticeable results. Military reports in October of 1922 substantiated the fact that the army had broken the strength of Irregular resistance throughout much of the country—despite the fact that the mopping up operation would take months and would at times degenerate into outrageous violations of decency on both sides. Intelligence reports from the 3rd Southern, for example, believed that the area was basically under control with the Irregulars suffering from a lack of organization. There was a similar report from the 2nd Southern that there were a "considerable amount of Irregulars loose in the area without any organization or without any attempt to support one another. . . . They go in for sniping and waiting for small convoys. They are badly off for clothing and boots." The 1st Northern claimed that the Irregulars in that area were "on the run all the time", and the Eastern area saw difficulties only in Dundalk and Dublin City.[45]

The army faced stiffer challenges in the southern part of the country. Although it had improved significantly since the early days of the war, Cork remained one area of concern:

> Irregulars are working mostly against the Army—sniping. Use women in towns and with columns. No adequate way of dealing with women. Morale of Enemy is bad. Have no incentive to fight. People turning more against them every day. Are against all military forces. Irregulars have not gone in for close ambush. Tried road mining but without success. Might be running short of stuff. . . . Do not attack with any heart.[46]

This particular analysis was prophetic in that it pointed out, amidst the details on the fighting, that the people were turning against all armies, against all military forces. This would be significant in the upcoming army mutiny of 1924.

Problem areas remained. Kerry, in particular, was—and remained until the end of the war—one of the worst areas in the country for the Free State army. According to the October report, the Irregulars were:

> Still in large numbers. . . . Keep all roads broken. As soon as a bridge is built up it is broken again that night. No railways running. Very hard to keep Tralee Fenit road open. Laborers terrorized and won't do any repair work. . . . 12,000 Irregulars. . . have looted Kenmare and robbed all shops. Comdt. O'Connor's father chased out of Kenmare. Father O'Sullivan kidnapped. Cumann na mBan the problem in Kerry.[47]

Kerry became increasingly difficult for the military to control, and it was the site of some of the worst atrocities of the war—Knocknagoshel, Ballyseedy, Cahirciveen and Countess Bridge.

Despite the problem with Kerry, in the fall of 1922, GHQ believed that, overall, the position of the army was satisfactory with numerous commands reporting progress in the restoration of peace and order. It also noted that special efforts were being made to keep the arteries of commerce open and trade flowing and thus decrease the economic hardship the people were suffering. In turn, the Irregulars were rapidly losing the sympathy of the people, and their morale was weakening.[48]

Mulcahy exhorted the army to take advantage of the loss of support for the Irregulars and actively cultivate the good will of the people:

> Every effort . . . [should] be made to regard with consideration the feelings of the civilian population. It will be remembered that practically all civilians are our friends and where the civilians are not friendly, all restraint and forbearance will be shown. Cases have arisen where the action of the troops shown certain lack of thoughtfulness, particularly in regard to the driving of motor cars, tenders, lorries etc. Careless driving will be avoided. Undue and unnecessary sounding of horns and alarms will not be permitted. Anything that could be construed by the people as Militarism must be avoided. All ranks should remember that they are the army of the people.[49]

Mulcahy was, as always, concerned about the reputation of the army. Sometimes his concern with image led him into harsh, unfair decisions. Such an instance occurred over the question of granting dependents' allowances to common law wives and illegitimate children. According to the army finance officer, in cases where dependants were being supported by the soldier for a reasonable time before enlistment, they would be eligible for dependants' allowance. In the finance officer's view, the criteria for the award was "bona fide permanent domestic basis". Despite this advice, Mulcahy refused to countenance such a decision. Not only did he hold that common law wives and illegitimate children should not be regarded as dependants, he also maintained that "when it is revealed that they exist, that the officer or other rank concerned should be dismissed from the Forces."[50] This type of decision gave Mulcahy the reputation among some of being self-righteous and priggish.

Moreover, Mulcahy could be curt and dismissive when he believed that a situation required action rather than discussion. Nor was he always sensitive to others in answering questions about the progress of the civil war. He was taciturn with his colleagues. He could be abrupt with others. For example, when asked by a special correspondent of the Press Association if he cared to reassure the people about the army's ability to deal with any Irregular challenge, Mulcahy replied that the people would not be more assured of the effectiveness and ability of the officers and men of the Army by his speaking of it. "Our most effective work", he said, "has always been done with our mouth shut."[51]

This impression of Mulcahy has to be balanced, however, against the fact Mulcahy cared deeply about those serving under him and could be exceedingly kind and considerate. For example, a week before Christmas in 1922, Mulcahy and his chief of staff, Sean MacMahon, visited Marlboro Hall Convalescent Home and had a brief conversation with every wounded soldier in the building.[52] Unfortunately, because of the policy of the executions with which he so clearly identified and because of some harsh decisions and statements, it was the unyielding, rigid persona which came to be associated in the popular mind with the commander-in-chief.

In its fall 1922 report, GHQ also evaluated its own progress in raising and training an army:

> The efficiency of the Army is being constantly raised, and it is hoped that in reasonable time any serious military activity of the Irregulars will become a matter of impossibility. In view of the fact that an army had to be hurriedly raised, organized, and trained practically at the moment when the portals of self-government were being opened to the country, errors of administration may creep in, but every effort is being made towards raising efficiency, as well as towards pursuing a course of rigid economy.[53]

But problems remained. Chief among these was the difficulty of maintaining discipline given the severe strains of a civil war, especially a civil war which had deteriorated from guerrilla action to simply hit and run. Neither side was free of dishonorable conduct. Neither side was free of inhumane actions.

It was not surprising that the areas which witnessed the worst lack of discipline were those in which the war dragged on the longest. Both sides seemed to have lost all decency as they stalked one another like animals of prey, shooting, ambushing, dynamiting at will. Kerry was a prime example.

Because Kerry was a Republican stronghold, the Free State troops were working under particularly adverse conditions. They could not count on the majority of the population to support them—either through fear of, or loyalty to, the Irregulars. The terrain of parts of Kerry made it ideal for the Irregulars to fade in and out of action, frustrating the attempts of the Free State troops to capture them. Even before the passage of the Emergency Powers Act, the Kerry command had seemingly carried out ad hoc executions in retaliation for the deaths of two railway men and the continued destruction of railroads.[54]

To curb Irregular activity, the Kerry command executed 19 people between September and December of 1922, a high number indeed. It also threatened to execute others, if their military activity did not cease. For example, on 20 December 1922, a military court in Kerry found three Irregulars guilty of possession of arms and ammunition and sentenced them to death. The GOC, Comdt. Gen. Murphy, suspended the execution of the sentences if the Irregulars ceased "(1) ambushes or attacks on National troops; (2) interference with railways on roads; and (3) interference with private property". If they did not, the convicted men would be put to death.[55] This strategy did not end the violence and both Irregular activity and Free State executions continued through the early months of 1923.

One tactic, moreover, which escalated the violence was the use of land mines. These mines exploded when either the pressure was released or when they were stepped on. Operation Reports of March 1923 from the Kerry Command claimed that the Irregulars used these land mines to blow up Free State troops who were clearing an arms and ammunition dump. Because of later events the Free State military report is worth quoting at length:

> As result of mine tragedy Castleisland, this morning, G.O.C. Kerry Command, has issued order that in future all mines will be lifted, and all dumps cleared by Irregular prisoners.
>
> Reference mine tragedy, Castleisland, details as follows:—Troops conducted search in Knocknagoshel located dump in Bairanarig Wood. It was covered with stones, and troops removed same, and finally encountered big rock. They were engaged in lifting it when trap mine exploded, and blew six of the party of nine to pieces. Arms, legs, flesh and pieces of uniforms found hundreds of yards away. Captain Stapelton had Machine Gun which was blown to atoms, and rifles carried by remainder of party suffered similarly. Five deaths have already resulted, and sixth victim cannot recover as his legs are shockingly mangled, and had to be amputated.[56]

The events at Knocknagoshel bear a direct relation to the disputed events the next day at Ballyseedy. There are at least two versions of the story.

According to Free State sources, on 7 March 1923 a party of Free State troops encountered a barricade of stones built across the road at Ballyseedy bridge, a few miles out. In consequences of [the] mine tragedy Castleisland, troops did not attempt to remove obstruction. Party returned to Tralee, and brought out batch of Irregular prisoners, who were instructed to remove the barricade. While engaged in doing so a trigger mine exploded, and eight of the prisoners [were] killed, and Captain Breslin, Lieut. Joseph Murtagh, and Sergt. Ennis wounded, the last two rather seriously.[57]

This Free State report distinctly differs from the account written by the Irregulars. According to their account, Irregular prisoners were deliberately blown up by the Free State troops as a reprisal for Knocknagoshel. In this version, the prisoners were "tied together with ropes, the boot laces of each tied to those of the prisoner on either side of him, so as to make all chance of escape impossible, and then [they] were dragged over the mines by FS officers and the mines exploded."[58] The people in the area claimed that, for days after, "the birds were eating the flesh off the trees at Ballyseedy Cross."[59] Miraculously, one prisoner survived, blown far enough away by the mine blast to escape. The Free State report from Kerry claimed he was insane;[60] the Irregulars published his tale of the deliberate dynamiting of prisoners far and wide.

Both sides do agree as to the denouement of the episode. That evening, there was a riot outside the Free State post by the families and friends of the Irregular prisoners. The Free State report blamed the local people for "disgraceful scenes" at the funerals of the prisoners killed in the "mine explosion" at Ballyseedy. Free State officers in Kerry claimed that

> Every facility for burial was accorded relatives by military authorities, who, also provided coffins for [the] dead. The coffins containing dead were handed over to relatives out-side Barrack gate. They removed the remains in public street, from coffins supplied by military, and transferred them to other coffins. Military coffins were then broken up, and left lying on roadway.[61]

The Irregular's account agreed with the fact that the relatives of the dead prisoners were angry and that a "frenzy" swept the crowd as, upon opening the coffins, they could not distinguish the bodies of their relatives. The crowd stoned the Free State soldiers.[62]

It also seemed that the Free State troops, perhaps under the influence of alcohol, did not show proper respect for the remains of the prisoners, and rumor has it that legs and arms were carelessly put into coffins—some with three legs and some with three arms, for example. The destruction of the coffins was a statement of the contempt which the relatives felt for the Free State and its troops. The scenes following the funerals at Ballyseedy were so bad that, within the month, the army issued a new regulation that all prisoners in Kerry shall be buried in the area in which the death has taken place.[63] Bodies, henceforth, would not be returned to their relatives.

The events of Ballyseedy were quickly followed by the same type of event in other places: Countess Bridge and Cahirciveen. At Countess Bridge, a mine exploded killing four prisoners and at Cahirciveen, five more prisoners were killed. In this instance a pro-Treaty officer, Lt. McCarthy, resigned in disgust over the raging violence. He claimed that the prisoners had been shot first and then blown up by mines.[64] A similar attempt at Castlemaine to force prisoners to clear mines was unsuccessful as the prisoners escaped.

The Republicans made good propaganda of these events. As early as 12 March, Lynch was writing to his adjutant-general that the "massacre of prisoners" in Kerry should be "expose[d] . . . to the utmost, getting out pamphlets for all country areas etc." Lynch also noted that the details of the events were being collected—including signed statements—and that a report was to be sent by special courier to Dublin. Lynch wanted to send it to all Senators and clergymen and even hoped to have it exposed in the Dáil.[65]

The events at Ballyseedy, Cahirciveen, and Countess Bridge sparked an official military inquiry. It was presided over by Major-General P. Daly, GOC, Kerry Command; Major-General Eamon Price from Portobello; and Colonel J. McGuiness, Kerry Command. The report denied that the prisoners had been killed as reprisals for Knocknagoshel and rejected the allegations of brutality and mistreatment of prisoners. It claimed that the mines had been laid by the Republicans, citing as an example the case of Cahirciveen where the Republicans had hoped to capture the town.[66] In the eyes of the military court, the Free State army was vindicated.

Mulcahy had to answer the charges against the army—his army—in the Dáil. He reported the results of the inquiry exonerating the army against the Republican charges. And he defended the soldiers in Kerry:

> The troops in Kerry have had to fight against every ugly form of warfare which the Irregulars could think of. They have . . . [had] 69 killed and 157 wounded, and their record there is such that it is inconceivable that they would be guilty of anything like the charges that are made against them in the Irregular statement. . . . On the other hand, the Irregulars in Kerry have stooped to outrage of every kind. Of the 69 of our men killed in that area, 17 lost their lives guarding food convoys to feed the people in outlying districts. The Knocknagoshel incident is typical of the methods of their warfare.[67]

Mulcahy reaffirmed Daly's decision to use prisoners for clearing barricades. But, he added two new qualifications. Clearing barricades would no longer normally be done in darkness and, more importantly, steps would be taken to detect the presence of mines before the prisoners began to remove the barricades.

The events at Ballyseedy, Cahirciveen and Countess Bridge remained controversial. The Republicans readily admitted that they obstructed and mined roads. They took credit for mining the roads at Knocknagoshel, and possibly Ballyseedy.[68] In light of the order that Free State troops were not to clear away any obstruction, it was not impossible that the prisoners were brought in to clear the obstructions. But it was not likely. A Free State investigation after the war into Ballyseedy claimed it was a reprisal.[69]

Even at the time, the verdict of the military court of inquiry did not allay the allegations against the army in Kerry. In the Dáil, Tom Johnson called for a non-military inquiry, claiming that the composition of the military court did not inspire confidence in the results.[70] Moreover, without a more impartial investigation, the conduct of the army in Kerry could be used by those government officials who were becoming displeased with the army as another indication of the problems plaguing the military.

Mulcahy did not see it this way. He replied to Johnson's criticism of the military court by saying that he saw no problem with having those who were responsible for the army in Kerry investigate the allegations. It was now up to the government to decide if it wanted an outside inquiry. Mulcahy then went on to voice his faith and confidence in Major-General Daly and his army in Kerry:

> As far as the Kerry officers were concerned, very few who know them, and very few, I think, of the civil population in Kerry will question their desire for discipline. . . . I have the fullest confidence that the honour of the Army is as deeply rooted in them as it is in any of us here at Headquarters or in any member of the Government.[71]

Mulcahy's handling of this affair was in keeping with his sense of loyalty. He would not forget the important role which Daly played at the beginning of the civil war, at a time when so many of his experienced officers deserted him. He would not now repay that loyalty with a vote of no confidence. In fact, Mulcahy's opinion of Daly remained so high that he would recommend him after the civil war for reappointment over a number of other officers. This recommendation would be strongly questioned by some of the civilian members of the government, at least in part, because of what happened in Kerry.

In general, it would have been out of character for Mulcahy not to publicly defend his officers from civilian attacks and Republican allegations. Mulcahy also was worried about the effect of these accusations on the morale of the army in Kerry in particular and the army as a whole. In this, the final stage of the war, he would not undermine their confidence or determination by siding with their critics.

Mulcahy erred. The charges against the army in Kerry were so serious that a civilian inquiry was the only way of establishing the truth of the matter. Lingering doubts and accusations would, in the long run, hurt both the Kerry command and the army in general. Mulcahy could not see that. His faith in the honor of the army and his disdain for the claims of Republican propaganda probably made it almost impossible for him to believe that his officers and men could do such things. And, for those who lacked his faith, Mulcahy could point to the results of an official military inquiry. To doubt their findings, was in his view, tantamount to challenging the honor of the army.

   Even before these events in Kerry, there were some on the Irregular side who were questioning the wisdom of continuing the war. Among the most important was Liam Deasy, deputy chief of staff of the Irregulars and recognized leader of Cork. Deasy had come to believe that victory in the field was now impossible and that to continue the struggle would be simply to destroy any hope that the wounds of civil war might heal in the near future.[72] Deasy also knew that the government's policy of executions had taken its toll on the Irregulars and he suspected that this policy would be intensified as the struggle continued. Thus, Deasy concluded that it was necessary to end the war.[73] For Deasy, the Irregulars were right in protesting the abandonment of the Republic. The tragedy was that it "did not end with the fall of the Four Courts".[74]

   It would seem that many of these ideas had crystallized in Deasy's mind before his capture by Free State troops on 18 January 1923, in Cahir, County Tipperary. Deasy was tried before a military court on charges of "having in his possession without proper authority, a long parabellum revolver and twenty-one rounds of ammunition", found guilty, and sentenced to death.[75] Deasy then requested a stay of execution in order to allow him time to discuss his ideas on ending the civil war. He requested an interview with Mulcahy. Mulcahy's response was simple and direct: An interview and a stay of execution would be granted only on the basis of immediate and unconditional surrender. Deasy agreed.[76] The execution was stayed and Deasy was moved to Dublin.

   Deasy undertook to convince his comrades of the futility of continuing the struggle. In letters to the ranking members of the Irregular executive and army council, Deasy asked them to consider:

   (a) The increasing strength of the F.S. army as evidenced by the present response to the recruiting appeal.

   (b) The decrease in strength of the IRA consequent on the recent numerous arrests.

   (c) The entirely defensive position of our Units in many Areas, and the general decrease in fighting.

   (d) The "War Weariness" so apparent in many areas.

   (e) The increasing support for the F.S. Government, consequent on our failure to combat the false propaganda.

(f) The serious situation which the executions have created; reprisals, counter-reprisals etc.[77]

Deasy believed that these conditions would lead to a situation where the war would be waged by both sides against the people and would soon deteriorate to where the British would intervene, sounding the death knell to nationalist interests. For these reasons, Deasy asked that the fighting stop.

One particularly interesting point he raised concerned the Irregular hope of aligning itself with "separatist elements" in the Free State army who, it was hoped, would be alienated by the repressive policy of the government. Having observed the Free State army during his arrest, Deasy concluded that

> candidly, I am convinced it has only made for better discipline among the Officers. To them it is only a matter of carrying out instructions, even though they are unpleasant. . . . You realize the hopes I had of eventually making for unity with the separatist elements under the old conditions—the only basis upon which real firm unity can be made—I cannot now from my experience hold out even the slightest hope of a response under present conditions.[78]

Deasy's appeal fell on deaf ears. The Irregular leaders rejected his proposals emphatically. Within a week, Liam Lynch, chief of staff of the Irregulars, wrote to Deasy, "on behalf of the Government and Army Command, that the proposal contained in your circular letter of the 30th of January, and the enclosure, cannot be considered".[79]

Deasy's appeal, however, did provide Mulcahy and the army leaders with good propaganda. On 9 February 1923, Mulcahy issued a proclamation announcing that "the government was prepared to offer amnesty to all persons in arms against the Government "who, on or before Sunday, February 18th 1923 surrender with arms to any officers of the National forces or through any intermediary."[80] Mulcahy believed that Deasy's appeal should be publicized to the rank and file and that they should have the opportunity of following Deasy's advice, regardless of the decision of their leaders. Mulcahy wanted them to surrender their weapons, admit their error, acknowledge the Dáil as the legitimate government and then go home in peace. Speaking in the Dáil about the offer of amnesty, Mulcahy said:

> Some of us feel very tied at any rate to the rank and file of these people who are fighting against us, or rather those people whom we are trying to prevent fighting against us. We know how they were misled into their present situation, and we know that if they are to be saved from a certain type of damnation they have to make a clean breast of it, and admit that they have gone the wrong road in the present instance.[81]

Mulcahy severely underestimated the strength of the hostile feelings which his policies had generated among the rank and file of the Irregulars. He might reach out to them, but they rejected him and his party, as subsequent elections would demonstrate.

Despite the fact that Lynch categorically rejected Deasy's peace moves, the Irregular chief of staff was worried about the effect it and the government's offer of amnesty would have on the morale of his troops. Lynch wrote to all his officers warning them of the dangers inherent in listening to such offers of peace. He denied the validity of Deasy's analysis and assured them that the general position was most satisfactory.[82] However, in a private letter, Lynch admitted that the Deasy incident hurt the Irregulars:

> The general situation here up to a few days ago was most satisfactory, and were it not for the Deasy incident. . . I am sure we would have matters all our own way within a few weeks. Owing to this incident it may take us some time to recover from it, but I am certain all will be right away.[83]

Deasy's appeal provided a good excuse for Irregular difficulties. Perhaps Lynch actually believed that the Irregular position was that strong. Perhaps the Deasy incident provided him with an excuse to explain away present difficulties to his Irish-American supporters.

Deasy's analysis of the situation proved correct. The civil war degenerated more and more as it dragged on and on. On the government's side, dissatisfaction was building in the cabinet over the army's performance. The chief dispute was between Kevin O'Higgins, the minister for home affairs, and Mulcahy, the minister for defence. The issue that was being ironed out was the relationship of the military to the civilian government.

Part of the problem was that Mulcahy failed as minister for defence to keep his colleagues properly informed. Time and again, the cabinet requested the presence of the minister for defence. Although Mulcahy was justifiably preoccupied with winning the civil war, he had an obligation to inform the cabinet as to the progress and problems of the army. This Mulcahy did not do.

Communication between Mulcahy and his cabinet colleagues was hampered by the fact that while most of the cabinet shared quarters in government buildings during the worst part of the war, Mulcahy and his staff stayed at Portobello. Thus the distance between the minister for defence and his colleagues was both symbolized and exacerbated by their different headquarters. More significant was Mulcahy's reticence to discuss military matters, even with cabinet colleagues. He believed that military matters were the concern of the army and not within the purview of the cabinet. He would give them general policy descriptions, but the details, the plans, the minutiae he kept to himself. Thus, cabinet members fell prey to rumors and gossip. The attorney-general, Hugh Kennedy, provided an incisive analysis of the climate of the times:

> individual ministers have in the course of their ordinary work, met persons day by day who gave them unofficial accounts of disquieting happenings and such accounts made deeper impressions because ministers were not in possession of authoritative information which to test and weigh the stories told. Such a state of affairs could only breed suspicion that all was not well, that things were being concealed, and necessarily give rise to a form of great anxiety opening the ear the more ready to every tale that offered.[84]

And, clearly, as the civil war dragged on, tongues wagged, willing minds believed, and fact and fiction became merged beyond recognition.

Even before the civil war had officially ended, a crisis point was reached. As minister for home affairs, O'Higgins was in charge of the civic guards and received monthly reports from them. These reports convinced him that, despite its extraordinary power and overwhelming numbers, the army was not moving quickly or efficiently enough against Irregular lawlessness. For this failure, O' Higgins blamed the leadership of the army, a leadership which he characterized as unbending and unimaginative.

Mulcahy rejected his colleague's analysis and judgment of the army. Mulcahy argued that the civic guard reports were not an accurate assessment of the situation in the country, but rather were written to curry favor with O'Higgins, to tell O' Higgins what he wanted to hear. According to Mulcahy, these monthly reports were written " in the spirit of wanting generally to prejudice the position of the Army and all persons in the Army. . . . And that these reports are provided with a very definite knowledge that they are asked for, for that reason."[85]

In January 1923, O' Higgins prepared a memorandum for a full cabinet meeting on the military situation, analyzing the state of the nation. He suggested that a special mobile force be created to deal with criminal violations and urged the army to cultivate better relations with the civilian population through more courteous conduct, stricter discipline and prompt payment of accounts and dependants' allowances. Furthermore, O'Higgins favored executions in every county in order to increase the psychological impact. He believed that "local executions would tend considerably to shorten the struggle."[86]

Not having received a satisfactory response to his memo, O' Higgins pressed on. His receipt of the civic guard reports for the month of February 1923 precipitated a cabinet crisis. A special meeting of the executive council was called for 27 March to consider the latest police analyses.[87] This time the result was dramatic. The meeting ended with the resignation of the army council: the commander-in-chief, Mulcahy; the chief of staff, Sean MacMahon; the adjutant-general, Gearoid O'Sullivan; and the quartermaster-general, Sean O'Murthuile.

In a letter to President Cosgrave, Mulcahy explained that cabinet discussion convinced him that he and the army council no longer had the confidence and trust of the cabinet. Specifically, he believed that his colleagues felt:

> 1. That progress made by the Army up to the end of February has not been satisfactory; 2. that the control of the Army is aloof from and is felt to be unresponsive to the Government; and 3. that there is some undefined divergence of purpose on the part of the Army, as from the Government.[88]

Although the army council disputed these charges, they felt that considering their grave responsibilities—literally deciding issues of life and death—they could not continue to exercise power in this atmosphere.[89] Not wishing "to make difficulties" for the government, they collectively tendered their resignation as the Army Council.[90]

The executive council refused to accept the resignation of the army council and, on 9 April, ordered the army council to continue to function as it had in the past.[91] It was not, however, a ringing endorsement of the army council. The generals' resignations would be accepted by basically the same cabinet only a year later. Rather the government did not want to send out the wrong message either to its supporters or its foes. It believed that the resignation of the army council at this time would be interpreted as a sign of deteriorating conditions in the country which would give heart to the now faltering Irregulars and would discourage its own followers.[92] Strategically, it made little sense to change the leadership of the army before the civil war was over. Perhaps also the executive council was unsure of the reaction of the army if its leaders were dismissed.

The cabinet did take some action, however, establishing a Council of Defence which would allow the executive committee more direct voice in army affairs. Its members were to include President Cosgrave; Kevin O'Higgins; the minister for industry and commerce, Joe McGrath; and Mulcahy. It was simply a compromise—a means of placating O'Higgins while not totally alienating Mulcahy. As an article in the *Morning Post* correctly claimed "the cabinet finally screwed up its courage, or to be more accurate, Kevin O'Higgins screwed up the rest of the cabinet's courage" to move against the senior officers of the army.[93] The cabinet moved, albeit slowly and cautiously.

The council of defence had a short life. Due in part to Mulcahy's resentment at this interference in the affairs of the army and to the successful conclusion of the civil war, this particular council of defence was allowed to lapse. Predictably, it received mixed reviews. O'Higgins believed that "the results secured justified the intervention" of the cabinet.[94] Mulcahy, on the other hand, maintained that it weakened Army control, interrupted the final operations against the Irregulars and "created the psychological position that certain groups of Army officers were encouraged to go behind the backs of the Army Authorities to Mr. Joe McGrath and another group to Mr O'Higgins".[95] The events of the army mutiny of 1924 proved Mulcahy's claim correct.

Despite controversy within the cabinet over civilian-military relations, the army itself pushed closer and closer to victory. More and more Irregulars were captured or killed. Their forces had dwindled significantly and Free State jails were bursting from overcrowding. By March, over 10,000 Republicans were in internment camps. Some of the prisoners went on hunger strike. One of the most famous cases was that of Mary MacSwiney, a doctrinaire Republican who went on hunger strike and forced the government to release her. Re-arrested a few months later, she was joined on another hunger strike by five other women—one of whom was Nellie Ryan, Mulcahy's sister-in-law.[96] Despite appeals and much personal anguish, the government released the women only after obtaining agreement that in the future "the fact of a prisoner being on hunger-strike should not affect the merits of the question of detention or release."[97] And, despite these individual protests, it was clearly just a matter of time. The 8,000 Irregulars left on the field were opposed by a Free State army of 40,000.[98] Victory would belong to the Free State.

Some of the leaders of the Republican cause sensed that the time had come to lay down arms. A series of meetings ensued. Lynch remained the most adamant against compromise and peace terms. Others, like de Valera, wanted to see the kind of terms they could negotiate with the Free State. After Deasy's appeal, there had been a renewed spurt of peace offers. The neutral IRA had fielded one team; the Church had organized two—one under the direction of the archbishop of Cashel, one under the direction of a papal envoy, Monsignor Luzio. Because the Free State leaders were not willing to compromise on essentials—and this is was what the Irregulars ultimately wanted—no group was successful. The government's terms were that the Irregular leaders must relinquish their arms and recognize the Dáil as the legitimate government. The Free State leaders would not yield in negotiations what they had fought a civil war for. They were on the verge on winning and would push on until they had won. As O'Higgins said, this was "not going to be a draw, with a replay in the autumn".[99]

The situation changed dramatically with the death of Liam Lynch. Lynch had been meeting with members of the Irregular government and army council to decide whether or not to continue the fight. Unable to agree, they adjourned, to resume on 10 April 1923. Travelling in the Knockmealdown Mountains, on his way to the next meeting, Lynch and his men were surprised by Free State troops.[100] Lynch was wounded in the encounter. He was found by Free State troops and taken to hospital. He died that evening. Lynch's death destroyed whatever was left of the Republican resistance. More than anyone else, he embodied the determination, the zeal and the will of the Republican forces. Liam

Lynch, like Michael Collins, was one of the many tragedies of the civil war, tragedies which deprived Ireland of the talent the country so desperately needed in the post-independence days.

Frank Aiken succeeded Lynch as chief of staff. He was in agreement with de Valera's position that the Republicans should try to arrange a peace settlement. De Valera tried to negotiate terms. Using Senators Jameson and Douglas as intermediaries, de Valera argued that the Republicans should be allowed to keep their arms, or at least store them until after the upcoming election, and insisted there should be no obstacle, that is, no oath, to prevent any representative from participating in the political life of the country. It was a bold attempt to win at the negotiating table much of which had been fought for and lost in the war. The government refused to be drawn into these attempts. It simply issued a document containing its terms:

> All political action in the country should be based on a recognition by every party in the State of the following principles of order: (a) that all political issues . . . shall be decided by the majority vote of the elected representatives of the people; (b) as a corollary to (a) that the people are entitled to have all lethal weapons within the country in the effective custody or control of the Executive Government.[101]

The government insisted that the Irregulars agree to all these terms completely and without qualification.

The government left their opponents little room to maneuver. The Republicans had few options left. Aiken issued an order to dump arms and to hold them for another day.[102] On 24 May 1923, de Valera issued his proclamation:

> Soldiers of Liberty! Legion of the rearguard! The Republic can no longer be defended successfully by your arms. Further sacrifices on your part would now be in vain, and continuance of the struggle in arms unwise in the national interest. Military victory must be allowed to rest for the moment with those who have destroyed the Republic.[103]

The war was over. The Republicans simply hid their weapons. There was no surrender of arms, no recognition of the legitimacy of the Free State. As the country had drifted into war, it now drifted into an uneasy peace. But the scars of the civil war cut deep, disfiguring the body politic, and marring the political, social and economic development of the Irish Free State.

EIGHT

Crisis in the Army—Resignation[1]

I cannot stand over condoning mutiny to such an extent as to foster it and to prejudice discipline in the Army.

Richard Mulcahy, ex-minister for defence

. . . but most people, we think, will have much sympathy with General Mulcahy's position. Mutiny has been condoned, and resignation has been the fate of those responsible persons who refused to condone it.

Irish Times, 20 March 1924

The civil war had left the country weary and disillusioned. The dreams of the revolutionary period seemed like misplaced illusions as the government confronted the harsh realities of post-war state-building. Among the myriad difficulties the new State faced were a political climate tainted with distrust, a collapsing economy, and a problematic relationship between the army and the state. In its relationship with the army, the government had to face the fact that it had authorized the creation of a large military establishment with extraordinary power and responsibility, and that it still needed the army to insure order throughout the country. The government's dependence on the army caused them grave anxiety and, more significantly, engendered a reaction against the army. The situation was further complicated by the fact that, at a time when the government was still unsure of its power and authority, it would undertake massive demobilization.

De Valera's proclamation and Frank Aiken's order to dump arms did not restore peace to Ireland. The main Irregular organization had been broken, but numerous groups of three or four soldiers, bent on avoiding capture and arrest, continued the fight against the Free State army. Too many guns had fallen into private hands and violence had become too much a part of daily life. The army was thus still involved in putting down lawlessness and trying to impose the rule of law.

The government, moreover, had to divert the army into duties usually performed by civilians and usually volatile: collecting rates, often from citizens who refused to pay; seizing cattle (prior to March 1923); enforcing court decrees and returning stolen property.[2] Troublesome questions also arose about the role of the army regarding strikes. General instructions decreed that troops were not to be used for strike duty or riot duty except when the absence of "effective civil authority" would cause "great breaches of the Peace". In all instances, officers were to consult with the civil authority, and only with the express permission of GHQ were troops to replace strikers.[3] It was obviously a sensitive situation. In the Waterford strike of 1923, for example, reports to the chief of staff praised the army for "affording protection to life and property with divided impartiality".[4] The Irregulars, however, used the strike to castigate the army as "the enemy of labour".[5]

These types of encounters placed a strain on military-civilian relations. The severity of the problem can be gauged by the intelligence reports for June 1923. While commending the army for treating civilians in a "more courteous and deferential manner",[6] intelligence also urged that "special precautions . . . be taken to prevent any derogatory conduct on the part of the members of the Army for the future. Excessive drinking, by officers especially, should be put down with a heavy hand."[7] Discipline remained a problem. In October 1923, for example, the adjutant-general's office felt it necessary to remind its officers and men that "severe disciplinary action will be taken in respect of any breach of discipline, whether same arises from neglect, omission, or misconduct". GHQ insisted that all regulations "be implicitly adhered to" and that the army perform its duties in an "efficient and soldier-like manner".[8]

The conduct of the army had political implications. As military activity receded, the Irregulars turned from the battle field to the political arena, setting their sights on victory at the polls. Their aim was to discredit the government and the army and win the support of the people. As one intelligence report indicated: "The gunmen will go behind the scenes and allow the politicians to take the field and to try and win the people to their side."[9] Weeks later, intelligence asserted "that a well-organized campaign is on foot to smash the present Government at the forthcoming election. With this end in view, every possible organisation, social or political, is being exploited".[10]

Government supporters also realized that the next round of the civil war would be fought at the polls and even before the civil war ended, had begun organizing themselves into a political party. In October of 1922, some supporters of the Treaty had met and decided to launch a political party. Mulcahy objected. He believed that it would be enough to select the best possible candidates in each constituency. He wrote to one of the party organizers:

> I do not think this is the time to launch a political organization of any kind. Particularly is it not a time to select a name for it. I don't think you can appeal for a general "rank and file" . . . support until you have got your new Parliament and the new Government had definitely sized up what its programme is going to be. . . . [Y]ou cannot with any justice to anybody define your 'objects' at the present time.[11]

Mulcahy showed himself to be a more astute politician than some of his civilian colleagues. Given the likelihood of retaliation against those who supported the Treaty and the atmosphere of suspicion in which party organizers were working, the government should have expected a cool reception. In fact, the people did not rush to join the new party.[12]

While Mulcahy would eventually become one of the leaders of the new party, Cumann na nGaedheal, his concern at this point was to secure a distance between the army and politics:

> Certain sections of the community regard the Army as the weapon of a particular political party, and this view had so much developed of late that in some Commands the Army is inclined to allow itself to become, through contact, infected with "political disease".[13]

GHQ stated that no officer or soldier could identify himself with any political party, party meeting or demonstration of any kind.[14] In particular, GHQ meant for the army to know and observe its place during the election of August 1923, and dispatched a special note regarding conduct at polling places:

> It must be clearly understood that the duties of these military Piquets on Election Day, are simply to protect Polling Booths, and to assist Police or preserve order. They must not express sympathy with any Party, nor must they pass comments on Elections or Personating Agents, nor any of the electors supporting any of the candidates.[15]

While the minister for defence and GHQ could issue directives and take steps to insure that officers and men observed correct procedures, there was no question but that the de-politicization of the army would be a slow process.

The needs of the new State also demanded a restructuring of the army, moving it from a war time to a peace time force, from a political and independent guerrilla force to a highly professional and disciplined army, unquestionably subject to civilian control. As noted, the army, both in its Volunteer days and during the civil war, had developed largely in response to the exigencies of the time. Now, GHQ wanted to impose a formal, centralized structure which would result in a permanent, professional establishment.

Mulcahy and the headquarters staff believed that a vital step in this transformation would be to initiate changes in the officer corps. During the early days of the civil war, officers were appointed primarily because of pre-Truce service and because of their power to persuade their colleagues to accept the Treaty and fight for the Free State.[16] Now, after the civil war, not only pre-Truce service, but also efficiency and suitability for the designated post were important criteria. The selection of officers became more formalized. GHQ established an officers training program at the Curragh camp. Although GHQ tried to appoint men who were already in positions of authority, some who had served bravely in both the Anglo-Irish struggle and civil war fell short of the higher standards and had to be replaced. Some protested that they were being treated unfairly.

Not only did GHQ have to replace unsuitable officers, it also had to demobilize surplus officers. During the war, the military establishment had burgeoned. By the end of the civil war, in May 1923, the army numbered 52,000 men and 3,000 officers. GHQ wanted to pare down these numbers to 30,000 men and 1,300 officers by January 1924. Final projections were for an army of 18,000 men. Given the high rate of unemployment in the Free State, and the changing nature of the army, demobilization would inevitably prove to be a difficult and delicate task. Men who once enjoyed the adventure and mystique of being "gunmen" were now being asked either to return to civilian life or to assume less prestigious positions within the army.

The efforts to professionalize and demobilize the army would trigger the events of the army mutiny of 1924. At issue were questions of power and prestige within the army. Mulcahy and his staff would be the targets of the dissatisfaction and the victims of the mutiny. In the end, the army would lose many of the men who had guaranteed the very existence of the Irish Free State.

Resistance to change was immediate. In January 1923, a group of pre-Truce officers founded the Irish Republican Army Organisation or the "Old IRA".[17] They felt they were being treated in a manner inconsistent with the sacrifices they had made for Ireland during the struggle for independence and sought more power and prestige within the army. Liam Tobin, Charles Dalton, Frank Thornton and Tom Cullen—all former members of Michael Collins' Intelligence Unit—were its founders.

The Old IRA held their first meetings in January and February 1923. Tobin was appointed chairman and Tom Cullen, organizer. Membership was available only to those officers with the proper "past and present outlook from a national point of view". Their objective was clear: a "strong voice in Army Policy, with a view of securing complete Independence when a suitable occasion arose". They urged their members to take "control of the vital sections of the Army and oust those undesirable persons who were and are holding those positions".[18]

Theirs was a provocative and clever statement of purpose. By merging nationalist aims with personal ambition, the Old IRA created an effective patriotic platform from which to attack Mulcahy and the senior officers of army. Its members posed a potent threat as they proselytized their views throughout the officer corps.

Even before Collins' death, the leaders of the Old IRA were beginning to feel "let down" and it was only the intimidating force of the late commander-in-chief's personality which had kept them in line. As Collins' successor, Mulcahy did not enjoy the same relationship with them. Mulcahy was more formal, more aloof, more reserved. He spent the war years at GHQ. The men of the Intelligence Unit were used to the informal atmosphere of Vaughan's Hotel. Consequently, there was not the same feeling of camaraderie and *esprit de corps* between them and Mulcahy.

The immediate cause of the schism between GHQ and the Old IRA was the reorganization of the IRB after Collins' death. Most of the officers of the Intelligence Unit were excluded from positions of power in this plan. Those who reorganized the IRB did not believe that the members of the Old IRA had previously held sufficiently important offices within the Brotherhood to warrant their inclusion in the upper echelons of power. Officers of the Old IRA blamed GHQ for their exclusion. They mistakenly believed that Mulcahy was the new head of the IRB and that he had rejected them. Although Sean O'Murthuile, the quartermaster-general, would later publicly take responsibility for the reorganization, recent evidence suggests that, in fact, Sean MacMahon, the chief of staff, succeeded Collins as head of the IRB.[19]

Because they were excluded from the upper echelons of the IRB, officers of the Old IRA believed they were also excluded from powerful positions in the army. In general, members of the Old IRA were dissatisfied with their new assignments in the army. Again they blamed GHQ whom they accused of supplanting them with men who had contributed much less than they to the Free State.[20] They were frustrated and bitter. The problem was that although they had performed well during the Troubles, many of these officers were, indeed, poorly suited to the bureaucratic work necessary in a professional, peace-time army.[21]

However, by focusing their complaints on the IRB, the dissident officers won the sympathy of some in the government who disapproved of a secret revolutionary society, especially within the army. Led by Kevin O'Higgins, these cabinet members argued that the IRB was harmful as well as unnecessary, weakening the soldiers' allegiance to the state and dividing the army into factions. They, therefore, were willing to listen to the complaints of the mutineers.

The Old IRA wasted little time in trying to redirect army policy. On 6 June 1923, they boldly sent a letter to President Cosgrave requesting a meeting with him and Mulcahy. Ostensibly, their purpose was to discuss the government's deviation from Collins' position on the Treaty. In particular, the officers wanted to place their views before Collins' successor, that is, Mulcahy, believing that a "genuine effort must now be made to keep absolutely to the forefront the ideals and objects for which the late Commander-in-Chief gave his life".[22] Their exclusion from the higher levels of the IRB and the army must have signaled to the officers of the Old IRA an unwelcome shift in nationalist policy and, equally significant, their own lack of power and prestige.

Their request precipitated a general policy discussion among Mulcahy, Cosgrave and Attorney-General Kennedy. The president's concern was political. He was worried that the Old IRA might move into politics and put up candidates for elections, possibly dividing Cumann na nGaedheal. Mulcahy was concerned about the army. Dismissing the grievances as vague grumbling, Mulcahy insisted that the army not tolerate this interference but rather proceed with the work of demobilization and professionalization.

During the summer of 1923, over Mulcahy's objections, the representatives of the Old IRA met several times with Joe McGrath, self-appointed mediator and minister for industry and commerce, President Cosgrave and Mulcahy himself. During these meetings, the disaffected officers were allowed to state their grievances and vent their frustrations. In this way, the government hoped to forestall an open and public split in the army or in the party. Elections, after all, were to be held in that August. The meetings, however, only raised the dissident officers' expectations and created false hopes. In reality, the Old IRA failed to effect any change in army policy.

Initially, Mulcahy was clearly against these meetings. At the first meeting, the disaffected officers had condemned both the reorganization of the IRB and the current composition of the army officer corps, and had demanded a committee of inquiry to investigate both the retention and demobilization of officers. They had ended their indictment of the army with a direct threat:

> It is time this bluff ended. We intend to end it. Until satisfactory arrangements are come to, we will expose this treachery and take what steps we consider necessary to bring about an honest, cleaner, and genuine effort to secure the Republic.[23]

Mulcahy was incensed. He left the room demanding to know why he should have been brought before the president to listen to such matters. He stated:

> I do not think that in any country in the world four officers would come in uniform and sit down in front of the Commander-in-Chief of that country and read in his presence that document.[24]

Mulcahy, however, succumbed to pressure, especially from Joe McGrath, to continue meeting with the leaders of the Old IRA. Assuming the role of the voice of the Old IRA in the government, McGrath defended the dissident officers, reiterating their arguments that they had been ostracized by GHQ, assigned unsuitable positions, and left out of the reconstitution of "other organizations" (the IRB). McGrath's own feelings of hostility also surfaced. He believed that he himself "had been slighted in a number of matters and that he felt like making an exposure of the whole business and that he was not going for the Dáil at the coming election".[25]

Thus, under pressure from his cabinet colleagues, Mulcahy held meetings with the dissident officers. Mulcahy flatly denied their contention that membership in the IRB was a prerequisite for positions of authority in the army. He pointed out that in the reorganization of the army, GHQ was obliged to fill each position with the most suitable officer. Once the transition from a wartime to a peacetime army was completed and the officer corps had a clearer idea of its duties, Mulcahy assured the representatives of the Old IRA that they would be satisfied.[26]

Lest the officers, however, regard these informal meetings as a means of supplanting the formal military command structures, he also warned them against circumventing the army's chain of command. He told them directly "that their interference with the authority of those responsible for the army or the assumption by them of any authority that did not come from their definite positions in the army could not be countenanced". Mulcahy also cautioned them about involving the army in discussions about the complete independence of Ireland.[27] They had to understand that the army was not to be used for political purposes and that, these meetings not withstanding, discipline would be enforced.

Mulcahy was later criticized for having softened toward, indeed, for seeming to accommodate, the Old IRA,[28] but his apparent inconsistencies were understandable in the political and historical context of 1923. Despite his own denials,[29] he probably tried to placate the dissident officers, at least until after the August elections. Mulcahy was under pressure from his cabinet colleagues to reach an accommodation with the Old IRA and he himself would be concerned about the effects of splitting Cumann na nGaedheal. In the fall, when all the votes had been counted, however, he took a firm stand against the Old IRA.

It was not simply political expediency, however. The memory of the tragic split in the army over the Treaty probably also motivated him. In a letter to the Old IRA, dated 27 July 1923, Mulcahy reaffirmed his wish to keep open the lines of communication with men who had done so much for Ireland. This was particularly important to him as he had witnessed the disastrous situation brought about by isolation and misunderstanding.[30] Consciously or not, Mulcahy repeated the pattern of 1922 in dealing with the dissident officers: negotiations, discussions, conferences, all aimed at holding the army together.

Paradoxically, however, the memory of the civil war also worked to harden Mulcahy's stance. The Free State army had finally ended its campaign against the Republicans. Not unreasonably, Mulcahy, the man who had engineered this victory, may have been distressed and dismayed that officers who had ostensibly fought for the Treaty, for acceptance of the Free State, were now trying to divide the country again. It must have confirmed his worst fears that some of his officers continued to see the army as a political force. This would explain his comment that the interviews were "distasteful to him and that the correspondence with the Tobin group was not profitable in any way".[31]

As of late summer, 1923, Mulcahy did not believe that the Old IRA was a serious threat. He evaluated their threats as "the bluff of children" and did not think them "capable . . . [doing] any damage",[32] an opinion he would shortly be forced to revise. He was counting on the reorganization scheme to alleviate most of the grievances. If, after reorganization, the officers' dissatisfaction continued, strict army discipline would be easier to enforce. Now, however, amid all the changes, Mulcahy felt that "the time was not opportune to face the problem direct in view of the military, political and financial situation."[33] Mulcahy's strategy, once again, was to play for time.

Mulcahy also had to worry about the effects of demobilization in swelling the ranks of the Old IRA. Intelligence reports repeatedly warned of the dangers of releasing large numbers of men into a situation of high unemployment.[34] The demobilization of non-commissioned officers and enlisted men had begun smoothly in June 1923. Men were discharged either for failure to meet the army's physical standards or for questionable conduct records. Some others simply chose to leave the army to return to civilian life. Problems arose, however, when GHQ began to discharge officers in September-October 1923.

After evaluating inspection reports and the recommendations of all heads of departments, staffs and commands, the council of defence—consisting of the minister for defence, the chief of staff, the adjutant-general, the quartermaster-general and one civilian member—prepared the first lists for demobilization under Defence Order No. 28.[35] Approximately 763 officers were dismissed, primarily for marked inefficiency or lack of discipline. In October, the Old IRA wrote to Mulcahy requesting him to prevent the demobilization of certain officers.[36] Mulcahy considered the letter improper and irregular; he never replied. In his view, any such attempt to dictate who should or should not remain in the National Army would be treated as a major breach of army discipline.[37] By ignoring the demands of the Old IRA in this case, Mulcahy defined the difference between airing grievances and influencing army policy.

Officers who had completed the officers training program at the Curragh were among the first to be released. Either positions were unavailable or the officers themselves were judged not suitable for command. The Curragh, therefore, became, as Col. M.J. Costello of Intelligence described it, a "hotbed" for the growth of a mutinous organisation".[38] The Old IRA wasted no time in turning the Curragh into a recruiting ground, preaching resentment and injustice among the pre-Truce officers of the camp. Their work soon yielded results.

The first protest against demobilization occurred at the Curragh on 9 November 1923, when seven officers refused to accept their papers. They were placed under arrest, charged with disobedience, and tried at a general court martial. As part of their defence, they claimed that as members of the Old IRA organisation, they had sworn an oath not to lay down their arms until Ireland had become an independent Republic.[39] The disturbance spread to about sixty other officers at the Curragh who protested against dismissing old Volunteers from the army while retaining ex-British Army officers. They refused to accept their demobilization papers, were removed from camp and denied separation pay and grants.[40]

The disturbance at the Curragh was a prelude to the mutiny four months later, the first in a series of events that culminated in the army crisis of March 1924. Unofficially, the Old IRA warned the government and GHQ of the potential trouble they could cause. The government took notice.

In response to the protest at the Curragh and against the wishes of Mulcahy, on 26 November 1923, the government formed a cabinet committee on demobilization consisting of the minister for education, MacNeill; finance, Blythe; and industry and commerce, McGrath. The committee's charge was to hear the complaints of pre-Truce officers concerning their dismissals, evaluate the validity of the charges against the retention of ex-British Army officers, and investigate the circumstances surrounding the arrest of the men at the Curragh. The committee received—and denied—sixty applications for reinstatement from officers who had rebelled at the Curragh.[41] The committee found it difficult to dispute with Mulcahy's repeated claim that the applicant was "surplus to requirement".[42] On 5 December, McGrath resigned from the committee because some of the officers, whose cases he believed should be decided by the committee, had already been demobilized.[43]

Although the cabinet committee achieved no tangible results, it enabled civilians once again to inquire into the workings of the army or, as Mulcahy saw it, to interfere in military business. Mulcahy contended that the incident at the Curragh would have ended any threat of mutiny, "were it not for the encouragement given these men by politicals",[44] especially in setting up the cabinet committee. Significantly and not surprisingly, Mulcahy's view further strained his relations with his cabinet colleagues.

The disturbance at the Curragh, the subsequent formation of the cabinet committee, and Mulcahy's growing estrangement from the rest of the government strengthened the Old IRA. Its growing power was evident. All the officers who had refused demobilization papers claimed membership in the Old IRA. Moreover, Old IRA leaders alleged that McGrath had guaranteed them that the cabinet committee's decisions would be binding on Mulcahy and the Army Council.[45] President Cosgrave had given McGrath just such a guarantee in order to induce the Minister to return to the committee. The Old IRA thus assumed that they had circumvented Mulcahy's refusal to retain some of their officers scheduled for demobilization.

These developments buoyed the spirit of the men of the Old IRA. Without even resorting to extreme measures, the Tobin-Dalton group had pressured the government into undermining the decisions of the army council, had acquired a voice in army policy. It set a bad precedent, conferring credibility and, at least, the appearance of power upon the Old IRA.

Intelligence realized that the Old IRA was a potential danger to the Free State. Their reports provided GHQ with information on membership, objectives, and arms.[46] As early as August 1923, Professor James Hogan, director of intelligence, warned Sean MacMahon, the chief of staff, that officers were organizing throughout the country and that "these officers have been asked to sit in judgment on the question of Army control and on their brother Officers. They have constituted themselves a final Court of Appeal."[47]

Intelligence continued to monitor the Old IRA. In its general monthly report for November 1923, it stated that:

> The Army situation requires very careful handling. There is a strong undercurrent of unrest among demobilized Officers, and Officers whose demobilization is pending. There is a widespread belief that certain influences are at work to retain the service of officers who never had any National outlook, while officers who have good records are being dispensed with. . . . It is to be feared that meetings and negotiations with Irregular leaders are by no means uncommon. There is a danger that, by continual propaganda and intrigue on the part of certain Army officers, the morale of the Army will be badly shaken.[48]

Unrest simmered through January 1924 when GHQ learned that the Old IRA intended to seize arms, take over a number of barracks, and issue terms to the government. Quietly, GHQ informed their commanding officers to prepare for trouble, and relocated certain troops. Immediate action forestalled any difficulties, but GHQ nevertheless grew anxious.

Mulcahy sent Cosgrave a memorandum on the situation. Mulcahy revised his earlier opinion that the Old IRA were simply bluffing: "The organisation [the Old IRA] may not be a very great danger [now] but in the near future it can possibly be a far greater danger than the Irregular one." Mulcahy insisted that the army hold to its course. He reaffirmed his intention not to retain any unsuitable or recalcitrant officer. Mulcahy reiterated his belief that decisions about demobilization and discipline should be made by the proper army authorities. Government interference, he argued, should be only on the basis of general principles that would be applicable to all cases and could be stated in a policy memorandum.[49] It was not an unreasonable position.

Furthermore, Mulcahy prophetically foresaw one major potential difficulty still to be overcome: "that these men must be weaned away from the idea and the use of the gun". The "gunmen" must be removed from the army. The department of industry and commerce through its resettlement bureau must help them settle into civilian life. Mulcahy criticized not only the resettlement board of the department of industry and commerce for not doing its job properly, but also its Minister, Joe McGrath. Mulcahy told the president that unless McGrath disassociated himself from the Old IRA and turned over whatever information he had to the army, the time would come when these officers would try to dictate unacceptable terms to the government, raising the possibility of another civil war.[50]

As a result of this memorandum, Mulcahy met President Cosgrave and Joe McGrath on 26 January 1924. Mulcahy seemed satisfied with the results. He believed the conference reaffirmed "the soundness of my proposals relating to demobilization etc. and that there was no element of danger in the situation".[51] Apparently both of his colleagues reassured him. McGrath convinced him that the Old IRA meant no harm—his recurring theme—and Cosgrave gave at least some support to the army's demobilization scheme. Mulcahy was too optimistic in his assessment of the meeting. The perils he had predicted remained. He erred in trusting Cosgrave and McGrath.

Throughout the first three months of 1924, demobilization proceeded according to the dictates and design of the army council. The cabinet committee proved ineffective in swaying army policy for the Old IRA. To the Tobin-Dalton group, the high hopes engendered by the Curragh incident proved illusory. They continued to remain outside the portals of power, frustrated and concerned that their powerlessness was undermining their credibility and weakening their organization.

Moreover, GHQ was taking steps to rein them in. On 3 March 1924, the adjutant-general's office ordered that:

> Officers will not leave their Command Areas without the written permission of the GOC of the Command, nor will they leave their Battalion Areas without the written permission of their Battalion Commandant. Officers on leave visiting Dublin will not call at GHQ unless so instructed by their GOC.[52]

This made it increasingly difficult for the Old IRA to organize and hold meetings. Perhaps headquarters had been alerted that a crisis was imminent; perhaps the generals were taking seriously the threat of the Tobin-Dalton group. Whatever their reason, it was a wise decision.

The Old IRA had indeed decided on a more radical course that led Liam Tobin and Charles Dalton to present an ultimatum to the Cosgrave government on 6 March 1924. The ultimatum demanded changes in the army and strongly protested the direction the Free State had taken since the Treaty. Dressing their demands in the rhetoric of republican nationalism, the mutineers declared that they and the Irish people had accepted the Treaty only as a stepping stone to a republic and that the government had betrayed their ideal. They demanded a meeting with government leaders to discuss their interpretation of the Treaty. On a practical level, they insisted on the removal of the army council and the immediate suspension of demobilization and reorganization of the army. If the government declined, they would take action to save the country from "the treachery that threatens to destroy the aspirations of the nation".[53] This was mutiny.

As news of the mutiny spread, officers throughout the country threw their support to the mutineers, a number of them absconding with arms and equipment.[54] The chief of staff, Sean MacMahon, feared that unless steps were taken at once ". . . with great tact and firmness, the Army will develop into an armed mob shortly".[55] Headquarters response was clear and resolute. Mutiny would not be tolerated:

> The Army must not be involved in any political crisis, even if the crisis develops from the mutiny, but must be forced into a military machine that will be the right arm of any Government the people wish to place in power.[56]

And Mulcahy told the press:

> Two Army officers have attempted to involve the Army in a challenge to the authority of the Government. This is an outrageous departure from the spirit of the Army. It will not be tolerated. Particularly will it not be tolerated by the officers and men of the Army who cherish its honour. They will stand over their posts and do their duty to-day in this new threat of danger in the same watchful, determined spirit that has always been the spirit of the Army.[57]

At first, the government seemed as resolute and uncompromising as Mulcahy and his staff. On 7 March 1924, the executive council ordered the arrest of the two signatories of the ultimatum,[58] for what President Cosgrave characterized to the Dáil as "a challenge to the democratic foundations of the State, to the very basis of parliamentary representation and of responsible government". The president refused to discuss any of the political issues mentioned in the ultimatum, claiming that "this Government has never discussed questions of politics with Army officers."[59] But, in fact, Tobin and Dalton met numerous times with members of the executive council, including at least once with the president himself. Perhaps the president did not consider the discussions with the Old IRA political. It was an interesting distinction. At best, Cosgrave's statement was misleading; at worst, a deliberate falsehood.

Following the president's explanation, Mulcahy outlined the military situation. Reports of officers absconding with arms had been received from Roscommon, Gormanston, Baldonnel and Templemore barracks. A few officers had resigned, particularly from the Dublin command. Mulcahy believed that:

> There is a certain atmosphere of threat, that a large number of Officers throughout the Army are preparing to resign if the threat contained in the letter to the Government is not carried out; that they are prepared to set themselves up in arms in defiance against the Government is another threat.[60]

During debate in the Dáil, McGrath repudiated the government's policy and contradicted the interpretation of Mulcahy and his officers. Although he claimed to disagree with the substance of the Tobin-Dalton document, McGrath charged that the "absolute muddling, mishandling and incompetency" of the department of defence had produced the present crisis.[61] In protest, he resigned his position as minister for industry and commerce. Thus, the military crisis generated a political crisis and the government faced both a potential revolt in the army and serious dissension within its own party.

In response to McGrath's charges, Cumann na nGaedheal held several meetings throughout the army crisis, with a "rather well regimented section within the party giving a certain qualified support to the mutineers".[62] By all accounts, McGrath was the star performer. Mulcahy also attended, but abstained from substantial debate with his colleague.[63]

McGrath defended the mutineers. He charged that the government had misunderstood Tobin and Dalton's motives and over-reacted to the ultimatum. It was not mutiny, but rather a dispute between two rival secret organizations, the IRB and the old IRA. As old friends and comrades, the mutinous officers should not, McGrath continued, be expected to adhere to a strict disciplinary code. Allowances must be made. In McGrath's view, the government was truly worried only about its image and the adverse publicity this incident could generate.[64]

McGrath's minimizing of the mutiny as nothing more that a faction fight provoked a lengthy discussion on the role of secret societies in the army. The exchange strengthened the convictions of those who, like O'Higgins and his ally, Patrick Hogan, the minister for agriculture, already favored changes in the army. Discussion on this issue spilled over into a cabinet meeting. Worried that the leaders of the army were tainted by their association with the IRB and therefore, unable to effectively deal with the mutineers, the executive council assigned Eoin O'Duffy, now chief of the civic guards, to manage the crisis and assume the position of general officer commanding the defence forces of Saorstát Éireann.[65] Mulcahy resented O'Duffy's appointment, characterizing him as an outsider who was out of touch with the military.[66] Ironically, the government seemed unaware that O'Duffy himself was a high-ranking member of the IRB.[67]

Mulcahy was clearly upset at the cabinet's decision and O'Duffy's appointment. Yet he remained quiet during the party debate on the army crisis and did not appear to actively defend himself against McGrath's charges. His silence is puzzling. Perhaps Mulcahy believed that it was not proper to discuss military affairs at an open party meeting, especially during a volatile crisis situation. Moreover, although it remains unclear how much the government had actually revealed to its party members, it is possible that Mulcahy refrained from defending headquarters' position because to do so he would have had to make public the discussions which they had held with the mutineers. Such revelations would have embarrassed both the minister himself and, even more so, the government. Perhaps Mulcahy believed that his position was so obviously correct that his colleagues would support him in the end.

Whatever his reasons, Mulcahy remained silent and, to some extent, McGrath persuaded Cumann na nGaedheal and the executive council to accept his interpretation. Both the government and the party wanted a compromise by which they could escape the crisis. Thus, they delegated McGrath to approach the mutineers and induce them to "undo, so far as they can, the mischief created by their actions". Thereafter the incident would be regarded as closed.[68] What else they agreed to is unclear. The mutineers alleged that the government promised, through McGrath, to establish an inquiry board to examine the army crisis, review the demobilization procedure, and offer lenient terms—reinstatement with no victimization—to those who mutinied.[69]

In fact, subsequent events support the mutineers' interpretation. On 12 March 1924, the day after the party meeting, the executive council ordered army authorities to stop the search for the mutineers, granted the mutineers an opportunity to return stolen property, and agreed that the minister for defence would review all individual resignations. Final decision would rest with the executive council. The government also agreed to establish an inquiry committee to investigate McGrath's charges of muddling, mishandling and incompetency in the department of defence. The inquiry would serve two purposes. It would meet one demand of the mutineers. It would also provide a useful cover to prevent full scale discussion in the Dáil. Taken together, these decisions met the basic demands of the mutineers and strongly suggests that some type of agreement was struck.

Furthermore, after these decisions were made, the government received another document from the mutineers in which they repented and rescinded the original ultimatum. The mutineers claimed that they had sent the earlier letter "with the sole object of exposing to the government and the

representatives of the people . . . a serious menace to the proper administration of the army".[70] They now professed their loyalty and allegiance to
the state, acknowledging the supremacy of civil authority over the military
and deploring the detrimental effects of secret societies within the army.
They made no mention of the treaty.

The government underwent a *volte face*. As of the evening of 12 March,
the mutiny was no longer a serious threat to the democratic institutions of
the Free State. It became merely a foolish action, not to be taken at face
value. Kevin O'Higgins articulated the government's position to the Dáil.
While acknowledging that the original ultimatum constituted "mutiny plus
treason", O'Higgins contended that these men had never really meant to
challenge the government, but rather had simply railed against the military
authorities and the abuses and irregularities they had witnessed in the
army. O'Higgins invoked enlightened pragmatism to justify the government's new attitude: "It is all opportunism, if you wish, but in the handling
of national affairs, and in the handling of very delicate situations, there
must needs be opportunism."[71] Later, the mutineers explained that they
had rescinded the original ultimatum in return for the government's
agreeing to their demands. The second document was "to enable the
government to explain its change of front to the Dáil and the public".[72]

Dáil members demanded more information. The government hid behind
a shield of benign ignorance and vagueness. It would not explain; it would
not elaborate. It made no mention of McGrath's role. No hint was given of
the negotiations with the mutineers. The President even refused to provide
the Dáil with details of the inquiry. In this regard, the government was
guilty of the worst of political back room dealings. As an editorial in the
Irish Times observed:

> Mutiny is mutiny, and with all respect for Kevin O'Higgins, who
> must have been acutely uncomfortable yesterday, twenty-four hours
> cannot change it into a merely frank expression of military
> discontent, not even twenty-four hours of treatment in the secret
> alembic of the Cumann na nGaedheal.[73]

Mulcahy agreed. He favored much harsher terms. He argued that the
similarity of statements of resignation among officers from various parts of
the country indicated a conspiracy which "did not intend to confine itself to
resignation alone". Mulcahy urged President Cosgrave to accept the resignations immediately, to preclude the officers' reconsidering their decision.
Furthermore, Mulcahy recommended that all officers who had left their
posts or were absent without leave be charged with a suitable offence as part
of a conspiracy to mutiny. Pending the investigation of a court martial, they
should be under open arrest. Those officers who had absconded with arms
or taken other definite action, Mulcahy argued, should face harsher treatment. He proposed that, in addition to being charged with mutiny, they be

held under closed arrest until the stolen materiel was returned.[74] These measures would enunciate clearly and unequivocally that his ministry would not tolerate such conduct. Most of all, Mulcahy believed that a strong stance was necessary to discourage further action on the part of the mutineers. He felt the mutiny still posed a serious threat to the state, regardless of well-intentioned phrases to the contrary.

Records prove Mulcahy correct. Army archives reveal that the Old IRA had approached non-commissioned officers to ascertain what support they could expect in the event that they staged a *coup d'etat*.[75] Moreover, these same archives indicate that there was also concern that the mutiny would expand to include ex-army officers who were serving in the Guards. A confidential letter sent to General O'Duffy, after the crisis had subsided, accused the Old IRA of asking the ex-army officers for support at the time of their demobilization. Some, the letter implied, might have sympathized with the revolt, but none promised "active support for Tobin and Co."[76] Evidence also indicates that the Old IRA planned to seize government buildings, presuming that some members of the guards were "all right and expected to stand with the mutineers".[77]

Furthermore, the possibility existed that the mutineers would link up with the anti-Treaty forces. Intelligence reports verify this concern, indicating that there were a number of meetings between the two groups. It is not clear how much and at what level the contact between the groups was made, but it was a worrisome possibility.[78] All these attempts to broaden their base of support suggest that the Old IRA was a serious threat to the State.

Rumors of violence filled Dáil corridors, GHQ meeting rooms, shops and pubs throughout Ireland—and Intelligence reports. Army headquarters continued to receive intelligence reports of political intrigue, alleged assassination plots, and a possible *coup d'etat*. It had to be extremely unsettling for Mulcahy and his staff to read of the wild threats of the gunmen desirous of "plugging all and sundry";[79] or more specifically, to read reports which stated that the Old IRA was planning to assassinate cabinet members.[80] Mulcahy was worried about these rumors and about the unpredictable and unstable nature of some of the mutineers.[81]

Thus, when GHQ learned of an Old IRA meeting on 19 March at Devlin's public house in Parnell Street—an establishment formerly used by Michael Collins during the Anglo-Irish war—they decided to act. Probably the purpose of the meeting was to stage a coup or formulate plans to kidnap the entire cabinet.[82] Therefore, the minister for defence and the adjutant-general ordered a raid. The army arrested eleven mutinous officers, and confiscated a small quantity of arms and ammunition. Mulcahy did not consult General O'Duffy or civilian members of the cabinet.

The raid at Devlin's immediately sparked controversy. The mutineers alleged that the Parnell Street raid was a "deliberate attempt to provoke resistance in order to be able to suppress the 'conspiracy' in the most sure and final manner . . . the wiping out of the chief members of the IRA Organisation in bloodshed". Their officers, on the other hand, wanted to avoid bloodshed and "a new outbreak of hostilities" and therefore surrendered.[83]

The army authorities believed the raid was necessary to avoid a more serious challenge to the government. Intelligence reports support their concern. For example, one report stated that "one of the principle items on their [the Old IRA] programme on the occasion of the 'bust up' was the seizure of Government Buildings." Squads of Old IRA officers, the report continued, were to kidnap the governor general and the wife of the GOC Dublin, Mrs Hogan, and assassinate certain officers of the army.[84] Later, there was talk of assassinations, in particular of Kevin O'Higgins, Major General Dan Hogan and a number of other officers.[85] In light of the information available to them, had Mulcahy and his staff ignored the Parnell Street meeting, they would have been derelict in their duties. GHQ had just finished with one civil war and could ill afford a re-enactment of the Four Courts. In this respect, they were successful. The Parnell Street raid, for all practical purposes, ended any real threat of mutiny.

Attention now shifted away from the mutineers to the army council. The executive council met the morning after the Parnell Street raid on 19 March. President Cosgrave was ill and therefore did not attend. Once again there was a general debate on the army, sparked this time by the activities of the previous evening. At least a majority of the cabinet contended that the raid had violated government policy. Mulcahy disagreed, citing the Defence Forces Act and the army's obligation to uphold the law. Neither the executive council, Mulcahy contended, nor any arrangements made with the mutineers should subvert or supersede the law. He argued that the arrested officers had violated military code and endangered the state. The rest of the cabinet countered that the minister and his staff had overstepped their authority and jeopardized the peace of the nation. This, they said, was worse than mutiny. It was mutiny plus treason. Interestingly, whereas the government had treated the mutineers with restraint and understanding, it was ruthless, almost vengeful toward the Army Council. Subject to Cosgrave's approval, the executive council demanded the immediate resignations of the chief of staff, the adjutant-general, and the quartermaster-general from their administrative posts, and recommended to President Cosgrave that Mulcahy too be removed from his office as minster for defence. General O'Duffy was to assume complete control of the army.[86]

Having left the cabinet meeting to allow further and, most likely, more candid discussion, Mulcahy met his staff, unaware that his colleagues would seek his resignation. When a telephone call from O'Higgins made it clear that the cabinet demanded the immediate resignation of the army council—despite Mulcahy's assertion that he could not allow critical positions to become vacant in the midst of a crisis—he resigned in protest.[87]

In accordance with the cabinet's demand, adjutant-general O'Sullivan and quartermaster-general O'Murthuile resigned both their administrative posts and their commissions. The chief of staff, General MacMahon, who was in Cork trying to keep that command calm and loyal at the time of the raid, refused to resign unless the reasons for his dismissal were clearly and specifically stated. He also demanded the opportunity to refute such charges. MacMahon believed that his resignation "would be equivalent to an expression of acquiescence in a policy that will ultimately involve the Army in a political crisis".[88] Despite his protests, however, MacMahon's allegiance to the government was never seriously in question nor did he genuinely intend to challenge the decision of the government. His letter does, however, point out the difficulties confronting the army council. Although its members were being slandered by unnamed accusers, vilified by rumor, sacrificed to gossip and dismissed without explanation, military discipline prevented them from retaliating. They could only resign.

In spite of their harsh treatment by the government, Mulcahy and the army council made certain that military discipline continued to prevail in the army. Mulcahy told his officer corps that he believed "that General O'Duffy will get absolute and scrupulous service from every officer in the army, not touched with mutiny".[89] When Mulcahy's brother, an army officer, approached him and asked what the army should do about the dismissals, Mulcahy emphatically told him to do nothing and return to his regular duties.[90] Similarly, when an officer suggested that GHQ could repudiate the government's measures, MacMahon reprimanded him sharply.[91] And, according to O'Murthuile, when he and O'Sullivan summoned their subordinates at GHQ and "advised them to stand loyal to the Government and forget us, some of these officers ventured to express surprise that we were accepting the situation so calmly".[92] Despite the rumblings of discontent over how the senior officers had been treated by the government, the army, in particular the officer corps, followed the example of the army council and accepted the decision of the government. By acknowledging the right of the cabinet to dismiss the generals, the army showed that it had progressed from a politicized volunteer force to a professional, disciplined military body. Ironically, this evolution was primarily the work of the army council and the minister for defence, those very men who were now being dismissed because of the alleged undisciplined, political spirit which the cabinet believed animated the military.

When the government announced its dismissal of the army council in the Dáil, there was little or no protest. Except for Mulcahy's speeches, few deputies were concerned about the firing of the three generals. It was a rather perverse twist of reason that the men who put down the mutiny were being treated severely while the men who actually threatened the State were being petted and pampered. But Joe McGrath had good political skills and a vocal following in the Dáil. He exploited the dissatisfaction prevalent in

Cumann na nGaedheal and portrayed the mutineers as loyal soldiers who had distinguished themselves in the war for independence and were now being treated shabbily. It made good copy. McGrath, moreover, talked of splitting the party[93] and tied the defence of the mutineers to the political ambitions of some of the deputies.

Furthermore, the mutiny brought forth all the antipathy towards the army that had festered within the government and the Dáil since the civil war. Having conspicuously failed to assert its control over the mutineers, in order to save face, the government needed to affirm its authority over the leaders of the army. By blaming the mutiny on the army leaders, on the way in which Mulcahy and headquarters had reorganized and demobilized the military, the cabinet and the Dáil were able to vent their frustrations and exorcise the fears accumulated during the civil war. Especially among opposition members of the Dáil who had not been kept properly informed during the mutiny,[94] the army crisis activated an anti-military spirit, a backlash to the horrors, the excesses and even the very fact of the civil war.

During the debate on the army crisis, Mulcahy stood alone. By failing to be more politic, more sensitive toward his civilian colleagues, he had isolated himself. Mulcahy's reserve prevented him from appealing to the Dáil as McGrath had. Mulcahy's loyalty prevented him from threatening to split the party. In this instance, he was out maneuvered by McGrath, on the one hand, and the government, on the other. Moreover, the entire debate was rather restricted. The cabinet and Dáil alike deemed the proposed army inquiry to be the proper forum for examining the crisis.

In one respect, however, the Dáil debates were significant. They revealed in vivid detail the wide chasm of distrust separating the cabinet and the army leaders. Speaking for the cabinet, Kevin O'Higgins justified the cabinet's decision to replace the army council. He explained that the Parnell Street raid deviated from both the cabinet's intention and its policy. Moreover, the army chiefs had acted without the imprimatur of General O'Duffy, the man who had been specifically appointed to handle the upheaval. It could very well have resulted in disaster.

But the raid, O'Higgins cautioned, was not the sole reason for the army council's dismissal. Rather "the view was expressed at the executive council that this particular personnel was not the personnel to deal with a mutinous revolt". Regardless of the value of their past services to the State, regardless of the validity of the charges against them, the members of the army council were simply no longer useful, O'Higgins argued. He denied the accusation that the government had capitulated to the demands of the mutineers. The cabinet, he explained, somewhat lamely, had reached its decision in spite of the ultimatum, not because of it.[95]

O'Higgins contended that the cabinet was dissatisfied with the present state of the army. He charged that the army was racked by secret societies, that it was not governed by an impersonal disciplinary code and that a proprietary attitude had developed among members of the army council. O'Higgins then levelled his most stinging accusation: the executive council feared that "the Army was not unequivocally, unquestionably, without reserve, simply the instrument of the people's will."[96]

Mulcahy refuted O'Higgins' charges, characterizing them as "an absolute mis-statement of fact". Were it true that the army was not the obedient servant of the State, he argued, the executive council would not have taken "the extraordinary step" of removing the three principal officers of the army.[97] Only the army's unequivocal loyalty to the government, he told the Dáil, permitted the cabinet to dismiss the army council *en masse*. Mulcahy criticized the cabinet for relying on rumor and gossip, ignoring the fact that it had been his responsibility to keep his cabinet colleagues informed.

Mulcahy countered O'Higgins version of the Parnell Street raid with his own, reiterating what he had argued in the cabinet meeting. He explained his failure to consult O'Duffy by arguing that O'Duffy refused to assume responsibility or issue orders until his position was completely defined.[98] The raid itself, he maintained, was carried out in accordance with the law and the canons of military discipline. He could not be so lax in maintaining discipline as to

> allow officers, either by deserting their posts, or by taking away material belonging to the Army, or by engaging in a conspiracy that might have had disastrous results, to talk and meet openly and publicly in the streets or in the country.[99]

He himself, Mulcahy explained, had resigned because he could not "stand over condoning mutiny to such an extent as to foster it and to prejudice discipline in the Army".[100]

Even though he stood alone in the Dáil, Mulcahy was not alone in censuring the government for having condoned mutiny. O'Higgins' disclaimer notwithstanding, some complained that the government indeed appeared to have acquiesced to the ultimatum. The delay in the reorganization of the army, another of the mutineers' demands, strengthened this perception. As an editorial in the *Irish Times* pointed out:

> Everyone will agree with Mr. O'Higgins that the establishment of discipline in the Army is a vital necessity; but most people, we think, will have much sympathy with General Mulcahy's position. Mutiny has been condoned, and resignation has been the fate of those responsible persons who refused to condone it. Soldiers are simple men, but they can put "two and two together". The "two and two" in this case are represented by the facts that the mutinous ultimatum demanded the removal of the Army Council and the Army Council has been removed.[101]

According to the mutineers, the dismissal of the army council vindicated their actions.[102]

In fact, the government's official position on the Parnell Street raid was undermined by its subsequent policy *vis-à-vis* the detention of the men arrested during the raid. They were released on parole on 21 March 1924. McGrath objected. Since the army had violated the agreement between the government and the mutineers, he said, the arrested men should have been unconditionally released. O'Higgins disagreed. Astonishingly, O'Higgins now claimed that:

> when it was undeniable that a mutinous revolt seemed imminent and seemed under Providence inevitable, it would not be a proper thing to release these prisoners without at least some assurance being given by them that they would not become leaders in any such mutinous revolt.[103]

In so arguing, O'Higgins contradicted himself and his fellow cabinet members' earlier claim. If a "mutinous revolt seemed imminent", the Parnell Street raid was justified. As Mulcahy claimed, army officials would have been irresponsible to have acted otherwise. By acknowledging the seriousness of the meeting at Devlin's public house, the cabinet revealed their true feelings about the army council and the Parnell Street raid. The executive council had simply used the raid to purge Mulcahy and the army council in one bold stroke. The raid crystallized their festering discontent with the army. Critics of the army could use it to convince their colleagues that the senior officers had to be dismissed. Just as mutiny had been transformed into folly, now the "worse than mutiny" raid became a response to an apparently "mutinous revolt". The government made no effort to explain its inconsistency.

The army mutiny of 1924 was the final echo of the civil war, the last vestige of the Volunteer mentality of an independent, political army. The mutiny precipitated a cabinet crisis during which two ministers resigned and the army council was dismissed. Moreover, it brought to a climax the conflict between Kevin O'Higgins and the new breed of leaders and Richard Mulcahy and the veteran officers. The antagonism between the two men and two groups was not personal, but rather the result of differences in strategy, technique and philosophy. By forcing Mulcahy's resignation, O'Higgins and his followers prevailed and emerged victorious.

By resigning on the command of the government—regardless of the validity of the government's decision—the army council upheld the right of the government to control the army. The government's policy was one of compromise, vacillation and inconsistency. Despite the excuses and disclaimers, the fact remained that the Cosgrave government was willing to come to terms with men who had threatened the stability of the state. It was the leaders of the army who refused to condone mutiny. Only with respect to the three generals and the minister for defence did the cabinet act decisively. The cabinet gambled on the loyalty of the army council—and won. If the army council had defied the order to resign and had publicly argued that it was being sacrificed to the demands of the mutineers, if they had called upon the IRB for support, they could have moved Ireland to the verge of another civil war or a military *coup d'état*. The generals had a following in the army, stemming from their work in the early nationalist movement, and a following in the IRB. The *Irish Times* had spoken for many when it argued that the generals were being treated unfairly and that dismissing loyal men at the behest of the mutineers was an insult to those officers who had obeyed orders and upheld discipline. The generals could have used their dismissals effectively, had they so desired. The government was fortunate that the army council believed in the obedience of the military to civilian authority. By submitting their resignations on the demand of the government, by strongly discouraging even talk of repudiating the cabinet's decision among subordinate officers, and by appearing before the Army Inquiry Committee a few weeks later, the army council adhered to and upheld the principle that the Irish army was subordinate to the Irish government.

NINE

The Army Inquiry Committee[1]

We, Sir, because of our appointment, have had to suffer in silence the insinuations and innuendos that the Army has at its head Officers in whom there is not full confidence.

Letter from MacMahon, O'Murthuile
and O'Sullivan to Mulcahy

To allay criticism and possible embarrassment, and to satisfy McGrath and the mutineers, the government established the promised committee to investigate the recent disturbances in the army. It was a smart decision. By the time the army inquiry committee had issued its report in June 1924, both the political and military crises had been sufficiently defused to preclude the Dáil from re-igniting them.

Moreover, by its limited mandate and lack of power, the government ensured that the inquiry would focus on those who quelled the mutiny rather than the mutiny itself. The committee's mandate was "to enquire into the facts and matters which have caused or led up to the undisciplined and mutinous or insubordinate conduct lately manifested in the Army". The terms of reference were expanded to include an investigation into the state of discipline and an evaluation of the charges of "muddling, misman- agement and incompetency in the administration of the army".[2] Thus, the events of the mutiny itself fell outside the scope of the inquiry, conveniently saving the government from scrutiny.

Moreover, the executive council had severely handicapped the committee by withholding the power of subpoena and the right to examine witnesses under oath. In addition, the hearings were closed to the public and the evidence remained confidential, preventing Dáil deputies and the public from fully evaluating the committee's final report.

The committee chair was J. Creed Meredith, a judge who in the pre-1916 period had been one of John Redmond's nominees to the Volunteer executive. He was scathing of Mulcahy and hostile to the army authorities. Among others, the committee also included Patrick McGilligan, who succeeded McGrath as minister for industry and commerce and was an ally of Kevin O'Higgins.[3]

Although they agreed to participate, Mulcahy and his generals rankled at the arrangements. In fact, when the government first announced its intention to hold an inquiry, the three senior officers wrote to Mulcahy requesting a public investigation:

> We, Sir, because of our appointment, have had to suffer in silence the insinuations and innuendos that the Army has, at its head, Officers in whom there is not full confidence. We have also had, for the past year or more, to suffer the interference with Army discipline, with utter disregard of consequences, displayed by certain Army Officers and others who have now, by threats of revolution and mutiny, created a situation unprecedented in the history of regularly governed countries.[4]

The generals wanted to defend themselves openly and "to place the responsibility for these recent regrettable happenings on the proper shoulders regardless of what may be thus involved".[5]

Mulcahy pressed the government for a public investigation under expanded terms of reference, one that would investigate the events of the mutiny, one that could compel testimony under oath and assess responsibility. He agreed, however, to accept the limited format to "see the nature of the evidence in black and white, and in order to give myself and the officers concerned in this inquiry an opportunity of putting down in black and white what we desire to put down".[6] He clearly believed that any investigation would vindicate the army council.

Thus despite their dissatisfaction, Mulcahy and his staff agreed to appear before the inquiry. The mutineers, however, claimed that they had been betrayed by the government and would not now trust the President's promise that there would be no victimization.[7] McGrath would not testify without the mutineers' evidence to substantiate his charges.[8] Lacking subpoena powers, the inquiry committee could not compel them to appear. Thus, it turned its attention to Mulcahy and the army council.

The hearing concentrated on four main topics: the origins of the mutiny; demobilization; the relationship of the Irish Republican Brotherhood to the army; and the general condition of the army. After completing its investigation, the committee submitted to the executive council an official report, generally favorable to the army leaders, which was subsequently published.

The chair of the committee, Meredith, however, signed the published report with reservations and then submitted his own draft report to the cabinet. It was not published because it contained references to the evidence which was not to be made public.[9] Meredith agreed in principle with the official findings, but went further and harshly criticized Mulcahy, in particular, his handling of the crisis. Nevertheless, although believing that Mulcahy may have been guilty of "mismanagement", Meredith dismissed as invalid the charges of "muddling or incompetence".[10]

With respect to the development of the Old IRA and the genesis of the mutiny, the evidence presented to the committee confirmed both the judgment of General Headquarters as well as the evaluations made by the Intelligence staff. The mutineers had been a problem even to Michael Collins. After his death, they distrusted and were antagonistic to the new leadership at GHQ.[11] They deeply resented their loss of power and position, and some, at least, aspired to positions for which they were not qualified.[12] Although they may have been excellent "gunmen", they could not readily accept discipline or submit to authority.[13] The Old IRA organization grew out of their shared experiences and common frustrations.

The inquiry committee heard conflicting testimony on the efficacy of the strategy that headquarters followed once it learned of the subversive intentions of the Old IRA. According to Sean MacMahon, the former chief of staff, Headquarters

> decided that the information we had as to their intentions was such that we could not have anything to do with them in the matter of parley, that our duty was to see that Army Officers were reasoned back to their simple Army allegiance; that the time must come when if it is not possible to do this, these Officers must be asked to resign from the Army, that the Army must be our first and last consideration.[14]

Professor Hogan, former director of Intelligence, criticized this position. He contended that GHQ should have confronted the members of the Old IRA as soon as their efforts to subvert the allegiance of other officers and to foment rebellion became clear.[15] He believed they should have been told either to desist from their activities or resign from the army. Not surprisingly, Mulcahy disagreed. When he came before the inquiry committee, he testified that, but for the politicians who intervened and who encouraged the mutineers, headquarters would have peacefully completed its reorganization and retrained and reassigned its officers.[16]

In its report, the committee concluded that the Old IRA was a mutinous organization bent on using the army for political purposes and engaged in conduct "wholly incompatible with discipline and the obedience which an Army must render to the Government of any Constitutional State".[17] Although he agreed with the rest of the committee, in his private report, Chairman Meredith condemned Mulcahy for meeting and corresponding with the mutineers during the summer of 1923; for his lack of sympathy for their grievances; and more importantly, for inconsistent and misleading behavior and for failing to confront the Old IRA "in a direct and straightforward manner". Meredith said that in assuring the mutineers that he would listen to their concerns, Mulcahy appeared willing "at least in his private capacity, to go behind the back of the cabinet and join hands with an [mutinous] organization . . . and assist the organization in getting control of the Army for a particular purpose".[18]

And then, Meredith continued, Mulcahy "exasperated" the Old IRA and intensified its sense of grievance by ignoring its specific demands. The chairman also reproached Mulcahy for underestimating the mutineers and signs of trouble. Although Meredith agreed that, once the Old IRA came into existence, mutiny was inevitable, he also believed that Mulcahy's handling of the situation "in his own way" increased the threat the mutineers posed. Meredith said that

> it is impossible to exonerate General Mulcahy from all blame in respect of his handling of the admittedly difficult problem of dealing with the IRA Organization and the group that promoted it. There was mismanagement on his part.[19]

Meredith's accusation are only partially valid. True, Mulcahy was ambiguous and, to a degree, inconsistent with the mutineers. With the benefit of two months hindsight, Meredith easily argued the wisdom of a different course. Meredith's analysis of Mulcahy's action, however, misgauged completely the climate of the times, the political machinations of the cabinet, and the history from which the army had emerged. As a result, his attack on Mulcahy was too harsh and his criticism unfair.

Meredith ignored Mulcahy's intentions to preserve army unity and prevent the outbreak of another civil war. To a large extent, the meetings with the Old IRA paralleled negotiations with the Republicans in 1922 when Mulcahy and Collins worked to mend the rift in the army. Difficulties with the Old IRA occurred soon after the conclusion of the civil war, amid lingering violence and a readiness to resort to the gun. Understandably, Mulcahy wanted to avoid another confrontation. By not challenging the mutineers in a "direct and straightforward manner", Mulcahy was able to stall for time and draw other officers—possible recruits for the Old IRA—into a disciplined routine. Delay also eased President Cosgrave's fear that the Old IRA might organize politically and disrupt the elections of August 1923. In his critique, moreover, Meredith omitted mention of the pressure President Cosgrave and McGrath brought to bear on Mulcahy to continue meeting with the Tobin–Dalton faction. It was not a decision Mulcahy had made alone.

In this context, Meredith was rather naive, not to say self-righteous, to have said that "If you have a cause you can stand over, the time is always ripe to face problems in a direct and straightforward manner".[20] In so saying Meredith demonstrated a lack of political savvy and contradicted the expressed policy of the government as articulated in the Dáil on 12 March 1924 by Kevin O'Higgins: ". . . in the handling of national affairs, and in the handling of very delicate situations, there must needs be opportunism".[21]

Meredith's charge that Mulcahy was guilty of giving at least the appearance of complicity in using the army for political purposes has more credibility. On the advice of others in the cabinet, and against his better judgment, Mulcahy held the meetings. While this may not have been a wise decision, Mulcahy did try to limit the scope of the discussions. In correspondence with the mutineers, Mulcahy made clear that he would deal directly with the Old IRA for:

> the *consideration* of any representations they may wish to make on "matters which are considered vital to the progress of the Army on National lines with a view to the complete independence of Ireland"—it being understood that this is, of necessity, a personal and private arrangement and not indicative of sectionalism of any kind in the Army.[22] (Emphasis added.)

Mulcahy most likely meant that he would listen to the complaints and grievances of the Tobin-Dalton group, but was not promising them any power or influence. This was not what the Old IRA understood. As Meredith noted, when they failed to effect change, the mutineers cried foul, charging the government with "empty promises".[23]

Meredith's report provided an important insight into Mulcahy's style, his manner of handling situations "in his own way". Faced with intense criticism of the army in the cabinet, Mulcahy became defensive and hence less flexible, less open to suggestions for change. When he could not dissuade his cabinet colleagues from "interfering" in army affairs, his recourse was to continue to do things in his own way, at times circumventing or thwarting the wishes of the cabinet. Convinced of the eventual efficacy of the army's reorganization plan, Mulcahy concentrated on pushing through this plan, believing the results would vindicate and justify his methods. His approach, unfortunately, not only increased tension in the cabinet, but also contributed to the cabinet's frustration with the minister and with the army.

During demobilization, for example, Mulcahy steadfastly pursued his own policy. In November 1923, the government had set up a cabinet committee to investigate the claims of several officers at the Curragh who refused to accept their demobilization papers. Mulcahy withheld from its members the files they would need until he had completed reorganization. Before the committee had taken any action, he had already dismissed many applicants as "surplus" and had drawn up the final lists of officers to be retained, demobilized or placed on reserve. Meredith accused Mulcahy of denying the applicants the special consideration they were promised and, therefore, of thwarting the will of the executive council.[24] In this instance, Meredith was accurate. Although Mulcahy could have argued that the executive council had the authority to prevent reorganization, he knew any delay would have been dangerous. Thus, Mulcahy prevented the committee from interfering in demobilization. He had done things "in his own way".

The inquiry committee generally endorsed the actions of GHQ in dealing with demobilization. In light of the large number of men who were to be released, the high rate of unemployment, the claims of pre-Truce soldiers, the territorial rivalries, and the transition to a peace-time force, the committee stated: "We believe that in all the circumstances the Army Council honestly endeavoured to deal fairly with the question of demobilization".[25] On the specific complaint of the Old IRA about the number of ex-British soldiers in the army, testimony revealed that, in fact, only a few ex-British officers were retained.[26] The committee found that the dissidents had used this issue as propaganda to foment dissatisfaction and unite disparate individuals,[27] as a rallying point around which the Old IRA could fashion an army "officered and controlled by men of, or in sympathy with, their views".[28]

According to the committee, the Curragh episode forged the link between demobilization and the mutiny and "may have influenced subsequent mutineers by producing the impression that mutinous conduct would not be severely punished".[29] These words vindicated the position of Mulcahy and the army council that cabinet interference in army affairs undermined both discipline and the authority of army officials.

Chairman Meredith, however, viewed Mulcahy's charge of interference as "unproved and ungenerous".[30] He himself strongly doubted that, but for the meddling of certain politicians, the mutiny would never have taken hold. To have established the council of defence and the cabinet committee on demobilization, Meredith said, was within the purview of the executive council. As members of the executive council, both O'Higgins and McGrath acted in accordance with their duties. Interestingly, Meredith did not condemn O'Higgins for secretly and repeatedly communicating with a disgruntled officer without the knowledge of the minister for defence—a clear violation both of the code of military conduct and of the accepted norm of behaviour among cabinet colleagues.

Moreover, Meredith particularly exonerated McGrath, as a "well-intentioned peacemaker", editorializing that "well-intentioned peacemakers do not generally fare well in this country and deputy McGrath seems only to have suffered the usual fate of those who try to throw oil on the troubled waters".[31] Meredith was extremely kind and extremely inaccurate. Although an active intermediary, McGrath was also a spokesman for the mutineers in the cabinet, the Dáil and the Cumann na nGaedheal party. Meredith also chose to ignore McGrath's healthy political ambitions. Meredith's bias weakened his credibility. He was as unsympathetic to Mulcahy as he was sympathetic to McGrath. Perhaps his own personal past caused him to identify with ill-fated peacemakers. Perhaps his tenure on the Volunteers committee as one of Redmond's nominees and one of the two Redmondites who "remained above the fray and tried to be co-operative" with the original members of the IRB-dominated Executive[32] prejudiced his interpretation.

Now, in 1924, Meredith, as well as the rest of the inquiry committee, had to once again deal with the IRB and untangle a web of accusations and counter-accusations about the revitalization of the Irish Republican Brotherhood and its power in the army. The role of the IRB had been a central issue in the army mutiny. As self-proclaimed rivals of the Brotherhood, Old IRA members had, in their original ultimatum, called for the dismissal of the army council citing it as the core of the revitalized IRB. This charge also caused the government to assert that the leaders of the army were unable to deal effectively with the mutineers.

The committee heard conflicting evidence on the reorganization or resurrection of the IRB. Witnesses who opposed the army council—in particular O'Higgins—deemed that the Brotherhood had died after the conclusion of the Anglo-Irish war and that it should have been left moribund.[33] O'Higgins charged that the IRB was revived only to combat the Old IRA; that to revitalize the IRB, officers from various parts of the country had met at Portobello Barracks (Dublin) under the chairmanship of O'Murthuile. O'Higgins claimed that when he confronted Mulcahy with this information during a cabinet meeting, Mulcahy denied it and disputed O'Higgins' assertion that GHQ was practically the "inner" or "upper" circle of the Brotherhood. Other sources, however, confirmed to O'Higgins that his suspicions were accurate.[34]

The army council refuted these charges, emphatically denying that the IRB had ever ceased to exist.[35] The officers admitted that a reorganization of the Brotherhood had occurred sometime between the end of 1922 and the beginning of 1923, necessitated not by the formation of the Old IRA, however, but by the Republicans' attempt to take over the organization.[36] Upon learning of this threatened coup, the senior pro-Treaty members of the IRB took steps to ensure that the IRB would remain in control of those loyal to the Irish Free State.[37] Recent historical research supports this claim.[38]

Although the inquiry committee seemed to accept the army council's explanation, it concluded that the IRB was detrimental to the army, that members of the old IRA perceived the reorganization to be directed at them and that members of the IRB and the Old IRA both failed "to appreciate their position as servants of the State".[39] This last judgment was unfair, as was the assessment of the Old IRA and the IRB as similar organizations. They differed in aims, outlook and appeal. The greatest distinction, however, was that the officers of the Old IRA issued an ultimatum to the government and threatened rebellion. The army council had resigned on demand of the government and the IRB had neither threatened rebellion nor issued an ultimatum. That was a qualitative difference.

Moreover, the leaders of the IRB were definitely sensitive to the anomaly of perpetuating a secret revolutionary society in a now independent state. Because of the delicate political situation in 1922-23—that is, the continuing attempts of the British and Irish governments to agree on the meaning of dominion status—IRB members who were also in the government were not involved in the reorganization. This avoided the possibility that "members of the government might be inhibited in their relations with the British if it could be said that the IRB was functioning with their full knowledge and connivance".[40] Theoretically, at least, the Brotherhood was still dedicated to an independent 32-county republic whereas Ireland was a 26-county dominion within the British Commonwealth. Its very existence might have alarmed British politicians. Moreover, IRB activities on behalf on Catholics in Northern Ireland would have caused difficulties between London and Dublin.

IRB leaders showed similar discretion regarding the army. According to Mulcahy, "no [IRB] member ever attended any meeting in his capacity as an Army officer" and all IRB meetings were attended by army officers and civilians alike.[41] Similarly, General O'Murthuile explained, in dealings with Mulcahy when he was minister for defence,

> General Mulcahy, himself, though he was informed, was never placed in the position that he would have to stand over everything we did. He was more of a free lance in this matter. It was not fair, we felt, that General Mulcahy should be bound by any steps we proposed to take and that he should be free in view of his position and of the responsibilities he would have, but that he would be in a position to know whether anything that happened was a danger or otherwise to the Government.[42]

Mulcahy was, of course, a member of the IRB, but most probably, became inactive after its reorganization and relied on his subordinates to keep him informed. What the IRB would have disclosed to a minister for defence who was not part of the secret society is an interesting matter for speculation.

According to the inquiry committee, the IRB's discretion and sensitivity did not justify keeping their reorganization secret. Its report reprimanded Mulcahy for failing to take "the earliest opportunity of informing the executive council of the proposed reorganization of the IRB".[43] In this instance, the committee's judgment was indeed correct. Mulcahy's neglect allowed rumor to replace fact and amplified the distrust between Mulcahy and the rest of the cabinet.

Although opponents of the IRB over and over expressed their suspicions that membership in the Brotherhood influenced promotion and advancement in the army, they were unable to produce any specific proof. Patrick Hogan, minister for agriculture, was typical: "I sensed it was there [IRB influence], at least I had sensed that there were things happening which I could not explain by ordinary reasoning".[44] Members of the army council steadfastly denied the charges and demanded concrete evidence to support these allegations.[45]

In its report, the inquiry committee stated that "it has not been proved to us that any appointment or promotions were made by reason of being a member of, or influence corruptly exercised, by the IRB."[46] Current literature concurs, judging that "Mulcahy and others involved in the IRB reorganization were not promoting members of the IRB in the national army at the expense of others."[47] But, the inquiry committee also said that a secret society within the army created a "natural suspicion" among non-members and "undermined confidence in the impartiality of the army council and higher commands".[48] For those whose ambitions exceeded their capabilities, whose inadequacies held them down, the IRB provided a convenient excuse for their failure.

The generals made clear in their testimony that, prior to the mutiny, they had been poised to break the link between the army and the IRB. They had planned to insert into the new defence Forces Act of August, 1924, a clause forbidding members of the army from belonging to any secret society. They had expected unquestioning compliance.[49] Prior to 1924, to ensure the survival of the Free State, the generals felt that they and other senior officers should guide the IRB. Now, having shepherded the army through the Anglo-Irish war of independence and the civil war, Sean O'Murthuile, speaking for the army council, advised the committee that

> the future activities of the IRB should be directed toward turning to the social and political atmosphere with the programme of any Government working towards the National and economic advancement of the Irish people without regard to parties or party influence.[50]

O'Murthuile's sentiments are reminiscent of Mulcahy's prediction to Kevin O'Higgins in June 1923 that the IRB would become an open society in the near future.[51] Mulcahy himself hoped that a transformed IRB would take the lead in implementing nationalist ideals.[52] He believed the distrust among some members of the executive council was unfounded, charging his colleagues with using the IRB "as a stick to beat us".[53]

Despite Mulcahy's and the generals' aspirations for the IRB, the committee concluded this phase of its investigation with a stinging indictment of the generals:

> We consider that the reorganization of the IRB, carried out as it appears to have been by the actual heads of the Army, was a disastrous error of judgment, and accentuated a mutiny which might not have occurred at all, and which could have been more firmly suppressed if those in authority had not weakened their position by leaving themselves open to the charge of acting in the interest of a hostile secret society.[54]

The question of the IRB was clearly a delicate issue. The split in the army and the exigencies of civil war made the decision to reorganize the

Brotherhood understandable. By 1924, however, the climate was such that not only was the Brotherhood unnecessary but, as Mulcahy perceived, gave the opponents of the leaders of the army a strong argument to use against them.

When the inquiry committee arrived at the final issue on its agenda, the overall condition of the army, most witnesses agreed that army discipline was good and steadily getting better.[55] Professor Hogan, former head of Intelligence, reported "an extraordinary improvement" in the army during the period from December 1922 until April 1923, and a slight breakdown in control with the cessation of hostilities.[56] The consensus traced the causes of most disciplinary problems to inexperience and the remaining vestiges of a guerrilla army, which likely would fade after time, training, and refinements of the military system.

O'Higgins disagreed. During his testimony, he reiterated the accusations he had made in the Dáil. Specifically, he charged:

> (a) that the Army was breaking up into factions, societies or combinations;
>
> (b) that the personal equation was too much in evidence in the Army, and was re-acting most unfavourably on discipline;
>
> (c) that the Army was not unequivocally, unquestionably, without reserve, simply the instrument of the people's will;
>
> (d) that the ex-minister for defence [Mulcahy] throughout the year previous to his resignation did not stand for stern, impersonal discipline in the Army and that the names of certain officers were submitted to the executive council for rank and position under the reorganization scheme against whom grave charges had been made without being satisfactorily rebutted.[57]

During his testimony, O'Higgins revealed that, in September 1922, in a clear breach of discipline, a disgruntled army officer, Colonel Jephson O'Connell, had sought him out saying that "the condition of the army demanded the immediate attention of the Government."[58] Without informing the minister for defence, O'Higgins obtained damaging information about the army from O'Connell throughout the next year. O'Connell reinforced O'Higgins' own feelings about the shortcomings of the army.

O'Higgins' testimony evolved into a vicious attack on Mulcahy—much of which was unjustified. O'Higgins accused Mulcahy of trying to "buy off" the mutineers with choice positions in the reorganization scheme but failed because "the price was not big enough".[59] There was, however, no evidence to support his position. Any special consideration which may have been shown to the mutineers stemmed from the fact that they were all pre-Truce officers. Under general army policy, all such officers were placed in a special category.

O'Higgins also castigated Mulcahy for conferring with the Tobin-Dalton group instead of vindicating "outraged discipline".[60] But President Cosgrave, not Mulcahy, had initiated the meetings and the president had discussed their progress with Mulcahy, giving at least the appearance of sanctioned governmental policy and endowing O'Higgins' condemnation with a false ring. O'Higgins' obsession with the state of discipline in the army was fanned and fueled by his secret meetings with Jephson O'Connell. He failed to realize, however, that these meetings themselves helped undermine army discipline by encouraging an officer to circumvent army authorities and seek redress for grievances outside the established channels.

Actual events of the mutiny refute O'Higgins' charge that Mulcahy failed to vindicate outraged discipline. Mulcahy and the army council clearly took strong, decisive action. Ironically, after they had done so, they were dismissed by the executive council with O'Higgins leading the attack. O'Higgins himself was no model of strict, impartial discipline when he excused a clear act of mutiny as a "foolish action" not to be taken at face value.

Moreover, O'Higgins' charge of lax discipline stemmed, not from the mutiny, but from a case of assault and battery. Mulcahy had received conflicting legal advice on the advisability of instituting court martial proceedings against the three officers accused of criminal conduct. All authorities agreed, however, that there was insufficient evidence for a conviction. Mulcahy retained these officers in the reorganization scheme. O'Higgins was scandalized and claimed that this affair (known as the Kenmare case) sounded "the death knell of either discipline or efficiency in the Army".[61] O'Higgins exaggerated. However, the inquiry committee did believe that, in light of the publicity and the officers rank, Mulcahy should have publicly probed the charges. Mulcahy's failure to do this was, in the opinion of the committee, a "grave error of judgment" which "encourag[ed] suspicion in the minds of officers and others that the army authorities were disposed to hush up charges against persons high in authority".[62]

Finally, O'Higgins accused Mulcahy of not understanding and not fulfilling his role as minister for defence and member of the executive council. O'Higgins told the committee:

> I could not get away from the impressions that the minister for defence came to the executive council not so much as a colleague to do business with colleagues as in the capacity of a delegate . . . almost as man coming to the executive council to hold a watching brief for . . . the Army in the executive council. . . . There was a lack of candour. There was a cloud bank between the Army and the executive council. . . . It was as if what went on within the Army was no business of the other members of the executive council.[63]

This was perhaps O'Higgins most valid criticism. Mulcahy was an army man who identified himself more as commander-in-chief than as minister for defence. The experience of the Anglo-Irish struggle and the civil war colored his outlook. As assistant minister for defence and chief of staff during the Anglo-Irish war, Mulcahy helped to establish and shape the army. The subsequent civil war strengthened the bonds among the generals at GHQ, as they strove to defeat the IRA and forge a professional army. While his civilian colleagues were housed together, working to make the Free State a reality, Mulcahy was at headquarters, laboring to ensure that the Free State would survive. Mulcahy was thus separated both physically and mentally from his cabinet colleagues. The distance dimmed Mulcahy's appreciation of the fears and frustrations of his colleagues *vis-à-vis* the army. The distance also dimmed his colleagues' appreciation of the obstacles the army faced and the progress it had made. Their constant carping set Mulcahy on edge and made him more likely to act as if he were holding "a watching brief" for the army.

Overall, the inquiry committee handed down what Mulcahy termed a "grudging" vindication of the generals. It found no evidence to support the charges of muddling, mismanagement and incompetence on the part of MacMahon, the chief of staff; no charges relevant to the investigation against O'Murthuile, the quartermaster-general, although it believed he had committed a disastrous error of judgment in reorganizing the IRB; no evidence that O'Sullivan, the adjutant-general, had been negligent or had tried to shield offenders in handling cases involving high-ranking officers.[64]

When the inquiry committee's report was introduced to the Dáil, Mulcahy introduced what was tantamount to a motion of censure of the executive council. On 26 June 1924, he moved that the Dáil condemn as "as contrary to the best interests of the State the ill-considered action of the Executive Council"[65] in removing the army council and the "subsequent failure of the Executive Council to act upon the Report of the Army Inquiry Committee". It was a futile gesture.

The Dáil debate on Mulcahy's motion was unimpressive. Because the executive council refused to publish either the evidence presented to the committee or the chairman's reservations, the deputies heard mostly a reiteration of previously articulated positions. But it was President Cosgrave who set the tone of the government's position and probably reflected the feelings of most of the Dáil deputies when he said:

> That particular incident which occurred three months ago is an incident which in my opinion, ought to be dead and buried and ought not to be resurrected, no matter what its influence was either at that time or now.[66]

Not surprisingly, the motion to censure the executive council was defeated.

President Cosgrave thus ended the army crisis, using the reluctance of deputies to tamper with a matter which did indeed seemed "dead and buried". The threat of mutiny had been defused; the Free State was safe; the government was still in power. Success, however, came at a price, paid by the men who would not countenance mutiny. Mulcahy, MacMahon, O'Murthuile and O'Sullivan were the primary victims of the mutiny—they who had created a disciplined, non-political army. Their resignations upheld the principle of unquestioned obedience to the government and set an example for all the army. Out of the crisis of mutiny came the affirmation that Ireland was to be governed by the will of the people and not by the dictates of her generals.

On the surface, the government and its political party, Cumann na nGaedheal, surmounted the immediate challenge to their supremacy posed by the army mutiny. Though Mulcahy and McGrath resigned from the executive council, the government maintained its vigor and vitality. With no difficulty, it survived Mulcahy's vote of no confidence. McGrath and his coterie in the Dáil formed their own party, but it was short-lived and of little significance.

In truth, however, the crisis inflicted long-term damage on both the government and Cumann na nGaedheal. The government alienated those who supported the mutineers as well as those who supported the army council. Mulcahy and McGrath represented a particular type of nationalist, one who was associated with both the Gaelic League and the war for independence. They were, therefore, identified with the cultural and political manifestations of revolutionary nationalism. Their departures, the last of the men who had actively fought in the war of independence, weakened the identification of the government with its revolutionary origins. Their resignations, which the cabinet accepted without too much heartrending—especially Mulcahy's—could be interpreted as a turning away from the nationalist tradition. This was of particular significance because, since the death of Michael Collins in August 1922, Cumann na nGaedheal had been without a national hero to rival Eamon de Valera, leader of anti-Treatyites.

The government's brightest star, Kevin O'Higgins, while extraordinarily talented, was not of the mould from which popular, revolutionary idols were cast. He was known for his passion for honoring the terms of the Treaty and asserting Ireland's position in the British Commonwealth—a passion hardly calculated to bestir a nationalist population. O'Higgins, in fact, boasted that, after Mulcahy and McGrath had resigned, "he and his colleagues in government were the most conservative revolutionaries who ever lived".[67] In a private letter, he revealed his hostility to traditional nationalist ideals:

> None of these fellows care a curse about the country or the people in the country. McGilligan, who wasn't "out in 16," has no particular "record" and no particular "Gaelic soul", has done more

in two weeks than his predecessor [McGrath] in two years. . . . I have come to the conclusion that men like Hogan, McGilligan . . . could do more for the country in a year and (even for the realisation of all its ideals) than all the Clans and Brotherhoods could effect in a generation.[68]

After the mutiny and after the government failed to successfully alter the boundary with Northern Ireland, the party no longer appeared to be in the mainstream nationalist tradition. If not overtly pro-British, it was at least perceived as the Commonwealth party. Mulcahy believed that the mutiny of 1924 had a disastrous effect, "reducing the prestige of the Government" and leaving the "directing force, in the parliamentary party and in the government, completely denuded of those people and names who stood for the Griffith approach and policy, in relation to industrial development".[69] The army crisis of 1924 thus contributed to the decay and stagnation which would beset Cumann na nGaedheal and hence unwittingly aided the coming ascendancy of de Valera and Fianna Fáil.

On a personal level, the army crisis marked Mulcahy's demise. Although he would be back in government, eventually to become party leader, never again would he enjoy the power and the prestige that he had in 1924. Mulcahy himself believed that his own personal position and influence had been "broken down particularly by the 1924 episode".[70]

When he was minister for defence, Mulcahy was one of the most powerful members of the government—the man whose judgments would determine whether the Free State would survive the Irregular challenge. He earned greater respect among his colleagues for his military service but greater criticism for his political failings. Mulcahy underestimated his civilian colleagues' concern with the power the army had accrued during the civil war and, with the advent of peace, with their desire to vindicate the principle of civil supremacy. Although he was personally and powerfully affected by former comrades turning their guns on one another, and sincerely motivated to prevent a recurrence, Mulcahy ignored the sensitivities of others in the cabinet to the horror of civil war. In so doing, he exacerbated the anti-military feelings in the cabinet and stirred political resentment. His decisions regarding demobilization and the Parnell Street raid, for example, circumvented government policy. His resentment of O'Duffy typified his view that the army, not outsiders, would solve the army's problems. In essence, Mulcahy was an "army man", laudably loyal to his staff and military comrades. His zealous protection of his prerogatives as minister for defence and his equally zealous resentment of criticism of the army meant that, more and more, Mulcahy became the army's presence in the government.

Despite his defensiveness, despite his posture as the army's presence in the cabinet, Mulcahy was totally dedicated to the formation and development of an Irish army which would be blindly loyal to any Irish government and removed from political involvement. His attitude toward the government's demand for his and the army council's resignation testified to that belief. Mulcahy fought the civil war to uphold the principle of majority rule and affirm the right of the people to choose a government that would carry out their will. He would not, two years later, repudiate those principles for personal ambition or power.

Mulcahy and the army council demonstrated that peaceful change in the leadership of the army was not only possible but desirable. It signified and signalled the commitment of this revolutionary elite to democratic principles. Their message to their followers was that recourse to violence was not an acceptable alternative nor was it to be a habit, a way of life for Ireland. The resignations of Mulcahy and his generals upheld and affirmed the supremacy of constitutional rule in Ireland, finally and firmly deciding the question of who would rule the Free State.

Epilogue

After 1924, Richard Mulcahy moved off the center stage of Irish political life, relinquishing his leading role in dramatic events to become part of the supporting cast. Though he remained an important figure—a cabinet minister, a senior statesman, a party leader—he would never again achieve the power and status he enjoyed during the revolutionary period.

During the fight for independence and the civil war, Mulcahy had flourished. Mulcahy was an architect of the guerrilla war which forced the British to concede dominion status to the Irish. He was the guiding spirit behind the civil war which insured the survival of the state. Mulcahy was well suited to be both chief of staff and commander-in-chief. His dedication and zeal coupled with his methodical concentration and absorption in his work were an important part of the success of these military encounters.

One testimony to his achievements ironically came from the British. According to David Neligan, a Castle detective who worked for Collins' intelligence unit, when the British found some of Mulcahy's papers, a British staff officer "expressed astonishment at the professional competence displayed as Mulcahy of course was self-trained and knew Sandhurst only on the map".[1] In his capacity as chief of staff and commander-in-chief, Mulcahy developed a general headquarters staff which reflected this professional competence and which was an important component in the success of the IRA and the Free State army.

Mulcahy was the linchpin of general headquarters—overseeing the struggle, coordinating strategy and informing his officers of current developments. Again it was an adversary, a foe in the civil war, who acknowledged the important role which the chief of staff played during the Anglo-Irish war, recalling how "when we used to meet for Group Staff Meetings in the old days, the C.S. was always ex officio, was the nucleus and co-ordinating link of each group."[2] In this way, Mulcahy kept the threads of the revolutionary movement together. And, it must be remembered, Mulcahy did all this with a price on his head: "He rivalled Collins for the dangerous honour of being the most 'wanted' man in Ireland and a huge reward was offered for his capture."[3] In the civil war, after Collins' death, it was Mulcahy who was the figure of strength who steadied the army and held it together. And it was Mulcahy's stature and determination which pushed the army on to victory.

Mulcahy, moreover, played an important role in setting boundaries and articulating parameters during the Anglo-Irish war and the civil war. He was more successful in restraining his officers and men in the struggle against the British than he was in the civil war. Ironically, his most controversial policy, the executions, was an attempt to restrain and control the violence of the army. Despite its intent, however, this policy, coupled with the Mountjoy executions, injured both the reputation and political viability of Mulcahy and his cabinet colleagues.

One of Mulcahy's most significant contributions, however, came after the war of independence and the civil war: his insistence on de-politicizing the army. Contemporary history is rife with examples of armies that interfered in politics immediately after the struggle for independence and then continued to interfere in, if not control, the political process. That this did not happen in Ireland must be credited to the work of General Richard Mulcahy and his staff. It was Mulcahy's determination to separate the military from politics that effectively removed the Irish army from the political process. It was because of his effort that the army remained on the sidelines in 1932, when, within ten years of the civil war, Eamon de Valera and Fianna Fáil assumed the power of government. This was a remarkable tribute to Mulcahy and his staff.

Mulcahy was not as successful as minister for defence. Although he recognized and adhered to the principle of civilian control of the army, Mulcahy, nevertheless, distrusted and was hostile to politicians intruding themselves and their beliefs on the military. His experience during the Anglo-Irish war with an essentially civilian minister for defence and president, evidenced to him their inadequate understanding of military matters. In Mulcahy's eyes, whenever they attempted to dictate military policy or strategy, the result was disastrous. In the civil war, his experience was similar. Mulcahy was convinced that his civilian colleagues did not appreciate the military situation—the conditions in which the Army labored, the strains, the dangers involved in fighting a war which had degenerated into wanton violence. Attempts by his colleagues to have a voice in army affairs (for example, the cabinet committee on demobilization) were, in Mulcahy's view, again nothing short of disastrous. And, during the crisis of 1924, he steadfastly maintained that this type of political interference fuelled the flame of mutiny. All these experiences reinforced his insistence on doing things "his own way", convinced that he knew better than his civilian colleagues what was good for the army.

Moreover, Mulcahy blamed the politicians for their lack of leadership leading up to the civil war, for exacerbating the bitterness and hostility surrounding the Treaty. He was, therefore, more intolerant of their criticisms and overzealously defended his officers and men against charges and accusations. When legitimate questions about the conduct of the Free State troops were raised, Mulcahy justified the army's actions by contrasting them with the atrocities of the Irregulars and dwelling on the perilously difficult situation in which the army found itself. He failed to see that simply saying the Free State army is better than the Irregulars did not absolve the army of charges of misconduct. The civil war exacerbated Mulcahy's sense of loyalty and skewed his judgment. Deserted by trusted comrades like Lynch, Mulcahy felt especially protective of those who remained loyal to him and Collins. Unfortunately, this allegiance strengthened the perception of his civilian colleagues that Mulcahy was an "army man".

As minister for defence, Mulcahy failed to recognize and address the growing anti-military sentiment both in the cabinet and in the Dail. He neglected to sufficiently inform the other ministers about military matters during the civil war. These failures fostered and enhanced the credibility of the anti-army faction in the cabinet. Similarly, Mulcahy was not attuned to his civilian colleagues' concern about the power the army had amassed during the civil war. Nor did he notice how anxious they were to insure that the army remain the loyal servant of the civilian government. Mulcahy simply did not recognize how deeply the atrocities of both the Free State troops and the Irregulars had affected members of the Dáil and the government and how much it fuelled anti-military feeling. He paid for his blindness and insensitivity. Mulcahy was a victim of the cabinet's fear of, and anger against, the army. His resignation and the resignation of his senior officers were demanded to atone for the sins of the military.

Perhaps one reason for Mulcahy's lack of sensitivity to his civilian colleague's concern about the military was rooted in his perception of the army. For Mulcahy, the army was more than simply a fighting force. It was an agent for fostering national ideals. That was one reason why, for example, in October 1922, Mulcahy founded the Army School of Music. Mulcahy is quoted as saying: "I want, in the first place, bands for the Army. I want to have bands that will dispense music and musical understanding in the highest terms to the people."[4] Thus, in Mulcahy's view, the Army School of Music would be an instrument for bringing good music to the people, traditional Irish music as well as the classical masters. And, it would foster the development of Irish music as well. To accomplish this aim, Wilhelm Fritz Brase, well-known and well-thought of in German military band circles, was brought to Ireland. Under Mulcahy's patronage and Brase's direction, the Irish Military Band made sufficient progress to hold its first concert in October 1923. The concert was described as "an unqualified success and laid the foundation for the reputation the bands have enjoyed ever since".[5] Taken together with Mulcahy's desire for an Irish speaking battalion, it was clear that Mulcahy saw in the army a positive force for lifting the cultural and education level of the country.

For Mulcahy, the Irish language, Irish music—all of Irish culture—remained an integral part of his nationalist vision. He never lost the sense that this was what was vital to the life of the nation. Thus, one of his first acts as minister for education in 1948 was to double the grant for the Irish Folklore Commission. In his view, Irish society had to provide for the material, cultural and spiritual life of its people. Mulcahy believed it was necessary "to develop the spirit without which, not only can material wealth not be sufficiently developed, but that being developed it cannot be made to secure the real happiness and integrity of a people".[6] His vision was of a free, united, Christian, Irish-speaking Ireland—virtuous and prosperous.

Mulcahy thought in terms of the good of the entire nation. For example, as leader of Fine Gael, Mulcahy would not oppose legislation simply for the sake of harassing the government. Nor would he engage in criticism for the sake of personal or party aggrandizement. To him, the nation, not the party, not any individual, came first.[7] Mulcahy, moreover, had an expansive vision. His own intellectual curiosity was far reaching, ranging from a fascination with the latest technology to a deep interest in history. He was not an isolationist, but rather envisioned Ireland taking her place among the nations of the world. Nor was his nationalism exclusive. Mulcahy never succumbed to religious sectarianism. For him, all were "children of the nation".[8] Although he deplored the violence in the North, and was clearly involved in arming IRA units for the defence of Catholics, it was not, to him, a question of religion, a question of being anti-Protestant. In 1950, on the occasion of the Limerick Holy Year Exhibition, Mulcahy wrote:

> Now, that we have achieved freedom for ourselves, for our spiritual values and for our native way of life, we know too, and we are glad, that we have great tolerance and that we respect and would always safeguard the religious beliefs of those who differ from the majority.[9]

After 1924, Mulcahy never again donned a military uniform but rather spent the rest of his life in politics. He remained active in politics for almost three more decades. Mulcahy returned to the front bench of Cumann na nGaedheal in 1927 as minister for local government and public health. He succeeded Cosgrave as party leader in 1944 and was most responsible for organizing the coalition governments in 1948 and 1954. In both inter-party governments, Mulcahy served as minister for education and was the first minister for the Gaeltacht in the 1954 government.

Mulcahy brought to his political career the same loyalty and dedication which he had given the army. He spent endless hours working for Cumann na nGaedheal and then Fine Gael—travelling all over Ireland, organizing, attending meetings, giving speeches. When the fortunes of Fine Gael faltered—at one point its number of seats in the Dáil dropped to an all-time low of 28—Mulcahy toiled unceasingly to hold the party together. As leader of the party, he increased both its visibility and its electoral record—raising its seats in the Dail from 30 to 50 in a ten year period. He spent years touring the country on behalf of the party, reaching out to the people. For example, in 1944, he informed Fine Gael TDs that he was willing "to go to any part of the country" to speak to the people.[10] The next year, Mulcahy repeated his offer, telling party members that he would be free every Sunday from April through June and "wished to place himself at the disposal of the Party for meetings in the country."[11]

Mulcahy also realized, however, that members of the Dáil had to improve their visibility, had to make an impact on their constituencies, if the fortunes of Fine Gael were to improve. He, therefore, tried to motivate his deputies, urging them to ask questions in the Dáil, to take up local issues and to arrange for publicity in the local press.[12] His determination kept the party alive and functioning in the parliamentary process, assuring its role in the opposition and bringing it into coalition government twice during his term as leader of the party.

Moreover, in the early years of the party, after his resignation from the government in 1924, Mulcahy played an important role as mediator between the two wings of the Cumann na nGaedheal party. As noted, after the resignation of Mulcahy and McGrath, the perception developed that the party was moving away from its nationalist commitment to a more conservative, Anglicized position. There was a significant and vocal segment within the party who opposed this drift and who, on a number of occasions, presented the government with direct and serious challenges to its leadership. In these instances, Mulcahy was the one most active in defusing hostility and effecting a compromise.

For example, in October of 1924, following the mutiny, the standing committee of Cumann na nGaedheal issued a searing and direct repudiation of the Cosgrave administration's policy. This "October Manifesto" articulated the disappointments, frustrations and festering grievances which had been building for the last year. The government's response was to dismiss the charges and try to circumvent the standing committee and set up its own organizing committee. It was Mulcahy who devised the compromise which prevented the party from splintering once again.[13] As mediator, as senior statesman, as a nationalist with impeccable credentials, Mulcahy used his considerable influence to hold Cumann na nGaedheal together.

One issue which seriously threatened to rupture Cumann na nGaedheal was that of the status of Northern Ireland. Like many of his colleagues, Mulcahy was outraged by the findings of the Boundary Commission. Not only would nationalists in the North remain under Unionist control, there was also talk that the Free State would lose some of its territory. To Mulcahy, this was in direct contradiction to what the British had promised the Irish delegation during the Treaty negotiations. To prove that neither Collins not Griffith had renounced the idea of a united Ireland, that this was not the intention of either those who negotiated or those who voted for the Treaty, he urged Cosgrave to publish the documents relating to the Treaty. To him, it was a question of vindicating the honor and integrity of dead comrades.[14] Thus, he could not have been pleased with the final settlement which made no change in the boundary, which brought Irish unity no closer. Throughout his life, Mulcahy rejected partition and espoused the peaceful reunification of the country.

Mulcahy remained active in the party during its amalgamation into Fine Gael and its brief flirtation with the Blueshirt movement. He was, in fact, a member of the national executive of the Blueshirts. To him, however, it was less a matter of embracing Fascism or denouncing Communism than a fear of a replay of the civil war. When a meeting that Mulcahy was addressing during the election of 1932 was disrupted and attempts were made to wreck the platform,[15] it must have seemed that the days of 1922 when the anti-Treaty IRA members would not allow free speech to "traitors" were indeed back again. When de Valera assumed power, neither Mulcahy not his colleagues believed that the new government would guarantee their basic rights—freedom of speech, freedom of the press, and freedom of assembly. Thus, they turned to the Army Comrades Association and then to the Blueshirts for protection. Moreover, the aims of the Army Comrades Association reflected Mulcahy's earlier aspirations for the army. The Army Comrades Association saw its mission not only to safeguard the right of free speech but also to preserve the Irish language and "all that is best in the National Tradition" and to foster "patriotic idealism by honouring the memory of all the heroic dead who worked and suffered for Ireland and especially of Griffith, Collins and O'Higgins".[16] It was a platform which represented some of Mulcahy's most cherished objectives.

During World War II—the "Emergency" as it was known in Ireland—Mulcahy and Fine Gael supported the government's policy of neutrality. In fact, they believed that the crisis engendered by the war was of such magnitude that it required an all-party government. De Valera thought otherwise. The government, however, did inaugurate defence conferences to keep the opposition parties informed as to the progress and perils of neutrality. Mulcahy was one of the participants for Fine Gael. He was extremely dissatisfied with these meetings, believing that it was "nothing but a stultifying humiliation to be listening to explanations of Defence policy from ministerial members".[17] For Mulcahy, meeting with de Valera simply made the "situation seem very unreal"[18] and Mulcahy doubted that de Valera had a coherent strategy regarding defence. In fact, by May, 1940, Mulcahy's advised the party "that the spirit of Dev's approach was such that we should leave him to himself until circumstances brought him to a different kind of attitude".[19] De Valera, however, remained indifferent to calls for more meaningful cooperation. Nevertheless, in spite of the doubts and difficulties, Fine Gael upheld the position of Irish neutrality.

Despite all of his political activity, despite the number of years he spent in the political arena, Mulcahy was not truly at ease as a politician. In private he could be quite gracious and charming. He listened patiently to those who needed his help and went out of his way to aid those who needed assistance. In social conversations, he was congenial and engaging. However, his shy and reserved demeanor often led him to be perceived as cold and aloof. His public speeches were often difficult to follow. Although he had a number of dedicated followers in Cumann na nGaedheal, Mulcahy was not a charismatic figure.

Politics, to Mulcahy, seemed a duty, a sacred commitment, not something he relished. It was not a lack of confidence or a lack of dedication. He just never seemed as comfortable on a party platform as he had been at GHQ. Nor did Mulcahy have the flair, the *élan* associated with dominant political figures. Mulcahy attained his power and stature in the army and in politics because of his commitment, intelligence, concern and hard work. He inspired by example. Mulcahy's relationship with Collins illustrates this point. The two men worked extremely well together, accomplished much, and maintained a valued friendship. Mulcahy submerged his ego and was content to leave a great deal of the glamour and public recognition to Collins. Those in the army knew his achievements, his accomplishments. The public mind, however, identified Collins as the man who won the Anglo-Irish war. More than anything else, Mulcahy did not seem to have that passion for power, that personal burning desire for self-aggrandizement that would make him seek power and status as the nation's leader.

Mulcahy, for example, did not try to split the party in 1924 and set himself up as a rival leader to Cosgrave. His loyalty to the government and the party would not permit it. Not surprisingly, Cosgrave would later praise Mulcahy for his "great qualities of restraint and self-sacrifice".[20] Mulcahy waited patiently to return to the cabinet, chairing the commission of Inquiry into the Irish-speaking districts and remaining active in the Cumann na nGaedheal party. In 1926, however, when Mulcahy asked Cosgrave about the possibility of his returning to the cabinet after the next election, Cosgrave demurred. The members of the Cumann na nGaedheal party, however, thought otherwise. In 1927, they elected Mulcahy to the executive committee of the party, effectively ushering him back into the cabinet.[21] However reluctantly, Cosgrave appointed him minister for local government and public health.

Mulcahy's lack of self-aggrandizement was most conspicuous, perhaps, during the negotiations for the inter-party government in 1948. The idea for a coalition originated with Mulcahy. He canvassed the various parties and brought them all together. He understood that his role in the civil war would make him unacceptable to some as Taoiseach—a post he could have rightfully claimed as leader of the largest political party in the coalition. Thus, he chose the relatively minor position of minister of education. Mulcahy persuaded John A. Costello of Fine Gael to become Taoiseach.

Mulcahy saw it as his responsibility to insure that the Coalition went forward. As party leader, Mulcahy recognized that it was in the interests of Fine Gael to be back in power after sixteen years in opposition. But, perhaps even more important, Mulcahy saw it at his duty to oust de Valera, to finally force de Valera and Fianna Fáil out of office and out of power.

More than anyone else, Mulcahy blamed de Valera for the civil war. He believed that the civil war assumed the scale it did because de Valera persuaded Liam Lynch, with his tremendous influence in the Southern divisions, to go against the Treaty. In Mulcahy's eyes, de Valera had destroyed the wonderful harmony of the revolutionary movement and had led good IRA comrades astray. For these offences, Mulcahy never forgave him.[22]

Because Mulcahy believed that de Valera had betrayed the revolutionary movement for personal power, not principle, he could never trust de Valera as a political leader. Mulcahy remained suspicious of both his motives and actions and doubted his commitment to democratic representative government. De Valera came to embody all that Mulcahy despised in politics and politicians. Mulcahy characterized de Valera as a leader whose nationalism was "narrow, vindictive and dominated by Party spirit", a "Fianna Fáil tiger" that "tasted more and more blood" which served only to "increase its lust for power".[23] To the end of his life, Mulcahy refused to accept de Valera's popularity and dominance of Irish political life.

Mulcahy retired from politics in 1959 and died in 1971. He was remembered as a "soldier-patriot-politician", a "formidable personality" who bore "that certain austerity and high-mindedness which went with so many of his comrades in the days of resurgence".[24] Ernest Blythe, a fellow minister in the Cosgrave government, described Mulcahy as "the most prominent and effective spokesman of Fine Gael".[25] John A. Costello, the man whom Mulcahy convinced to lead the Coalition government, paid tribute to Mulcahy's unselfishness and dedication: "In any situation where there appeared to be a conflict between his personal and his public interests, he unhesitatingly left aside all his own interest. He is a man of idealistic principle".[26] And he was remembered by his secretary in the department of education as a man who "at all times [was] affably courteous . . . never ill-humored or impatient . . . of quick intelligence . . . a great Christian gentlemen".[27]

Richard Mulcahy is important in Irish history for his many accomplishment, achievements and successes. Indeed, his importance would be assured if only for his contributions to the war for independence and the civil war. But his significance goes much deeper. Mulcahy's ideas and beliefs illustrate much about the diversity of Irish nationalism, the nature of the revolutionary struggle and the pervasiveness of the colonial experience.

Mulcahy upheld a particular type of nationalism which did not find expression in the leadership of either Cosgrave or de Valera. Because of the civil war, it is customary to divide nationalist opinion into either pro- or anti-Treaty. Such division, however, masks the diversity which was contained within the nationalist movement. It is not sufficient to say that Mulcahy was pro-Treaty. Mulcahy's position is more accurately represented by the terms middle-class, Gaelic League, Sinn Féin, Volunteer, IRB and also pro-Treaty. Those who also held this outlook had no spiritual home after the death of Collins and the ascendancy of Cosgrave and O'Higgins. Mulcahy became their leader. He voiced their demands, articulated their frustrations and understood their discontent. Their significance lay not in their numbers but rather in the fact that they provide an important clue to the malaise, the disenchantment which permeated the Irish Free State during the initial years of its existence and which translated into the appalling electoral record of Cumann na nGaedheal and Fine Gael. It is remarkable that the party responsible for ushering the Free State into existence—Cumann na nGaedheal/Fine Gael—would never again hold power on its own and would be in government only as part of a coalition. When he became leader of Fine Gael, Mulcahy tried to recoup some of the energy and enthusiasm of the earlier nationalist movement, but the years in power had enabled de Valera to dominate much of the nationalist space. Although Mulcahy did succeed in ousting de Valera from government, it was only through a coalition. Years after Cosgrave and O'Higgins, Fine Gael would still be perceived as the pro-Commonwealth, pro-British party.

Mulcahy's career is also significant for the perspective it casts on the nature of the Irish struggle for independence. His career is a testimony to the evolutionary nature of the Irish revolution. While there may have been some zealots who saw clearly and cleverly plotted the guerrilla war of independence, they were not many nor was Mulcahy one of them. In this, he was representative of a significant group within the nationalist movement. To say he and they stumbled into a guerrilla war would be to overstate the case. But neither did they leap confidently from one step to another. Perhaps it is most accurate to say they walked a cautious path into the revolutionary struggle. They were pushed onwards by British policy and prejudice. They were also prodded by their more radical colleagues.

Mulcahy was not an unwilling revolutionary, but he was essentially a middle class nationalist who was radicalized by the circumstances and events of the drive for independence. In this, Mulcahy typified a significant segment of the population who, although committed nationalists, had to be drawn into an armed struggle, had to be gradually convinced that a sustained guerrilla war with England was the answer. Many of his decisions— his initial displeasure at Soloheadbeg, his concern less the struggle become too bloody too quickly—reflect his understanding of the attitudes and beliefs of this group within the nationalist movement. Because he appreciated their feelings, Mulcahy could bring them along with him as he traveled the road to a full scale guerrilla war.

Finally, Mulcahy's career typified the dilemma of the colonized, rebelling against political domination but caught in a web of British cultural domination, conscious of and responding to the negative portrait which the British painted of the Irish. This sensitivity and concern informed many of the decisions which characterized Mulcahy's tenure as chief of staff. Only within this colonial context are many of his attitudes understandable. For years, the Irish had been demeaned by British stereotypes which characterized them as lazy, drunken, inefficient, superstitious and morally deficient. Mulcahy seemed determined to disprove this myth of Irish inferiority and to demonstrate to the British that the Irish, in particular the Irish army, was a disciplined, controlled, and efficient organization which would acquit itself with honor in any situation. Thus Mulcahy went to the lengths he did to ensure that the army—even the bandmasters[28]—would act honorably and reflect well upon the nation. Thus Mulcahy would not sanction allowances for common law unions, those irregular relationships outside the bounds of conventional marriages. Thus Mulcahy tried his best to impose a boundary on the guerrilla struggle and ensure that authorized procedures protected the army from criticism and reproach. To him, it was war with honor.

Admired and praised by his colleagues, idolized by a small but distinct faction of the Fine Gael party, Mulcahy has nevertheless been excluded from the pantheon of Irish heroes. The civil war tarnished his reputation. More than anyone else, he was tarred with the memory of the executions, of the brutality of the civil war. Perhaps tributes to Mulcahy raise once again painful issues of the civil war which are easier kept buried and forgotten. However, in light of his important contributions to the modern Irish state, this neglect is ill deserved. As John A. Costello said of Mulcahy:

> He served his country well, but it was not appreciated. I personally have never come across any man who was so selfless in public or national affairs.[29]

Richard Mulcahy—soldier and statesman—deserves to be recognized as one of the foremost patriots of the revolutionary era.

Translation of a speech delivered by General Mulcahy on introducing the Democratic Programme for the acceptance of Dáil Éireann at its first meeting on the 21st January 1919

A Chean Comhairle and Members of the Dáil, I offer you this programme and I ask you to accept it willingly and to put its intentions into effect exactly in your actions and in your laws. For a long time our Country and our People have been under the tyranny and under the bonds of our enemies. Today we are breaking those bonds and we are dispelling that tyranny from our Country but the mark of both bond and tyranny lie on her. Work and organised industry are the great arteries of a Country's life blood, that blood that gives live and health to its body and energy to its soul. These arteries are badly bruised, and even broken, as a result of the tyranny that has been among us. There is not a proper running in the blood. Because of that there are ugly growths here and there on the body of our Country in our cities, in our towns and even in our countryside. These growths indicate to us a disease that will grow and that will, perhaps, kill our Country unless they are cured. If we want our country to exist and to be a living country not only must we free it, but we must restore its health. Let us do it with efficiency and with careful thought. Let us clearly understand in doing this what our Country is. This, Ireland, that has been a dream and prophecy to every single one of its children from their earliest youth. Let us understand in the first place that it is this country here of ours, beautiful with the beauty of God gave it, rich with the labours of its people, bright with their laughter, pleasant with their gaiety, holy with their faith and with their goodwill. Let us understand too, that it is this people of ours living in gaiety and peace among the riches that God bestowed on them, and gaining by their industry from those riches their sustenance. And when we set ourselves to regulate by our laws the application of our people's industry to our Country's riches let us do it in such a way as will prevent the spiteful and the robber stealing the riches for themselves to the impoverishment of the People.

A Nation cannot be fully free in which even a small section of its people have not freedom. A Nation cannot be said fully to live in spirit, or materially, while there is denied to any section of its people a share of the wealth and the riches that God bestowed around them to make them living and to sustain life in them. Therefore, I ask you to accept this programme. Let us enshrine it in our laws, and let us ever remember in our actions our People whom it is our responsibility to teach and to defend.

Notes

AICT	Army Inquiry Committee Testimony
Mul.P	Mulcahy Papers (housed in UCDA)
NLI	National Library of Ireland
PN	Personal Narrative by Richard Mulcahy (private collection)
SPOD	State Papers Office, Dublin
UCDA	University College Dublin Archives

CHAPTER ONE

1. The two classic works in this area are F. Fanon, *The Wretched of the Earth* and A. Memmi, *The Colonizer and the Colonized*. On the Irish experience, see, for example, the work of L.P. Curtis, *Anglo-Saxon and Celts* and *Apes and Angels*; and N. Lebow, *White Britain and Black Ireland*.
2. PN No.1, p.34, Personal Narrative files are all in possession of the author.
3. Ibid. No.2, p.1.
4. Ibid. No.2, p.4.
5. Ibid. No.1, p.13.
6. Mul.P, P7/D/26.
7. PN No. 2, p.13.
8. Ibid. p.21.
9. Ibid. p.27.
10. Transcript of Telefís Éireann programme of 2 February 1966, Mul.P P7/D/29.
11. PN No.2, p.9.
12. Ibid. p.14.
13. Ibid. p.14.
14. Ibid. p.15.
15. Mulcahy's comments must be analyzed in light of the later controversy surrounding the IRB. During both the Anglo-Irish war and the mutiny of 1924, critics charged that the oath of the IRB undermined its members' loyalty to the state and that the Brotherhood's presence in the army interfered with its command structure, thwarted discipline, and encouraged cliques and rivalries. Its opponents deemed the IRB an anachronistic and subversive influence on the new state. These disputes, which will be discussed in detail later, may very well have colored Mulcahy's recollections of his years in the IRB. Mulcahy was always a staunch defender of the IRB. Therefore, he consistently downplayed the question of the oath, in particular, and the influence of the Brotherhood in general.
16. PN No.2, p.2.
17. Ibid. p.20.
18. Ibid. p.15.
19. Ibid. No. 1, p.5.
20. Ibid. No. 2, p.23.
21. Ibid. pp.25–26.
22. Ibid. p.28.
23. Ibid. p.27.
24. Transcript of Telefís Éireann programme of 2 February 1966, Mul.P, P7/D/29.
25. The two others were located in Dublin and in the Galtee area of

Tipperary. The Volunteers had also set up smaller camps throughout the country for general training.
26. PN No.3 and No.4.
27. Ibid. No.3 and No.4.
28. Transcript of Telefís Éireann programme of 2 February 1966, Mul.P, P7/D/29.
29. PN No.3 and No.4, p.51.
30. Mul.P, P7/D/18.
31. Mul.P, P7/D/24. See also Mul.P, P7/D/30 and P7/D/18.
32. Mul.P, P7/D/18.
33. Ibid.
34. Ibid.
35. Ibid.
36. Ibid.
37. Col. J.V. Lawless, "Ashbourne, 1916", Mul.P, P7/D/25.
38. Transcript of Telefís Éireann broadcast on 2 February 1966, Mul.P, P7/D/29. See also Mul.P, P7/D/2.
39. Conversation with Denis McCullough, Mul.P, P7/D/14.
40. Note on Pearse, Mul.P, P7/D/29.
41. Mul.P, P7/D/19.
42. Pearse at Arbour Hill, Mul.P, P7/D/18.
43. Transcript of Telefís Éireann broadcast on 2 February 1966, Mul.P, P7/D/29.
44. Transcript of Radio Éireann broadcast on 21 April 1966, Mul.P, P7/D/30.
45. Ernie O'Malley, *On Another Man's Wounds* (1979), pp.30–40; See also James Stephens, *The Insurrection in Dublin* (1916; 1978), *passim*.
46. One need only think of the burnings of the Boer farms or the use of concentration camps during the Boer war or, in India, of the massacre at Amritsar.
47. Charles Townshend, *Political Violence in Ireland* (1983), p.308. Townshend also cites General Maxwell's orders concerning the arrest of prisoners. Maxwell wanted those people arrested —"dangerous Sinn Feiners" as he called them—"who have actually supported the movement throughout the country, even though they have not taken part in the rising" (ibid.)
48. PN No.4, p.4.
49. Knutsford and Frongoch, PN No.4. Knutsford was a small jail used as a prison for convicted British soldiers. It must have been a rather frightening experience as, during the night, the Irish prisoners could often hear their British counterparts screaming from tortuous physical punishment.
50. Mul.P, P7/C/42.
51. Letter from Mulcahy, 13 July 1916, Mul.P, P7/C/55.
52. Note on Frongoch, PN No.4. See also Mulcahy's notes on P. Beaslai's *Michael Collins and the Making of a New Ireland*, Mul.P, P7/D/67.
53. Both Margery Forester and T.P. Coogan in their respective biographies of Collins imply that the Volunteers were thinking in terms of an upcoming guerrilla war. Forester does not provide a source for her information. Coogan is more tentative. He suggests that the Boer War may have inspired the Volunteers in Frongoch to start thinking of guerilla tactics. I have found no evidence in my research that the Volunteer leaders were actually thinking in terms of guerilla warfare at this time.
54. The Question of the Chief of Staff Position, Mul.P, P7/D/96.
55. Note on Frongoch, PN No.4.
56. Florence O'Donoghue, "The Re-Organisation of the Irish Volunteers, 1916–1917", *Capuchin Annual*, Vol. 34, 1967, p.383.
57. Richard Mulcahy, "The Irish Volunteer Convention 27 October 1917," *Capuchin Annual*, Vol.34, 1967, p.405.
58. Talk given by Richard Mulcahy to the Members of the 1916–21 Club, Mul.P, P7/D/66.
59. Mul.P, P7/D/18. In his funeral oration, Collins said: "Nothing additional remains to be said. That volley which we have just heard is the only speech which it is proper to make above the grave of a dead Fenian." T.P. Coogan, *Michael Collins* (1990), p.74.
60. The other directors were Diarmuid Lynch, Communications; Michael Staines, Supply; Rory O'Connor, Engineering. Richard Mulcahy, "The

Irish Volunteer Convention 27 October 1917," *Capuchin Annual*, Vol.34, 1967, p.408.

61. PN No.5, p.2.
62. Richard Mulcahy, "The Irish Volunteer Convention 27 October 1917," *Capuchin Annual*, p.409.
63. Florence O'Donoghue, "The Re-Organisation of the Irish Volunteers, 1916–1917", p.385.

CHAPTER TWO

1. Florence O'Donoghue, Guerrilla Warfare in Ireland 1919–1921, Mul.P, P7/D/1.
2. Florence O'Donoghue, "The Re-Organisation of the Irish Volunteers 1916–1917," p.384.
3. Richard Mulcahy, "Conscription and the General Headquarters' Staff," *Capuchin Annual*, Vol.35, 1968, p.386.
4. Ibid., p.392.
5. PN No.5, p.2.
6. Ernie O'Malley, *On Another Man's Wounds*, p.79.
7. Ibid., p.75. O'Malley is wrong in asserting that Mulcahy was assistant chief of staff. He was chief of staff. In the reorganized de Valera cabinet of 1919, he would be assistant minister for defence.
8. PN No.5, pp.12–13.
9. Florence O'Donoghue, "The Re-Organisation of the Irish Volunteers 1916–1917," p.383.
10. Florence O'Donoghue, Guerrilla Warfare in Ireland, Mul.P, P7/D/1.
11. Charles Townshend, *The British Campaign in Ireland 1919–1921* (1975), pp.6–7.
12. *An t-Oglach*, Vol.1, No.8, 16 December 1918.
13. The latest biography of Collins by T.P. Coogan indicates that Collins was one of the earliest leaders to switch from passive to active resistance.
14. Richard Mulcahy, "The Irish Volunteer Convention 27 October, 1917", p.408.
15. The Question of the Chief of Staff Position, Mul.P, P7/D/96.

16. Sinn Féin Standing Committee Minutes, Mul.P, P7/D/39.
17. Diary, Mul.P, P7/C/33.
18. Talk given to the Members of the 1916–21 Club, Mul.P, P7/D/66.
19. Sinn Féin Standing Committee Minutes, 31 December 1918, Mul.P, P7/D/39.
20. Talk given by Richard Mulcahy to the Members of the 1916–21 Club, Mul.P, P7/C/66.
21. Brian Farrell, *The Founding of Dáil Éireann* (1971), p.48. The interpretation of these figures continues to be a source of much debate. See, for example, David Fitzpatrick's article, "The Geography of Irish Nationalism," in *Past and Present*, lxxvii (1978).
22. *Minutes of the Proceedings of the First Parliament of the Republic of Ireland*: 16.
23. Florence O'Donoghue, Guerrilla Warfare in Ireland, Mul.P, P7/D/1.
24. Translation of Speech Delivered by General Mulcahy on Introducing the Democratic Programme for the Acceptance of Dáil Éireann at its First Meeting on the 21st January, 1919, Mul.P, P7/C/97. For the complete text, see Appendix to this book.
25. Talk with M.V. Sugrue, Mul.P, P7/D/94.
26. Note on the differences between Cathal Brugha and Stack and other members of the Volunteers executive and cabinet, Mul.P, P7/D/96.
27. Richard Mulcahy, "Conscription and the General Headquarters Staff," p.383.
28. In Innishannon in County Cork, a policeman lost his life in a scuffle with the Volunteers. Cathal Brugha apparently was furious about the Innishannon incident and threatened an inquiry of the Volunteer executive. However, his rage soon cooled and the matter was hushed up; cf. Note on the Differences between Cathal Brugha and Stack and Other Members of the Volunteer Executive and Cabinet, Mul.P, P7/D/96.
29. Michael Brennan, *The War in Clare* (1980), p.37.

30. Conversation between Mulcahy and Sean MacEoin in Notes by MacEoin, Mul.P, P7/D/3.
31. Dan Breen, *My Fight For Irish Freedom* (1944 edition), pp.68–69.
32. Talk with M.V. Sugrue, Mul.P, P7/D/94.
33. Michael Brennan, *The War in Clare*, p.38.
34. Comments on P. Beaslai, *Michael Collins and the Making of a New Ireland*, Mul.P, P7/D/67.
35. Some Special Points as Regards Propaganda in Ircland, Mul.P, P7/A/42.
36. Compare, for example, Tom Barry, *Guerrilla Days in Ireland* or Dan Breen, *My Fight For Irish Freedom* with the work of Charles Townshend, *The British Campaign in Ireland 1919-1921*, or his article "The Irish Republican Army and the Development of Guerrilla Warfare," *English Historical Review*, xiv (1979) p.321. The phrase "social banditry" is taken from Townshend, "The Irish Republican Army and the Development of Guerrilla Warfare".
37. Quoted in P. Beaslai, *Michael Collins and the Making of a New Ireland*, Vol.1, p.275.
38. Charles Townshend, "The Irish Republican Army and the Development of Guerrilla Warfare," p.321.
39. Mul.P, P7/D/1; Talk with M.V. Sugrue, Mul.P, P7/D/94.
40. Talk given to the Members of the 1916–21 Club, Mul.P, P7/D/66.
41. On a personal note, it was during this time, June, 1919, when Mulcahy married Josephine (Min) Ryan, a woman who was active in the nationalist movement and whose family was also prominent in nationalist activities. They eventually had six children. Most of the Ryan family would go anti-Treaty and one of Mulcahy's sisters-in-law would even go on hunger strike while in prison. See below, Chapter 7.
42. The Question of the Chief of Staff Position, Mul.P, P7/D/96.
43. Comments on P. Beaslai, *Michael Collins and the Making of a New Ireland*, Mul.P, P7/D/67.
44. Richard Mulcahy, "The Irish Volunteer Convention 27 October 1917," *Capuchin Annual*.
45. Ibid, p.410.
46. *Minutes of the Proceedings of the First Parliament of the Republic of Ireland*: 46–47.
47. Ibid.,152–153.
48. Ibid., 151–152. Alderman T. Kelly made this argument in what was a remarkably short debate. Kelly said that "In his opinion the two bodies should remain separate. He reminded them of the fate of the Volunteers of 1782. A time might come when a military demonstration might be necessary."
49. General Orders, New Series, Order No.11, 23 July 1920, Mul.P, P7/A/45.
50. It is not clear when the term IRA replaced that of the Volunteers. General Headquarters Staff continued to use the term Volunteer at least into 1921, although IRA was used popularly before that. I have used the taking of the oath as a kind of demarcation point and will, after that date, use the two names interchangeably.
51. General Order, New Series, Order No.9, 19 June 1920, Mul.P, P7/A/45.
52. Notes on Cathal Brugha, Mul.P, P7/D/86.
53. Mul.P, P7/C/96.
54. General discussion about the independence movement among Dr Mulcahy, General Mulcahy and Mrs Mulcahy, Mul.P, P7/D/100.
55. Mulcahy sees the return of de Valera as a decisive event in altering his relationship with Brugha. Notes on Cathal Brugha, Mul.P, P7/D/86. Mulcahy's view of de Valera will be discussed later in this book.
56. General discussion about the independence movement among Dr Mulcahy, General Mulcahy and Mrs Mulcahy, Mul.P, P7/D/100.
57. Note on the difference between Cathal Brugha and Stack and other members of the Volunteer executive and cabinet, Mul.P.
58. Charles Townshend, "The Irish Republican Army and the Development of Guerrilla Warfare," p.341.

59. The Question of the Chief of Staff position, Mul.P, P7/D/96.

60. Dan Breen, *My Fight for Irish Freedom* (1944 edition) p.156; this phrase is used extensively in Mulcahy's writings. See, for example, his article, "Chief of Staff 1919," *Capuchin Annual*, Vol.36, 1969.

61. Richard Mulcahy, "Chief of Staff 1919," *Capuchin Annual*, p.351.

62. Dan Breen, *My Fight For Irish Freedom* (revised edition, 1975), p.38.

63. Mul.P, P7/D/2.

64. On 21 November 1920, members of the Squad killed eleven alleged British spies sent to infiltrate GHQ. Under the guise of commercial travellers, they mingled with ordinary people—domestics, mail carriers, delivery people, for example—and could, therefore, pick up stray, but significant, bits of information. They became a direct threat to the security of GHQ. These alleged spies even interviewed a number of staff and Squad members under the pretense of helping GHQ acquire arms—almost a guaranteed means of at least a first interview. Collins struck as soon as he realized the threat these men were to his organization and GHQ. Mulcahy's position on Bloody Sunday was that they destroyed "a very dangerous and cleverly planned spy organisation whose purpose was to destroy the Directing Corps. of the Volunteers." Letter from Mulcahy to Hector G.C. Legge, 14 April 1959, Mul.P, P7c/2.

65. Margery Forester, *Michael Collins—The Lost Leader*, p.124.

66. Dan Breen, *My Fight For Irish Freedom* (1944 edition), p.156.

67. O'Murthuile Manuscript, p.70, Mul.P, P7/A/209. Mulcahy in a conversation later on in his life dismisses O'Murthuile's comments as inaccurate.

68. Quoted in Leon O'Broin, *Michael Collins* (1980), p.49.

69. This point is substantiated in the latest biography of Collins. T.P. Coogan, *Michael Collins* (1990).

70. Memo to adjutant general from brigade commandant, Sligo, 4 April 1920, Collins Papers, Department of Defence Archives, Reel No.9, A/0512, NLI.

71. Memo to brigade commandant, Sligo, from adjutant general, April, 1920, Collins Papers, Department of Defence Archives, Reel No.9, A/0512, NLI.

72. Memo to director of organisation from adjutant, Leitrim Brigade, 28 May 1920, Collins Papers, Department of Defence Archives, Reel No.9, A/0510, NLI.

73. Richard Mulcahy, "Chief of Staff 1919," pp.351–352.

74. Ibid., p.352.

75. Charles Townshend, *Political Violence in Ireland*, p.335.

76. Richard Mulcahy, "Chief of Staff 1919," p.352. In this article, Mulcahy estimates about 500 police barracks were destroyed. In his Talk given to the Members of the 1916–21 Club, P7/D/66, he used the figure of 300. Townshend uses the figure of 400. I chose to use Townshend's figure.

77. Mul.P, P7/C/42.

CHAPTER THREE

1. Mul.P, P7/D/131.

2. General Orders, New Series, Order No.4, 26 May 1920, Mul.P, P7/A/45.

3. Letter from chief of staff to minister for defence, 14 May 1921, Mul.P, P7/A/18.

4. See, for example, David Fitzpatrick, *Politics and Irish Life 1913–21*; Charles Townshend, *Political Violence in Ireland*; or, from the point of view of the participants, Tom Barry, *Guerrilla Days in Ireland*.

5. General Orders, New Series, No.15, 3 December 1920, Mul.P, P7/A/45.

6. Talk given to the Members of the 1916–21 Club, Mul.P, P7/D/66.

7. Ernie O'Malley in *On Another Man's Wounds* gives a vivid picture of his activities as a training officer.

8. Memo to brigade commandant, Cork, No.1 from chief of staff, 14 May 1921, Mul.P, P7/A/18.

9. Memo from chief of staff to O/C, 1st Southern Division, 17 June 1921, Mul.P, P7/A/21.

10. Tom Barry, *Guerrilla Days in Ireland* (Irish Press edition, 1949), p.23.

11. Memo from chief of staff to brigade commandant, Kerry No.2, 21 March 1921, Mul.P, P7/A/38.

12. Memo to adjutant-general from chief of staff, 7 June 1921, Mul.P, P7/A/ 19.

13. Memo to brigade commandant, West Connemara, from the chief of staff, 19 April 1921, Mul.P, P7/A/19. Reports from officers and Mulcahy's replies are predominantly found in the files P7/A/17, 18 and 19.

14. Memo to brigade commandant, West Connemara, from the chief of staff, 18 April 1921, Mul.P, P7/A/19.

15. Memo to brigade commandant, Offaly No.2, from chief of staff, 21 April 1921, Mul.P, P7/A/17.

16. Ibid.

17. Memo to brigade commandant, Sligo, from chief of staff, 6 June 1921, Mul.P, P7/A/19.

18. Memo to brigade commandant, Cork No.3, from chief of staff, 31 May 1921, Mul.P, P7/A/18.

19. Memo to brigade commandant, East Donegal, from chief of staff, 26 April 1921, Mul.P, P7/A/17; Memo to brigade commandant, West Limerick, from the chief of staff, 23 March 1921, Mul.P, P7/A/17.

20. Memo to GHQ, Organiser, North Cavan, from chief of staff, 24 May 1921, Mul.P, P7/A/18.

21. Memo to brigade commandant, South Wexford, from chief of staff, 13 May 1921, Mul.P, P7/A/17.

22. Memo to chief of staff from the O/C, Mid-Clare, 28 May 1921, Mul.P, P7/A/18.

23. Memo to minister for defence from chief of staff, 17 June 1921, Mul.P, P7/A/20.

24. Draft memorandum, Mul.P, P7/A/20.

25. Charles Townshend, *The British Campaign in Ireland*, pp.71–72.

26. See, for example, the memo to the chief of staff from HQ, Cork No.2 Brigade, 3 March 1921, asking for permission to destroy a particular line. Mul.P, P7/A/17.

27. Memo to O/C, 1st Southern Division, from adjutant, Kerry No.3 Brigade, 20 May 1921, Mul.P, P7/A/21.

28. Memo to chief of staff from divisional adjutant, 1st Southern Division, 24 May 1921; memo to O/C, 1st Southern Division, from chief of staff, 16 June 1921, Mul.P, P7/A/21.

29. General Orders, New Series, Order No.12, 1 November 1920, Mul.P, P7/A/45, UCDA.

30. Memo to adjutant general from minister for home affairs, 10 June 1921, Mul.P, P7/A/20.

31. Memo to chief of staff from adjutant general, 21 June 1921, Mul.P, P7/A/20.

32. *Minutes of the Proceedings of the First Parliament of the Republic of Ireland*: 241.

33. Ibid.: 247–248.

34. Mul.P, P7/D/2.

35. See, for example, memo to adjutant general from adjutant, Cork No.2 Brigade, 24 June 1920, Collins Papers, Department of Defence Archives, P917, NLI.

36. Memo to brigade commandant Kerry No.2 from adjutant general, 1920, Collins Papers, Department of Defence Archives, P916, NLI.

37. General Orders, New Series, Order No.10, 19 June 1920, Mul.P, P7/A/45.

38. Staff memo on Emigration, n.d., Mul.P, P7/A/18.

39. Memo to adjutant general from Cork No.1 Brigade, 26 March 1921, Mul.P, P7/A/17.

40. Memo to minister for defence from chief of staff, 30 March 1921, Mul.P, P7/A /17.

41. Dail Order, 8 April 1921, Mul.P, P7/A/17.

42. Question of a Disciplinary Code, Staff Memo, 30 March 1921, Mul.P, P7/A/17.

43. General Orders, New Series, Order No.18, 2 April 1921, Mul.P, P7/A/45.

44. Quoted in Charles Townshend, *The British Campaign in Ireland*, p.122. His source is a memo by the Secretary of State for War, 10 November 1920, C.59A(20), CAB.23. About this statement, Townshend writes, "These remarkable admissions were never made elsewhere" (ibid.).

45. Memo to brigade commandant, Belfast, from the chief of staff, 18 March 1921, Mul.P, P7/A/17, *UCDA*.

46. Memo to minister for defence from chief of staff, 14 May 1921, Mul.P, P7/A/18.

47. Memo to adjutant general from chief of staff, 24 June 1921, Mul.P, P7/A/45.

48. General Orders, New Series, Order No.26, 22 June 1921, Mul.P, P7/A/45.

49. Memo to minister for defence from chief of staff, 5 July 1921, Mul.P, P7/A/21.

50. Memo to chief of staff from Commandant, Cork No.2 Brigade, 19 March 1921, Mul.P, P7/A/17.

51. Memo to O/C, First Southern Division, from chief of staff, 17 June 1921, Mul.P, P7/A/21.

52. Memo to chief of staff from O/C, Tuam Brigade, 28 June 1921, Mul.P, P7/A/20.

53. Memo to adjutant general from Cork No.1 Brigade, 26 March 1921, Mul.P, P7/A/17.

54. General Orders, New Series, General Order No.19, 20 April 1921, Mul.P, P7/A/35.

55. General Orders, New Series, Order No.24, 9 June 1921, Mul.P, P7/A/45.

56. Memo to adjutant general from chief of staff, 6 June 1921, Mul.P, P7/A/45.

57. General Orders, New Series, Order No.20, 20 April 1921, Mul.P, P7/A/45.

58. Memo to chief of staff from intelligence officer, 1st Southern Division, June 1921, Mul.P, P7/A/20. The question of spying is dealt with predominantly in files P7/A/17, 18, 19, and 20.

59. General Orders, New Series, Order No.20, 20 April 1921, Mul.P, P7/A/45.

60. General Orders, New Series, Order No.13, 9 November 1920, Mul.P, P7/A/45.

61. Memo to chief of staff from brigade commandant, South Roscommon, 14 February 1921, Mul.P, P7/A/17.

62. Report of the 1st Southern Division, 29 October 1921, Collins Papers, Department of Defence Archives, Reel No.10, Ref.A/26, NLI.

63. Memo to chief of staff from O/C, 1st Southern Division, 11 July 1921, Mul.P, P7/A/21.

64. Correspondence between the chief of staff and the divisional commandant, 1st Southern Division, May-June 1921, Mul.P, P7/A/20.

65. Report on Capture and Execution of Three Military Officers, 20 June 1921, Mul.P, P7/A/20.

66. Talk with M.V. Sugrue, Mul.P, P7/D/94.

67. Memo to chief of staff from GHQ Cork No.2 Brigade, 12 March 1921, Mul.P, P7/A/17.

68. The Divisional Idea, Mul.P, P7/A/47.

69. See Mul.P, P7/A/47, UCDA for a number of these directives to various divisions.

70. Memo to brigade commandant, Cork No.2, from chief of staff, 8 March 1921, Mul.P, P7/A/17.

71. The Divisional Idea, Mul.P, P7/A/47.

72. O'Donoghue, Guerrilla Warfare in Ireland, Mul.P, P7/D/1; Notes on the Origin of Divisional System, Collins Papers, Department of Defence Archives, Reel No.10, Ref. No.0629, NLI.

73. General Instructions to Divisional Commandants, Organisation Department, Mul.P, P7/A/17.

74. Divisional Journals, Mul.P, P7/A/21.

75. Tom Barry, *Guerilla Days in Ireland*, Anvil Press edition, pp.148–149.

76. Ernie O'Malley, *On Another Man's Wounds*, p.307.

77. Tom Barry, *Guerilla Days in Ireland*, Anvil Press edition, pp.146–148; *On Another Man's Wounds*, pp.307–308.

78. Charles Townshend, *Political Violence in Ireland*, p.337.

79. Memo to chief of staff from O/C, 3rd Southern Division, 30 June 1921, Mul.P, P7/A/22.

80. *Guerilla Days in Ireland*, Anvil Press edition, p.165.

81. O'Murthuile manuscript, pp.209–210, Mul.P, P7a/209.

82. Memo from chief of staff to each officer, 2 May 1921, Mul.P, P7/A/20.

83. Captured Papers, Mul.P, P7/A/21. For information on the activities of the IRA in England, see the Reports of the Department of Engineering entitled Operations Abroad, 3 June 1921, Mul.P, P7/A/19; 16 July 1921, Mul.P, P7/A/21.

84. Memo to director of purchasing from chief of staff, 22 March 1921, Mul.P, P7/A/17.

85. Memo to director of munitions from the chief of staff, 6 June 1921, Mul.P, P7/A/19.

86. Allocation of the New Machine Gun [probably a staff memo], Mul.P, P7/A/18.

87. Charles Townshend, *The British Campaign in Ireland*, p.181.

88. Margery Forester, *Michael Collins*, p.196.

89. Comments of P. Beaslai, *Michael Collins and the Making of a New Ireland*, Mul.P, P7/D/67.

90. Army-Dail Relations, Mul.P, P7/D/2.

CHAPTER FOUR

1. Memo to officers commanding all units from the chief of staff, 9 July 1921, Mul.P, P7/A/21. On the same day, de Valera issued a proclamation to the nation: "During the period of the truce each individual soldier and citizen must regard himself [*sic*] as a custodian of the nation's honour. Your discipline must prove in the most convincing manner that this is the struggle of an organised nation. In the negotiations now initiated your representatives will do their utmost to secure a just and peaceful termination of this struggle, but history, particularly our own history, and the character of the issue to be decided are a warning against undue confidence. An unbending determination to endure all that may still be necessary, and fortitude such as you have shown in all your recent sufferings— these alone will lead you to the peace you desire. Should force be resumed against our nation, you must be ready on your part once more to resist. Thus [*sic*] alone will you secure the final abandonment of force, and the acceptance of justice and reason as the arbiter." Mul.P, P7/A/21.

2. Sean Collins Powell, "Details of the Anglo-Irish Conflict, 1916–1921", Collins Papers, Department of Defence Archives, Microfilm Reel No.921, NLI.

3. List of Executions for 1921, Collins Papers, Department of Defence Archives, Microfilm Reel No.920, NLI.

4. Ernie O'Malley, *On Another Man's Wounds*, p.342.

5. Liam Deasy, *Brother Against Brother* (1982), p.23.

6. Memo to O/C, 1st Southern Division from chief of staff, 20 July 1921, Mul.P, P7/A/22.

7. Draft Notes, Mul.P, P7/A/21.

8. Michael Brennan, *The War in Clare*, p.106.

9. Mul.P, P7/D/48.

10. Comments on P. Beaslai, *Michael Collins and the Making of a New Ireland*, Mul.P, P7/D/67.

11. Mul.P, P7/D/48.

12. Quoted in Dorothy Macardle, *The Irish Republic* (1968), pp.434–435. There was some disagreement over the actual terms of the truce. The British, for example, argued that the IRA had agreed to prohibit the use of arms and to cease military manoeuvres. These terms would obviously have been unacceptable to the IRA.

13. *Dáil Debates*, Private Session, 14 September 1921. This is the phrase used in a letter from the British Prime Minister, Lloyd George, to de Valera. De Valera accepted it as the basis of negotiations.

14. The Military Situation in Ireland at the End of September 1921, Captured British Intelligence Document, Mul.P, P7/A/37.
15. Charles Townshend, *The British Campaign in Ireland 1919–1921*, p.199.
16. Quoted in Rex Taylor, *Michael Collins* (1970), p.110.
17. British Intelligence Instructions, 23 August 1921, Captured British Intelligence Documents, Mul.P, P7/A/23.
18. Memorandum, General Headquarters, July, 1921, Mul.P, P7/A/24. For additional information, see also, Report from the Director/Chemicals to the Chief/Staff for Months Ending August and September 1921, Mul.P, P7/A/24.
19. Sheila Lawlor, *Britain and Ireland 1914–1923* (1983), p.114.
20. Memo to quartermaster general from chief of staff, 31 October 1921, Mul.P, P7/A/26.
21. Memo to minister for defence from quartermaster general, 19 December 1921, Ernie O'Malley Papers, P17a/2, UCDA.
    The report is given at the bottom of this page:
22. Ernie O'Malley, *The Singing Flame*, p.15.
23. Memo to O/C, South Roscommon brigade from chief of staff, 3 October 1921, Mul.P, P7/A/26.
24. Ernie O'Malley, *The Singing Flame*, p.22.
25. Report on the Officers Training Camp, 3rd Southern Division, 25 November 1921, Mul.P, P7/A/27.
26. Report to director of training, 29 September 1921, Mul.P, P7/A/27.
27. Report of the chief of staff's visit to the South Wexford Training Camp, 12 September 1921, Mul.P, P7/A/25.
28. Memo to O/C, 2nd Southern Division from adjutant general, 20 September 1921, Ernie O'Malley Papers, P17b/134, UCDA.
29. Ibid.
30. Captured British Intelligence documents contained in a memo to the chief of staff from the deputy director of information, 25 October 1921, Mul.P, P7/A/26.
31. Memo on flying columns, 9 November 1921, Mul.P, P7/A/29.
32. Memo to head of each Department from Oific an Runaidhe (Secretary's office), 24 November 1921, Mul.P, P7/A/28.
33. Comments on P. Beaslai, *Michael Collins and the Making of a New Ireland*, Mul.P, P7/D/67.
34. Memo to quartermaster, 1st Southern Division, from adjutant general, GHQ, 28 October 1921, Mul.P, P7/A/36.
35. Memo to adjutant general, GHQ, from divisional adjutant, 1st Southern Division, 1 November 1921, Mul.P, P7/A/31.

Importation of Munitions		
Description	From 16 August 1920 to 11 July 1921	From 11 July 1921 to 17 December 1921
Machine Guns	6	51
Rifles	96	313
Revs. & Autos.	522	637
Rifle Ammn.	21,673	18,232
Rev. & Auto. Ammn.	45,680	63,675
ShotGun Ammn.	24,629	16,574
Grenade Manuf.	2,209 completed	15,000 completed* 12,000 part grenades
Explosive Manuf.	1,900 lbs.	40,000 lbs.*
	*approximately	

36. Memo to Seamus Ó Duibir, TD, from chief of staff, 16 November 1921, Mul.P, P7/A/28.
37. Memo to O/C, Dublin, from the chief of staff, 4 October 1921, Mul.P, P7/A/26.
38. Ernie O'Malley, *The Singing Flame*, p.12.
39. Memo to O/C, 1st Southern Division, from chief of staff, 31 October 1921, Mul.P, P7/A/28.
40. Memo to chief of staff from chief of police, 25 August 1921, Mul.P, P7/A/23.
41. Memo to adjutant general from O/C, 1st Southern Division, 6 October 1921, Mul.P, P7/A/26.
42. List of Decisions at Meeting of the Ministry held on Friday, 21st [October 1921], Mul.P, P7/A/36.
43. Memo to chief of staff from minister for defence, 24 October 1921, Mul.P, P7/A/30.
44. General Orders, New Series, Order No.30, 4 November 1921, Mul.P, P7/A/45, Memo to minister for defence from chief of staff, 4 November 1921, Mul.P, P7/A/37.
45. Memo to GHQ from O/C, 1st Western Division, 10 November 1922, Mul.P, P7/A/27.
46. Memo to O/C, West Connemara from chief of staff, 24 September 1921, Mul.P, P7/A/24.
47. Memo to O/C, 1st Eastern Division from chief of staff, 21 September 1921, Mul.P, P7/A/36.
48. Memo from O/C, 5th Battalion, Dublin Brigade, n.d., Mul.P, P7/A/30.
49. Letter to Mr Peter O'Loghlin, County Clare, from the chief of staff, 4 October 1921, Mul.P, P7/A/26.
50. Correspondence between Mulcahy and Collins, October-November, 1921, Collins Papers, Department of Defence Archives, P911, NLI.
51. Special Memorandum, 25 October 1921, Ernie O'Malley Papers, P17a/2, UCDA.
52. Memo to O/C, 2nd Southern Division from director of organisation, 7 July 1921, Mul.P, P7/A/22.
53. Staff Memo, n.d. [probably Truce period], Mul.P, P7/A/31.
54. Extract from the O/C, 1st Northern Division in a memo to the chief of staff from the director of organisation, 26 June 1921, Mul.P, P7/A/ 22.
55. Memo to President de Valera from Michael Collins, 29 June 1921, D.E.2/446, SPOD.
56. Memo from minister for defence, 21 October 1921, Mul.P, P7/A/36; memo to adjutant general from the O/C, 1st Southern Division, 21 November 1921, Mul.P, P7/A/30.
57. Memo to adjutant general from chief of staff, 1 October 1921, Mul.P, P7/A/28.
58. Report of Training Meeting, GHQ, 10 November (most probably 1921), Mul.P, P7/A/29.
59. *Dáil Debates* 28 April 1922, no volumn, p. 340.
60. Mul.P, P7/A/28.
61. Memo to minister for defence from minister for agriculture, 6 October 1921, Mul.P, P7/A/37.
62. Memo to O/C, Cork No.1 Brigade from O/C, 5th Battalion, 28 October 1922, Mul.P, P7/A/37.
63. Memo to minister for labour from Thomas Foran, Irish Transport and General Workers Union, 15 September 1921, Mul.P, P7/A/30.
64. Memo to chief of staff from O/C, 1st Southern Division, 13 October 1921, Mul.P, P7/A/34.
65. Correspondence concerning unemployment demonstration, September, 1921, Mul.P, P7/A/24.
66. Ibid.
67. Talk between General Michael Brennan and General Richard Mulcahy, 1 May 1963, Mul.P, P7/D/2.
68. Memorandum Re: Confiscated Farms, October, 1921, Mul.P, P7/A/29.
69. For information on relations between the police and IRA, see Mul.P, P7/A/26, P7/A/34.
70. Memo to minister for defence from minister for home affairs, 30 Samham 1921, Mul.P, P7/A/34; Memorandum,

n.d. [probably Truce period] Mul.P, P7/A/29.

71. Correspondence concerning incident at Milltown Infants School, September-October 1921, Mul.P, P7/A/26.
72. Memo to chief of staff from O/C, Mid-Limerick Brigade, 7 October 1921, Mul.P, P7/A/27.
73. Memo to O/C, Mid-Limerick Brigade, from chief of staff, 18 October 1921, Mul.P, P7/A/27.
74. Memo to minister for defence from chief of staff, 10 November 1921, Mul.P, P7/A/29.
75. Memo to chief of staff from O/C, 1st Southern Division, 2 November 1921, Mul.P, P7/A/29.
76. Memo to adjutant general from O/C, 2nd Northern Division, 30 September 1921, Mul.P, P7/A/36.
77. Weekly Memorandum, 21 October 1921, issued by order of the chief of staff, Mul.P, P7/A/34.
78. Memo to minister for defence from chief of staff, October, 1921, Mul.P, P7a/35.
79. Memo to Michael Collins from chief of staff, 7 November 1921, Mul.P, P7/A/28.
80. Captured Enemy Document, Breaches of the Truce, Ernie O'Malley Papers, P/17a/9, UCDA; Collins Papers, Department of Defence Archives, NLI.
81. Report to chief of staff from chief liaison officer, Martial Law Area, 26 August 1921, Mul.P, P7/A/23.
82. Report to adjutant general from chief liaison officer, 6 October 1921, Mul.P, P7/A/24; memo to chief of staff from chief liaison officer, Martial Law Area, 19 October 1921, Mul.P, P7/A 26.
83. Memo to chief liaison officer from chief of staff, 5 October 1921, Mul.P, P7/A/26.
84. Memo to adjutant general from Michael Collins, 1 November 1921, Mul.P, P7/A/26.
85. Copy of Communications from *Examiner* [Cork] Office, July, 1921, Mul.P, P7/A/22.

86. Memo to O/C, 1st Southern Division from chief of staff, 22 July 1921, Mul.P, P7/A/22.
87. Memo to chief of staff from chief liaison officer, Martial Law Area, 19 October 1921, Mul.P, P7/A/26.
88. Discussion among Dr Mulcahy, General and Mrs Mulcahy, 23 December 1961, Mul.P, P7/D/100.
89. Correspondence between chief of staff and O/C, 1st Southern Division, 4-13 October 1921, Mul.P, P7/A/26.
90. For information on the difficulties in Clare, see Mul.P, P7/A/28; in South Roscommon, P7/A/27; in Limerick, P7/A/28; and in Kerry, P7/A/28.
91. Memo to chief of staff from O/C, 1st Southern Division, 4 October 1921, Mul.P, P7/A/26.
92. Dorothy Macardle, *The Irish Republic*, p.492. This interpretation is also upheld by Joseph Curran, Leon O'Broin and Sheila Lawlor.
93. Both Macardle and Curran hold this interpretation. Moreover, Forester credits Collins with holding a similar sentiment. See Margery Forester, *Michael Collins—The Lost Leader*, p.265.
94. Note on the difference between Cathal Brugha and Stack and other members of the Volunteer executive and cabinet, Mul.P, P7/D/96.
95. Michael Brennan, *The War in Clare*, p.106.
96. Memo to adjutant general from minister for defence, 30 July 1921, Mul.P, P7a/1, *UCDA*.
97. Memo to minister for defence from chief of staff, 2 September 1921, Mul.P, P7a/1.
98. Memo to chief of staff from minister for defence, 6 September 1921, Mul.P, P7a/1.
99. Memo to chief of staff from adjutant general, 12 September 1921, Mul.P, P7a/1.
100. Memo to Risteard Ó Maolcatha, TD from minister for defence, 13 September 1921, Mul.P, P7a/1.
101. Memo to president from chief of staff, n.d. [probably September, 1921],

Mul.P, P7a/1. In a later discussion of the event, Mulcahy dates his letter to the President as either the 13th or 14th of September, 1921. See The Chapter on the New Army, Mul.P, P7/D/1.

102. The Chapter on the New Army, Mul.P, P7/D/1.

103. Memo to minister for defence from chief of staff, 18 October 1921, Mul.P, P7/A/27.

104. Memo to president from chief of staff, 19 October 1921, Mul.P, P7/A/27.

105. It is not clear if Mulcahy had a meeting with de Valera after the incident in September or in October. He himself seems to indicate at one time that the meeting took place after the September incident (The Chapter on the New Army, P7/D/1) and at another time that it took place after the October incident (Note on the Differences Between Cathal Brugha and Stack and Other Members of the Volunteer Executive and Cabinet, P7/D/96). As Mulcahy's original note to the president, dated 19 October 1921, specifically requests a meeting, I have placed the meeting after the October incident.

106. Memo to chief of staff from minister for defence, 16 November 1921, Mul.P, P7a/2.

107. Memo to minister for defence from O/C, 5th Northern Division, 25 November 1921, Mul.P, P7/A/37.

108. Notes of Frank Aiken, Ernie O'Malley Papers, P17a/93, UCDA.

109. Mulcahy's recommendations for his staff were:

Deputy chief of staff: Eoin O'Duffy
Assistant chief of staff: J.J. O'Connell
Adjutant general: G. O'Sullivan
Quartermaster general: S. MacMahon
Director of information: M. Collins
Director of organisation: E. Price
Director of engineering: R. O'Connor
Director of training: E. Dalton
Director of munitions: Sean Russell
Director of chemicals: J. O'Donovan
Director of purchases: Liam Mellows
Assistant director of purchases: J. Vise

110. Memo to minister for defence from chief of staff, 16 November 1921, Mul.P, P7a/2.

111. Correspondence between minister for defence and chief of staff, November 1921, Mul.P, P7a/2.

112. Memo to minister for defence from O/C, 1st Southern Division, 6 December 1921, Mul.P, P7a/5.

113. Memo to minister for defence from chief of staff, 22 November 1921, Mul.P, P7a/2. Collins wrote to Mulcahy from London about the meeting, suggesting a meeting of GHQ staff before the cabinet meeting and also suggesting that Mulcahy include some directors who had "wide knowledge of the Staff and the things that were done during the days when it was hard work to organise and to run the Old Army." Note on the Difference Between Cathal Brugha and Stack and Other Members of the Volunteer Executive and Cabinet, Mul.P, P7/D/96.

114. Note on the Differences between Cathal Brugha and Stack and Other Members of the Volunteer Executive and Cabinet, Mul.P, P7/D/96.

115. Ibid.

116. Sheila Lawlor, *Britain and Ireland 1914–23*, p.119.

117. Charles Townshend, "The Irish Republican Army and the Development of Guerrilla Warfare, 1916–1921," p.341.

118. Sheila Lawlor, *Britain and Ireland 1914–23*, p.119.

119. Comments on P. Beaslai, *Michael Collins and the Making of a New Ireland*, Mul.P, P7/D/67.

120. Ibid.

121. Quoted in Dorothy Macardle, *The Irish Republic*, p.544.

CHAPTER FIVE

1. Like the army, the IRB also split on the Treaty. At a meeting on 10 December 1921, the Supreme Council voted to accept the Treaty, but it was not a unanimous decision. Four of the sixteen members opposed the agree-

ment. The Council issued the following order: "The Supreme Council, having due regard to the Constitution of the Organisation, has decided that the present Peace Treaty between Ireland and Great Britain should be ratified. Members of the Organisation, however, who have to take public action as representatives are given freedom of action in the matter."

Throughout the country, various local IRB units rejected the order to accept the Treaty and the entire South Munster division declared against the Treaty. Collins, now president of the Supreme Council, was unable to convince his IRB colleagues of the wisdom of accepting the Treaty. The split in the IRB, as well as its order allowing members to vote their conscience, undermined the argument used by de Valera and others that the IRB was one of the major forces behind the Treaty's majority in the Dail. Cf. Joseph Curran, *The Birth of the Irish Free State* (1981), pp.144–146; Hopkinson, *Green Against Green*, (1988), pp.44–45.

2. Notes of Frank Aiken, Ernie O'Malley Papers, P17a/93, UCDA.
3. Statement of Dr Jim Ryan, Ernie O'Malley Papers, P17b/103, UCDA.
4. Ibid. In his recollections, Ryan says Eoin O'Duffy was initially against the Treaty and told Mulcahy that the army would not stand for it.
5. Those who favored the Treaty at GHQ were Collins, Mulcahy, MacMahon, O'Sullivan, O'Duffy, O'Connell, Dalton, and Beaslai; those who opposed the Treaty were Mellows, O'Connor, Russell and O'Donovan.
6. Note on the Conversation with Cruise O'Brien, 28 December 1962, Mul.P, P7/D/1.
7. *Treaty Debates*, Private Session, 14 December 1921, p.133.
8. Note on the Conversation with Cruise O'Brien, 28 December 1962, Mul.P, P7/D/1.
9. Ibid. It is interesting to note the similarity between Collins' reply

and the statement which de Valera subsequently made when he joined the Four Courts/Irregular army.
10. Ernie O'Malley, *The Singing Flame*, pp.42–44.
11. Statement of 1st Southern Division, 10 December 1921, Mul.P, P7/A/32.
12. *Treaty Debates*, 22 December 1922 p.142.
13. Ibid., p.143.
14. Ibid., p.143.
15. Ibid., p.142.
16. Conversation among Dr Mulcahy, General Mulcahy and Mrs Mulcahy, 23 December 1961, Mul.P, P7/D/100.
17. Letter to Richard Mulcahy from Tom Greene, TD, 27 December 1921, Mul.P, P7/A/32.
18. Letter to Richard Mulcahy, TD, unsigned ["from a once great admirer of yours"], n.d., Mul.P, P7/A/31.
19. Letter to Richard Mulcahy from L. Wilson, late of GPO, 26 December 1921, Mul.P, P7/A/33.
20. Letter to Commandant McKeon, TD from Dan Breen, 19 December 1921, Mul.P, P7/A/33.
21. *Treaty Debates*, Private Session, 17 December 1921, pp.266–267.
22. *Treaty Debates*, 4 January 1922, p.229.
23. *Treaty Debates*, Private Session, 17 December 1921, pp.225–226.
24. Ibid., 14 December 1921, p.128. Brugha reiterated this claim throughout the debates. See, for example, his comments of 17 December 1921.
25. Sheila Lawlor makes an interesting distinction when she writes "The Volunteers were a-political rather than anti-political, though within, it must be said in many cases, an ideological context . . ." (*Britain and Ireland*, p.123). The distinction she draws between the IRA's antipathy to what I would call party politics and what the Volunteers viewed as the inherent nature of politics to seek compromise, and their involvement in and commitment to political ideals is a valid one.
26. *Treaty Debates*, 6 January 1922, p.290.

27. Florence O'Donoghue, *No Other Law*, (1954), p.196.

28. *Treaty Debates*, 6 January 1922, p.289. Also included in the note was a listing of the Brigades which supported their divisional commandants in opposing the Treaty: "1st Southern Division: Cork, Nos. 1, 2, 3, 4, 5 Brigade. Kerry, Nos. 1, 2, 3 Brigade; West Limerick Brigade; Waterford Brigade; Dublin Brigade; 3rd Southern Division: Tipperary No.1 Brigade; Offaly No.2 Brigade; Leix Brigade."

29. *Treaty Debates* (Private Session), 16 December 1921, p.182. The document was handed to J.J. Walsh.

30. Ibid., 14 December 1921, p.128.

31. Ibid., 16 December 1921, p.182.

32. Ibid., 14 December 1921, p.134.

33. Ibid., p.134.

34. Ibid., p.132.

35. Ibid., p.132.

36. Ibid.

37. Memo to divisional adjutant, 1st Southern Division, from O/C, Cork No.1 Brigade, 19 December 1921, Mul.P, P7/A/33.

38. Memo to chief of staff from minister for defence, 29 December 1921, Mul.P, P7/A/33.

39. Copy of Communications Sent to Liaison Officer appended to letter to Richard Mulcahy, TD from W.J. Fahy, Secretary of County Cork Association Irish Farmers' Union, 31 December 1921, Mul.P, P7/A/32.

40. Memo to chief of staff from O/C 1st Southern Division, 4 January 1922, Mul.P, P7/A/32.

41. Memo to O/C, 1st Southern Division, from O/C, Cork No.1 Brigade, 31 December 1921, Mul.P, P7/A/32.

42. Memo to O/C, 1st Southern Division, from O/C, Cork No.1 Brigade, 30 December 1921, Mul.P, P7/A/32.

43. Memo to chief of staff from O/C, 1st Southern Division, 4 January 1922, Mul.P, P7/A/32.

44. Diary, 1965, Mul.P, P7c/35.

45. *Treaty Debates*, 7 January 1922, p.347.

46. Ibid., p.424.

47. This is the position of General Sean McKeon. Quoted in Calton Younger, *Ireland's Civil War* (1968), p.235. The political situation was somewhat confused. There was the Dáil government under Griffith and the Provisional Government under Collins. Most ministers held the same portfolio under both governments. As noted, Mulcahy did not.

48. Memo to minister for defence from Eamon de Valera, 6 March 1922, Mul.P, P7/B/191.

49. Notes of Frank Aiken, Ernie O'Malley Papers, P17a/93, UCDA.

50. Memo to Richard Mulcahy, TD, from Rory O'Connor, Liam Mellowes, James O'Donovan, Sean Russell, Oscar Traynor, A. McDonnell, Liam Lynch, M. McCormack, Thomas Maguire, William Pilkinton, M. Mac Giollarnaid, 11 January 1922, Mul.P, P7/B/191. There is also a note appended to the above letter stating that the O/C 2nd Southern Division, Ernie O'Malley, supports the request but his signature was not available for some hours. The note also states that "it is understood that other Divisional Commandants are also in agreement."

51. Memo to Oscar Traynor, O/C, Dublin Brigade, from minister for defence and chief of staff, 13 January 1922, Mul.P, P7/B/191.

52. Memo to chief of staff from Liam Lynch, 13 January 1922, Mul.P, P7/B/191.

53. Minutes of the Provisional Government, 17 February 1922, Vol.1, G1/1, SPOD.

54. Quoted in M. Forester, *Michael Collins—The Lost Leader*, p.278.

55. Memo to chief of staff from Rory O'Connor, Chairman, Acting Military Council, IRA, 18 January 1922, Mul.P, P7/B/191. O'Connor referred to his initial letter to Mulcahy as the letter of 12 January 1922. The original document was, however, dated 11 January 1922. This accounts for the discrepancy in some of the accounts

of the negotiations. See, for example, Calton Younger, *Ireland's Civil War*, pp. 234–235.

56. In attendance were the minister for defence, the chief of staff, the adjutant general, the quartermaster general, the directors of training, engineering, munitions, chemicals, publicity, and the commandants of the following divisions: 3rd Southern, 4th Western, 5th Northern, 1st Eastern and Midland; and the commandants of the following brigades:- No.1 Dublin, No.2 Dublin, Wexford North, Wexford South and Carlow. The minister for defence presided.

57. Memo to all divisional and brigade commandants and for transmission to all ranks, 21 January 1922, Mul.P, P7/B/191.

58. Ibid.

59. Ibid.

60. Ernie O'Malley, *The Singing Flame*, p.53.

61. Memo to all divisional and brigade commandants and for transmission to all ranks, 21 January 1922, Mul.P, P7/B/191.

62. Sean O'Murthuile Manuscript, Mul.P, P7a/208.

63. *Dáil Debates*, 1 March 1922, no volumn, p.140.

64. Florence O'Donoghue in *No Other Law* (pp.203–204) states very clearly, in fact, that Mulcahy did not get these guarantees from the IRA.

65. Memo to Ceann Conganta an Airm from Commandant on Staff, As son Ceann Fuirinne, 14 March 1922, Collins Papers, Ms. 22,127 (iii), NLI.

66. Memo to O/C, Cork No.1 Brigade from minister for defence, 12 May 1922, Mul.P, P7/B/193.

67. Joseph Curran, *The Birth of the Irish Free State, 1921–1923*, p.163.

68. *Dáil Debates*, 28 April 1922, cols. 334–335.

69. Report of director of organization on the 2nd Southern Division, 9 February 1922, Mul.P, P7/B/191. Compare the statement O'Malley gave on February 1922 to the portrayal of the incident which he gives in *The Sing-*

ing Flame. He wrote: "By breaking away from General Headquarters we would not receive any arms or ammunition. We would find it difficult to maintain men in barracks. We would be isolated. It was a definite step, however. Our brigades would know exactly for what they stood, to whom they were giving allegiance. We would find it difficult to get food; we would have to cut down staffs. Many of the men would have to return to their homes" [p.54].

70. *Dáil Debates*, 26 April 1922, col.249.

71. Ibid., col.255.

72. *The Singing Flame*, pp.60–61.

73. Interview between Mayor O'Mara, Limerick, and President Griffith, 9 March 1922, Mul.P, P7/B/191.

74. For a discussion of the problems of the Mid-Limerick Brigade in November of 1921, see Collins Papers, Department of Defence Archives, Microfilm Reel No.10, NLI.

75. Sheila Lawlor, *Britain and Ireland, 1914–1923*, p.164.

76. Memo to assistant chief of staff from M. Brennan, 8 March 1922, Collins Papers, Ms.22,127 (iii), NLI.

77. Memo to assistant chief of staff from M. Brennan, n.d. (most likely early March), Collins Papers, Ms 22,127 (iii), NLI.

78. Notes of Frank Aiken, Ernie O'Malley Papers, P17a/93.

79. Ernie O'Malley, *The Singing Flame*, pp.58–61.

80. National Army, 1922, Ginger O'Connell Collection in the Ernie O'Malley Papers, P17b/134.

81. Interview between Mayor O'Mara, Limerick, and President Griffith, 9 March 1922, Mul.P, P7/B/191.

82. Ibid.

83. Memo to minister for defence from Eamon de Valera, 6 March 1922, Mul.P, P7/B/191.

84. Liam Deasy, *Brother Against Brother*, pp.37–38; Mul.P, P7/B/191.

85. Quoted in Joseph Curran, *The Birth of the Irish Free State, 1921–1923*, p. 171.

86. Report from Sean Hurley to GHQ on Limerick Crisis, 12 March 1922, Collins Papers, Ms.22,127 (iii), NLI.
87. Ernie O'Malley, *The Singing Flame*, p.61.
88. Calton Younger, *Ireland's Civil War*, pp.244–245.
89. Gresham Hotel Protest, 12 March 1922, J.J. O'Connell Papers, Ms.22,126, NLI; Ginger O'Connell Collection in the Ernie O'Malley Papers, P17b/134, UCDA.
90. J.J. O'Connell Papers, Ms. 22,126, NLI.
91. Ibid.
92. According to an entry in the Mulcahy papers labelled Michael Collins' diary, there was, for example, a special meeting of the Supreme Council on 18 March 1922. Both Lynch and Mulcahy attended. Mul.P, P7a/62.
93. Statement on the genesis of the Army situation, n.d., Mul.P, P7/B/191.
94. Memo to minister for defence from minister for foreign affairs, 24 March 1922, Mul.P, P7/B/191.
95. *Dáil Debates*, 26 April 1922, col.255.
96. Cabinet Notes, Convention, 15 March 1922, Mul.P, P7/B/192.
97. *Dáil Debates*, 26 April 1922, col.252.
98. Army, Negotiations for Unification, S1233, SPOD.
99. Ibid.
100. Minutes of the Provisional Government, Vol.1, G1/1, SPOD.
101. Cabinet Notes, Convention, 15 March 1922, Mul.P, P7/B/192.
102. Sheila Lawlor, *Britain and Ireland, 1914–1923*, p.166.
103. Offer made by minister for defence at a meeting of the 1st Southern Division on 20 March 1922, Mul.P, P7/B/191.
104. Memo to chief of staff from minister for defence, 23 March 1922, Mul.P, P7/A/49.
105. Ibid.
106. *Dáil Debates*, 28 April 1922, no volumn, p.351.
107. Intelligence report, 26 March 1922, Mul.P, P7/B/191.
108. Dorothy Macardle, *The Irish Republic*, p.616.
109. Ronan Fanning, *Independent Ireland* (1983), p.12; Curran, *The Birth of the Irish Free State*, p.181.

CHAPTER SIX

1. *Dáil Debates*, 26 April 1922, no volume, pp.249–250.
2. Ibid, p.250.
3. Memo to Arthur Griffith from the minister for defence, 24 March 1922, Mul.P, P7/B/152.
4. Joseph Curran, *The Birth of the Irish Free State*, p.178.
5. Ibid., pp.178–179; Liam Deasy, *Brother against Brother*, p.42.
6. *Dáil Debates*, 28 April 1922, no volume, p.335.
7. Joseph Curran, *The Birth of the Irish Free State*, p.179.
8. Sheila Lawlor, *Britain and Ireland*, p.185.
9. *Dáil Debates*, 28 April 1922, no volume, p.335.
10. O' Murthuile Manuscript, pp.190–193, Mul.P, P7a/208.
11. Memo entitled Suggestions by Sean Moylan in conversation on Friday, 21 April 1922, Mul.P, P7/B/152.
12. Letter to Dan Breen from Paddy Daly, 27 April 1922, Mul.P, P7/B/192.
13. Chronology, Mul.P, P7/B/192.
14. The ten officers were: Dan Breen, Tom Hales, Humphrey Murphy, Sean O'Hegarty and F. O'Donoghue for the anti-Treaty side; Sean Boylan, Mulcahy, O'Duffy, O'Sullivan, and Collins for the Treaty side.
15. The Army Truce—How it came about, n.d., Mul.P, P7/B/192.
16. *Dáil Debates*, 3 May 1922, no volume, p.357.
17. Ibid., 3 May 1922, p.359.
18. Ibid., 3 May 1922, p.367.
19. The Army Truce, Mul.P, P7/B/192. Certainly not everyone responded positively to O'Hegarty's speech or even to the Truce. When O'Hegarty finished his presentation to the Dail, for example, Liam Mellows characterized it as a "political dodge." Mellowes pointed out quite simply

that as long as the Treaty remained, there could be no unity. That was *sine qua non* of the radical Republican position. *Dáil Debates*, 3 May 1922, col.360.

20. Memo to each member of the Defence Council, not signed, [seems to be from the minister for defence], 21 April 1922, Mul.P, P7/B/192.

21. Untitled memo [seems to be Intelligence Report on Republican views or report of conversation], 28 April 1922, Mul.P, P7/B/191.

22. Dáil Committee Report, 10 May 1922; Report of the Republican Delegation, Mul.P, P7/A/63.

23. *Dáil Debates*, 19 May 1922, no volume, p.473.

24. For a full and interesting discussion of the reactions to and implications of the Collins-de Valera Pact, see Joseph Curran, *The Birth of the Irish Free State*, pp.188-190.

25. Letter to Joseph McGarrity from Eamon de Valera, 10 September 1922, McGarrity Papers, Ms 17,440, NLI.

26. Memorandum on Proposals Made Toward Army Unification, n.d. (pre-Collins-de Valera Pact), Mul.P, P7/B/192.

27. Memorandum on Proposals for Agreement from Liam Lynch, 8 May 1922, Mul.P, P7/B/193.

28. Memo to General O'Duffy from Liam Lynch, 12 May 1922, Mul.P, P7/B/193.

29. Note on the bottom of memo to General O'Duffy from Liam Lynch, 12 May 1922, Mul.P, P7/B/193.

30. Diary, 14 May 1922, Mul.P, P7/B/193.

31. For a list of the truce violations, see Mul.P, P7/B/192.

32. Memo to minister for defence from Sean O'Hegarty, n.d. (most likely, mid-May), Mul.P, P7/B/192.

33. Memo to O/C, Cork No.1 Brigade, from minister for defence, 12 May 1922, Mul.P, P7/B/193.

34. Ibid.

35. Unsigned and undated copy of a letter from Cork officers, Mul.P, P7/B/193.

36. Memo to chief of staff [O'Duffy] from Capt. Dennehy, 1st Battalion, 1st Cork Brigade, 3 June 1922, Mul.P, P7/B/26.

37. Memo to minister for defence from the chief of staff, 27 May 1922, Mul.P, P7/B/193.

38. Memo to chief of staff from Liam Lynch, 13 January 1922, Mul.P, P7/B/191.

39. Sheila Lawlor, *Britain and Ireland*, pp.164-165.

40. Memo to Michael Collins from minister for defence, 26 May 1922, Mul.P, P7/B/193. According to Mulcahy's memo, the Four Courts executive agreed to cease commandeering cars or private property. They also agreed to restore cars and property which they had taken over. Moreover, according to this same memo all buildings—save those occupied by refugees from Belfast— were to be evacuated. However, for some reason, the Four Courts building was exempt from this.

41. Memo to minister for defence from chief of staff, 22 May 1922, Mul.P, P7/B/192.

42. Memorandum, n.d. (most likely early June, 1922), Mul.P, P7/B/192.

43. Minutes of the Provisional Government, 5 June 1922, P.G.28, Vol.2, G1/2, SPOD; Mul.P, P7/B/243.

44. Memo to Commandant Sean O'Hegarty from minister for defence, 6adh Meithimh [June] 1922, Mul.P, P7/B/192.

45. Ibid.

46. Memo to minister for defence from Liam Lynch, 7 June 1922, Mul.P, P7/B/192. Lynch's distribution of office differs from Mulcahy's in that the government has the director of publicity and there is an agreed adjutant general. This was one of O'Duffy's suggestions. However, another document has the government with both the adjutant general and the quartermaster general. The confusion on this point is heightened because a number of documents of this period are not dated or signed. Lynch's references

to specific memos and proposals are evidence that they refer to this period, but the actual distribution of offices remains unclear. See Mul.P, P7/B/192.

47. Minutes of the Provisional Government, 7 June 1922, P.G.30, Vol.1, G1/2, SPOD; Mul.P, P7/B/243.

48. Guarantee Given by Liam Lynch, 8 June 1922, Mul.P, P7/B/192.

49. Memo to minister for defence from Ernie O'Malley, Secretary to the Executive, 10 June 1922, Mul.P, P7/B/192.

50. Army Position, June 1922, Mul.P, P7/D/3.

51. Memo to Secretary, Four Courts executive, from the minister for defence, 12 June 1922, Mul.P, P7/B/192.

52. Minutes of the Provisional Government, 12 June 1922, P.G.33, Vol.II, G1/2, SPOD.

53. Memorandum handed to minister for defence on Thursday, 15 June, by Messrs. Rory O'Connor and E. O'Malley, representing the Forces at the Four Courts, Mul.P, P7/B/192.

54. Quoted in F. O'Donoghue, *No Other Law*, p.203.

55. The results of the election were pro-Treaty candidates, 58 seats; anti-Treaty candidates, 35 seats; Labour, 17; Farmers,7; Independents,7; and Dublin University, 4.

56. In a craftily constructed letter to Collins, Lloyd George claimed that the British had evidence that clearly connected the men who had been arrested for Wilson's murder to the Irish Republican Army. He then went on to blame the Four Courts Executive (Letter to Michael Collins from Lloyd George, 22 June 1922, Mul.P, P7/B/244). The implication was that the evidence connected them to the Four Courts. This was not true. Tim Pat Coogan suggests that the evidence might have implicated Collins himself. On this issue and the question of Collins' responsibility for ordering Wilson's death, see T. P. Coogan, *Michael Collins*, pp. 372–375; Michael

Hopkinson, *Green Against Green*, pp.112–114; Joseph Curran, *The Birth of the Irish Free State*, pp.224–225.

57. Ernie O'Malley, *The Singing Flame*, pp.88–89.

58. Minutes of the Provisional Government, 27 June 1922, P.G. 37, G1/2. Vol II, SPOD.

59. Joseph Curran, *The Birth of the Irish Free State*, p.229.

60. Minutes of the Provisional Government, 27 June 1922, P.G. 37, G1/2, Vol. II, SPOD.

61. Ernie O'Malley, *The Singing Flame*, p.95.

62. Republican Proclamation, 28 June 1922, Mul.P, P7a/76.

63. Official Statement, 28 June 1922, Mul.P, P7/B/244.

64. Government Address, 15 July 1922, Mul.P, P7/B/29.

65. Unidentified and undated memo in Mul.P, P7/B/28. This memo seems to be part of a collection of documents from Collins. It is also quoted in Beaslai's book, *Michael Collins and the Making of a New Ireland*, Vol. II, pp.411–412. In a letter to a friend, Collins states that he wrote the memo in early July, 1922. The reference in the letter to the surrender of O'Connor and Mellowes substantiates this date.

66. Conversation among Dr Mulcahy, General Mulcahy and Mrs Mulcahy, 23 December 1961, Mul.P, P7/D/100.

67. Ibid.

68. Note on [conversation with] Liam Deasy, 18 October 1962, Mul.P, P7/D/45. This is basically the same interpretation that Deasy gives in *Brother Against Brother*, pp.46–47.

69. *Brother Against Brother*, pp.46–47.

70. Minutes of the Provisional Government, 30 June 1922, P.G. 44, G1/2, Vol. II, SPOD.

71. Joseph Curran, *The Birth of the Irish Free State*, pp.236–237.

72. Undated, unsigned memo, Mul.P, P7/B/28; P. Beaslai, *Michael Collins and the Making of a New Ireland*, vol. II, pp.411–412. There were also

numerous moves to re-establish peace talks during the fighting in Dublin. See *The Birth of the Irish Free State*, pp.235–236.

73. Notes of Frank Aiken, Ernie O'Malley Papers, P17a/93, UCDA.
74. Memo to minister for defence from Frank Aiken, 16 July 1922, Mul.P, P7/B/192.
75. Ibid.
76. Minutes of the Provisional Government, 28 June 1922, Mul.P, P7/B/244.
77. Memo, 5 July 1922, Adjutant General memo file, Military Archives, Dublin.
78. Minutes of the Provisional Government, 6, 7 and 8 July, Mul.P, P7/B/244.
79. Report on Situation in Cork, 19 July 1922, Mul.P, P7/B/40.
80. Captured Irregular Correspondence, Memo to O/C, 1st Southern Division, from Liam Lynch, chief of staff, 22 August 1922, A/0992/7, Military Archives, Dublin.
81. Memo to acting chairman from commander-in-chief, 25 July 1922, Mul.P, P7/B/29.
82. Conversation among Dr Mulcahy, General Mulcahy and Mrs Mulcahy, 23 December 1961, Mul.P, P7/D/100.
83. Minutes of the Provisional Government, 12 July 1922, P.G.58, G1/2, Vol. II, SPOD; Mul.P, P7/B/244.
84. Quoted in Calton Younger, *Ireland's Civil War*, p.343.
85. Minutes of the Provisional Government, 21 July 1922, P.G. 72, G1/2, Vol. II, SPOD.
86. Memo to Lt. Gen. O'Connell from commander-in-chief, 16 July 1922, Collins Papers, Ms 22,127 (i), NLI.
87. Memo to chief of staff from Michael Collins, 15 July 1922, General Orders, Military Archives, Dublin.
88. General Order No.13, 8 August 1922, Military Archives, Dublin.
89. Conversation among Dr Mulcahy, General Mulcahy and Mrs Mulcahy, 23 December 1961, Mul.P, P7/D/100.
90. For more detail on these complaints, see Mul.P, P7/B/45 and P7/B/43. The men from the North of Ireland who were sent down to the Curragh camp for training were particularly in need of clothing. In a memo to the quartermaster general, the chief of staff authorized payment for some non-uniformed clothing. This was necessary because "many of them will, of necessity, be very badly off from the point of view of suits, underclothing, [boots], etc." Mul.P, P7/B/78.
91. See Chapter 8 for a discussion of this issue in the army mutiny of 1924.
92. Quartermaster General's Department, Regulation No. 42, 15 August 1922, Mul.P, P7/B/152.
93. Memo to chief of the general staff from O'Duffy, G.O.C., South Western Command, Mul.P., P7/B/40.
94. Memo, 21 August 1922, Adjutant General memo file, Military Archives, Dublin.
95. Captured Irregular Correspondence, Memo to the assistant quartermaster, 1st Southern Division, from the divisional adjutant, 31 January 1923, A/09921/1, Military Archives, Dublin.
96. Diary, Notes on Visits to Military Headquarters throughout the Country, Mul.P, P7c/27.
97. Captured Irregular Correspondence, Memo to chief of staff from acting assistant chief of staff, 25 July 1922, Ginger O'Connell Collection in the Ernie O'Malley Papers, P17b/134, UCDA.
98. Memo, General Situation, from commander-in-chief, 26 July 1922, Mul.P, P7/B/28.
99. Ibid.
100. Calton Younger, *Ireland's Civil War*, p.394.
101. Memo to Michael Collins from W.T. Cosgrave, 27 July 1922, Mul.P, P7/B/29.
102. Memo to Government from commander-in-chief, 29 July 1922, Mul.P, P7/B/29.
103. Quoted in Calton Younger, *Ireland's Civil War*, p.347.
104. Memo on the General Position on the Army, to the acting chairman of

the Provisional Government from the commander-in-chief, 5 August 1922, Mul.P, P7/B/29. While the report was issued in Collins' name alone, correspondence between Collins and Mulcahy indicates joint authorship.

105. Report on the Situation in Cork, 19 July 1922, Mul.P, P7/B/40.

106. Joseph Curran, *The Birth of the Irish Free State*, pp.243-244.

107. Report on Situation in Cork, 19 July 1922, Mul.P, P7/B/40.

108. Captured Irregular Correspondence, Memo to Ernie O'Malley from Sean Moylan, 10 July 1922, Mul.P, P7a/80.

109. Captured Irregular Correspondence, Memo to O/C, 1st Southern Division from chief of staff, 24 August 1922, A/0992/7, Military Archives, Dublin.

110. Memorandum, 7 August 1922, Mul.P, P7/B/43.

111. Memo to chief of staff from Michael Collins, General, commander-in-chief, 4 August 1922, Mul.P, P7/ B/43.

112. Quoted in a memo to chief of the general staff from Michael Collins, General, commander-in-chief, 26 July 1922, Mul.P, P7/B/43.

113. Ibid.

114. Memo to commander-in-chief from the chief of staff, 28 July 1922, Mul.P, P7/B/43.

115. Ibid.

116. Quoted in Calton Younger, *Ireland's Civil War*, p.439.

117. Statement issued by General Mulcahy, Collins Papers, Ms 22,604, NLI.

118. Captured Irregular Correspondence, Memo to the O/C, 1st Southern Division, from chief of staff, Liam Lynch, 28 August 1922, A/0992/1, Military Archives, Dublin.

119. Calton Younger, *Ireland's Civil War*, p.444.

120. General Mulcahy's Oration at the Graveside, Mul.P, P7/D/72.

CHAPTER SEVEN

1. For a discussion of Cosgrave's election, see Brian Farrell, *Chairman or Chief*, (1971), p.18.

2. Conversation among Dr Mulcahy, General Mulcahy and Mrs Mulcahy, 23 December 1961, Mul.P, P7/D/100.

3. Notes on Conversation on the 19th August 1963 with Lieut. General Peadar McMahon, Mul.P, P7/D/3.

4. Minutes of the Provisional Government, 23 August 1922, P.6.98. 61/3, Vol.III, SPOD.

5. It is interesting to note that just prior to Collins' death, the Cabinet decided that commissions to officers in the national army were to be issued over the signatures of both the commander-in-chief and the minister for defence (Minutes of the Provisional Government, 31 July 1922, P.6.79, b1/3, Vol.III, SPOD) and that, pending the approval of the commander-in-chief, that when such commission were so issued, they would be "deemed to be issued with our authority and on our behalf." Minutes of the Provisional Government, 2 August 1922, P.6.79, b1/3, Vol.III, SPOD.

6. This information is based on a letter in the Mulcahy papers which is unaddressed and unsigned, but is noted as received 25 July 1922. If the date is accurate, it would mean that the government, or at least Collins and Mulcahy, were considering another election strictly on the Treaty. The clause which speaks of the cessation of hostilities would seem to indicate that it had to be after the Four Courts attack and the preface states very clearly that the government wanted to give the Republican leaders a chance "to realise the position created by Military operation during the past month". This would certainly seem to place it toward the end of July. Mul.P, P7/B/192.

7. Ginger O'Connell Collection in the Ernie O'Malley Papers, P17b/134, UCDA.

8. Minutes of the Provisional Government, 5 September 1922, P.G.108, G1/3, Vol.III, SPOD; Mul.P, P7/B/245.

9. Comments on Calton Younger's *Ireland's Civil War*, Mul.P, P7/D/93.
10. Ibid.
11. Letter to Joe McGarrity from de Valera, 10 September 1922, McGarrity Papers, Ms 17,440, NLI.
12. National Anthem, Mul.P, P7/D/13l.
13. Minutes of the Provisional Government, 15 September l922, P.G.6(a), Gl/3, Vol.III, SPOD.
14. *Dáil Debates*, 27 September 1922, Vol.1, cols.802–804.
15. Ibid, 25 September 1922, Vol.1, cols.807–809.
16. Ibid, 27 September 1922, Vol.1, cols.807–808.
17. Ibid., cols.807–809.
18. Ibid., cols.849–850.
19. Ibid., col.849.
20. Ibid., cols.848–850.
21. Ibid., col.830.
22. Minutes of the Meetings of the Provisional Government, P.G. 28(a), G1/3, Vol.III, SPOD.
23. *Dáil Debates*, 17 November 1922, Vol.1, cols.2263–2264.
24. Ibid., col.2265.
25. Ibid., cols.2267–2268.
26. Ibid., cols.2273–2275.
27. Ibid., cols.2273–2275.
28. *Irish Times,* 8 December 1922.
29. Mul.P, P7/B/85.
30. *Dáil Debates*, 8 December 1922, Vol.2, col.55.
31. Ibid., col.49.
32. Ibid., cols.51–52.
33. Ibid., cols.53–54.
34. *Irish Independent*, 9 December 1922.
35. Quoted in Dermot Keogh, *The Vatican, the Bishops and Irish Politics 1919–1939* (Cambridge 1986), p.98.
36. Ibid.
37. *Irish Times*, 3 November 1922.
38. *Irish Independent*, 11 December 1922.
39. *Freeman's Journal*, 21 December 1922.
40. The total of 77 executions is the commonly used figure. However, a list of executions in the Military Archives puts the total at 79. Since there is no indication who compiled the list or when it was compiled, I have chosen to stick with the generally accepted figure of 77. For the list of executions, see file A/0770, Military Archives, Dublin. For a report on the execution of the five Free State soldiers, see the *Irish Independent*, 9 January 1923.
41. The phrase is Liam Lynch's. Letter to Joe McGarrity from Liam Lynch, 21 December 1922, McGarrity Papers, Ms17,455, NLI.
42. In the 1923 election, standing in Dublin City, North, Mulcahy received 22,205 votes as compared to 10,518 votes and 4,233 for the other two candidates—one of whom was his brother-in-law, Sean T. O'Kelly. Mulcahy received 40% of the total valid poll. Compare this to Mulcahy's showing in the two elections of 1927 (June and September) wherein he received only 18.4% and 22.3% of the total valid poll respectively. This point is also made in Conversation among Dr Mulcahy, General Mulcahy and Mrs Mulcahy, 23 December 1961, Mul.P, P7/D/100.
43. Killing in both the Tan War and the Civil War, Mul.P, P7/D/32.
44. The National Anthem, Mul.P, P7/D/131. For a more complete record of the documents issued by de Valera and Lynch, see Mulcahy's speech of 20 October 1932, *Dáil Debates*, Vol.44, cols. 222–243. This speech is incorrectly cited in Mul.P, P7/D/131 as being given on 30 October 1932.
45. Intelligence Report, 16 October 1922, Mul.P, P7/B/245.
46. Ibid.
47. Ibid.
48. Headings on the Army Position, n.d. [November, 1922?], Mul.P, P7/B/71.
49. Draft Orders suggested by the commander-in-chief, 25 October 1922, Staff and Army Council Memoranda File, Military Archives, Dublin.
50. Staff Memo No.12, 8 September 1922, Staff and Army Council Memoranda File, Military Archives, Dublin.
51. *Irish Independent*, 1 December 1922.

52. Ibid., 18 December 1922.
53. Headings on the Army Position, n.d. [November 1922?], Mul.P, P7/B/71.
54. Talk with Dave Neligan, 13 March 1967, Mul.P, P7/D/51.
55. *Irish Independent*, 20 December 1922.
56. Operations Report, Kerry Command, 6 March 1923, K/29, Military Archives, Dublin.
57. Operations Report, Kerry Command, 7 March 1923, K/29, Military Archives, Dublin.
58. Irregular Report, H. Murphy, O/C Kerry No.1 Brigade to Liam Lynch, chief of staff, n.d., O'Donovan Papers, Ms 22 956, NLI.
59. Dorothy Macardle, *Tragedies of Kerry* (1946?), pp.14–17.
60. Operations Report, Kerry Command, 9 March 1923, K/32, Military Archives, Dublin.
61. Operations Report, Kerry Command, 13 March 1923, K/30, Military Archives, Dublin.
62. Dorothy Macardle, *Tragedies of Kerry*, pp.14–17.
63. Ibid., Eoin Neeson, *The Civil War in Ireland*, Cork: (1966), p.293.
64. Dorothy Macardle, *The Irish Republic*, (1968), pp.765–766.
65. Memo from Irregular chief of staff to adjutant general, 12 March 1923, O'Donovan Papers, Ms 22,956, NLI.
66. Letter to chief of staff from GOC Kerry Command, 11 April 1923, O'Donovan Papers, Ms 22,956, NLI, *Dáil Debates*, 17 April 1923, Vol.3, cols.188–190.
67. *Dáil Debates*, 17 April 1923, Vol.3, cols. 188, 190.
68. Michael Hopkinson, *Green Against Green* (1988), p.241.
69. Ibid.
70. *Dáil Debates*, 17 April 1923, Vol.3, col.188.
71. Ibid.
72. Liam Deasy, *Brother Against Brother*, pp.111–113.
73. Letter to Seamus O'Donovan from Liam Deasy, 30 January 1923, O'Donovan Papers, Ms. 22,306, NLI.
74. *Brother Against Brother*, p.113.
75. Quoted from Mulcahy's speech to the Dáil, *Dáil Debates*, 9 February 1923, Vol.2, cols. 1469–1470.
76. Deasy agreed to the following statement: "I have undertaken for the future of Ireland to accept and aid in an immediate and unconditional surrender of all arms and men as required by General Mulcahy." He also agreed to another condition: "In pursuance of this undertaking I . . . appeal for a similar undertaking and acceptance from the following:

E. de Valera   F. Aiken
P. Ruttledge   F. Barrett
A. Stack   T. Barry
N. Colivet   S. McSweeney
D. O'Callaghan   Seamus Robinson
Liam Lynch   Humphrey Murphy
Conn Moloney Seamus O'Donovan
T. Derrig   Frank Carty

and for the immediate and unconditional surrender of themselves after issue by them of an order for this surrender on the part of all those associated with them, together with their arms and equipment." *Brother Against Brother*, pp.115–116; O'Donovan Papers, Ms 22,306, NLI.
77. Letter to Seamus O'Donovan from Liam Deasy, 30 January 1923, O'Donovan Papers, Ms 22,306, NLI.
78. Ibid.
79. Letter to Liam Deasy from Liam Lynch, 5 February 1923, O'Donovan Papers, Ms 22,306, NLI.
80. *Irish Independent*, 9 February 1923.
81. *Dáil Debates*, 9 February 1923, Vol.2, cols.1473–1474.
82. Letter to O/C Commands, Divisions and Independent Brigades from Liam Lynch, chief of staff, 2 February 1923, McGarrity Papers, Ms 17,455, NLI.
83. Letter to Joe McGarrity from Liam Lynch, 5 February 1923, McGarrity Papers, Ms 17,455, NLI.
84. Memorandum, Hugh Kennedy, 2 April 1923, Kennedy Papers, P4/II/43, UCDA.
85. Defence Council Meeting, 3 May 1923, Mul.P, P7/C/322.

86. O'Higgins, AICT, Mul.P, P7/C/23.
87. Cabinet Minutes, C1/74, SPOD.
88. Mul.P, P7/B/178.
89. Mulcahy, AICT, Mul.P, P7/C/35.
90. Mul.P, P7/B/178.
91. Cabinet Minutes, C1/81, Vol.II, SPOD.
92. Hugh Kennedy, Memorandum, 2 April 1923, Kennedy Papers, P4/II/43, UCDA.
93. The *Morning Post* article was actually read aloud in the Dáil. *Dáil Debates*, 12 April 1923, Vol.3, cols.59–60.
94. O'Higgins, AICT, Mul.P, P7/C/37.
95. Mulcahy, Testimony before the Army Inquiry Committee, Mul.P, P7/C/37.
96. Charlotte H. Fallon, *Soul of Fire* (1986), p.97.
97. Quoted in Charlotte Fallon, *Soul of Fire*, p.99.
98. Joseph Curran, *The Birth of the Irish Free State*, p.271.
99. Quoted in Joseph Curran, *The Birth of the Irish Free State*, p.271.
100. The Military Archives in Dublin has an impressive collection of maps which demonstrate how the Free State army was closing in on Lynch and his men.
101. Cabinet minutes, C1/102, 8 May 1923, G2/2, Vol.II, SPOD.
102. Dorothy Macardle, *The Irish Republic*, p.781.
103. Longford and O'Neill, *Eamon de Valera* (1971), p.222.

CHAPTER EIGHT

1. Portions of this chapter are reprinted from the author's earlier book, *Almost A Rebellion: The Irish Army Mutiny of 1924* (1985), *passim*.
2. Intelligence Report, 17 May 1923, Military Archives, Dublin; General Staff Special Memo No.4, 22 March 1923, Military Archives, Dublin.
3. General Staff Instruction No.6, 30 May 1923, Military Archives, Dublin.
4. General Weekly Summary for Week Ending 30 June 1923, Military Archives, Dublin.
5. Intelligence Report, 14 June 1923, Military Archives, Dublin.
6. Intelligence Report, 2 June 1923, General Staff Weekly Survey–Army Reports, Military Archives, Dublin.
7. Intelligence Report, 14 June 1923, S/1235, Military Archives, Dublin.
8. Memo of adjutant general, Memo No.5, 6 October 1923, Military Archives, Dublin.
9. Intelligence Reports, 7 May 1923, S/1235, Military Archives, Dublin.
10. Intelligence Report, 14 June 1923, S/1235, Military Archives, Dublin.
11. Letter to Dan McCarthy, unsigned but appears to be from Richard Mulcahy, 12 October 1922, Mul.P, P7/B/325.
12. For a discussion of the origins of the Cumann na nGaedheal party, see the author's "After the Revolution: The Formative Years of Cumann na nGaedheal," in *The Uses of the Past* edited by Eyler and Garratt (1988).
13. General Weekly Summary for Week Ending 23 June 1923, Military Archives, Dublin.
14. General Staff Instructions No.11, 19 June 1923, Military Archives, Dublin.
15. Operations Memo No.12, Department of the chief of the general staff, 10 August 1923, Military Archives, Dublin.
16. Costello, AICT, Mul.P, P7/C/25.
17. While this organization came to be known as the Irish Republican Army Organization or IRAO, most of the documents for this period refer to it as the Old IRA. Following the documents of the period, I have chosen to use the term Old IRA.
18. Tobin Mutiny File, Mul.P, P7B/195.
19. Conversation between General Mulcahy and General Sean MacEoin; tape in possession of the author.
20. For example, Dalton and Tobin were not satisfied with their positions as Adjutant of the Air Services and ADC to the Governor General respectively. Similarly, although Thornton was to be appointed a brigade major, he wanted to be named director of intelligence.

21. Interview with Col. Dan Bryan, Dublin, 18 March 1975.
22. Tobin Mutiny File, Mul.P, P7/B/195.
23. Ibid.
24. Ibid.
25. Ibid.
26. Ibid.
27. Ibid.
28. See the comments of Chairman Meredith discussed below regarding this matter.
29. Tobin Mutiny File, Mul.P, P7/B/195.
30. Ibid.
31. Ibid.
32. Mulcahy, AICT, Mul.P, P7/C/36.
33. Ibid; Tobin Mutiny File, Mul.P, P7/B/195.
34. Chief of staff, General Weekly Report No.5 for Week Ending 23 June 1923, Military Archives, Dublin; chief of staff, Supplement to General Survey for Week Ending 14 July 1923, Military Archives, Dublin.
35. According to Defence Order No.28, three classes of officers were to be demobilized: 1) Officers whose work was unsatisfactory; 2) Post-Truce officers who had no special qualifications; 3) Pre-Truce officers who were surplus to requirements. A demobilization grant of five pounds was offered to each man, in addition to the continuation of his full salary for two months and half pay for the following two months. A special grant was given to pre-Truce officers based on the nature and extent of their service from 1919 to 1921 in the Anglo-Irish war, the degree to which their lifestyle had been interrupted, and the service rendered in the National Army during the Civil War. To help the demobilized men ease back into civilian life, a resettlement bureau was established under the auspices of the Ministry for Industry and Commerce. *Dáil Debates*, V (1923) cols. 717–718.
36. Tobin Mutiny File, Mul.P, P7/B/195.
37. Mulcahy, AICT, Mul.P, P7/C/36.
38. Costello, AICT, Mul.P, P7/C/25.
39. O'Connor, AICT, Mul.P, P7/C/1.
40. Subsequently, all but 14 officers applied for and were granted demobilization papers. After the army crisis, papers were sent to the remaining officers and all but one accepted them.
41. Cabinet Minutes, CAB 2/22, SPOD.
42. Mulcahy, AICT, Mul.P, P7/C/37.
43. Mulcahy, AICT, Mul.P, P7/C/10.
44. Mulcahy, AICT, Mul.P, P7/C/37.
45. Irish Republican Army Organisation pamphlet, *The Truth About the Army Crisis* (Dublin, n.d.), p.7.
46. Costello, AICT, Mul.P, P7/C/25.
47. Professor Hogan, AICT, Mul.P, P7/C/6.
48. Intelligence Department, General Monthly Report of November, 1923, Military Archives, Dublin.
49. Tobin Mutiny File, Mul.P, P7/B/195.
50. Ibid.
51. Ibid.
52. General Routine Orders, Order No. 24, 3 March 1924, Military Archives, Dublin.
53. *The Truth About the Army Crisis*, p.12.
54. Before the crisis was over, 49 officers resigned from the army, including 3 major-generals, 5 colonels, 17 commandants, 12 captains and 12 lieutenants (MacMahon, AICT, Mul.P, P7/C/35). Furthermore, 50 officers absconded with war materials, which included Lewis guns, rifles, grenades and revolvers. Correspondence between GOC Dublin Command and the office of the chief of staff, 2 April and 9 April 1924, Ms/358/3, Military Archives, Dublin.
55. MacMahon, AICT, Mul.P, P7/C/14.
56. Ibid.
57. *Irish Independent*, 10 May 1924.
58. Cabinet Minutes, CAB2/60, SPOD.
59. *Dáil Debates*, VI (1924), col.1896. Dáil Debates, 11 March 1924, Vol. 6, col. 1896.
60. Ibid.
61. Ibid., col. 1897.
62. O'Higgins, AICT, Mul.P, P7/C/23.
63. P. Hogan, AICT, Mul.P, P7/C/24.
64. *Irish Independent*, 19 May 1924.
65. Cabinet Minutes, CAB 2/62, SPOD. For all practical purposes, the execu-

tive council had abolished the position of commander-in-chief. Hence O'Duffy's title of general officer commanding the defence forces of Saorstát Éireann and later also inspector general of the defence forces.

66. *Dáil Debates*, 19 March 1924, Vol.6, col.2218. O'Duffy, of course, was formerly a senior officer in the army. He had been chief of staff during the hiatus between the ratification of the Treaty and the outbreak of civil war. During the civil war, he was general in command South Western Division. Mulcahy's characterization of him as an outsider was a bit strong. See Chapter 6, *passim*.

67. J. Bowyer Bell, *The Secret Army* (1980), p.67. Bell also says that O'Duffy resigned as treasurer of the IRA on his appointment, but cites no sources for this information.

68. *Dáil Debates*, 26 March 1924, Vol.6, col.2367.

69. *The Truth About the Army Crisis*, p.14.

70. Ibid.

71. *Dáil Debates*, 12 March 1924, Vol.6, cols. 1996–2001.

72. *The Truth About the Army Crisis*, p.14.

73. *Irish Times*, 13 March 1924.

74. Tobin Mutiny File, Mul.P, P7/B/196.

75. Intelligence Report, May, 1924, S/21.501, Military Archives, Dublin.

76. Confidential Letter to O'Duffy, April, 1924, Ms/388/8, Military Archives, Dublin.

77. Intelligence Report, 22 March 1924, Military Archives, Dublin.

78. Current historiography claims that members of the Old IRA approached the quartermaster general of the Republican army about the possibility of staging a joint coup (O'Neill and O'Fiannachta, *De Valera* (1970), vol.2, p.155). I have seen no evidence of this in the army intelligence files, but these files do contain an order by Frank Aiken stating that "no demobilized or resigned officer is to be taken into the ranks of the IRA unless there is good reason to show that such are acting on principle and not from any motive of self-interest." Intelligence Reports, April, 1924, Ms 388/5, Military Archive, Dublin.

79. Intelligence Report, 7 February 1924, Military Archives, Dublin.

80. Tobin Mutiny File, Mul.P, P7/B/195.

81. Interview with Col. Dan Bryan, 18 March 1975, Dublin.

82. Leon O'Broin, *Revolutionary Underground* (1976), p.212.

83. *The Truth About the Army Crisis*, p.15.

84. Intelligence Report, 22 March 1924, Military Archives, Dublin.

85. Intelligence Report, 1 April 1924, Military Archives, Dublin.

86. Cabinet minutes, CAB 2/68, SPOD.

87. O'Murthuile manuscript, Mul.P, P7a/209.

88. Tobin Mutiny File, Mul.P, P7/B/196.

89. *Freeman's Journal,* 20 March 1924.

90. Interview with General Patrick Mulcahy, 12 July 1981, Dublin.

91. Telephone interview with Lt. Gen. M.J. Costello, 8 September 1975, Dublin.

92. O'Murthuile manuscript, Mul.P, P7a/209.

93. Intelligence Report, 1 April 1924, Military Archives, Dublin.

94. Throughout the army crisis, the Government acted as if the mutiny were an internal affair and did not inform the Labour party as to what was going on. The Labour leader, Mr Johnson, told the *Irish Independent* (10 March 1924): "I don't know any more about the business that I have read in the newspapers."

95. *Dáil Debates*, 19 March 1924, Vol.6, cols.2215–2219.

96. Ibid., col.2217.

97. Ibid., col.2230.

98. Ibid., col.2232.

99. Ibid., col.2226.

100. Ibid., cols. 2225–2226.

101. *Irish Times*, 20 March 1924. This view was also expressed by other newspapers, like the *Manchester Guardian*.

102. *The Truth About the Army Crisis*, p.15.
103. *Dáil Debates*, 26 March 1924, Vol.6, col.2363.

CHAPTER NINE

1. Portions of this chapter are reprinted from the author's earlier book, *Almost a Rebellion: The Irish Army Mutiny of 1924* (1985), *passim.*
2. *Dáil Debates*, 27 March 1924, Vol.6, cols. 2502–2503.
3. In addition to Meredith and McGilligan, the members of the Committee were Gerald Fitzgibbon, a former Dáil deputy and an ally of McGrath, who could look after the interest of the mutineers; D.J. Gorey, TD, Farmer's Party; and Major Bryan Cooper, TD, Independents. The Labour Party refused to nominate anyone because its leadership felt that the inquiry should be a committee of the Dáil, responsible solely to it, with all the power and stature such status would confer.
4. Tobin Mutiny File, Mul.P, P7/B/196.
5. Ibid.
6. *Dáil Debates*, 3 April 1924, Vol.6, col.2825.
7. Ibid., col.2669.
8. Army Mutiny File, S3678B, SPOD.
9. Cabinet Minutes, CAB2/106 and CAB2/108, SPOD.
10. Chairman's Draft Report, Mul.P, P7/C/41.
11. Professor Hogan, AICT, Mul.P, P7/C/25.
12. *Report of the Army Inquiry Committee* (1924), p.6.
13. O'Sullivan, AICT, Mul.P, P7/C/12.
14. MacMahon, AICT, Mul.P, P7/C/29.
15. Professor Hogan, AICT, Mul.P, P7/C/25.
16. Mulcahy, AICT, Mul.P, P7/C/10.
17. *Report of the Army Inquiry Committee*, p.6.
18. Chairman's Draft Report, Mul.P, P7/C/41.
19. Ibid.
20. Ibid.

21. *Dáil Debates*, 12 March 1924, vol.6, col.2000.
22. Tobin Mutiny File, Mul.P, P7/B/195.
23. *The Truth About the Army Crisis*, p.5.
24. Chairman's Draft Report, Mul.P, P7/C/41.
25. *Report of the Army Inquiry Committee*, p.5.
26. According to Sean MacMahon, the former chief of staff, the number of ex-officers from other armies who had been retained in the Irish Free State army was 155, of whom 80 had pre-Truce service. Of the remaining 75 officers, 40 were technical officers with specialized skills which the army needed, such as medical or legal training. Furthermore, MacMahon estimated that, before reorganization, the army had been composed of approximately 25 per cent post-Truce and 75 percent pre-Truce officers. After reorganization, approximately 90 percent were pre-Truce officers and only 10 percent post-Truce. MacMahon, AICT, Mul.P, P7/C/35.
27. This point was made by various witnesses. See Costello, AICT, Mul.P, P7/C/25; Russell, AICT, Mul.P, P7/C/29; Professor Hogan, AICT, Mul.P, P7/C/29.
28. *Report of the Army Inquiry Committee*, p.6.
29. Ibid., p.8.
30. Chairman's Draft Report, Mul.P, P7/C/41.
31. Ibid.
32. Ruth Dudley Edwards, *Patrick Pearse: The Triumph of Failure* (1977), p.213. Edwards credits Willie Redmond with being the other conciliatory nominee.
33. O'Higgins, AICT, Mul.P, P7/C/23; P. Hogan, AICT, Mul.P, P7/C/24.
34. O'Higgins, AICT, Mul.P, P7/C/23.
35. Mulcahy, AICT, Mul.P, P7/C/10.
36. O'Murthuile, AICT, Mul.P, P7/C/32; Mulcahy, AICT, Mul.P, P7/C/36.
37. O'Sullivan, AICT, Mul.P, P7/C/12.
38. See, for example, Leon O'Broin, *Revolutionary Underground*; and John

O'Beirne-Ranelagh, "The IRB From the Treaty to 1924," *Irish Historical Studies* 20 (March, 1976): 26–39.

39. *Report of the Army Inquiry Committee*, p.6.
40. Leon O'Broin, *Revolutionary Underground*, p.214.
41. Mulcahy, AICT, Mul.P, P7/C/10.
42. O'Murthuile, AICT, Mul.P, P7/C/32.
43. *Report of the Army Inquiry Committee*, p.9.
44. P. Hogan, AICT, Mul.P, P7/C/24.
45. O'Sullivan, AICT, Mul.P, P7/C/12.
46. *Report of the Army Inquiry Committee*, p.7.
47. John O'Beirne-Ranelagh, "The IRB from the Treaty to 1924," p.38.
48. *Report of the Army Inquiry Committee*, p.7.
49. Mulcahy, AICT, Mul.P, P7/C/10; O'Murthuile, AICT, Mul.P, P7/C/32; MacMahon, AICT, Mul.P, P7/C/36.
50. O'Murthuile, AICT, Mul.P, P7/C/13.
51. Mulcahy, AICT, Mul.P, P7/C/10.
52. Mul.P, P7/D/67.
53. Mulcahy, AICT, Mul.P, P7/C/35.
54. *Report of the Army Inquiry Committee*, p.6.
55. Col. Henry, AICT, Mul.P, p7/C/25; Davitt, AICT, Mul.P, P7/C/24; O'Sullivan, AICT, Mul.P, P7/C/32.
56. Professor Hogan, AICT, Mul.P, P7/C/25.
57. O'Higgins, AICT, Mul.P, P7/C/21.
58. Ibid.
59. O'Higgins, AICT, Mul.P., P7/C/23, UCDA.
60. Ibid.
61. Ibid.
62. *Report of the Army Inquiry Committee*, p.9.
63. O'Higgins, AICT, Mul.P, P7/C/23.
64. *Report of the Army Inquiry Committee*, p.9. Despite the committee's findings, only General MacMahon was reissued his commission.
65. *Dáil Debates*, 10 April 1924, Vol.7, col.3110.
66. Ibid., col.3150.
67. Ronan Fanning, *Independent Ireland* (Dublin: Helicon Limited, 1983), p.52.
68. Letter to Mrs Powell from Kevin O'Higgins, 19 May 1924, Mul.P, P7/C/8.
69. Mul.P, P7/D/3.
70. Mul.P, P7/D/50.

EPILOGUE

1. Dave Neligan, "The Spy in the Castle," *Irish Independent*, 16 February 1967.
2. Letter to the Irregular chief of staff from the director of chemicals and munitions, 27 January 1923, Irregular Correspondence, O'Donovan Papers, Ms 22,306, NLI.
3. Dave Neligan, "The Spy in the Castle," *Irish Independent*, 16 February, 1967.
4. Col. J. Brennock, "Army School of Music," *An Cosantóir*, October 1973, p.335.
5. Ibid., p.338.
6. Mul.P, P7/D/2.
7. Interview with Chief Justice Tom O'Higgins, Dublin, 29 June 1984.
8. Interview with Dr Rafferty, Secretary to the Department of Education, Dublin, July 1981.
9. Speech on the Occasion of the Limerick Holy Year Exhibition, 1950, Mul.P, P7/C/49.
10. Fine Gael Parliamentary Party Minutes, 19 April 1944, P/39.
11. Ibid., 22 March 1945, P/39.
12. Ibid., 16 May 1946, P/39.
13. For a discussion of the dissension within the Cumann na nGaedheal party, see Maryann Gialanella Valiulis, "After the Revolution: The Formative Years of Cumann na nGaedheal," in *The Uses of the Past Essays on Irish Culture* edited by Eyler and Garratt (1988).
14. Mul.P, P7/C/97.
15. *Irish Times*, 13 February 1932.
16. "A.C.A. Note on Draft Constitution," Mul.P, P7/C/44.
17. "Notes from Defence Conference Meeting, 25 July 1940, Mul.P, P7a/212.
18. Memorandum concerning meeting with Mulcahy, de Valera, Dillon,

O'Kelly, 24 May 1940, Mul.P, P7a/210.

19. Memorandum regarding meeting with J.M.O'Sullivan, McGilligan, Dillon, Cosgrave, Mulcahy, Hayes, O'Higgins, 25 May 1940, Mul.P, P7a/210.

20. Minutes of the meeting of the Fine Gael Party, 21 July 1937, Cumann na nGaedheal Party Minute Books, P/39.

21. Conversation among General Mulcahy, Mrs Mulcahy and Dr Mulcahy, December, 1961, Mul.P, P7/D/160; Conversation between General Mulcahy and Dr Mulcahy, Mul.P, P7/D/105.

22. For a discussion of Mulcahy's attitude and the attitude of Cumann na nGaedheal and Fine Gael, see the author's article, "The Man They Could Never Forgive—The View of the Opposition: Eamon de Valera and the Civil War," in *De Valera and His Times*, ed. J.P. O'Carroll and John A. Murphy (Cork: Cork University Press, 1983), pp.92–100.

23. Mul.P, P7/C/119; Comments on P. Beaslai, *Michael Collins and the Making of a New Ireland*, vol.II, 114–115.

24. *Irish Times*, 17 December, 1971.

25. Ibid.

26. "Mr John A. Costello Remembers", *Irish Times*, September 1967, Mul.P, P7/D/116.

27. Dr T. Rafferty, A Personal Memory of General Mulcahy, Document in possession of the author.

28. General Staff Memo No.21 of 18 June 1923 states: "As the bandsmen will be very much under observation during engagements particular care will be taken towards ensuring that they are smart and soldierly in appearance and that their behaviour generally will reflect credit on the Army." Military Archives.

29. "Mr John A. Costello Remembers," *Irish Times*, September 1967, Mul.P, P7/D/116.

Bibliography

PRIMARY SOURCES

University College, Dublin, Archives
  Ernest Blythe Papers
  Cumann na nGaedheal Party Minute Books
  Eoin MacNeill Papers
  Patrick McGilligan Papers
  Ernie O'Malley Papers
  Hugh Kennedy Papers
  Richard Mulcahy Papers

Military Archives, Dublin
  Adjutant General File
  Captured Irregular Correspondence
  General Staff Instructions
  General Weekly Surveys
  Intelligence Reports
  Inspection Reports
  Operations Reports

National Library of Ireland
  Michael Collins Papers
  J.J. O'Connell Papers
  Sean McGarrity Papers
  James L. O'Donovan Papers
  Military Report, Ballyseedy Inquiry

State Paper Office, Dublin
  Minutes of the Provisional Government
  Minutes of the Executive Council
  Government Material

Official Publications
  Minutes of the Proceedings of the First Parliament of the Republic of Ireland
  Private Sessions of the Second Dáil
  Debate on the Treaty Between Great Britain and Ireland
  Dáil Debates, 1922–1924

Newspapers
  Freeman's Journal
  Irish Independent
  Irish Times

Interviews
  Fr Fergus Barrett, OFM, Dublin, 1981
  Liam Cosgrave, Dublin, 1984
  Sean MacBride, Dublin, Telephone Interview, 1984
  General Patrick Mulcahy, Dublin, 1981
  Dr Risteárd Mulcahy, Dublin, 1981; 1985
  Dr Leon O'Broin, Dublin, 1984
  Chief Justice Thomas O'Higgins, Dublin, 1984
  Mrs O'Higgins McCoy, Dublin, 1981
  Dr Terence Rafferty, Dublin, 1981
  Richard Ryan, Dublin, 1984
  I also spoke informally to Néillí Mulcahy Bacon, Elizabeth Mulcahy Burney,
  Padraig Mulcahy, and Sean Mulcahy.

SELECT SECONDARY SOURCES

Barry, Tom. *Guerrilla Days in Ireland.* Dublin: Irish Press, Ltd., 1949.
Beaslai, Piaras. *Michael Collins and the Making of a New Ireland.* 2 vols. New York:
  Harper and Brothers n.d..
Bell Bowyer, J. *The Secret Army.* Massachusetts: MIT Press Edition, 1980.
Breen, Dan. *My Fight for Irish Freedom.* Dublin: Talbot Press, 1944; revised edition,
  Anvil Books, 1975.
Brennan, Michael. *The War in Clare.* Dublin: Irish Academic Press, 1980.
Brennock, Col. J. "Army School of Music." *An Cosantóir* (October, 1973): 335-341.
Coogan, T.P. *Michael Collins.* London: Hutchinson, 1990.
Curran, Joseph. *The Birth of the Irish Free State 1921-1923.* Alabama: University of
  Alabama Press, 1981.
Davis, Richard. *Arthur Griffith.* Dundalk: Dundalgan Press, 1976.
Deasy, Liam. *Brother Against Brother.* Cork: Mercier Press, 1982.
Edwards Ruth Dudley, *Patrick Pearse: The Triumph of Failure.* London: Victor
  Gollancz, 1977.
Fallon, Charlotte. *Soul of Fire.* Cork: Mercier Press, 1986.
Fanning, Ronan. *Independent Ireland.* Dublin: Helicon, 1983.
Farrell, Brian. *The Founding of Dáil Éireann.* Dublin: Gill and Macmillan, 1971.
———. *Chairman or Chief.* Dublin: Gill and Macmillan, 1971.
Fitzpatrick, David. *Politics and Irish Life 1913-21.* Dublin: Gill and Macmillan,
  1977.
———. "The Geography of Irish Nationalism". *Past and Present,* lxxvii (1978).
Forester, Margery. *Michael Collins, The Lost Leader.* London: Sphere Books, 1972.
Foster, Roy. *Modern Ireland, 1600-1972.* London: Penguin Press, 1988.
Garvin, T. *The Evolution of Irish Nationalist Politics.* Dublin: Gill and Macmillan,
  1981.
Hopkinson, Michael. *Green Against Green.* Dublin: Gill and Macmillan, 1988.
Keogh, Dermot. *The Vatican, the Bishops and Irish Politics 1919-1939.* Cambridge:
  Cambridge University Press, 1986.
Lawlor, Sheila. *Britain and Ireland 1914-1923.* Dublin: Gill and Macmillan, 1983.
Lee, Joseph. *Ireland 1912-1985 Politics and Society.* Cambridge: Cambridge
  University Press, 1989.
Longford and O'Neill. *Eamon de Valera.* Boston: Houghton Mifflin, 1971.
Macardle, Dorothy. *The Irish Republic.* London: Transworld Publishers, 1968.
———. *Tragedies of Kerry.* Dublin: Irish Book Bureau.
Macready, General Sir Nevil. *Annals of an Active Life.* 2 Vols. London: Hutchinson,
  1924.

Mulcahy, Richard. "Chief of Staff 1919". *Capuchin Annual,* Vol. 36 (1969).
——. "Conscription and the General Headquarters Staff". *Capuchin Annual*, Vol. 35 (1968).
Mulcahy, Richard. "The Irish Volunteer Convention 27 October 1917". *Capuchin Annual*, Vol. 34 (1967).
Neeson, Eoin. *The Civil War in Ireland.* Cork: Mercier Press, 1966.
O'Broin, Leon. *Michael Collins.* Dublin: Gill and Macmillan, 1980.
——. *Revolutionary Underground.* Dublin: Gill and Macmillan, 1976.
O'Donoghue, Florence. *No Other Law.* Dublin: Irish Press, 1954.
——. "Re-Organisation of the Irish Volunteers 1916-1917". *Capuchin Annual*, Vol. 34 (1967).
O'Malley, Ernie. *On Another Man's Wounds.* Dublin: Anvil Books, 1979 reprint.
——. *The Singing Flame.* Dublin: Anvil Books Ltd., 1978.
Ranelagh, J. O'Beirne. "The IRB from the Treaty to 1924". *Irish Historical Studies,* XX (1976).
Stephens, James. *The Insurrection in Dublin.* Gerrards Cross: Colin Smythe, 1978 edition.
Taylor, Rex. *Michael Collins.* London: New English Library, 1970.
Townshend, Charles. *Political Violence in Ireland.* Oxford: Clarendon Press, 1983.
——. *The British Campaign in Ireland 1919–1921.* Oxford: Oxford University Press, 1975.
——. "The Irish Republican Army and the Development of Guerrilla Warfare". *English Historical Review*, XIV (1979).
Valiulis, Maryann Gialanella. *Almost a Rebellion: The Irish Army Mutiny of 1924.* Cork: Tower Books, 1985.
——. "After the Revolution: The Formative Years of Cumann na nGaedheal", in *The Uses of the Past Essays on Irish Culture*, edited by Eyler and Garratt, 131–143. Delaware: University of Delaware Press, 1988.
——. "'The Man They Could Never Forgive'—Eamon de Valera and the Civil War", in *De Valera and His Times*, edited by O'Carroll and Murphy, 92-100. Cork: Cork University Press, 1983.
White, Terence deVere. *Kevin O'Higgins.* London: Methuen, 1948.
Younger, Calton. *Ireland's Civil War.* London: Fontana Books, 1968.

Index